Lecture Notes in Computer Science 13173

More information about this subseries at https://link.springer.com/bookseries/7410

Vincent Grosso · Thomas Pöppelmann (Eds.)

Smart Card Research and Advanced Applications

20th International Conference, CARDIS 2021
Lübeck, Germany, November 11–12, 2021
Revised Selected Papers

Editors
Vincent Grosso (iD)
Jean Monnet University
Saint-Etienne, France

Thomas Pöppelmann
Infineon Technologies
Neubiberg, Germany

ISSN 0302-9743 ISSN 1611-3349 (electronic)
Lecture Notes in Computer Science
ISBN 978-3-030-97347-6 ISBN 978-3-030-97348-3 (eBook)
https://doi.org/10.1007/978-3-030-97348-3

LNCS Sublibrary: SL4 – Security and Cryptology

This Springer imprint is published by the registered company Springer Nature Switzerland AG
The registered company address is: Gewerbestrasse 11, 6330 Cham, Switzerland

Preface

These are the proceedings of the 20th International Conference on Smart Card Research and Advanced Applications (CARDIS 2021). This year's CARDIS was held in a hybrid manner in Lübeck, Germany, and took place online from November 11 to November 12, 2021. It was organized by the Institute for IT Security of the Universität zu Lübeck, Germany.

Since 1994, CARDIS has been the venue for security experts from industry and academia to exchange ideas on the security of smart cards and related applications. Smart cards play an important role in our day-to-day life through their use in banking cards, SIM cards, electronic ID documents, and passports. Moreover, smart card technology is increasingly used in embedded systems to protect the Internet of Things (IoT), machine-to-machine communication (M2M), or automotive applications. Independent of the application, what has stayed a constant over the years is the need to prevent always advancing remote and physical attacks. Therefore, the scope of the conference has widened and now covers all aspects of the design, development, deployment, evaluation, penetration testing, and application of smart cards and secure embedded systems.

The present volume contains 16 papers that were selected from 32 submissions. The 31 members of the Program Committee evaluated the submissions, wrote 102 reviews, and engaged in thorough discussions on the merits of each paper. Three invited talks completed the technical program. Nele Mentens presented recent results on flexible electronics in her keynote "Security challenges and opportunities in emerging device technologies: a case study on flexible electronics". Christine van Vredendaal discussed challenges of post-quantum cryptography and of the NIST standardization process in her keynote "Challenges of Post-Quantum Cryptography in the Embedded World". Axel Poschmann gave insights on supply chain security in his keynote "Lessons Learned from Securing the Supply Chain of a High-Security Smartphone".

Organizing a conference is always a hard task, but it is even more complex nowadays with the COVID-19 crisis. We would like to express our deepest gratitude to Thomas Eisenbarth and all the members of his team who enabled CARDIS 2021 to succeed. We thank the authors who submitted their work and the reviewers who volunteered to review and discuss the submitted papers. We greatly appreciate the amazing work of our invited speakers who gave entertaining and insightful presentations. We would like to thank Springer for publishing the accepted papers in the LNCS collection and the sponsors Riscure, Infineon, hardwear.io, NewAE, NXP, Rambus, and Thales for their generous financial support. We are grateful to the CARDIS steering committee for allowing us to serve as the program chairs of such a well-recognized conference. Finally, we thank all presenters, participants, and session chairs, physically and online, for their support in making this CARDIS edition a great success.

December 2021   Vincent Grosso
                                                                                    Thomas Pöppelmann

Organization

General Chair

Thomas Eisenbarth   University of Lübeck, Germany

Program Committee Chairs

Vincent Grosso   CNRS and Université Jean Monnet, France
Thomas Pöppelmann   Infineon Technologies, Germany

Steering Committee

Sonia Belaïd   CryptoExperts, France
Begül Bilgin   Rambus Cryptography Research, The Netherlands
Thomas Eisenbarth   University of Lübeck, Germany
Jean-Bernard Fischer   Nagravision, Switzerland
Aurélien Francillon   EURECOM, France
Tim Güneysu   Ruhr-Universität Bochum, Germany
Marc Joye   Zama, USA
Konstantinos Markantonakis   Royal Holloway, University of London, UK
Amir Moradi   University of Cologne, Germany
Svetla Nikova   KU Leuven, Belgium
Jean-Jacques Quisquater   Université catholique de Louvain, Belgium
Francesco Regazzoni   University of Amsterdam, The Netherlands
Françis-Xavier Standaert   Université catholique de Louvain, Belgium
Yannick Teglia   Thales, France

Program Committee

Diego Aranha   Aarhus University, Denmark
Josep Balasch   KU Leuven, Belgium
Davide Bellizia   Université catholique de Louvain, Belgium
Shivam Bhasin   NTU, Singapore
Ileana Buhan   Radboud University, The Netherlands
Eleonora Cagli   CEA-Leti, Université Grenoble Alpes, France
Jan-Pieter D'Anvers   KU Leuven, Belgium
François Durvaux   Silex Insight and Université catholique de Louvain, Belgium

Domenic Forte	University of Florida, USA
Benoît Gérard	DGA-MI, France
Patrick Haddad	STM, France
Kerstin Lemke-Rust	Hochschule Bohn-Rhein-Sieg, Germany
Pierre-Yvan Liardet	eShard, France
Roel Maes	Intrinsic ID, The Netherlands
Cuauhtemoc Mancillas Lopez	CINVESTAV-IPN, Mexico
Nele Mentens	Leiden University, The Netherlands
Amir Moradi	Ruhr-Universität Bochum, Germany
Debdeep Mukhopadhyay	IIT Kharagpur, India
Colin O'Flynn	NewAE Technology Inc., Canada
David Oswald	University of Birmingham, UK
Peter Pessl	Infineon Technologies, Germany
Stjepan Picek	TU Delft, The Netherlands
Romain Poussier	NTU, Singapore
Francesco Regazzoni	University of Amsterdam, The Netherlands
Thomas Roche	NinjaLab, France
Pascal Sasdrich	Ruhr University Bochum, Germany
Tobias Schneider	NXP Semiconductors, Austria
Peter Schwabe	MPI-SP, Germany, and Radboud University, The Netherlands
Johanna Sepulveda	Airbus, Germany
Yannick Teglia	Thales, France
Yuval Yarom	University of Adelaide and Data61, Australia

Additional Reviewers

Manaar Alam	Nicolai Müller
Michel Agoyan	Kit Murdock
Florian Bache	Sioli O'Connell
Matteo Bocchi	Brisbane Ovilla-Martinez
Olivier Bronchain	Owen Pemberton
Nicolas Bruneau	Prasanna Ravi
Jean-François Dhem	Tania Richmond
Daniele Fronte	Sayandeep Saha
Dirmanto Jap	Aein Rezaei Shahmirzadi
Alberto Martinez-Herrera	Marvin Staib

Contents

Public-Key Cryptography

Secure Implementations

Side-Channel Attacks

Single-Trace Fragment Template Attack on a 32-Bit Implementation of Keccak

Shih-Chun You[ID] and Markus G. Kuhn[✉][ID]

Department of Computer Science and Technology, University of Cambridge,
Cambridge CB3 0FD, UK
{scy27,mgk25}@cl.cam.ac.uk

Abstract. Template attacks model side-channel leakage information using Gaussian multivariate distributions. They have been quite successful in directly reconstructing individual bits of 8-bit parallel buses and registers from power traces. However, extending their use directly to larger word sizes, such as 32-bit buses, becomes impractical. Here we show that it is possible to use an LDA-based stochastic model to independently build templates for just byte fragments of such a word, to predict the exact values of its four member bytes, instead of only overall Hamming weights. We demonstrate this technique to reconstruct the arbitrary-length inputs of SHA3-512 and some other Keccak sponge functions implemented on a 32-bit Cortex-M4 device. The quality of these templates was high enough such that remaining errors in their predictions could be eliminated via belief propagation on a factor-graph network (SASCA). In our experiments, we already reliably recovered SHA3-512 inputs up to 719 bytes long (10 invocations of the permutation), and reconstructing even longer inputs should be just a matter of making longer recordings.

Keywords: Template attack · SASCA · Keccak · SHA-3 · 32-bit device

1 Introduction

1.1 Motivation and Background

Since the National Institute of Standards and Technology (NIST) standardized *Secure Hash Algorithm 3* (SHA-3) [13] in 2015, several variants of Differential Power Analysis (DPA) [9,17,18] have been used to reconstruct the keys in Keccak-based message authentication codes (MAC-Keccak). These attacks require multiple accesses to the SHA-3$(K\|M)$ function, with a known and varying message M, and their recorded power traces, to recover the fixed and unknown key K.

S.-C. You—Supported by the Cambridge Trust and the Ministry of Education, Taiwan.

V. Grosso and T. Pöppelmann (Eds.): CARDIS 2021, LNCS 13173, pp. 3–23, 2022.
https://doi.org/10.1007/978-3-030-97348-3_1

Later, in 2020, two different approaches for single-trace recovery strategies appeared. Kannwischer et al. [7] used Soft Analytical Side-Channel Analysis (SASCA) [19] to recover a 128 or 256-bit secret S used in Keccak-f[1600]($S\|M$), given known message M, based on simulated noisy Hamming-weight information of intermediate values in this permutation. They concluded that their method was very successful on a simulated 8-bit or 16-bit device, but the situation was not yet clear on 32-bit devices, where they successfully recovered 128-bit keys only under some conditions, such as a lower noise level, but not 256-bit keys. They also suggested their SASCA approach may reach a higher success rate with a leakage model bearing more information than just Hamming weights.

We introduced the other approach in [21]. On an ATxmega256A3U [1] 8-bit device, we used an enumeration procedure based on 600 rank tables for the intermediate bytes. Each rank table lists all 256 candidate bytes in descending order of probability, as predicted by LDA-based stochastic-model templates. This enumeration technique could reconstruct a complete intermediate state from a single trace and then invert it to determine all Keccak-f[1600] input and output bits. By repeating the same procedure on every invocation of Keccák-f[1600] in the absorbing stage of the Keccak sponge function, we can recover arbitrary-length SHA3-512 inputs.

Therefore, encouraged by both these results, we now target a more ambitious goal, namely to reconstruct the complete arbitrary-length input of SHA-3 or SHAKE functions implemented on a 32-bit device, from a single trace. To achieve this target, we will have to figure out how to practically build templates for a 32-bit bus that can obtain far more information about a 32-bit state than just the Hamming weight.

Choudary and Kuhn [3] used template attacks based on Linear Discriminant Analysis (LDA) to directly recover from a single load instruction the exact value of a byte, and not just its Hamming weight. They also looked at extending their method to states with more than 8 bits. However, directly building templates for a 32-bit value is not practical this way.

1.2   Contributions and Paper Structure

We introduce the *fragment template attack*, to extract information about individual bits from power traces that observe activity on 32-bit parallel data buses. To achieve this, we apply the LDA technique to project the data onto subspaces where the projected data are only related to a fragment (e.g., a byte or a nibble) of the full 32-bit word, and then independently build templates for these fragments, to enable us to reconstruct their values independently and within a reasonable run time.

We built fragment templates for intermediate states in the Keccak-f[1600] permutation implemented on a 32-bit device, the STM32F303RCT7 CPU on a ChipWhisperer-Lite board [14]. We found that the resulting estimates are good enough for a SASCA attack, i.e. to error-correct the template-attack information with the help of a loopy belief-propagation factor graph based on the structure of the rounds of the Keccak-f[1600] permutation.

In this paper, we first introduce and review some of the prior work that our technique is based on (Sect. 2), namely the LDA-based stochastic model templates and SASCA. Section 3 then explains our methodology, including how we build fragment templates and our modification of a previous use of SASCA against Keccak, and how to combine the results from multiple invocations of Keccak-$f[1600]$ in the absorbing stage of a Keccak sponge function to calculate full arbitrary-length inputs. The evaluation of our experiments in Sect. 4 shows how parameters such as the number of rounds observed and the number of known bits at the input of Keccak-$f[1600]$ affect the success probability of our attack.

2   Preliminaries and Notation

2.1   LDA-based Templates on Keccak

The Template Attack with Stochastic Models. Following the original template attack (TA) introduced by Chari et al. [2], the "stochastic" model $\mathcal{F}_9$ by Schindler et al. [15], and the use of Fisher's Linear Discriminant Analysis (LDA) by Standaert and Archambeau [16] for dimensionality reduction of traces, Choudary and Kuhn [3] combined these into an LDA-based template profiling stage for a $\mathcal{F}_9$ model as follows. Firstly, record the traces and group them according to the target byte value $b \in \{0, \ldots, 255\}$, where trace $\mathbf{x}_{b,t}$ observed target value b, with $t \in \{1, \ldots, n_b\}$ enumerating the traces in that group. When building a template for a target byte b, treat each member bit ($b[0]$ to $b[7]$) as an independent variable, and then use a multivariate linear regression to calculate for each point in time coefficients c_0 to c_7 and a constant c_8 to predict the expected values of samples as $\bar{x}_b = \sum_{l=0}^{7}(b[l] \cdot c_l) + c_8$, the $\mathcal{F}_9$ stochastic model. We write

$$\bar{\mathbf{x}}_b = \sum_{l=0}^{7}(b[l] \cdot \mathbf{c}_l) + \mathbf{c}_8$$

to represent the expected vector of an entire m-sample trace, where $\mathbf{c}_0, \ldots, \mathbf{c}_8 \in \mathbb{R}^m$. From these, build two covariance matrices, $\mathbf{B}$ representing the signal, and $\mathbf{\Sigma}$ representing the noise, as

$$\mathbf{B} = \frac{1}{\sum_b n_b} \sum_b n_b (\bar{\mathbf{x}}_b - \bar{\mathbf{x}})(\bar{\mathbf{x}}_b - \bar{\mathbf{x}})^{\mathsf{T}},$$

$$\mathbf{\Sigma} = \frac{1}{\sum_b n_b} \sum_b \sum_{t=1}^{n_b}(\mathbf{x}_{b,t} - \bar{\mathbf{x}}_b)(\mathbf{x}_{b,t} - \bar{\mathbf{x}}_b)^{\mathsf{T}},$$

where $\bar{\mathbf{x}}$ is the average of all 256 expected vectors $\bar{\mathbf{x}}_b$.

Dimensionality Reduction. In the LDA step, project the m-sample traces $\mathbf{x}_{b,t}$ onto the m' largest eigenvectors of $\mathbf{\Sigma}^{-1}\mathbf{B}$, to obtain dimensionality-reduced m'-sample traces $\mathbf{x}_{b,t,\text{proj}}$, where $m' \ll m$, and the signal-to-noise ratio in the new subspace is larger. Likewise, the expected traces $\bar{\mathbf{x}}_b$ as well as the attack trace $\mathbf{x}_a$ can be projected into the same subspace as $\bar{\mathbf{x}}_{b,\text{proj}}, \mathbf{x}_{a,\text{proj}} \in \mathbb{R}^{m'}$.

With all these traces projected into the new subspace, we now can build a pooled covariance matrix

$$\mathbf{S} = \frac{1}{\sum_b n_b} \sum_b \sum_{t=1}^{n_b} (\mathbf{x}_{b,t,\text{proj}} - \bar{\mathbf{x}}_{b,\text{proj}})(\mathbf{x}_{b,t,\text{proj}} - \bar{\mathbf{x}}_{b,\text{proj}})^\mathsf{T},$$

such that the probability density of the attack trace $x_{a,\text{proj}}$ can be modelled as

$$f(\mathbf{x}_{a,\text{proj}}|\bar{\mathbf{x}}_{b,\text{proj}}, \mathbf{S})$$
$$= \frac{1}{\sqrt{(2\pi)^{m'}|\mathbf{S}|}} \exp\left(-\frac{1}{2}(\mathbf{x}_{a,\text{proj}} - \bar{\mathbf{x}}_{b,\text{proj}})^\mathsf{T} \mathbf{S}^{-1}(\mathbf{x}_{a,\text{proj}} - \bar{\mathbf{x}}_{b,\text{proj}})\right).$$

Having this likelihood calculated for all 256 values b, we can sort them in descending order to generate a rank table of all candidates, or we can normalize these likelihoods to build a probability table.

If the originally recorded trace length and sampling frequency are very high, prior sample selection or resampling steps are needed to make the above LDA matrix operations feasible. Like in [21], we therefore used sample-rate reduction and sample selection based on multivariate linear regression as initial dimensionality reduction steps before applying LDA compression (see Sect. 4.2).

Template Attack on an 8-Bit Implementation of Keccak. In [21] we used the above LDA-based template attack already to recover 600 intermediate bytes from single invocations of the Keccak-f[1600] permutation on an ATxmega256A3U 8-bit microcontroller. This permutation is the sequence of five steps $(\theta, \rho, \pi, \chi, \iota)$, which iterate for 24 rounds. We reuse here the same notation for the intermediate states α_Ω, α'_Ω, β_Ω and β'_Ω between these steps, defined for the Ωth round as

$$\textbf{Input} \xrightarrow{\theta} \alpha_0 \xrightarrow{\rho,\pi} \alpha'_0 \xrightarrow{\chi} \beta_0 \xrightarrow{\iota} \beta'_0 \xrightarrow{\theta} \alpha_1 \xrightarrow{\rho,\pi} \cdots \xrightarrow{\chi} \beta_{23} \xrightarrow{\iota} \textbf{Output}.$$

We use three variables, $i, j \in \mathbb{Z}_5$, $h \in \mathbb{Z}_8$ to label the 200 bytes of these states, where "$\in \mathbb{Z}_n$" shall imply arithmetic modulo n. For example, the first byte in the first lane of α'_0 is $\alpha'_0[0,0,0]$, and its least significant bit is $\alpha'_0[0,0,0][0]$. In addition to this bytewise notation, we also use a bitwise notation with bit index $k \in \mathbb{Z}_{64}$ and a "$\hat{}$" on the variable, as in $\hat{\alpha}'_0[i,j,k] = \alpha'_0[i,j,h][l]$ for $k = 8 \times h + l$ and $l \in \{0, \ldots, 7\}$.

Given an attack trace, in [21] we used 600 templates to generate the rank table for each of the 200 intermediate bytes in each of the three states α'_0, β_0 and α_1, so that all the correct candidates in α'_0 can be found through the three-level enumeration.

2.2   Soft Analytical Side-Channel Analysis on Keccak

Belief Propagation and SASCA. Veyrat-Charvillon et al. [19] introduced SASCA, which is an inference technique for template attacks on cryptographic algorithms based on the belief-propagation algorithm [10, Chapter 26]. The idea behind SASCA is that all the probability information available to the attacker is represented as a *factor graph*, where there are two types of nodes called "variable", representing the intermediate states of the cryptographic algorithm, and "factor", representing how these intermediate states depend on each other and on the observed traces. Each of these nodes is only connected to nodes of the respective other type (i.e., the factor graph is a bipartite graph), and information can flow through these connections. The factor graph therefore reflects the mathematical structure of the cryptographic algorithm, which then influences the updating of the probability estimates of the variables accordingly during the execution of the belief-propagation or sum-product message-passing algorithm.

While the variable nodes represent the intermediate values in the cryptographic algorithm, we can separate the factor nodes into two subtypes, "observation factors" and "constraint factors". Observation factors $f_m(x_n)$ represent observed probabilities of the values of their only connected variable x_n, here usually from a template-based likelihood. Constraint factors $f_m(\mathbf{x}_m)$ are connected to more than one variable $(x_{n_1}, \ldots, x_{n_{k_m}}) = \mathbf{x}_m$ (where $\mathcal{N}(m) = \{n_1, \ldots, n_{k_m}\}$ shall denote the set of indices of these variables) with a mathematical equation as the constraint. The information flow can be thought of as messages passed between variable nodes x_n and factor nodes f_m, which in practice are stored in a table, and from which the marginal probabilities of all the candidate values of each variable can be calculated. On a connection, the information flow is bidirectional, where a message from a variable x_n to a factor f_m is denoted as $q_{n \to m}$, and a message from a factor f_m to a variable x_n as $r_{m \to n}$. Each of these messages is a function of a value ξ of x_n. The probability of a candidate $x_n = \xi$ in message $q_{n \to m}$ is:

$$q_{n \to m}(x_n = \xi) = \prod_{m' \neq m} r_{m' \to n}(x_n = \xi),$$

which means the probability passing from a variable to a factor is the product of the probabilities of the same candidate in all the messages r passing from all other factors connected to this variable. Meanwhile, the probability of a candidate $x_n = \xi$ in the message $r_{m \to n}$ is:

$$r_{m \to n}(x_n = \xi) = \sum_{\mathbf{w}} \left[f_m(x_n = \xi, \mathbf{x}_m \backslash x_n = \mathbf{w}) \prod_{n' \in \mathcal{N}(m) \backslash n} q_{n' \to m}(x_{n'} = w_{n'}) \right],$$

where

$$f_m(\mathbf{x}_m = \mathbf{v}) = \begin{cases} 1, & \text{constraint holds with } \mathbf{x}_m = \mathbf{v}, \\ 0, & \text{otherwise.} \end{cases}$$

In other words, the probability passed from factor f_m to variable x_n is the sum of the product of the probabilities of the candidates in the messages q passed from the other variables $x_{n'}$ connected to factor f_m, where these candidates combined with the candidate $x_n = \xi$ match the constraint in f_m. For the special case of an observation factor this reduces to:

$$r_{m \to n}(x_n = \xi) = f_m(x_n = \xi),$$

where $f_m(x_n)$ is the probability table observed from the templates, instead of a constraint function. To obtain the final probability P_n of candidates $x_n = \xi$, we need the product

$$Z_n(x_n = \xi) = \prod_m r_{m \to n}(x_n = \xi)$$

of the probabilities in all the messages r passed to the same variable x_n and then normalize the result as

$$P_n(x_n = \xi) = \frac{Z_n(x_n = \xi)}{\sum_{\xi'} Z_n(x_n = \xi')}.$$

This is how the probabilities can be updated recursively through a tree structure. The algorithm terminates on tree-shaped factor graphs once the number of steps has reached the diameter of the tree. However, in most SASCA networks of cryptographic algorithms, the factor graph is less likely to be a tree structure. Instead, it probably features loops, which means that this recursive belief propagation will not terminate to output exact probabilities.

MacKay describes an easy solution [10, Chapter 26] called loopy belief propagation (loopy-BP). The main idea is to initialize all the values in the table for all messages q with one, then alternatingly update all the messages in the table for r and then q, with renormalization when the probability values become too small. Then terminate when a steady state has been reached.

Apply Loopy Belief Propagation to Keccak. Kannwischer et al. [7] demonstrate how they use loopy-BP given noisy Hamming-weight information of intermediate values. Their simulated attacks targeted the secret first 128 or 256 bits of the input of a Keccak-$f[1600]$ permutation, with the remaining input bits being known. They first introduce a bitwise (i.e., $\xi \in \{0, 1\}$) loopy-BP network. In this case, many constraint factors and variables in the bit permutation step ρ and π are no longer needed: firstly, we can simply connect the output of step θ to the input of step χ following the permutation rules of the two steps instead, and secondly, step ι XORs some round constant in the first lane, so we only need to swap the output probabilities corresponding to 0 and 1 of step χ there. Therefore, we only need to include one of the two states α_Ω and α'_Ω in the factor graph, and one of β_Ω and β'_Ω.

As for the most complicated step, θ, the corresponding equation is

$$\hat{\alpha}_\Omega[i,j,k] = \bigoplus_{j=0}^{4} \hat{\beta}'_{\Omega-1}[i-1,j,k] \oplus \bigoplus_{j=0}^{4} \hat{\beta}'_{\Omega-1}[i+1,j,k-1] \oplus \hat{\beta}'_{\Omega-1}[i,j,k].$$

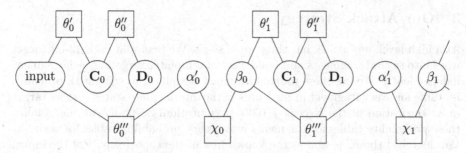

Fig. 1. The loopy-BP graph structure for the Keccak-f permutation, showing the node relations for the first two rounds. Variable nodes are in circles, constraint factors in squares. Observation factors are not shown here. Each state variable shown here actually represents 1600 or 320 single-bit variable nodes, respectively.

If we directly designed a constraint factor following this equation, it would connect to 12 variables. Instead, Kannwischer et al. [7, Fig. 1] separated it into three equations

$$\hat{\mathbf{C}}_\Omega[i,k] = \bigoplus_{j=0}^{4} \hat{\beta}'_{\Omega-1}[i,j,k], \qquad (\theta')$$

$$\hat{\mathbf{D}}_\Omega[i,k] = \hat{\mathbf{C}}_\Omega[i-1,k] \oplus \hat{\mathbf{C}}_\Omega[i+1,k-1], \qquad (\theta'')$$

$$\hat{\alpha}_\Omega[i,j,k] = \hat{\mathbf{D}}_\Omega[i,k] \oplus \hat{\beta}'_{\Omega-1}[i,j,k], \qquad (\theta''')$$

where $\hat{\mathbf{C}}$ and $\hat{\mathbf{D}}$ are additional 320-bit intermediate states (which we will also refer to as $\mathbf{C}$ and $\mathbf{D}$ bytewise). They then use these three substeps of θ to build the constraint factors in their graph.[1]

For step χ, they suggest to combine the five-bit input and output in a row (where j and k are fixed) into a single constraint factor node, instead of connecting these ten bits with five separate nodes connecting to three input bits and one output bit. They claim this will increase the efficiency of information transmission from $\hat{\beta}$ to $\hat{\alpha}'$ nodes. Figure 1 shows the resulting factor graph.

They terminate the loopy-BP procedure if the total entropy of all the variables drops to 0, or if the probabilities in the network no longer change, or after 50 iterations.

They simulated attacks on devices with 8, 16, or 32-bit words, of which their leakage model provides noisy Hamming weights. They state that the bitwise factor graph is not suitable for processing Hamming weights because marginalization will discard the information in the joint distribution of the bits in the target word, leading to bad attack performance. Therefore, they developed a "clustering" technique to deal with Hamming-weight information, which combines e.g. eight bits into one variable (i.e., $\xi \in \mathbb{Z}_{256}$).

---

[1] $\hat{\beta}'[i,j,k]$, $\hat{\mathbf{C}}[i,k]$, $\hat{\mathbf{D}}[i,k]$, $\hat{\alpha}[i,j,k]$ here are equivalent to I, P, T, O, respectively in [7].

3   Our Attack Strategy

At a high level, our attack has three main steps. We first split each 32-bit target word into several fragments and build a set of templates targeting each fragment independently. We use these profiled fragment templates to generate a probability table for every fragment in the words of the intermediate states that we target in an invocation of the Keccak-$f[1600]$ permutation. Secondly, we marginalize these probability tables for fragments into binary probability tables for each bit. We then feed these, as well as the known bits in the capacity part of the input, into the loopy-BP network for error correction. Recall that the capacity input has all 0 bits in the first invocation in a Keccak sponge function, and in later invocations it is the same as the capacity output of the previous invocation. The third step is to calculate the complete input and output of this invocation. Repeat this for each invocation. In the end, by XORing consecutive rate parts, we find the complete padded input of the Keccak sponge function.

3.1   Template Attack on Word Fragments

If we were to directly apply an LDA-based stochastic-model template [3] on each intermediate 32-bit word, we first would use multivariate linear regression, treating the 32 member bits as independent variables, to calculate the expected value for each candidate. We could then build templates for these candidates, to which the attack traces can be compared. However, with 2^{32} candidates, this approach is neither efficient nor practical. Therefore, we instead separate an intermediate word into fragments, here four bytes, and independently build templates for each. We hope that by limiting the candidate set to just the values of one fragment f at a time, treating the values of the other fragments as noise, based on the resulting per-fragment inter-class scatter $\mathbf{B}_f$ and total (pooled) intra-class scatter $\mathbf{\Sigma}_f$, the LDA can project the traces onto different subspaces, where each projection maximizes the signal-to-noise ratio for just one byte at a time.

More specifically, applying the LDA procedure directly on an intermediate 32-bit word, of value v, the matrices $\mathbf{B}$ and $\mathbf{\Sigma}$ would be

$$\mathbf{B} = \sum_{v=0}^{2^{32}-1} n_v (\bar{\mathbf{x}}_v - \bar{\mathbf{x}})(\bar{\mathbf{x}}_v - \bar{\mathbf{x}})^{\mathsf{T}} \bigg/ \sum_{v=0}^{2^{32}-1} n_v,$$

$$\mathbf{\Sigma} = \sum_{v=0}^{2^{32}-1} \sum_{t=1}^{n_v} (\mathbf{x}_{v,t} - \bar{\mathbf{x}}_v)(\mathbf{x}_{v,t} - \bar{\mathbf{x}}_v)^{\mathsf{T}} \bigg/ \sum_{v=0}^{2^{32}-1} n_v,$$

where $\bar{\mathbf{x}}_v$ is the expected value of traces corresponding to v with

$$\bar{\mathbf{x}}_v = \sum_{l=0}^{31} (v[l] \cdot \mathbf{c}_l) + \mathbf{c}_{32}, \tag{1}$$

where $\mathbf{c}_l$ is the coefficient vector of bit $v[l]$, and $\mathbf{c}_{32}$ is the constant vector.

Instead, our LDA procedure takes the same training traces, but profiles the template with only eight bits at a time. We split each word value $v \in \mathbb{Z}_{2^{32}}$ into four byte fragments $v \mapsto (F_0(v), \ldots, F_3(v))$ with $F_f(v) = \sum_{l=0}^{7} v[8f + l] \cdot 2^l$. Let $V_{f,b} = \{v \mid F_f(v) = b\}$ be the set of all 32-bit values where fragment number f has value b. For each f, we can apply the $\mathcal{F}_9$ stochastic model to obtain the 256 expected trace vectors

$$\bar{\mathbf{x}}_{f,b} = \sum_{l=0}^{7} b[l] \cdot \mathbf{c}_{f,l} + \mathbf{c}_{f,8}, \tag{2}$$

from the traces $\mathbf{x}_{v,t}$ with $v \in V_{f,b}$, respectively. We then calculate the inter-class scatter $\mathbf{B}_f$ and the total intra-class scatter $\boldsymbol{\Sigma}_f$:

$$\mathbf{B}_f = \sum_{b=0}^{255} \sum_{v \in V_{f,b}} n_v (\bar{\mathbf{x}}_{f,b} - \bar{\mathbf{x}})(\bar{\mathbf{x}}_{f,b} - \bar{\mathbf{x}})^\mathsf{T} \bigg/ \sum_{b=0}^{255} \sum_{v \in V_{f,b}} n_v,$$

$$\boldsymbol{\Sigma}_f = \sum_{b=0}^{255} \sum_{v \in V_{f,b}} \sum_{t=1}^{n_v} (\mathbf{x}_{v,t} - \bar{\mathbf{x}}_{f,b})(\mathbf{x}_{v,t} - \bar{\mathbf{x}}_{f,b})^\mathsf{T} \bigg/ \sum_{b=0}^{255} \sum_{v \in V_{f,b}} n_v.$$

Now the inter-class scatter $\mathbf{B}_f$ only contains the signals from fragment number f, and the signals from the other three bytes no longer count in the inter-class scatter, but instead contribute to the total intra-class scatter $\boldsymbol{\Sigma}_f$. In other words, they are considered to be switching noise in this model.

After we project the profiling and attack traces via these two matrices to the new m'-dimensional subspace ($m' = 8$ in this paper), we can calculate the pooled covariance matrix and combine it with the projected expected traces as the template for this target byte in the intermediate word.

Note that in practice, with far less than 2^{32} profiling traces acquired, an efficient implementation will exploit the fact that many n_v will be zero, by iterating over recorded traces rather than all v. Alternative schemes for partitioning a 32-bit word into fragments might be useful as well, such as $11 + 11 + 10$ bits, or grouping bits into fragments by distance of coefficient $\mathbf{c}_l$.

3.2   Bitwise Loopy Belief Propagation on Factor Graphs

After our templates generate the per-fragment probability tables for the selected intermediate states, we marginalize these tables to eight binary tables of their member bits and then use a bitwise loopy-BP network as the error-correction procedure. Kannwischer et al. [7] state that the probability of a bit calculated by marginalizing the Hamming weight will lose much information available in the joint distribution of the unit's member bits, but we believe that the information loss caused by marginalization may not be a severe problem in our experiments: our templates are based on the stochastic model $\mathcal{F}_9$ [15], where bits in the target bytes are viewed as independent binary variables. With the assumption of mutual independence, this model already, to some extent, gives up exploiting information from a joint distribution across bits. Since we have already bitwisely marginalized probabilities, the clustering technique is not required.

Besides that main difference, we made a number of other changes compared to Kannwischer et al. Firstly, instead of their "layer-after-layer" message updating, in a single iteration we simply update all $r_{m \to n}$ messages in the factor graphs before we update all $q_{n \to m}$ messages. Secondly, we terminate the loopy-BP algorithm after either reaching a steady state, or a maximum iteration count of 200. We found that checking the total entropy value helped little, so we dropped this termination check. Thirdly, their factor graph appears to cover only the first two rounds [7, Sect. 4.5] whereas we tested different factor graphs that cover the first two, three, or four rounds, respectively, to take more side-channel information into account. Finally, after not finding consistent improvements when trying different damping rates, we present our results without damping.

We did not acquire any side-channel observations for the input. Instead its observation factors set the capacity part of the Keccak-f[1600] input according to the sponge construct with probability one to all-zero for the first invocation, and, also with probability one, to the verified output of the previous invocation in subsequent invocations. The rate-part bits of the input are the only variables without any observation factor connected.

3.3   Dealing with Multiple Invocations

We slightly modify the procedure to recover the full padded input of a Keccak sponge function from [21] as follows.

After the loopy-BP algorithm reaches a steady state, we select in α_0' for each bit variable the candidate with the higher probability to decide on our prediction for that intermediate bit. However, the correctness of that state is not yet ensured. Therefore, we feed the predicted α_0' bits into the inverse functions of π, ρ, and θ, to calculate the corresponding input. Then we check if its capacity part matches the expected value (e.g., all zero at the first invocation). If it passes this check, we accept our α_0' prediction, and calculate from that the predicted output of the invocation. Otherwise, we consider the attempt to have failed and terminate. The reason for using the α_0' prediction instead of using the loopy-BP results of the rate part in the input variable node directly is that the latter does not benefit from this consistency check against the capacity part.

For a sponge function with more than one invocation, we repeat what we have done for the first invocation, however now the capacity of the input is verified instead against the capacity of the output of the previous invocation.

After recovering the input and output of every invocation, the remaining steps for calculating the complete padded sponge-function input are straightforward, involving XORing the rate-part inputs and outputs, as described in [21] and Fig. 2.

4   Experiments

4.1   Keccak Implementation and the Target Board

Our experiments target the 32-bit processor STM32F303RCT7, which has one ARM Cortex-M4 core, on a ChipWhisperer-Lite (CW-Lite) board [5]. Our

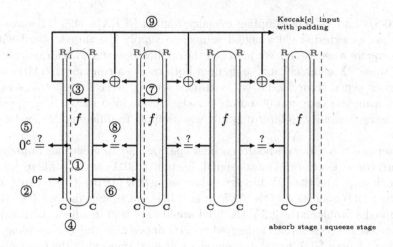

Fig. 2. The procedure to reconstruct input (and output) of sponge function Keccak[c] by template attack: ① generate the probability tables for the target intermediate states in the first Keccak-f[1600] permutation and marginalize them to binary tables; ② add the observation-factor for the capacity part of the input, which is all 0; ③ run the loopy-BP network, terminate and calculate the input and output of this invocation from state α_0' ④, and then ⑤ check consistency of the input capacity part; ⑥ add the observation-factor for the capacity part of the input, where the bits match the capacity part of the output from the previous invocation; ⑦ repeat template recovery, table marginalization, and loopy-BP on latter invocations in the absorb stage; ⑧ repeat step ⑤; ⑨ XOR the rate parts of consecutive invocations and concatenate these XOR results to find the padded Keccak[c] input.

Keccak implementation is based on the official reference C code [20] and our test application implements the four SHA-3 functions (SHA3-224, SHA3-256, SHA3-384, SHA3-512) and two extendable output functions (SHAKE128, SHAKE256). This device stores the intermediate states that we target as a sequence of fifty 32-bit words. We used the default compiler settings of the ChipWhisperer 5.2.1 software, such as optimization for space (-Os with arm-none-eabi-gcc v9.2.1).

4.2   Trace Recording

The ChipWhisperer-Lite board also includes a power-analysis oscilloscope, but that can record no more than 24 kilosamples per trace (at up to 105 MS/s). However, we wanted to record at least 15,000 clock cycles per trace, to cover at least four rounds of the Keccak-f[1600] permutation. That would have left us with very few points per clock cycle (PPC). To separate signals from 32 data bits processed in parallel, more samples per clock cycle will give us more dimensions in the signal space to achieve this. At the same time we wanted to preserve the phase lock between the oscilloscope's sampling clock and the CPU clock. Therefore, we used instead an NI PXIe-5160 [11] 10-bit oscilloscope, which can sample at 2.5 GS/s into 2 GB of sampling memory, and an NI PXIe-5423 [12] wave generator, as an external clock signal source, to supply the target board with a 5 MHz square wave signal. We installed the oscilloscope and waveform generator in the same PXIe chassis and configured both to use a common 100 MHz reference clock signal from the latter. With this setting, we collected traces at the highest sampling rate, at 500 points per clock cycle (500 PPC). This provided us with the flexibility to later digitally downsample to different PPC values, as needed.

After not using the on-board oscilloscope, we had to create an impedance-matched connection for the power signal. We used a $50\,\Omega$ coaxial cable to connect the oscilloscope and the CW-Lite's measure connector (JP10) [6]. However, JP10 taps the VDD connection of the CPU after a $13\,\Omega$ source impedance (R66+R67). This posed a problem: the 3.3 V DC level would have lead to a high current drain with the oscilloscope input configured to $50\,\Omega$ impedance and DC coupling, but if we don't have a $50\,\Omega$ impedance match on at least one end of the transmission line, reflections will add a lot of ripples to the recorded waveform. Therefore, we connected the coaxial cable to JP10 via a $37\,\Omega$ resistor (to better match the $50\,\Omega$ impedance of the cable) and a 10 nF capacitor (to block the 3.3 V DC component). Together with the $50\,\Omega$ impedance of the oscilloscope input, this capacitor forms a high-pass filter with a time constant of $0.5\,\mu s$ (2.5 clock cycles), or a 3 dB cutoff frequency of about 320 kHz. This way, we both avoid ringing on the cable, by terminating it at both ends, and use AC coupling with an impulse response that decays within a few clock cycles.

We recorded traces while the device executed SHA3-512 on random inputs that each require 10 invocations of the Keccak-f[1600] permutation. At 2.5 GS/s, each 7,500,000-sample trace we recorded covers the first four complete rounds of Keccak-f[1600], and we recorded that for each invocation of the permutation. To exclude the possibility of trigger accidents (none were detected), we checked that all traces recorded have a Pearson correlation of at least 0.98 with the mean trace. Overall, we recorded 16 000 traces for interesting-clock-cycle detection, 64 000 for template building, and 1 000 for model evaluation. For the traces recorded for testing, see Sec. 4.4.

4.3 SASCA Model Building and Evaluation

Interesting Clock Cycle Detection. Treating each bit in the intermediate byte as an independent variable, in [21] we had used multivariate linear regression to find the coefficient of determination (R^2) of these eight variables, and for the voltage-peak point in each clock cycle, we had evaluated the correlation with the intermediate byte. Using a selection threshold of $R^2 > 0.09$, we had created far shorter training traces for each intermediate byte to build its LDA-based template.

To detect the interesting clock cycle sets (ICs) for a 32-bit device, we assume that the four bytes in the same word will share the same sets. Therefore, we make a small change to our method for 8-bit devices. Rather than estimating the correlation between the samples and the 32-bit intermediate value with a

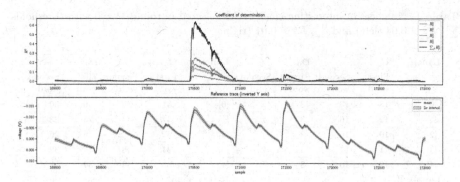

Fig. 3. The corresponding four R_f^2 values of $(\alpha'_0[0,0,0],\dots,\alpha'_0[0,0,3])$ for each sample based on the 16 000 detection traces and their sum representing the detection results of the full 32-bit word (above), as well as the mean trace and the 2σ interval (below) at the same time samples.

32-bit linear regression, as in Eq. (1), which would need more traces to build, we instead estimate the correlation by adding the four R_f^2 values calculated from the independently built 8-bit model (2) of each fragment byte in this 32-bit intermediate value. While this may be less accurate, due to slight overfitting, it significantly reduces the number of traces required.

Figure 3 shows a small part of a mean trace, covering the 32-bit word consisting of $(\alpha'_0[0,0,0],\dots,\alpha'_0[0,0,3])$, along with the corresponding four R_f^2 values for each point, based on the 16 000 detection traces. Most of the data dependency is limited to one clock cycle in the time interval shown. We also can see that the R values peak near the voltage peak, and can use this to speed up the selection of samples from our 500 PPC data. We sum 50 voltage samples around each voltage peak, and calculate $\sum_f R_f^2$ for that to decide whether this entire clock cycle should be included. Table 1 shows the number of interesting clock cycles selected for each intermediate word in the first round, with two different thresholds (0.04 and 0.01); the results of the omitted other three rounds are similar. We used the lower threshold $\sum_f R_f^2 > 0.01$. The SNR values of the points selected were in the range 0.01 to 3.43.

Template Building and Validation. Considering the run time for building templates, we only wanted to deal with at most 2000 samples per trace after selecting the ICs. Given the numbers in Table 1, we therefore decided to resample the training traces from 500 PPC down to 10 PPC, by averaging 50 consecutive samples into one, effectively reducing the sampling rate to 50 MHz.

Using the 1000 traces in the validation set, Table 2 shows the resulting success rate and guessing entropy (as in [21]) for α'_0, while Table 3, 4, 5 show the corresponding results for intermediate states β_0, $\mathbf{C}_0$ and $\mathbf{D}_0$, respectively. The omitted data for other rounds looks similar. Our results for α'_0 and β_0 are not as good as the ones for the 8-bit processor in [21], and possibly not good enough for our enumeration procedure there, but they are suitable for SASCA. Note that,

Table 1. Numbers of interesting clock cycles selected in round $\Omega = 0$ with thresholds $\sum_f R_f^2 > 0.04$ (left) and $\sum_f R_f^2 > 0.01$ (right)

Lane[i]	C_0		D_0		Lane[i]	C_0		D_0	
	First word	Second word	First word	Second word		First word	Second word	First word	Second word
[0]	13	15	3	2	[0]	31	35	36	30
[1]	12	16	3	1	[1]	31	33	25	33
[2]	10	16	3	1	[2]	32	35	25	26
[3]	11	17	3	2	[3]	31	38	17	32
[4]	12	16	3	1	[4]	35	36	34	55
Lane[i,j]	α_0'		β_0		**Lane[i,j]**	α_0'		β_0	
	First word	Second word	First word	Second word		First word	Second word	First word	Second word
[0,0]	21	35	28	39	[0,0]	55	69	48	66
[1,0]	73	90	54	68	[1,0]	130	139	91	114
[2,0]	67	89	53	68	[2,0]	125	141	88	112
[3,0]	68	88	49	66	[3,0]	120	142	88	111
[4,0]	71	88	54	68	[4,0]	136	158	96	111
[0,1]	64	85	47	61	[0,1]	120	147	86	111
[1,1]	71	87	56	69	[1,1]	124	144	92	111
[2,1]	67	80	46	61	[2,1]	129	143	85	103
[3,1]	71	89	53	70	[3,1]	127	141	91	110
[4,1]	69	74	48	55	[4,1]	141	144	100	103
[0,2]	61	90	49	70	[0,2]	143	166	87	113
[1,2]	68	84	51	67	[1,2]	121	135	89	110
[2,2]	66	87	48	64	[2,2]	126	142	90	113
[3,2]	73	84	52	68	[3,2]	133	148	92	109
[4,2]	73	91	59	69	[4,2]	134	162	101	116
[0,3]	64	88	47	64	[0,3]	120	145	87	112
[1,3]	63	88	43	61	[1,3]	115	140	84	112
[2,3]	71	90	54	69	[2,3]	131	146	96	112
[3,3]	68	89	55	73	[3,3]	116	144	90	115
[4,3]	77	85	50	58	[4,3]	143	158	106	112
[0,4]	75	74	50	62	[0,4]	133	146	102	106
[1,4]	79	90	49	67	[1,4]	134	146	104	117
[2,4]	64	86	50	65	[2,4]	122	137	83	111
[3,4]	65	91	52	70	[3,4]	131	140	87	110
[4,4]	65	82	45	60	[4,4]	135	153	83	126

similar to the 8-bit experiments in [21], the results for the first lane of state α' in every round are worse than those for the other lanes in the same state. This is because this lane is not rotated in steps π or ρ, resulting in fewer interesting clock cycles for the bits in this lane.

Since we use the marginal probabilities in the loopy-BP network, we also show in Table 6 the average number of correct bits in different intermediate states from the 1000 validation traces. Because the probability tables are binary after

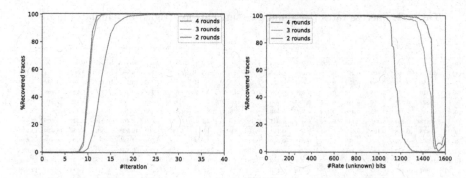

Fig. 4. Percentage of successfully recovered traces for the different factor-graph networks (with different numbers of rounds observed), as a function of the number of loopy-BP iterations (left) and the number of unknown input bits (right).

marginalization, we define whether a bit is successfully predicted by checking if the probability of the correct candidate bit is higher than 0.5. The marginalized results also show that our templates predicted the state α'_Ω more successfully in these four rounds than the other states.

We also tried other choices of fragment size besides 4×8 bits: $11 + 11 + 10$ bits, 8×4 bits, 16×2 bits and 32×1 bit. We found that the choice of fragment size plays little role in the results after marginalization. As an example, Table 8 compares the performance of these different fragment sizes for the first bit in α'_0 after marginalization. Therefore, the fragment size can be chosen here to optimize computation time. For 11-bit fragments, calculating probability tables for 2^{11} candidates dominates the testing stage. On the other hand, with 32 1-bit fragments, the profiling stage takes longer, as we need to calculate a separate Σ_f for each fragment for LDA, the most time-consuming profiling step. Therefore, for our experiments with single-bit marginalization, the use of 4×8-bit fragment templates seemed a good compromise.

Evaluation on Different Networks. We now evaluate how well the loopy-BP algorithm works when fed with marginalized binary probability tables from a single validation trace, along with 1024 known bits in the capacity part of the input. Table 7 shows the number of validation traces reaching a steady state, along with statistics on the number of iterations required, and the number of validation traces where all intermediate bits were recovered. We provide results from three networks, covering two, three, and four rounds, respectively. Although intermediate values of all the validation traces are successfully recovered in these three networks, we can see that we will need fewer iterations to reach a steady state with the four-round network. Figure 4 (left) shows the percentage of successfully recovered traces (defined as all the bits of α'_0 being recovered correctly) out of the 1000 validation traces for these three factor-graph networks as a function of the number of loopy-BP iterations. It takes fewer iterations to completely recover state α'_0 than it takes for the network to stabilize. It appears that the

Table 2. Success rates (left) and guessing entropy (right) of templates in α_0'

(i, j)	\[success\] h=0	1	2	3	4	5	6	7	\[entropy\] h=0	1	2	3	4	5	6	7
(0, 0)	0.036	0.046	0.021	0.023	0.029	0.050	0.012	0.015	47.918	37.603	72.631	66.417	58.449	36.038	84.323	69.128
(1, 0)	0.534	0.580	0.192	0.203	0.176	0.426	0.338	0.463	2.914	2.228	9.998	9.484	10.852	3.305	5.991	3.168
(2, 0)	0.459	0.558	0.259	0.152	0.206	0.457	0.352	0.386	3.296	2.191	7.754	13.492	10.111	2.793	4.998	4.433
(3, 0)	0.376	0.213	0.248	0.469	0.289	-0.306	0.291	0.612	3.878	10.928	7.214	3.287	6.476	5.613	5.836	2.142
(4, 0)	0.522	0.377	0.370	0.246	0.275	0.384	0.506	0.351	2.576	4.329	4.455	7.112	8.444	4.172	2.976	5.131
(0, 1)	0.450	0.273	0.133	0.348	0.412	0.393	0.145	0.405	3.304	6.886	21.260	3.147	3.947	3.788	13.872	2.868
(1, 1)	0.473	0.242	0.435	0.449	0.342	0.373	0.347	0.487	2.725	7.374	2.801	3.769	5.946	4.577	5.000	3.175
(2, 1)	0.878	0.358	0.109	0.149	0.791	0.389	0.151	0.163	1.161	4.434	21.005	16.938	1.381	4.054	16.640	12.926
(3, 1)	0.360	0.332	0.259	0.279	0.173	0.358	0.366	0.531	4.909	4.014	7.500	7.730	13.265	3.903	5.013	2.675
(4, 1)	0.598	0.337	0.140	0.447	0.432	0.230	0.068	0.307	2.005	4.753	18.085	3.258	3.421	8.237	30.208	3.685
(0, 2)	0.717	0.292	0.110	0.140	0.790	0.427	0.162	0.284	1.573	5.369	22.824	15.404	1.378	3.447	12.988	7.555
(1, 2)	0.807	0.457	0.182	0.135	0.610	0.539	0.173	0.196	1.295	3.155	12.805	16.964	2.118	2.141	13.294	12.928
(2, 2)	0.423	0.214	0.110	0.789	0.383	0.277	0.176	0.777	3.110	8.532	21.392	1.404	5.061	6.394	13.671	1.291
(3, 2)	0.789	0.554	0.233	0.164	0.608	0.423	0.219	0.242	1.308	2.049	9.743	14.054	2.401	3.065	11.262	8.953
(4, 2)	0.435	0.255	0.533	0.357	0.268	0.390	0.601	0.537	2.866	6.688	2.319	5.176	8.416	4.756	1.986	2.902
(0, 3)	0.517	0.240	0.112	0.424	0.387	0.364	0.168	0.554	2.555	8.155	22.583	2.758	4.980	4.951	14.281	2.157
(1, 3)	0.740	0.318	0.118	0.124	0.577	0.460	0.217	0.305	1.509	5.179	17.242	16.478	2.061	3.089	9.198	6.468
(2, 3)	0.599	0.609	0.248	0.195	0.358	0.709	0.256	0.230	2.029	1.885	8.480	12.055	5.119	1.573	8.126	8.616
(3, 3)	0.359	0.295	0.362	0.277	0.271	0.388	0.559	0.382	4.863	5.171	4.425	6.750	9.046	4.186	2.511	5.356
(4, 3)	0.517	0.263	0.228	0.807	0.263	0.187	0.132	0.885	2.509	7.140	9.502	1.275	7.513	11.743	17.919	1.167
(0, 4)	0.635	0.424	0.122	0.290	0.445	0.288	0.061	0.183	1.866	3.518	19.914	4.703	3.229	6.271	33.439	7.764
(1, 4)	0.522	0.234	0.282	0.747	0.211	0.160	0.164	0.845	2.620	9.101	8.051	1.582	10.651	13.080	14.079	1.306
(2, 4)	0.767	0.504	0.151	0.138	0.411	0.503	0.273	0.267	1.549	2.537	13.825	18.494	3.763	2.569	7.648	8.671
(3, 4)	0.633	0.571	0.148	0.140	0.250	0.621	0.265	0.382	2.066	2.134	15.311	16.691	7.488	1.926	8.879	4.935
(4, 4)	0.860	0.359	0.111	0.178	0.838	0.397	0.146	0.203	1.212	4.708	25.596	12.427	1.255	4.436	19.452	9.656

Table 3. Success rates (left) and guessing entropy (right) of templates in β_0

(i, j)	\[success\] h=0	1	2	3	4	5	6	7	\[entropy\] h=0	1	2	3	4	5	6	7
(0, 0)	0.063	0.060	0.026	0.034	0.035	0.039	0.022	0.017	29.099	31.206	66.016	55.164	49.097	41.215	77.061	72.161
(1, 0)	0.067	0.084	0.039	0.034	0.035	0.065	0.035	0.058	41.296	27.599	51.756	51.166	51.967	35.532	52.942	43.689
(2, 0)	0.055	0.073	0.049	0.043	0.046	0.070	0.039	0.052	45.505	31.928	47.914	52.142	52.209	34.579	52.971	48.676
(3, 0)	0.061	0.049	0.030	0.057	0.052	0.058	0.046	0.052	46.225	38.049	48.516	43.621	45.427	39.180	53.513	44.922
(4, 0)	0.045	0.066	0.059	0.044	0.056	0.080	0.048	0.051	44.973	33.773	41.436	53.657	45.342	29.965	45.826	47.460
(0, 1)	0.054	0.053	0.028	0.056	0.056	0.050	0.036	0.054	42.920	37.477	55.296	43.037	47.861	39.370	62.768	47.697
(1, 1)	0.062	0.052	0.061	0.054	0.049	0.043	0.043	0.043	44.062	41.569	43.692	47.447	49.794	41.370	51.363	48.475
(2, 1)	0.096	0.045	0.034	0.041	0.063	0.068	0.022	0.029	37.942	35.927	58.811	53.895	39.371	37.991	61.425	57.728
(3, 1)	0.047	0.063	0.043	0.055	0.045	0.055	0.038	0.064	49.000	33.408	47.756	51.132	54.896	38.350	52.300	44.095
(4, 1)	0.081	0.055	0.032	0.063	0.073	0.047	0.020	0.049	39.393	34.967	55.991	43.244	38.900	35.159	70.819	49.384
(0, 2)	0.055	0.062	0.029	0.033	0.067	0.056	0.029	0.035	40.071	34.954	57.510	54.016	40.775	36.531	61.750	54.218
(1, 2)	0.070	0.059	0.032	0.050	0.059	0.054	0.025	0.033	37.223	35.369	53.714	52.559	43.220	38.293	61.419	59.342
(2, 2)	0.064	0.049	0.028	0.065	0.049	0.057	0.029	0.040	42.703	38.837	58.793	42.058	44.949	41.459	63.710	40.046
(3, 2)	0.076	0.073	0.050	0.028	0.049	0.057	0.029	0.040	38.453	34.161	51.291	54.249	44.727	36.590	60.970	54.708
(4, 2)	0.064	0.072	0.080	0.053	0.051	0.064	0.065	0.058	40.264	35.120	43.146	49.255	43.270	33.627	44.398	47.326
(0, 3)	0.048	0.061	0.031	0.054	0.051	0.058	0.025	0.050	41.919	38.271	58.745	46.345	45.974	39.711	64.287	47.035
(1, 3)	0.088	0.062	0.031	0.030	0.051	0.085	0.032	0.050	35.889	34.639	56.862	54.783	43.745	32.077	56.285	52.072
(2, 3)	0.065	0.079	0.046	0.049	0.043	0.080	0.042	0.033	39.466	29.259	47.707	52.404	47.964	28.582	53.567	55.279
(3, 3)	0.055	0.067	0.053	0.038	0.044	0.065	0.050	0.050	47.758	34.515	41.710	50.016	45.893	35.975	51.737	50.468
(4, 3)	0.062	0.067	0.043	0.066	0.051	0.056	0.018	0.061	36.454	33.344	46.953	38.291	38.767	35.921	63.725	36.496
(0, 4)	0.063	0.080	0.028	0.063	0.050	0.044	0.022	0.031	36.658	30.434	57.476	47.138	45.926	38.289	73.197	47.420
(1, 4)	0.064	0.056	0.045	0.060	0.049	0.048	0.032	0.057	41.344	35.637	47.295	43.026	50.578	45.520	64.383	42.099
(2, 4)	0.073	0.074	0.037	0.025	0.048	0.072	0.044	0.054	38.915	32.309	55.223	55.883	42.468	35.518	55.496	49.946
(3, 4)	0.057	0.084	0.030	0.045	0.032	0.083	0.025	0.054	42.077	29.945	53.072	53.553	51.580	35.255	56.883	48.758
(4, 4)	0.077	0.061	0.020	0.041	0.163	0.144	0.038	0.055	37.359	38.467	61.073	50.593	15.980	21.212	53.895	33.795

two-round network takes more iterations to recover all validation traces correctly than the larger networks.

Figure 4 (right) shows the percentage of successfully recovered traces out of 1000 validation traces when we provide different numbers of known bits (not just 1024), to explore the situation when the size of the rate parts (r unknown

Table 4. Success rates (left) and guessing entropy (right) of templates in C_0

(i,j)	h								(i,j)	h							
	0	1	2	3	4	5	6	7		0	1	2	3	4	5	6	7
$(0,0)$	0.027	0.036	0.016	0.030	0.041	0.060	0.019	0.042	$(0,0)$	58.015	39.596	65.977	51.890	42.605	31.637	76.724	49.012
$(1,0)$	0.025	0.044	0.020	0.039	0.034	0.066	0.015	0.036	$(1,0)$	58.307	40.936	69.313	49.246	43.310	32.581	77.534	46.917
$(2,0)$	0.027	0.043	0.027	0.039	0.047	0.051	0.018	0.043	$(2,0)$	56.889	42.208	66.796	51.466	36.740	33.989	72.759	47.559
$(3,0)$	0.032	0.047	0.017	0.045	0.045	0.056	0.015	0.046	$(3,0)$	59.543	41.348	68.157	51.589	38.406	31.291	74.440	44.055
$(4,0)$	0.026	0.048	0.022	0.037	0.066	0.075	0.018	0.048	$(4,0)$	60.075	39.145	69.823	49.706	33.487	29.861	65.547	43.852

Table 5. Success rates (left) and guessing entropy (right) of templates in D_0

(i,j)	h								(i,j)	h							
	0	1	2	3	4	5	6	7		0	1	2	3	4	5	6	7
$(0,0)$	0.013	0.020	0.006	0.012	0.016	0.010	0.008	0.013	$(0,0)$	91.069	84.318	92.714	87.537	84.127	73.385	93.005	85.368
$(1,0)$	0.013	0.016	0.010	0.016	0.016	0.016	0.008	0.015	$(1,0)$	87.800	84.453	89.139	86.089	78.383	78.650	90.992	80.381
$(2,0)$	0.008	0.016	0.011	0.014	0.012	0.021	0.005	0.016	$(2,0)$	89.727	86.831	89.815	88.058	76.028	78.165	92.148	84.787
$(3,0)$	0.010	0.020	0.009	0.013	0.016	0.019	0.012	0.011	$(3,0)$	93.462	83.278	92.638	84.953	84.579	70.239	92.599	82.877
$(4,0)$	0.017	0.006	0.011	0.012	0.020	0.020	0.009	0.019	$(4,0)$	91.890	81.804	90.937	88.506	80.511	76.263	91.385	76.724

Table 6. Average (μ) and standard deviation (σ) of the number of correct bits found after marginalization of the byte tables (out of 1600 bits in α'_Ω and β_Ω, and 320 bits in C_Ω and D_Ω, respectively).

State	α'_0	β_0	α'_1	β_1	α'_2	β_2	α'_3	β_3
μ	1353.432	1093.831	1352.345	1094.108	1353.010	1095.214	1353.998	1095.555
σ	15.854	17.746	16.313	17.103	16.028	17.255	15.243	17.265
State	C_0	D_0	C_1	D_1	C_2	D_2	C_3	D_3
μ	211.007	187.974	211.480	187.722	211.509	187.489	211.051	187.565
σ	7.992	9.049	8.181	7.999	8.230	7.774	8.077	8.189

Table 7. Results of terminating bitwise SASCA on the 32-bit device

Network	#Steady	#Iteration				#Correct traces								
		Median	Mean	σ	Max	Input	α'_0	β_0	α'_1	β_1	α'_2	β_2	α'_3	β_3
4-round	1000	25	25.421	0.573	28	1000	1000	1000	1000	1000	1000	1000	1000	1000
3-round	1000	30	30.331	1.247	34	1000	1000	1000	1000	1000	1000	1000	N/A	N/A
2-round	1000	51	51.710	4.391	72	1000	1000	1000	1000	1000	N/A	N/A	N/A	N/A

Table 8. Fragment size had little influence on accuracy of bit prediction, as illustrated here for the first bit in α'_0, using several metrics: predicted marginalized probability of correct candidate from the first trace (Prob.), number of correct bit predictions over 1000 validation traces (#Success), maximum and average deviation ($|\epsilon|$) of probability among these 1000 trials from the predictions made by four-byte fragment templates.

Fragments	$11 + 11 + 10$ bits	4×8 bits	8×4 bits	16×2 bits	32×1 bit
Prob.	0.752437	0.750506	0.752002	0.752274	0.751888
#Success	729	730	733	733	732
Max $|\epsilon|$	0.026377	–	0.010587	0.013578	0.013906
Average $|\epsilon|$	0.002809	–	0.001652	0.001872	0.002043

bits) and capacity parts (c known bits) of the permutation input vary in different sponge functions. When the number of unknown bits increases beyond half of the full state, including up to the $1600 - 128 \times 2 = 1344$ unknown bits in SHAKE128, the four-round network performs better than the others. Therefore we chose the four-round network for our final version of the attack.

4.4 Loopy Belief-Propagation Results

Results for the SHA-3 and SHAKE Functions. We recorded five groups of 1000 test traces. Each group had a different range of SHA3-512 input lengths, requiring 1, 2, 4, 5, or 10 invocations of Keccak-f[1600] to absorb, respectively. Table 9 shows the number of successfully recovered inputs for each of these test traces, and related statistics on the number of iterations required. We can see that all the inputs were successfully recovered, after about 25–30 iterations.[2]

Apart from SHA3-512, we also recorded test traces for other Keccak[c] sponge functions, including the other three SHA-3 variants and the two SHAKE extendable output functions. It is noteworthy that, because our SASCA network of Keccak-f[1600] relies on the capacity part of the output of the previous invocation, the functions with a shorter capacity part (c known bits) may encounter a lower success rate or may require more iterations to reach a steady state. Table 10 shows some results of these five functions with inputs that can be absorbed in one or two invocations. We can see the results meet our expectation that the shorter the capacity part, the lower the number of inputs we successfully recover, and the more iterations we need to reach a steady state, despite all success rates remaining close to 1. It is also noteworthy that in the same function, if the success rate for inputs requiring one invocation is p, that for inputs requiring two invocations should be p^2, which is also consistent with our results.

Apart from our final four-round version, we have also tried these experiments with the three-round network. Table 11 shows the results of recovering 1000 inputs with one invocation from the test traces of the six SHA-3 or SHAKE functions. It appears that the four-round network provides better results, suggesting that recording longer traces covering more rounds helps to push the success rate much closer to 1.

---

[2] Recall that Kannwischer et al.'s results [7] for their *all-zero public input* set, which is similar to our experiments with very short Keccak[c] input, were worse than those for their *random public input* set. We did not observe such variability in our setting, i.e. the success rates or the number of iterations required did not significantly vary with the input length of Keccak[c], even down to just one byte.

Table 9. Results of recovering the SHA3-512 inputs with multiple invocations of Keccak-f[1600] permutation.

#Invocations	#Traces recovered	#Iteration			
		Median	Mean	σ	Max
1	1000	25	25.399	0.804	28
2	1000	26	25.629	0.619	29
4	1000	26	25.575	0.611	29
5	1000	26	25.615	0.621	31
10	1000	25	25.364	0.552	28

Table 10. Results of recovering the functions in the SHA-3 family with one and two invocations by the four-round network.

Function	c	r	#Inv.	#Rec.	#Iteration*			
					Median	Mean	σ	Max
SHA3-512	1024	576	1	1000	25	25.399	0.804	28
			2	1000	26	25.629	0.619	29
SHA3-384	768	832	1	1000	27	26.838	0.942	29
			2	1000	27	27.061	0.662	30
SHA3-256	512	1088	1	1000	29	28.646	1.246	32
			2	998	29	28.679	0.761	33
SHAKE256			1	997	29	29.054	1.272	34
			2	996	29	28.996	0.926	37
SHA3-224	448	1152	1	1000	29	29.106	1.255	33
			2	996	29	29.440	0.971	37
SHAKE128	256	1344	1	979	31	30.897	1.512	39
			2	971	31	31.206	1.212	39

*Only invocations that reached a steady state are taken into account.

Table 11. Results of recovering the functions in the SHA-3 family with one invocation by the three-round network.

Function	c	r	#Rec.	#Iteration*			
				Median	Mean	σ	Max
SHA3-512	1024	576	1000	30	30.064	1.720	35
SHA3-384	768	832	1000	34	34.066	2.057	41
SHA3-256	512	1088	999	38	38.023	2.924	46
SHAKE256			999	39	38.789	2.727	50
SHA3-224	448	1152	992	39	39.284	2.947	52
SHAKE128	256	1344	921	43	43.512	5.033	107

*Only invocations that reached a steady state are taken into account.

5   Conclusion and Outlook

With the help of LDA-based dimensionality reduction, we successfully built fragment templates that generate separate probability tables for each byte in the 32-bit words of the targeted intermediate states. The quality of our templates is sufficient for creating per-bit marginalized observation factors from which a bitwise loopy-BP network can reconstruct the full input and output of each invocation of Keccak-f[1600], using also knowledge about a part of its input, as given by the sponge construction. From that we can easily reconstruct the padded arbitrary-length inputs of the Keccak sponge functions. Interestingly, our results so far indicate that, although the Keccak[c] functions with a longer capacity have cryptographically a higher security margin, that actually helps in our attack strategy. Our results suggest that this method will also work for Keccak-based sponge functions with a shorter capacity, especially when observing more rounds by recording longer traces. We also expect that this attack strategy can easily be applied to other SHA-3-derived functions, such as cSHAKE, KMAC, TupleHash and ParallelHash, defined in NIST Special Publication 800-185 [8], which also use the Keccak[256] or Keccak[512] functions, except for different padding methods.

Our fragment templates reconstruct full-state information stored in larger word sizes (such as 32 bits) than are practical with regular template or stochastic-method attacks, by using the LDA technique to project traces onto subspaces that are only related to a manageable part of the state. Further improvements should be possible, for example lowering the R^2 threshold to include more interesting clock cycles may help to build templates with even higher success rates, at the expense of more computational time required for profiling. We expect this fragment-template technique can be extended beyond attacks on SHA-3 related functions. Also, so far we have only demonstrated this technique using the same board for profiling and attack, therefore its portability remains to be investigated; however LDA-based techniques have previously already been shown to help with portability of templates across boards [4].

Data and source code used are available at:

https://www.cl.cam.ac.uk/research/security/datasets/sha3-32bit/

References

1. Atmel Corporation: AVR XMEGA Microcontrollers. http://www.atmel.com/products/microcontrollers/avr/avr_xmega.aspx. Accessed Mar 2014
2. Chari, S., Rao, J.R., Rohatgi, P.: Template attacks. In: Kaliski, B.S., Koç, K., Paar, C. (eds.) CHES 2002. LNCS, vol. 2523, pp. 13–28. Springer, Heidelberg (2003). https://doi.org/10.1007/3-540-36400-5_3
3. Choudary, M.O., Kuhn, M.G.: Efficient stochastic methods: profiled attacks beyond 8 bits. In: Joye, M., Moradi, A. (eds.) CARDIS 2014. LNCS, vol. 8968, pp. 85–103. Springer, Cham (2015). https://doi.org/10.1007/978-3-319-16763-3_6

4. Choudary, M.O., Kuhn, M.G.: Efficient, portable template attacks. IEEE Trans. Inf. Forensics Secur. **13**(2), 490–501 (2018). https://doi.org/10.1109/TIFS.2017.2757440

5. CW1173: ChipWhisperer-Lite product data sheet, 13 February 2018. https://media.newae.com/datasheets/NAE-CW1173_datasheet.pdf

6. ChipWhisperer-Lite arm edition, schematic, rev 03. https://github.com/newaetech/chipwhisperer/raw/develop/hardware/capture/chipwhisperer-lite-32bit/cw-lite-arm-main.pdf

7. Kannwischer, M.J., Pessl, P., Primas, R.: Single-trace attacks on Keccak. IACR Trans. Crypt. Hardware Embed. Syst. **2020**(3), 243–268 (2020). https://doi.org/10.13154/tches.v2020.i3.243-268

8. Kelsey, J., Chang, S., Perlner, R.: SHA-3 derived functions: cSHAKE, KMAC. TupleHash ParallelHash (2016). https://doi.org/10.6028/NIST.SP.800-185

9. Luo, P., Fei, Y., Fang, X., Ding, A.A., Kaeli, D.R., Leeser, M.: Side-channel analysis of MAC-Keccak hardware implementations. IACR Cryptology ePrint Archive **2015**, 411 (2015). https://doi.org/10.1145/2768566.2768567

10. MacKay, D.J.C.: Information Theory, Inference and Learning Algorithms. Cambridge University Press, Cambridge (2003)

11. NI PXIe-5160. http://www.ni.com/en-gb/support/model.pxie-5160.html

12. NI PXIe-5423. http://www.ni.com/en-gb/support/model.pxie-5423.html

13. NIST: SHA-3 standard: permutation-based hash and extendable-output functions, August 2015. https://doi.org/10.6028/NIST.FIPS.202. FIPS PUB 202

14. O'Flynn, C., Chen, Z.D.: ChipWhisperer: an open-source platform for hardware embedded security research. In: Prouff, E. (ed.) COSADE 2014. LNCS, vol. 8622, pp. 243–260. Springer, Cham (2014). https://doi.org/10.1007/978-3-319-10175-0_17

15. Schindler, W., Lemke, K., Paar, C.: A stochastic model for differential side channel cryptanalysis. In: Rao, J.R., Sunar, B. (eds.) CHES 2005. LNCS, vol. 3659, pp. 30–46. Springer, Heidelberg (2005). https://doi.org/10.1007/11545262_3

16. Standaert, F.-X., Archambeau, C.: Using subspace-based template attacks to compare and combine power and electromagnetic information leakages. In: Oswald, E., Rohatgi, P. (eds.) CHES 2008. LNCS, vol. 5154, pp. 411–425. Springer, Heidelberg (2008). https://doi.org/10.1007/978-3-540-85053-3_26

17. Taha, M., Schaumont, P.: Differential power analysis of MAC-Keccak at any keylength. In: Sakiyama, K., Terada, M. (eds.) IWSEC 2013. LNCS, vol. 8231, pp. 68–82. Springer, Heidelberg (2013). https://doi.org/10.1007/978-3-642-41383-4_5

18. Taha, M., Schaumont, P.: Side-channel analysis of MAC-Keccak. In: 2013 IEEE International Symposium on Hardware-Oriented Security and Trust (HOST), pp. 125–130. IEEE (2013). https://doi.org/10.1109/HST.2013.6581577

19. Veyrat-Charvillon, N., Gérard, B., Standaert, F.-X.: Soft analytical side-channel attacks. In: Sarkar, P., Iwata, T. (eds.) ASIACRYPT 2014. LNCS, vol. 8873, pp. 282–296. Springer, Heidelberg (2014). https://doi.org/10.1007/978-3-662-45611-8_15

20. Extended Keccak code package. https://github.com/XKCP/XKCP. Accessed Apr 2019. lib/low/KeccakP-1600/Compact64/KeccakP-1600-compact64.c

21. You, S.-C., Kuhn, M.G.: A template attack to reconstruct the input of SHA-3 on an 8-bit device. In: Bertoni, G.M., Regazzoni, F. (eds.) COSADE 2020. LNCS, vol. 12244, pp. 25–42. Springer, Cham (2021). https://doi.org/10.1007/978-3-030-68773-1_2

Trace-to-Trace Translation for SCA

Christophe Genevey-Metat[1], Annelie Heuser[1]([✉]), and Benoît Gérard[1,2]

[1] Univ Rennes, Inria, CNRS, IRISA, Rennes, France
annelie.heuser@irisa.fr
[2] Direction Générale de l'Armement, Rennes, France

Abstract. Neural Networks (NN) have been built to solve universal function approximation problems. Some architectures as Convolutional Neural Networks (CNN) are dedicated to classification in the context of image distortion. They have naturally been considered in the community to perform side-channel attacks showing good results on traces exposing time misalignment. However, even where these timing distortions are not present, NN have produced better results than legacy attacks.

Recently in TCHES 2020, auto-encoders have been used as preprocessing for noise reduction. The main idea is to train an auto-encoder using as inputs noisy traces and less noisy traces so that the auto-encoder is able to remove part of the noise in the attack dataset.

We propose to extend this idea of using NN for pre-processing by not only considering the noise-reduction but to translate data between two side-channel domains. In a nutshell, clean (or less noisy) traces may not be available to an attacker, but similar traces that are *easier* to attack may be obtainable. Availability of such traces can be leveraged to learn how to translate *difficult* traces to *easy* ones to increase attackability.

Keywords: Side-channel analysis · Generative Adversarial Network · Profiled attacks · Neural networks · Electromagnetic emanations · Power consumption

1 Introduction

Physical side-channel analysis has been introduced at the end of the 90's in [9]. Since then, the interest of side-channel attacks has increased and new attacks and channels have been considered. Those attacks have been classified into two classes depending on the ability of the attacker to perform some prior training before attacking. Profiled attacks leverage the availability of training data to outperform non-profiled attacks by tuning the leakage model to best fit reality. Indeed profiled attacks are the most efficient ones since the model used is at worse as good as a generic model used in the non-profiled case. The reference for profiled attacks are Template Attacks (TA) [2] which are optimal as soon as the leakage fits the model used (usually a Gaussian model).

A few years ago, Deep Learning (DL) techniques have been introduced as new profiled attacks [11]. They have been shown to gain good performance even in the presence of countermeasures. As an example, the ASCAD database [14] contains

© Springer Nature Switzerland AG 2022
V. Grosso and T. Pöppelmann (Eds.): CARDIS 2021, LNCS 13173, pp. 24–43, 2022.
https://doi.org/10.1007/978-3-030-97348-3_2

traces corresponding to a masked implementation with artificial desynchronization. The database has been used in numerous works leading to high-performance attacks compared to classical techniques.

Related Work. Most of the works using DL techniques are based on convolutional neural networks [8,10,12,12,14,20]. Lately, some works go beyond this approach and have shown the advantage of using Generative Adversarial Networks (GAN)s for data augmentation [17] or Convolutional Auto-Encoders (CAE) for noise reduction [19]. In particular, Wang et al. investigated the use of Conditional Generative Adversarial Networks (CGAN) for data augmentation [17], which requires a labeled dataset. They show that increasing the amount of traces in the training dataset with traces generated by a CGAN can improve the performance of profiled attacks. As a result, they show that they can reach similar performances using only half of the original measured training traces.

Closer to our work, authors of [19] have investigated the capability of CAE to denoise/remove the effect of various hiding countermeasures. For this, they artificially added noise to the ASCAD datasets: Gaussian noise, shuffling, clock-jitter and random-delay. Their results show that auto-encoders are effective tools to improve the quality of traces and thus to increase the attack performance by targeting processed traces. This work is of interest since for the first time, NN are not considered for performing a full attack but only as a preprocessing step before applying a distinguisher. Actually, the approach does not need to be in a classical profiling context as we will detail in this paper and thus can be used as a prior process to any other classical side-channel attack.

To be able to learn how to *remove the noise*, the auto-encoder needs a training dataset containing the *noisy* traces and the corresponding *clean* traces. The main drawback of this approach is that the attacker must have access to those clean traces (e.g. traces without any countermeasure present). In many situations (e.g., when clock-jitter is present) the attacker might not be able to fulfill this requirement. We propose here to relax this constraint by considering an *easier* dataset instead of a *clean* one. That is, not using a noiseless version of the training dataset but some dataset obtained from a setup which is easier to attack. For this, we leverage on techniques designed to translate between two domains.

This Work. We aim at investigating how far we could extend the research topic from [19] by going beyond noise reduction and toward trace translation. The main goal is shared with the aforementioned paper since the finality is to improve attack traces for reaching better attack performances. To this end, we investigate the use of GAN, as they are known in the field of computer vision to be effective to generate synthetic data. They are for instance used to generate art, improve astronomical images, or to perform image-to-image translation.

In this paper, we adjust and tune two GAN architectures over a set of hyperparameters: (1) Speech Enhancement GAN (SEGAN) which has been designed for speech enhancement [13], (2) Pix2Pix [5] designed in the context of image translation or generation, and select the best performing one for our experiments.

Our main idea is to translate traces measured on "difficult" (e.g., complex, noisy) sources to "easier" ones, without the restriction of having clean and noisy traces from the same device, source, and implementation. We considered our traces as paired datasets, even if they come from different devices, because these traces contain the same intermediate variable. To make a proof of concept of our approach, we perform the following translation experiments:

1. from (less informative) electromagnetic (EM) to power consumption traces,
2. from one target device to another (STM32F1 to STM32F2, STM32F0 to STM32F2, STM32F2 to STM32F4).

The first case is motivated by the practical limitations of an attacker that may not be able to introduce a resistor on the target PCB to attack while being able to measure the power on a training device. The second one has been chosen to see if the translation goes beyond what could be seen as a (simple) scaling/shifting and is actually able to transform the leakage model (e.g. leakage shape and location).

2 Preliminaries

2.1 Side-Channel Analysis

In the side-channel adversary model one assumes that the attacker is able to measure side-channel information while knowing the plaintext or ciphertext plus some information about the internal structure of the implemented algorithm. Using this information the attacker is able to make predictions about parts of the secret key. Formally, a function of the cryptographic algorithm is processed taking as inputs (a part of) the secret key k^* and (a part of) the plaintext (or ciphertext) t. The attacker defines an internal state of the cryptographic algorithm y as a function of t and k^*, which is assumed to relate to the deterministic part of the measured leakage x. For example, in AES a common choice is the substitution output, i.e. $y(t, k^*) = \text{SBox}[t \oplus k^*]$, where $\text{SBox}[\cdot]$ is the substitution look-up table. We denote $y(\cdot, \cdot)$ as the label.

(Non-)Profiled Attacks. When performing a side-channel attack, an attacker has access to an attack dataset. That is, a set of traces which is obtained with some fixed secret that the attack aims at recovering. To extract information from these measurements, the attacker has to make some hypotheses about the least constrained leakage model. On top of that, profiled attacks have access to a training dataset that is a set of traces with known inputs/secrets obtained in similar conditions. The attacker may, for instance, acquire a clone device in order to extract such a training dataset.

Correlation Power Analysis (CPA). The most common non-profiled side-channel analysis technique is based on the Pearson correlation coefficient [1]. The attacker iterates over all possible values of the key k from the key-space and, knowing the ciphertext or plaintext t, computes $y(t, k)$ for each possible key prediction k. Given a certain amount of side-channel measurement traces x with corresponding t, he then calculates the Pearson correlation between x and $y(t, k)$. The most likely key prediction is the one that maximizes the correlation.

Neural Network Attacks. In our experiments, we will use three different networks for exploiting an *attack* dataset (that is, recovering the fixed key used to generate the traces). Those networks have been designed to target traces containing 700 time samples, and thus we reduced our traces to 700 points by selecting relevant windows based on Signal-to-Noise Ratio (SNR). The training is run for 100 epochs with batches of size 128. For each architecture, we selected the model reaching the best validation loss.

ASCAD Neural Network. Authors of [14] have introduced the first deeply studied neural network, that they refer to as *cnn_best*. In our experiments, we will refer to this network as ASCAD network (using its corresponding published parameters).

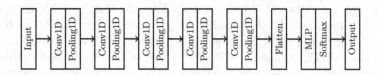

Fig. 1. ASCAD network

The ASCAD network, which is close to the architecture of VGG-16 [16] is depicted in Fig. 1. It is composed of five blocks with one convolutional layer by block, a number of filters equal to (64, 128, 256, 512, 512) with kernel size 11 (same padding), ReLU activation function, and an average pooling layer for each block. The CNN has two final dense layers of 4 096 units.

Variations of the ASCAD Network. Recently, lighter networks have been proposed in the side-channel context. To show that trace translation is not particular to one network, we additionally use:

1. the network proposed by Zaid et al. in [20] labeled as Zaid network,
2. the even lighter network presented by Wouters et al. in [18], labeled as NoConv1 network.

The Zaid network (depicted in Fig. 2(a)) is composed of one block with one convolutional layer, a number of filters equal to 4, with a kernel size 1 (same padding), SeLU activation functions, an batch normalization layer, and an average pooling layer. Finally, The Zaid network has two dense layers of 10 units.

The NoConv1 network (depicted in Fig. 2(b)) is composed of one block with one average pooling layer. The NoConv1 network has two dense layers of 10 units. Figure 2(b) gives an illustration of the NoConv1 network.

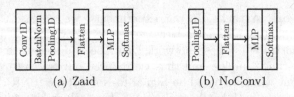

(a) Zaid   (b) NoConv1

Fig. 2. Additional networks

2.2 Datasets

We use the chipwhisperer light capture board combined with the CW308 UFO board to measure side-channel information from different STM32 devices. More precisely, we used the STM32F0 (Cortex-M0), STM32F1, STM32F2 (both Cortex-M3) and STM32F4 (Cortex-M4) target devices from the CW308 board[1].

On all devices, the beginning of an AES-128 encryption was measured, where we used the `TINYAES` implementation integrated in the chipwhisperer software. The chip frequency was set to 7.37 MHz and the measurements are sampled at 4×7.37 Ms/s. For the chipwhisperer light setup, power consumption is collected through the measurement shunt on the CW308 UFO board. To capture EM signals we used a Langer near-field EM probe (RF-U 5-2) connected to a 20dB amplifier[2]. On each device and source, we measured 100k traces for training and validating (used in a ratio of 80:20 for learning the translation and training the neural network attack), and 25k traces as an attack dataset with 25 different keys.

2.3 Evaluation Metrics and Targeted Value

Experiments have been performed to first-order leakage from the output of the AES substitution box (SBox): To evaluate the amount of leakage, we use the SNR. Let X denote the captured side-channel measurement, let Y be the label that is determined by the plaintext and the secret fixed key, then SNR gives the ratio between the deterministic data-dependent leakage and the remaining noise, i.e. $SNR = \frac{\mathbb{V}(\mathbb{E}(X|Y))}{\mathbb{E}(\mathbb{V}(X|Y))}$, where $\mathbb{E}(\cdot)$ is the expectation and $\mathbb{V}(\cdot)$ the variance of a random variable.

To evaluate the ability to retrieve the key, we use the Guessing Entropy (GE), which is the expected ranking of the secret key k^* within a vector of key guesses. In particular, the vector of key guesses $g_{i,1}, \ldots, g_{i,|K|}$ for the i-th measurement is calculated by mapping each key guess k to a label j with probability $\hat{p}_{i,j}$ and applying the maximum-likelihood principle over 1 to m measurements (where m is the number of measurements considered for the attack). The guessing entropy is then the expected position of the secret key k^* in the sorted vector of key

---

[1] https://rtfm.newae.com/Targets/UFO%20Targets/CW308T-STM32F.html.

[2] We do not claim that the setup, nor the position of the EM probe on the device is chosen optimally.

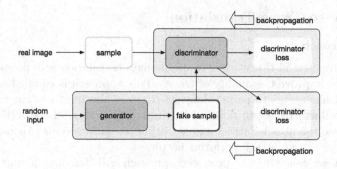

Fig. 3. General overview of GAN

guesses, where the sorting is applied to the probabilities in descending order. In other words, the guessing entropy gives the average amount of key guesses an attacker needs to perform before he reveals the secret key. In case his first guess is the secret key $GE = 0$.

2.4 GAN

GAN [4] falls into the class of generative modelling, meaning that it can be used to generate or output new synthetic data that could have plausibly been drawn from the original dataset. GAN is composed of two deep neural networks: the generator, and the discriminator. Generally speaking, the generator is used to generate new valid examples from the problem domain, whereas the discriminator is used to classify examples as real (from the domain) or fake (generated).

As illustrated in Fig. 3, the generator takes a fixed-length random vector as input and generates a sample in the domain, i.e., the space of real data. The random vector is typically drawn from a Gaussian distribution and it seeds the generative process. The discriminator model takes either an input from the real data or the generated one from the generator and predicts a binary class label of real or fake. The discriminator uses the discriminator loss for back-propagation, whereas the generator takes the generator loss produced by the discriminator.

Since its introduction in 2014, the interest of GAN has grown and many other GAN architectures have been proposed[3]. One particular class of GAN concentrates on the problem of image translation instead of pure image generation. One of the best-known architectures is Pix2Pix [6], it requires paired datasets.

Pix2Pix is trained to transform images from one domain into images that could plausibly belong to another domain. For example, a famous illustration in image translation transforms an drawing into a real image.

The interest of translation has been raised by different communities. For speech enhancement [13], authors implemented SEGAN to denoise audio waveforms. Contrary to the generator in standard GANs, the one of SEGAN takes as input a random vector plus a noisy signal data to produce the enhanced signal.

---

[3] Collection of GANs from several domains: https://github.com/hindupuravinash/the-gan-zoo.

3   Trace-to-Trace Translation

3.1   Approach

The idea proposed in this work is to use domain translation as a pre-processing technique to improve the quality of traces. This approach is enabled as soon as an attacker has access to paired datasets (that is, sharing the same intermediate target values) from two different settings. Indeed, one of the settings must correspond to the attack dataset and the other one corresponds to some settings for which the chosen attack performs better.

An attacker following the proposed approach will thus handle four different datasets. To smooth the description of the technique let us introduce some notation. The goal is to improve the attack on domain A traces by translating traces from the domain A to domain B. Datasets:

- the **original attack dataset** contains the traces from which the attacker wants to extract a secret key (thus from domain A);
- the **translation training dataset A** contains traces from domain A;
- the **translation training dataset B** contains traces from domain B that should be paired with the translation training dataset A;
- the **translated attack dataset** containing the translation from domain A to domain B of the *original attack dataset*.

Should this technique be used in a profiled setting, an additional fifth dataset would be added, namely

- the **training dataset** that contains training (thus labeled) traces from domain B used to train the profiled attack.

We want to bring the reader's attention to the fact that the only labeled dataset is the optional fifth one since translation training datasets only need to be paired (depending on the context, it may not necessarily imply being labeled).

Short Description. With these datasets in mind, the technique can be simply described in a very compacted form.

1. Train a *translator* to translate traces from domain A to domain B using *translation training datasets A and B*.
2. Use the trained *translator* to generate the *translated attack dataset* from the *original attack dataset on domain A*.
3. (optional) Train a profiled side-channel attack on the *training dataset* from domain B.
4. Attack the *translated attack dataset* to recover the key using an independent (un-)profiled attack.

Instantiating the Translator. As a first investigation of trace-to-trace translation, we propose to use GAN networks as a translator since they have shown to be efficient in several domains such as image translation [5], style transfer [7] or audio processing [13]. We do not claim that this architecture is an optimal choice for translation but its wide use makes it a relevant one for a first investigation. More details on the used GAN architecture are given in Sect. 3.3.

3.2   Experimental Methodology

For all our experiments on translation, we assess the improvements brought by the proposed preprocessing by applying both a profiled and a non-profiled attack. Let us recall that the attacker has an attack dataset from domain A and the improvement proposed is to translate them to domain B prior to the attack.

For the non-profiled scenario, the improvement consists in using the GAN to translate traces from a domain A to a domain B then apply CPA on translated (synthetic) traces. We compare this to the direct application of CPA to traces of domain A and thus generate two different graphs illustrating the attack success as a function of the number of traces used to attack.

Regarding the profiled scenario, the improvement consists in using the GAN to translate traces from a domain A to a domain B then apply a DL-based attack on translated (synthetic) traces. Obviously the DL-based attack should use a model trained on a training dataset from domain B.

For further comparison, we performed a complementary attack that consists in directly applying the DL-based attack using a model trained on domain B to the original attack dataset (from domain A). This additional experiment is only there as a witness experience and to demonstrate that the translation is indeed successful as both approaches use the same trained model.

3.3   Used GAN Architecture

We compared two architectures of GAN: Pix2Pix and SEGAN. Pix2Pix is well known for image translation, whereas SEGAN was designed to denoise audio-waveforms. We tuned both architectures over a set of hyperparameters, and selected the best performing model (see Table 1).

Table 1. Hyperparameter tuning

Hyperparameter	Range	SEGAN	Pix2Pix
		Selected	Selected
Optimizer	{Adam, RMSProp, SGD}	RMSProp	RMSProp
Activation function	{Tanh, LeakLy ReLU, PReLU}	Tanh	Tanh
Batch size	{64, 128, 256}	128	64[a]
Epochs	{25, 50, 100, 200}	200	200

[a]For SEGAN we tried four potential batch sizes, but as Pix2Pix is deeper than SEGAN, and we were limited by GPU memory in our setup, we could only test batch size of 64.

During the tuning phase, we used a paired dataset composed of $2 \times 100k$ traces (100k for each domain). These traces were split: 80k for the training and 20k for the validation. Since using the GE as a validation metric was too expensive on time, we saved the best model over training epochs based on the SNR obtained on translated traces. SNR can be directly computed on the validation dataset while using GE would require to translate a large attack dataset (with a few fixed keys). We kept the model providing the highest SNR peaks for each set of hyperparameters. A first analysis of the obtained SNR curves has shown that the best performances of Pix2Pix and SEGAN were obtained with Tanh as activation function and RMSprop as an optimizer. To better compare the obtained models, we additionally used 25k attack traces (translated traces with few fixed keys). Using them we computed the GE for all final models and chose the hyperparameters leading to the smallest one as summarized in Table 1.

The SEGAN architecture we selected for our experiments (after fine-tuning it) is close to the architecture of the original SEGAN [13] that is used for audio waveform translation.

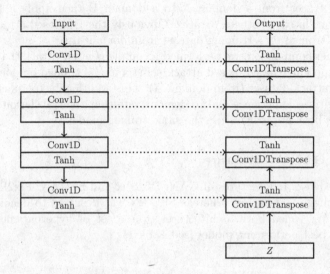

Fig. 4. Generator architecture (SEGAN)

The generator takes as input a 700-point trace coming from the original domain and outputs a 700-point synthetic trace, which is the translation to the target domain. The generator is an auto-encoder that is composed of an encoding part and a decoding part. The output value of the encoding part (or equivalently the input of the decoding part) lies in the so-called latent space. The latent representation of the trace has a shape equal to (2, 256) and this is where the random noise Z is added. The generator is illustrated in Fig. 4. The encoder is composed of four blocks with one convolutional layer per block, a number of filters equal to (32, 64, 128, 256) with kernel size 31 (same padding), followed by a Tanh activation function. The decoding part is composed of four blocks and one transposed convolutional layer per block, a number of filters equal to (128, 64, 32, 1) with kernel size 31 (same padding), followed by a Tanh activation function. Each block of the decoding part is concatenated with the output of each encoding block, represented by a dotted arrow in the Fig. 4, it is the principle of the U-Net architecture [15].

The discriminator takes as input a combination of two 700-point traces: one trace coming from the original domain and one trace coming from the target one. This last trace may directly come from the target domain (real trace) or it could be a generated trace (fake trace). The discriminator is trained to distinguish between real and fake. More precisely, the discriminator outputs the probability that a trace from the target domain is a translation from the original domain. The discriminator is illustrated in Fig. 5. It is composed of four blocks, and one convolutional layer per block, a number of filters equal to (32, 64, 128, 256) with a kernel size 31 (same padding), a Batch normalization layer, and a Tanh activation function. The discriminator has two final dense layers of 256 and 128 units.

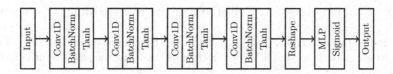

Fig. 5. Discriminator architecture (SEGAN)

As for SEGAN, we slightly adapted Pix2Pix to our datasets. The generator of the Pix2Pix takes as input a 700-point trace coming from the original domain and outputs a 700-point synthetic trace as SEGAN model. The generator is also an auto-encoder that is composed of an encoder part and decoder part. The Pix2Pix network didn't take latent representation between the encoder part and decoder part, but just one convolutional layer composed of 512 filters. The encoder part is composed of seven blocks with one convolutional layer per block, a number of filters equal to (32, 64, 128, 256, 256, 256, 256) with a kernel size of 11 (same padding), followed by a Batch Normalization layer and an activation function (see Table 1). The decoder part is composed of seven blocks and one transposed convolutional layer per block, a number of filters equal to (256, 256, 256, 256, 128, 64, 32) with a kernel size 11 (same padding), followed by a Batch Normalization layer and an activation function. The discriminator of the Pix2Pix is composed of five blocks with one convolutional layer per block, a number of filters equal to (32, 64, 128, 256, 1) with a kernel size of 11 (same padding). In the original paper [6] the discriminator part of the Pix2Pix is implemented as PatchGAN, which means that the discriminator will classify 70 × 70 patches of the input image as real or fake. In our case, we adapt the output of the discriminator to output one single value. During the tuning phase, Pix2Pix always provided lower performance (e.g., lower or less SNR peaks). Hence, SEGAN has been selected for our experiments on translation in the next sections.

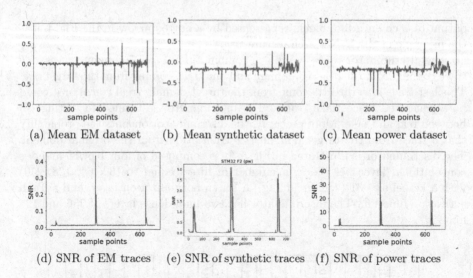

(a) Mean EM dataset   (b) Mean synthetic dataset   (c) Mean power dataset

(d) SNR of EM traces   (e) SNR of synthetic traces   (f) SNR of power traces

Fig. 6. Evaluation of STM32F2: (a)–(c) illustrates the mean trace and (d)–(f) the SNR of the attack dataset for the EM, power channel, and the translated synthetic trace dataset

4   Translation from EM to Power

In this scenario, we investigate the capability of GAN to translate traces from EM to power consumption on the same device. Depending on the device, we obtained various different SNR levels. For each device, we observed that the SNR corresponding to its EM and power traces have similar shapes while being of different magnitudes. From a quantitative point of view, the SNR value obtained from power traces is higher than from EM traces: in our setup EM measurements contain more noise. For the experiments presented in this section, **Domain A** will thus correspond to EM traces (that are harder to attack) and **Domain B** to power ones.

STM32F2. Figure 6 shows the mean trace of the attack dataset of the EM data, the synthetic dataset, and the power consumption, as well as their SNR levels. First, we observe a translation as indeed the mean translated synthetic trace is looking close to the mean trace of the power dataset, particularly for the second half. Next, the SNR value is low (close to 0.4) for the EM channel, whereas the SNR value is high (close to 50) for the power channel, but their shapes are similar. The synthetic dataset corresponds to the set generated by GAN, which was trained to translate traces from EM to the power channel. We observe that the shape of SNR is different compared to the shape of EM and power and that the leakage positions changed in time, while still being able to retrieve one (over three) leakage positions from the target domain. The SNR value of the synthetic dataset is close to 6, so the translation increases the magnitude and thus the amount of information. Still, the SNR value is lower than for the power channel, which means that some information could not be reproduced (as it may not be available in the EM trace).

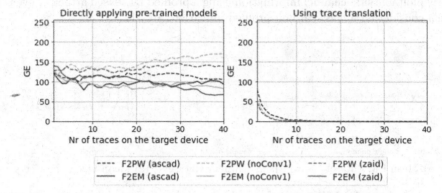

(a) GE for three networks; left: original EM dataset, right: translated synthetic dataset

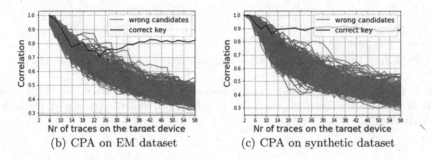

(b) CPA on EM dataset   (c) CPA on synthetic dataset

Fig. 7. Attack evaluation on STM32F2 EM (original and synthetic translated traces)

In Fig. 7 (top) we plot the GE in the profiled scenario when targeting the EM channel. First, we see that the performance is not specific to one network (ASCAD, Zaid, or noConv1). On the left side of the figure, one observes that when using directly the EM traces for attacking (labeled as F2EM), the attack does not succeed for any network. Next, similar performance can be observed when the network is trained on the power channel (labeled F2PW). Contrary the right plot shows that using the model trained on the power channel (F2PW) while attacking the translated synthetic traces, we observe that the attack rapidly converges towards a GE of 0 using less than 10 attack traces. We further evaluate the outcome in the scenario of non-profiled attacks. Figure 7 (bottom) illustrates CPA using directly the EM dataset and when using the translated synthetic traces. Without translation the correct key is found with approximately 30 traces, whereas with the translated synthetic dataset the key can be found using below 15 traces.

These results confirm that GAN is able to translate between the EM and power domain (i.e., F2PW not working on EM dataset, but on the translated dataset for the three networks), and further that the translation is increasing the exploitable side-channel information using a profiled DL-based attack or even when considering a classical non-profiled univariate attack.

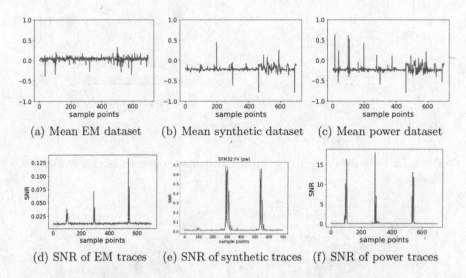

(a) Mean EM dataset   (b) Mean synthetic dataset   (c) Mean power dataset

(d) SNR of EM traces   (e) SNR of synthetic traces   (f) SNR of power traces

Fig. 8. Evaluation of STM32F4: (a)–(c) illustrates the (mean) trace and (d)–(f) the SNR of the attack dataset for the EM, power channel, and the translated synthetic trace dataset

STM32F4. Figure 8 (top) shows the mean trace obtained from STM32F4 of the dataset for EM/power measurements and the synthetic traces, where we visually observe a translation. In the bottom of the figure, we plot the SNR obtained with different attack datasets. The maximum SNR peak from the EM channel is close to 0.12, whereas it is close to 17.5 for the power channel, showing that the power channel is containing less noise. Again, the shape of the synthetic dataset is different compared to the original channels but in this experiment the translation preserved perfectly time locations. We observe that the SNR value of the synthetic attack set is improved by a factor 10.

Figure 9 (top) shows the GE obtained when targeting device STM32F4 with EM for all three networks. As for STM32F2, we observe on the left that attacking the EM channel using a model trained on EM (F4EM) or trained on power consumption (F4PW) does not converge within the given traces for any network. When using the translated synthetic traces and a model trained on the power channel (F4PW) GE reaches a mean rank equals to zero with only 20 traces for NoConv1 and around 30 traces for the other two networks. So, again by using the GAN translation, we could turn an unsuccessful attack into a successful one.

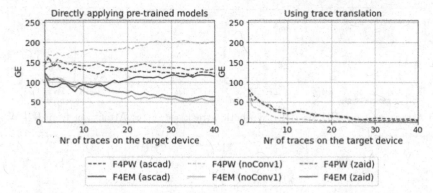

(a) GE for three networks; left: original EM, right: translated synthetic dataset

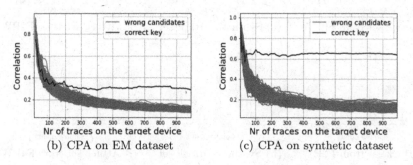

(b) CPA on EM dataset   (c) CPA on synthetic dataset

Fig. 9. Attack evaluation on STM32F4 EM (original and synthetic translated traces)

Figure 9 (bottom) shows that again the performance of CPA is improved as well. Using directly the EM dataset reveals the key using around 200 traces, while the attack succeeds using around 50 traces using the translated traces.

Summary. In this section, we demonstrate that a translation from EM to power consumption is possible and that it reduces the number of traces needed for a successful attack. On both datasets, the classical approach (attacking directly the noisy channel) with DL failed and we observe that directly using a network trained on the power channel (but without translating the attack dataset) leads to poor performances. Our results show that GANs can be used to translate traces from EM to power channel, and the synthetic traces combined with a network trained on the power channel is successful. Additionally, our results show that the performance of CPA is greatly improved when attacking on translated instead of the original traces.

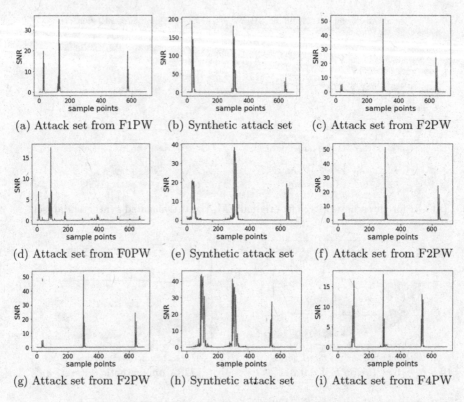

Fig. 10. SNR evaluation for each of scenarios considered: (a)–(c) F1PW translated to F2PW, (d)–(f) F0PW translated to F2PW, (g)–(i) F2PW translated to F4PW; left column domain A, middle column translated, right column domain B dataset.

5   Cross-Device Translation

In this scenario, we investigate the capability of GAN to translate traces captured from one device to another. For the experiments presented in this section, **Domain A** will thus correspond to traces from one chip and **Domain B** to traces from another chip.

STM32F1 Power to STM32F2 Power. In Fig. 10 (a)–(c), we plot the SNR evaluation obtained with different attack sets when translating F1 to F2 with power. The SNR value is close to 50 for F2, the synthetic attack set has an SNR value close to 200 (which is even larger than the target domain), and we can observe that GAN retrieved all three leakage positions from F2 which are at different time locations than F1.

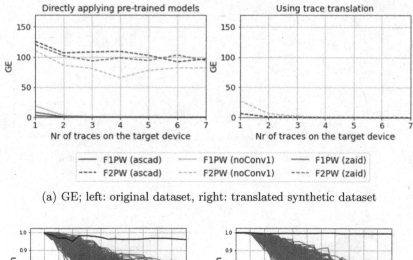

(a) GE; left: original dataset, right: translated synthetic dataset

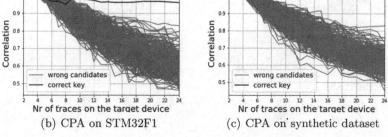

(b) CPA on STM32F1   (c) CPA on synthetic dataset

Fig. 11. Attack evaluation on STM32F1 (original and synthetic translated traces)

In Fig. 11 (top), we plot the GE obtained when we target F1 with power. Any of the DL-based attacks on the target domain (labeled F1PW) reaches a mean rank equal to zero below 2 traces. Using a model trained on F2 directly does not succeed, however, when translating to the domain F2, the ASCAD and Zaid networks succeed as well within 2 traces. Even though the performance using directly F2PW cannot be improved because of its high SNR by nature, this scenario shows that the translation into another domain is possible. For CPA (given at the bottom of the figure) we see that the performance can be improved due to translation. Attacking the original traces is successful within 8 traces, whereas the correct key is found on the synthetic traces using 2 traces.

STM32F0 Power to STM32F2 Power. In Fig. 10 (d)–(f), we plot the SNR evaluation when we translate F0 to F2 device with power. The SNR value is close to 50 for the F2 device, and the synthetic attack set has an SNR close to 12 (which is even smaller than the target domain), but again we can observe that GAN retrieved the leakage positions from F2, while being different in time and amount for F0 and F2.

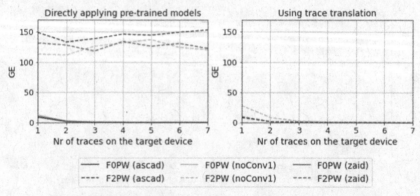

(a) GE; left: original dataset, right: translated synthetic dataset

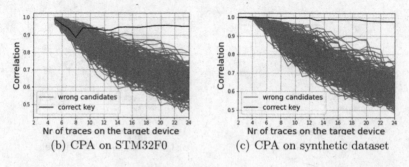

(b) CPA on STM32F0   (c) CPA on synthetic dataset

Fig. 12. Attack evaluation on STM32F0 (original and synthetic translated traces)

In Fig. 12 (top), we plot the GE obtained when we target F0 with power. As before, all DL-based attacks on the target domain (labeled F0PW) are already efficient (as the SNR is high enough), whereas the model trained on F2PW does not succeed on the original traces. Even though with a tiny difference, we observe that the best performance was obtained by applying GAN and the Zaid network.

As in the previous scenario, we see that the translation improves the attack-ability with CPA. On the original dataset, the key can be found using around 12 traces, whereas on the translated synthetic traces we see that the correct key can be found immediately using 2 traces.

STM32F2 Power to STM32F4 Power. Unlike the previous scenarios, we now consider to translate from a device with higher SNR to another one with lower SNR. This is driven by several aspects, for example, the investigation if the translation between domains is still successful (even though it may give less attackability), or an attacker may only have a dataset available with a tuned network for a device with less SNR. In Fig. 10 (g)–(i), we plot the SNR evaluation when we translate F2 to F4. The SNR value is close to 17.5 for the F4 device, the synthetic attack set has an SNR value close to 40 (which is still larger than the target domain), and we can observe that GAN has recovered all three leakage positions at the same time positions as F4.

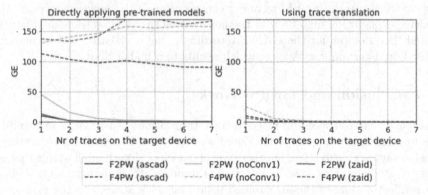

(a) GE for three networks; left: original EM dataset, right: translated synthetic dataset

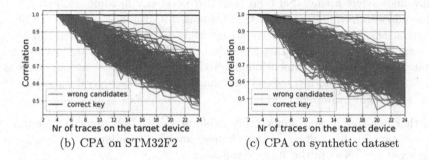

(b) CPA on STM32F2   (c) CPA on synthetic dataset

Fig. 13. Attack evaluation on STM32F2 (original and synthetic translated traces)

Figure 13 shows the GE obtained when targeting F2 with power. First, we see that indeed a translation to a higher noise domain is possible, as all networks trained on F4PW succeed on the translated dataset, but fail on the original dataset. Second, one can observe that the attack performance of the three neural networks is not degraded, but rather slightly improved. The increase may be explained by the fact, that even though F2 has a higher SNR peak, F4 contains three SNR peaks that are of a similar magnitude. We can see a similar behavior in the translated synthetic attack dataset, which shows three SNR peaks with comparable SNR levels. Indeed, when summing up all SNR values, the synthetic dataset achieves a higher value than F2.

The performance of CPA shows a degraded performance, which is expected as its an univariate attack, only considering one SNR peak at a time, where the magnitude of SNR is directly related to the success of CPA [3].

Summary. Our experiments show that a trace translation between devices is possible (lower to higher and higher to lower SNR) and the leakage positions of the target domain are retrieved by translation. Concerning the SNR amplitudes, we observed various behaviors. In two of the experiments, the synthetic traces lead to a significantly higher SNR than the target domain, which we did not observe when translating EM to power consumption in the previous section. An intuitive explanation may be that the noise of the two devices (domains) is not related (i.e., random for the GAN). Accordingly, the translation will be mainly focused on deterministic leakage, which results to a higher SNR.

6   Conclusion and Future Work

This paper derives successful trace-to-trace translations using GANs in two different contexts, which opens a new door for adversaries. To attack a noisy setting, an adversary is able to select another type of device or side-channel source that is easier to attack and use trace translation to improve attack performances. Using three different state-of-the-art profiled neural network attacks on the synthetic translated traces, we show that the translation is not particular to a network. To learn the translation between datasets, the approach in this paper does not require knowledge of the label (and thus the secret key in some contexts), but only requires to have paired datasets. This makes it also interesting in the non-profiled attacker model, demonstrated by using CPA in our experiments. We also want to point out that this technique is orthogonal to (and thus can be combined with) classical dimensionality reduction techniques. As our work is the first demonstration of trace-to-trace translation, we see several directions of future works. For example:

- further fine-tuning and architecture exploration of GAN networks for trace translation in the context of side-channel analysis (similarly as it has been achieved for CNNs in the state-of-the-art);
- exploration of the limitations of trace translation that may go beyond devices (of related types) and side-channel sources;
- further relaxation of the required datasets;
- applicability of protected implementations. We already applied our method to a hiding countermeasure (additional Gaussian noise) that showed similar success as the results presented in the paper. Another important research direction would be the investigation of masking countermeasures. However, this may need adaptions of the methodology to lead to successful translations due to the more complex algebraic links between the leakage and the labels.

Availability. Implementations for reproducing our results will be available at https://github.com/GeneveyC/Machine-learning-with-SCA.

References

1. Brier, E., Clavier, C., Olivier, F.: Correlation power analysis with a leakage model. In: Joye, M., Quisquater, J.-J. (eds.) CHES 2004. LNCS, vol. 3156, pp. 16–29. Springer, Heidelberg (2004). https://doi.org/10.1007/978-3-540-28632-5_2

2. Chari, S., Rao, J.R., Rohatgi, P.: Template attacks. In: Kaliski, B.S., Koç, K., Paar, C. (eds.) CHES 2002. LNCS, vol. 2523, pp. 13–28. Springer, Heidelberg (2003). https://doi.org/10.1007/3-540-36400-5_3

3. Fei, Y., Luo, Q., Ding, A.A.: A statistical model for DPA with novel algorithmic confusion analysis. In: Prouff, E., Schaumont, P. (eds.) CHES 2012. LNCS, vol. 7428, pp. 233–250. Springer, Heidelberg (2012). https://doi.org/10.1007/978-3-642-33027-8_14

4. Goodfellow, I.J., et al.: Generative adversarial networks (2014)

5. Isola, P., Zhu, J.Y., Zhou, T., Efros, A.A.: Image-to-image translation with conditional adversarial networks. In: CVPR (2017)

6. Isola, P., Zhu, J.Y., Zhou, T., Efros, A.A.: Image-to-image translation with conditional adversarial networks (2018)

7. Karras, T., Laine, S., Aila, T.: A style-based generator architecture for generative adversarial networks (2019)

8. Kim, J., Picek, S., Heuser, A., Bhasin, S., Hanjalic, A.: Make some noise. Unleashing the power of convolutional neural networks for profiled side-channel analysis. In: TCHES 2019, no. 3, pp. 148–179, May 2019

9. Kocher, P., Jaffe, J., Jun, B.: Differential power analysis. In: Wiener, M. (ed.) CRYPTO 1999. LNCS, vol. 1666, pp. 388–397. Springer, Heidelberg (1999). https://doi.org/10.1007/3-540-48405-1_25

10. Kubota, T., Yoshida, K., Shiozaki, M., Fujino, T.: Deep learning side-channel attack against hardware implementations of AES. In: 2019 22nd Euromicro Conference on Digital System Design (DSD), pp. 261–268, August 2019

11. Maghrebi, H., Portigliatti, T., Prouff, E.: Breaking cryptographic implementations using deep learning techniques. In: Carlet, C., Hasan, M.A., Saraswat, V. (eds.) SPACE 2016. LNCS, vol. 10076, pp. 3–26. Springer, Cham (2016). https://doi.org/10.1007/978-3-319-49445-6_1

12. Masure, L., Dumas, C., Prouff, E.: A comprehensive study of deep learning for side-channel analysis. In: TCHES 2020, no. 1, pp. 348–375 (2019)

13. Pascual, S., Bonafonte, A., Serrà, J.: SEGAN: Speech enhancement generative adversarial network (2017)

14. Prouff, E., Strullu, R., Benadjila, R., Cagli, E., Dumas, C.: Study of deep learning techniques for side-channel analysis and introduction to ASCAD database. Cryptology ePrint Archive, Report 2018/053 (2018). https://eprint.iacr.org/2018/053

15. Ronneberger, O., Fischer, P., Brox, T.: U-net: convolutional networks for biomedical image segmentation. In: Navab, N., Hornegger, J., Wells, W.M., Frangi, A.F. (eds.) MICCAI 2015. LNCS, vol. 9351, pp. 234–241. Springer, Cham (2015). https://doi.org/10.1007/978-3-319-24574-4_28

16. Simonyan, K., Zisserman, A.: Very deep convolutional networks for large-scale image recognition. CoRR abs/1409.1556 (2014). http://arxiv.org/abs/1409.1556

17. Wang, P., et al.: Enhancing the performance of practical profiling side-channel attacks using conditional generative adversarial networks (2020)

18. Wouters, L., Arribas, V., Gierlichs, B., Preneel, B.: Revisiting a methodology for efficient CNN architectures in profiling attacks. In: TCHES 2020, no. 3, pp. 147–168 (2020)

19. Wu, L., Picek, S.: Remove some noise: On pre-processing of side-channel measurements with autoencoders. In: TCHES 2020, no. 4, pp. 389–415 (2020)

20. Zaid, G., Bossuet, L., Habrard, A., Venelli, A.: Methodology for efficient CNN architectures in profiling attacks. In: TCHES 2020, no. 1, pp. 1–36 (2019)

Profiled Side-Channel Analysis
in the Efficient Attacker Framework

Stjepan Picek[1(✉)], Annelie Heuser[2], Guilherme Perin[1], and Sylvain Guilley[3]

[1] Delft University of Technology, Delft, The Netherlands
[2] Univ Rennes, Inria, CNRS, IRISA, Rennes, France
[3] Secure-IC S.A.S., Cesson-Sévigné, France

Abstract. Profiled side-channel attacks represent the most powerful category of side-channel attacks. There, the attacker has access to a clone device to profile its leaking behavior. Additionally, it is common to consider the attacker unbounded in power to allow the worst-case security analysis. This paper starts with a different premise where we are interested in the minimum power that the attacker requires to conduct a successful attack. We propose a new framework for profiled side-channel analysis that we call the Efficient Attacker Framework. With it, we require attacks to be as powerful as possible, but we also provide a setting that inherently allows a more objective analysis among attacks. To confirm our theoretical results, we provide an experimental evaluation of our framework in the context of deep learning-based side-channel analysis.

1 Introduction

Side-channel analysis (SCA) is a threat that exploits weaknesses in physical implementations of cryptographic algorithms rather than the algorithms themselves [1]. Profiled SCA performs the worst-case security analysis by considering the most powerful side-channel attacker with access to an open (the keys can be chosen or are known by the attacker) clone device. Additionally, the SCA community considers an attacker in the setting with unbounded power, e.g., the attacker can obtain any number of profiling or attack traces and has unlimited computational power.

In the last two decades, besides template attack and its variants [2,3], the SCA community started using machine learning to conduct profiled attacks. Those results proved to be highly competitive compared to template attack, and, in many scenarios, machine learning methods surpassed template attack performance [4–6]. Unfortunately, in these scenarios, the experimental setup is often arbitrarily limited, and no clear guidelines on the limitation of profiling traces or the hyperparameter tuning phase are offered or discussed.

More recently, the SCA community started to experiment with deep learning where such methods bested both template attack and other machine learning methods [7–9]. Again, no clear guidelines on the number of profiling traces

© Springer Nature Switzerland AG 2022
V. Grosso and T. Pöppelmann (Eds.): CARDIS 2021, LNCS 13173, pp. 44–63, 2022.
https://doi.org/10.1007/978-3-030-97348-3_3

were given or investigated. Simultaneously, the researchers started to give more attention to the hyperparameter tuning, but the results are still far from definitive ones, see, e.g., [10,11]. Consequently, there is an evident lack of evaluation guidelines/frameworks in the context of profiled analysis to understand various attacks' performance or how they compare. This gap is highly important as state-of-the-art results with deep learning successfully and efficiently break publicly available targets.

This paper aims to extend the currently used evaluation techniques to a framework that determines the least powerful attacker that can still reveal secret information. To achieve this, we evaluate the limit on 1) the number of measurements the attacker can collect in the training phase and 2) the number of hyperparameter tuning experiments. It could sound counter-intuitive to make such limitations as one can argue there is no reason why an attacker cannot collect a large number of measurements or run hyperparameter tuning as long as needed (or select an algorithm that has no hyperparameters to tune). We claim that there are several reasons for that:

1. By considering a scenario where an unlimited number of measurements are available, we "allow" less powerful attacks. More precisely, the attacker can use a larger set of measurements to compensate for less powerful profiling models.
2. By considering a scenario where a computationally unbounded attacker runs the analysis, one assumes the attacker can always find the best possible attack while that seldom happens in practice.
3. The target device may include a countermeasure that limits the number of exploitable measurements. The experimental setup can have constraints that limit the allowed length of the hyperparameter tuning phase.
4. Although taking measurements or running more experiments is "cheap", there is always a point where this is more effort than the target/secret is worth.
5. Having more measurements does not guarantee better results, especially in realistic scenarios. Consider the case where one device is used for profiling and the other for the attack, i.e., the portability setting (a realistic case that is usually simplified in research works where only a single device is used [7–9,12]). Then, adding more measurements to the profiling phase can cause machine learning methods to overfit[1] [12]. The same issue can happen due to a too detailed tuning phase.

As far as we know, there are no previous works considering profiling and realistic attacker evaluation frameworks. When the attacker is restricted, it is usually set as one of several tested scenarios (e.g., testing a classifier's performance with specific hyperparameters or a different number of measurements in the training phase). Alternatively, it is motivated by some limitations in the data acquisition or evaluation process.

In this paper, we present the following main contributions:

---

[1] Overfitting occurs when the learning model learns the data too well and cannot adapt to previously unseen data.

1. We propose a new framework for profiled side-channel analysis where we evaluate the minimum power of an attacker in the profiling phase to still be successful in the test phase. We also introduce a new threat model that differs from a common one by considering a more realistic attacker. The attacker in our threat model is still powerful from the computational perspective and the perspective of the learning models that can be built. In other words, we move from the problem of simply breaking the target (which is well-explored and with strong results, especially when considering deep learning) to a problem where we break the target with a minimal number of measurements and minimal hyperparameter tuning. We consider our framework to be intuitive and easily adaptable to many realistic scenarios.
2. We strengthen our results with an experimental evaluation conducted on publicly available datasets protected with masking countermeasures. We explore two commonly used leakage models and two neural network types.

The code is publicly available at https://github.com/AISyLab/EfficientAttackerFramework.

2   Existing Frameworks for Side-Channel Evaluation

2.1   Scientific Metrics

The most common evaluation metrics in the side-channel analysis are success rate (SR) and guessing entropy (GE) [13]. GE states the average number of key candidates an adversary needs to test to reveal the secret key after conducting a side-channel analysis. In particular, given Q traces in the attack phase, an attack outputs a key guessing vector $g = [g_1, g_2, \ldots, g_{|\mathcal{K}|}]$ in decreasing order of probability with $|\mathcal{K}|$ being the size of the keyspace. So, g_1 is the most likely and $g_{|\mathcal{K}|}$ the least likely key candidate. The guessing entropy is the average position of k_a^* in g over multiple experiments. The success rate is defined as the average empirical probability that g_1 equals the secret key k_a^*.

In practice, one may consider leakage models $Y(\cdot)$ that are bijective functions. Thus, each output probability calculated from the classifiers for $Y(k)$ directly relates to one key candidate k. When $Y(\cdot)$ is not bijective, several key candidates k may get assigned with the same output probabilities, which is why a single trace attack ($Q = 1$) may not be possible in the case of non-bijective leakage models. Further, to calculate the key guessing vector g over Q attack traces, the (log-)likelihood principle is used.

Remark 1. SR and GE are used for practical evaluations in both non-profiling and profiling scenarios. Typically, they are given over a range of traces used in the attack phase (i.e., for $q = 1, 2, \ldots, Q$). If these metrics are used in profiling scenarios, there are no clear guidelines for evaluating attacks. Most of the time, the number of training measurements N in the profiling stage is (arbitrary) fixed, making comparisons and meaningful conclusions on profiled side-channel attacks or resistance of implementations hard and unreliable in most scenarios.

Whitnall and Oswald introduced a more theoretical framework that aims at comparing distinguishing powers instead of estimators of attacks [14,15]. Accordingly, the profiling dataset N size does not play any role in this framework. The most popular metrics of the framework are the relative and absolute distinguishing margins in which the correct key's output score and the value for the highest-ranked alternative are compared.

Another approach to compare side-channel attacks uses closed-form expressions of distinguishers [16], enabling conclusions about distinguishers without the requirement of actual measurements. Unfortunately, only a few closed-form expressions of distinguishers have been achieved so far.

Regarding masking countermeasures, Duc et al. defined information-theoretical bounds on the success rate depending on the number of measurements, shares, and independent on the concrete estimated side-channel attack [17]. In [18], the authors provided information-theoretic tools to bound the model errors in side-channel evaluations concerning the choice of the leakage model.

Typically, to assess the performance of machine learning classifiers, accuracy is used [19]. A detailed comparison between accuracy (but also other machine learning metrics like precision, recall, F1) and guessing entropy/success rate is given in [6], which details that such metrics may not always be a proper choice for assessing the attack performance in side-channel analysis.

2.2   Practical Evaluation Testing

While most of these previous metrics are relevant in some contexts and scenarios, a different approach is required to make research statements in the context of profiled attacks. This issue becomes even more evident when looking at practical evaluation used in standardization processes. In practice, there are two main practical schemes:

1. Test-based schemes, such as NIST FIPS 140 [20] and its application to the mitigation of other attacks (part of Appendix F, in particular, non-invasive attacks ISO/IEC 17825 [21]).
2. Evaluation-based schemes, such as Common Criteria (CC, ISO/IEC 15408 [22]).

Interestingly, both FIPS 140 and CC pay attention to the limited amount of resources spent. When considering FIPS 140/ISO/IEC 17825, the requirement is more on the attack traces, but regarding CC, the evaluation of attacks is considered under two phases: identification (which matches with the training phase in the context of profiled side-channel attacks) and exploitation (which matches with the attack phase in the context of profiled side-channel attacks). Strictly speaking, the distinction is for CC version 2, but it still implicitly holds for version 3. Several factors are considered for the evaluations of attacks, namely: elapsed time, expertise, knowledge of the Target Of Evaluation (TOE), access to TOE, equipment, open samples. The first factor, elapsed time, directly connects with the acquisition of traces in the profiling phase and the hyperparameter tuning. Indeed, according to the guidance "Application of Attack Potential to Smartcards" [23], the score is considered:

- 0 if the profiling of the traces can be performed in less than one hour,
- 1 if the profiling of the traces can be performed in less than one day,
- 2 if the profiling of the traces can be performed in less than one week,
- 3 if the profiling of the traces can be performed in less than one month,
- 5 if the profiling of the traces cannot be performed in less than one month.

Accordingly, we see that the CC guidance favors attacks, realized with as little profiling effort as possible. This profiling effort can go in the direction of the number of required measurements, the number of experiments in the hyperparameter tuning phase, or both.

2.3 Practical Observations and Effects of Aging

Besides overfitting (see details in Sect. 1), another difficulty for profiled attacks is that the collection of side-channel traces becomes less reliable after a long period. Due to temperature and environmental conditions evolution over time, some trend noise must be added to the side-channel traces. For instance, this has been characterized by Heuser et al. in [24], where it is proven that trend noise drastically impedes SCA. Similar findings are confirmed by Cao et al. [25]. Efficient distinguishing situations, such as that depicted in Fig. 1 shows that the best number of traces to estimate a distinguisher is not always "the maximal".

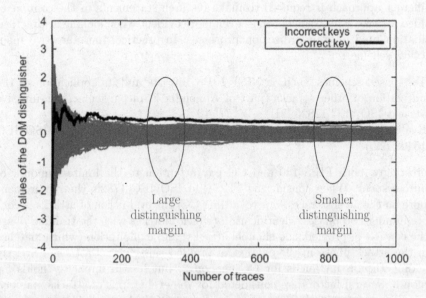

Fig. 1. Difference of Means (DoM) distinguisher estimation for all key bytes (the correct one and all incorrect ones).

This is illustrated on a simple "difference of means" attack representing side-channel attack on DPA contest 4.2 traces [26] (the second implementation (v4.2) is based on an improved version of the first version - v4).

3   The Efficient Attacker Framework

3.1   Threat Model

The adversary has access to a clone device running the target cryptographic algorithm. This device can be queried with a known key and plaintext while the corresponding leakage measurement is stored. Commonly, the adversary can have infinite queries to characterize a precise profiling model. There are no limits on how many experiments he can do to find such a profiling model. Next, the adversary queries the attack device with known plaintext to obtain the unknown key. The corresponding side-channel leakage measurement is compared to the characterized profiling model to recover the key.

In our threat model, the adversary has a limited number of queries to characterize a profiling model. Additionally, he has a limited number of experiments to conduct hyperparameter tuning. Note, while our framework allows various machine learning tasks, we concentrate on the classification task in this paper, as it is common in the profiled SCA [7–9].

3.2   Components of a Successful Attack

Current evaluations for profiled SCA mostly assume that the attacker is unbounded in his computational power. This assumption aims to provide the worst-case scenario for the designer, which should help assess the risk properly. Although the attacker is considered unbounded, he is always bounded, with bounds set ad-hoc, and there are no clear directions one should follow when modeling the realistic attacker.

First, we discuss two core assumptions we make in this research. These need to be fulfilled so that general meaningful comparisons between profiled attacks can be made, and our framework can provide exploitable results:

1. Attack must be possible. While our framework does not require the attacker always to succeed, the attack must be possible. For instance, having measurements completely uncorrelated with the labels (set of variables defined from a leakage model) will make our framework not useful. Still, no side-channel attack can succeed if there is no statistical connection between the measurements and labels. Consequently, this is not a drawback of our framework.
2. We consider only profiled (supervised) attacks, and therefore, profiling measurements need to allow learnability about the problem. Profiling measurements that are completely uncorrelated with the attack measurements would make our framework unusable. The hyperparameter tuning (if possible) must allow reaching a useful profiling model. Again, the profiled attacks cannot work if the previous conditions are not fulfilled, which does not represent our framework's disadvantage.

Next, we examine the three components of a successful attack. The worst-case (strongest) attacker will be unbounded in all three components. Simultaneously, fulfilling only one or two of those components accounts for more realistic settings one encounters in practice:

1. Quantity (the number of measurements) - there must be sufficient measurements in the profiling/test phase to conduct the attack, i.e., to build a reliable profiling model that generalizes to the unseen data. This criterion is a natural one and is already well-known in SCA as researchers usually report the attack's performance concerning a different number of measurements. There is much less research to determine the minimum number of measurements for a successful attack.
2. Quality (based on the available measurements, it must be possible to find the mapping f between the input (measurements) and output (labels)) - the measurements need to be of sufficient quality to conduct the attack. This condition could be translated into the requirement that the SNR should be sufficiently high or that the data need to have all information required to model the leakage correctly. Finally, this component includes the leakage model's quality, i.e., the considered leakage model provides sufficient information and the distribution of leakages. Again, like the previous component, this one is well addressed in the SCA community as researchers usually conduct various pre-processing steps, e.g., to select/transform features or align traces.
3. Learnability (hyperparameter tuning) - the attacker needs to learn the profiling model. This perspective also accounts for finding the best possible hyperparameters for the profiling model. The learnability is naturally connected with the quantity and quality components. This component is significantly less addressed, but more recent works show the SCA researchers becoming more interested in it [9–11,27], confirming our claims about the learnability importance. We note that while the researchers usually conduct various tuning procedures, they rarely report how difficult it was to find the hyperparameters used in the end.

We should not limit the quality component: if the attacker can obtain measurements, those measurements should be of the best possible quality. When discussing the quantity and learnability components, we can (and we must) evaluate the limit of the number of profiling measurements and experiments in the tuning phase since:

1. If always considering the extreme case of unbounded measurements in the profiling phase, we "allow" to utilize weaker attack, which may only work in this extreme scenario. On the other hand, if we consider the minimum number of available traces in the profiling phase while still succeeding in the attack phase, we promote efficient attacks.
2. Theoretically, the attacker who is unbounded in his capabilities could break cryptographic implementations even with a single measurement as he can always find the optimal attack. This reasoning suggests that ultimately, the designer could do nothing to stop the attack.

Remark 2. Having a limited number of measurements or time to conduct hyper-parameter tuning is a realistic occurrence in practical scenarios, as the attacker may be limited by time, resources, and also face implemented countermeasures, preventing him from taking an arbitrarily large number of side-channel measurements while knowing the secret key of the device.

To conclude, we need to consider an attacker who can perform a successful attack with the smallest possible number of profiling measurements N, where success is defined over a performance metric ρ with a threshold of δ. To reach that success, the attacker should use the smallest possible number of tuning experiments H (where h represents a specific set of hyperparameters, i.e., a specific profiling model).

Example 1. Consider ρ being the guessing entropy < 20, which is a common threshold value in the side-channel analysis, see, e.g., [6]. Then, the measure of the attacker's power is 1) the number of profiling traces N he needs to train a profiling model, which is then used on attack traces (of size Q) to break the implementation, 2) the number of experiments conducted before finding the hyperparameters resulting in a strong attack, or 3) both the number of profiling traces and hyperparameter tuning experiments.

3.3   Framework Description

The goal for machine learning classification task is to learn a mapping (model) f from $\mathcal{X}$ to $\mathcal{Y}$, i.e., $Y \leftarrow f(X, \theta)$ where X are samples drawn i.i.d. from set $\mathcal{X}$ and where the cardinality of X equals N. Let θ be the profiling model's parameters that result in the best possible approximation from h hyperparameter combinations. Additionally, let $\mathbf{g}_{Q,f} = [g_1, g_2, \ldots, g_{|\mathcal{K}|}]$ be the guessing vector from the profiled side-channel attack using Q traces in the attack phase, and the profiling model f built in the profiling phase as an input. In practice, the estimation of f depends on hyperparameters h, which we denote by f_h when the dependency is emphasized. Then, $\rho(g_{Q,f}, k_a^*)$ represents the performance metric of the profiled side-channel attack using the secret key k_a^* to evaluate the success.

For a given number of attack traces Q and $h_1, \ldots, h_H$ hyperparameter tuning selections (H being the number of different hyperparameter sets), the Efficient Attacker Framework aims at minimizing the number of profiling traces N to model the function f_{h_i} with hyperparameter selection h_i ($1 \leq i \leq H$), such that the performance metric is still below (or above) a certain threshold δ:

$$\min\{N \; : \; \rho(g_{Q, f_{h_i}}, k_a^*) < \delta\}, \text{ where } N, i \geq 1 \text{ and } i \leq H. \tag{1}$$

Algorithm 1 gives the procedure of the evaluation in the Efficient Attacker Framework, and a motivating example is given in Example 2. Note that the framework allows conducting experiments in parallel to the data acquisition phase. Indeed, one can start with evaluating the performance regardless of the number of already acquired measurements. For example, the attacker can assume

---

Static parameters: Maximum size H of hyperparameter models to consider, a performance metric ρ and a threshold value δ, e.g., GE < 20

Input   : Profiling and attacking device to collect traces from

Output   : Minimum number of profiling traces N

1 Capture a test dataset (with secret key k_a^*). Its size Q depends on the expected performance of the attack. For instance, this test dataset can be as small as one trace!

2 Training_set $\leftarrow \varnothing$

3 $N \leftarrow 0$

4 **while** *True* **do**

5   Capture one trace   `// A speed-up can be obtained by advancing faster, e.g., 10 by 10 traces`

6   Append them to Training_set, $N \leftarrow N + 1$

7   **for** $i = 1$; $i \leq H$; $i + +$ **do**

8   (Randomly) select hyperparameters h

9   Perform Training with selected hyperparameters and obtain a model f_h

10   Receive $\rho(g_{Q,f_{h_i}}, k_a^*)$

11   **if** $\rho < \delta$ **then**   `// The model is good enough`

12   store hyperparameter selection h

13   break

14 **return** *Minimum number of profiling traces N*

Algorithm 1: Conceptual evaluation procedure in the Efficient Attacker Framework.

the regime where he downloads new measurements every hour and repeats the experiments with an always-increasing number of measurements.

Algorithm 1 increases the number of profiling traces until the stop condition (statically defined) is satisfied. As a secondary objective, it attempts to reduce the search space for the hyperparameters models, with the learning phase to be as computationally efficient as possible.

Remark 3. Algorithm 1 considers both the number of profiling traces and hyperparameter tuning experiments, but this can be easily adjusted for only one of those options, extended or replaced by other performance evaluations. For instance, if using a template attack, there are no hyperparameters to tune, which means that only the number of profiling traces is relevant. On the other hand, if facing a setting where one cannot obtain enough measurements to reach δ, then the natural choice is not to limit the number of measurements even more but to consider the number of hyperparameter tuning experiments. While we consider the number of hyperparameter tuning experiments from the learnability perspective in this paper, this could be easily cast, for instance, to the selection of points of interest with template attack.

Example 2. A standard performance metric used in the side-channel analysis is guessing entropy with, e.g., a threshold $\delta = 20$. In the Efficient Attacker Framework, one would find the minimum number of profiling traces N and hyperparameter experiments H to reach a guessing entropy below 20 for a fixed number of Q attack traces. This setting ensures that key enumeration algorithms [28] (when attacking several key bytes, as in AES-128 where there are 16 bytes of the key that needs to be recovered simultaneously for a full key recovery attack) are efficient. Typically, Q ranges over a set of values. Experimental results are discussed in Sect. 4.

Remark 4. In practice, Algorithm 1 shall be evaluated several times to get an empirical estimation $\mathbb{E}(N)$ of the minimum number of profiling traces. This can be achieved by averaging several evaluations of Algorithm 1 (as done in non-profiled side-channel attack-oriented frameworks, see [13, §3.1]).

Remark 5. The Efficient Attacker Framework is evaluator-oriented and aims at unleashing profiled attacks even with frugal learning constraints. This reflects some situations where the number of interactions with the device is limited:

- by design, e.g., owing to enforcement of countermeasures such as limited number of cryptographic executions until system end-of-life, or
- by certification constraints such as limited "elapsed time" in the Common Evaluation Methodology (CEM [29, B.4.2.2]) of the Common Criteria.

Remark 6. If two profiling models exhibit very similar performance but require a radically different amount of resources, then a Pareto front of solutions (i.e., a set of non-dominated solutions) needs to be given where the designer can decide on a proper trade-off.

We reiterate that our framework is not designed to force the attacker to use a small number of measurements in the profiling phase or limit the number of experiments in the hyperparameter tuning phase. Instead, it forces the attacker (evaluator) to find the smallest number of traces and tuning experiments to attack the target successfully.

4 Experimental Evaluation

4.1 Datasets

The first dataset we consider is the ASCAD with a fixed key dataset. The measurements are obtained from an 8-bit AVR microcontroller running a masked AES-128 implementation, where the side-channel is electromagnetic emanation [30]. This dataset has the same key for the profiling and attack phase. There are 50 000 traces for profiling and 10 000 for the attack. We use a preselected window of 700 features for the raw trace, and we attack key byte 3, which is the first masked key byte, as commonly done in the literature [30].

The second dataset is a version of the ASCAD dataset with random keys (denoted ASCAD random keys dataset) in the profiling set. The dataset consists of 200 000 traces for profiling and 100 000 for the attack. We use a pre-selected window of 1 400 features for this dataset and attack key byte 3 (the first masked key byte).

4.2   Efficient Attacker Framework Evaluation

The Efficient Attacker Framework enables us to compare side-channel attacks and gives a fair comparison between leakage models. For deep learning-based side-channel attacks, it is often assumed to consider the most accurate leakage model, i.e., using the intermediate value as class variables (the Identity leakage model[2]) [9, 27, 31], which results in 2^b classes where b is the number of considered bits. In an unsupervised setting (i.e., non-profiled attacks), using the Hamming weight or the Hamming distance leakage model is a common choice, which results in $b + 1$ classes only. Using $b + 1$ Hamming weight/distance classes to guess a key value in $\{0, \ldots, 2^b - 1\}$ cannot result in a single trace attack on average. However, using the Hamming weight/distance leakage models may require fewer traces in the profiling phase to gain good quality estimates of the leakage models (as there are fewer classes to consider). It is, therefore, not straightforward to determine what leakage model is most suitable. Consequently, to give a fair comparison, one should include a dependency on the number of traces in the profiling phase, as done in the Efficient Attacker Framework.

As a metric, we consider guessing entropy (GE), and in particular, we give the minimum number of profiling and attack traces to reach GE < 20. We randomly define hyperparameters for every training procedure for multilayer perceptron (MLP) and convolutional neural networks (CNNs) according to the hyperparameter ranges provided in Table 1. This scenario represents an optimized random hyperparameter search since the hyperparameter ranges are chosen based on the optimized minimum and maximum values (the minimal and maximal values are selected based on related works) [9, 11, 27, 31]. The number of epochs is set to 50 (we observed that the models tend to overfit and degrade the generalization after 50 epochs), and the backpropagation algorithm optimizer is *Adam*. The weights and biases are initialized in a randomly uniform way. We use the batch normalization layer to avoid overfitting, which normalizes the input layer by adjusting and scaling the activations. For CNNs, a pooling layer (with hyperparameters range specified in Table 1) always comes after a convolution layer.

We do not explicitly discuss the time perspective here (e.g., the number of hours or days needed to conduct the experiments). Comparing the number of tuning experiments gives a fair evaluation, regardless of the time needed to run those experiments. We note that the number of tuning experiments up to

---

[2] By the "Identity leakage model", we mean that we do not assume the number of classes can be reduced owing to model degeneracy, as would be the case for instance in the "Hamming weight leakage model", where it is assumed that the leakage Y depends in X only through $w_H(X)$ (the Hamming weight of X).

Table 1. Hyperparameter search space for MLP and CNNs.

Hyperparameter	MLP			CNN		
	Min	Max	Step	Min	Max	Step
Learning rate	0.0001	0.001	0.0001	0.0001	0.001	0.0001
Mini-batch	100	1 000	100	100	1 000	100
Dense (fully-connected) layers	1	4	1	1	4	1
Neurons (for dense or fc layers)	100	400	100	100	400	100
Convolution layers	-	-	-	1	2	1
Filters	-	-	-	4	16	4
Kernel size	-	-	-	2	10	2
Stride	-	-	-	1	4	1
Pooling size	-	-	-	1	4	1
PoolingStride	-	-	-	1	4	1
Activation function (all layers)	ReLU, Tanh, ELU, or SELU					

50 is low, although we manage to break the target. There is no constraint on the number of experiments one can use with our framework. Additionally, as we work with guessing entropy, each attack is repeated 100 times, which gives much higher computational complexity than one could conclude solely based on the number of tuning experiments. Every figure contains the results for the Hamming weight and Identity (i.e., intermediate value) leakage models, as AES operates on $b = 8$ bits. We select the best neural network model out of 5, 10, 25, or 50 trained profiling models for each leakage model and a different number of profiling traces. More precisely, we compare the performance of a different number of profiling models (thus, forming ensembles) as done in [31]. Here, the main idea is to demonstrate that the *learnability* also represents an important dimension in our framework. All the graphs are to be viewed in color.

ASCAD Fixed Key Dataset. We depict results for the ASCAD fixed key dataset in Figs. 2 and 3, for MLP and CNN, respectively. For the CNN case, we also depict the results by using the architecture from [9]. The results confirm the importance of considering the number of profiling traces and hyperparameter tuning. In particular, for MLP in combination with the HW leakage model: 25 and 50 models behave the same for 30 000 profiling traces, indicating they are "equally" good. Nevertheless, restricting the number of profiling traces, e.g., to 20 000 reveals that 50 models reach better attack performance. Finally, many models perform better for 35 000 than 45 000 profiling traces, indicating that the data cannot fit the current network capacity.

ASCAD Random Keys Dataset. Figures 4 and 5 show results for the ASCAD with the random keys dataset. In Fig. 4, we give results for MLP with hyperparameters defined per Table 1. Notice that considering a different number of profiling traces shows radically different behaviors. The more important is to observe that the profiling traces component becomes not as relevant as increasing the number of searched MLP models, especially for the Identity leakage model

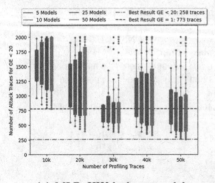

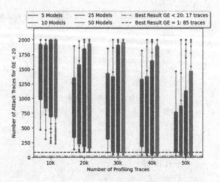

(a) MLP, HW leakage model.   (b) MLP, Identity leakage model.

Fig. 2. Profiled SCA on the ASCAD fixed key dataset with MLP.

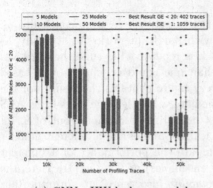

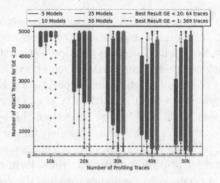

(a) CNNs, HW leakage model.   (b) CNNs, Identity leakage model.

Fig. 3. Profiled SCA on the ASCAD fixed key dataset with CNNs.

in Fig. 4b. For example, by keeping 40 000 profiling traces, the best number of attack traces after searching for five models is around 3 100 traces, while the minimum number of attack traces to reach GE< 20 with 50 models is close to 1 000 traces.

Figure 5 depicts the results for CNN architectures confirming the previous observations. In this particular example, we can immediately see how important it is to keep increasing the number of profiling traces as well as the number of searched models. This is expected as, due to the larger number of hyperparameter options, CNNs are more difficult to tune compared to MLP. In this case, the Efficient Attacker Framework reveals that increasing both components (profiling traces and learnability) makes the attack stronger.

4.3   Strong Adversary in the Efficient Attacker Framework

In the previous section, we evaluated our framework under the perspective of an adversary with strong side-channel capabilities (a profiled attack is mounted

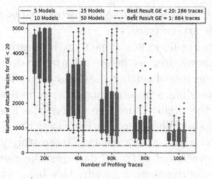

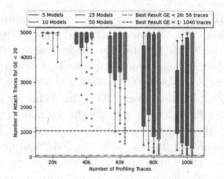

(a) MLP, HW leakage model.   (b) MLP, Identity leakage model.

Fig. 4. Profiled SCA on the ASCAD random keys dataset with MLP.

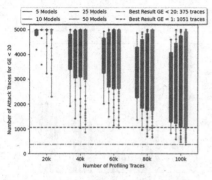

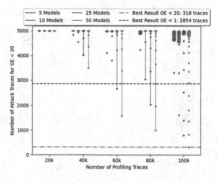

(a) CNNs, HW leakage model.   (b) CNNs, Identity leakage model.

Fig. 5. Profiled SCA on the ASCAD with random keys dataset with CNNs.

over optimal trace interval containing leaky points-of-interests). However, this same adversary executes a random search and does not possess an optimal neural network model. In this section, we consider state-of-the-art models from [9] and [27], which provide carefully tuned CNN models for the ASCAD dataset. This way, an adversary is considered strong from both side-channel and deep learning perspectives. As the hyperparameters are already chosen, we again run 50 models for each fixed number of profiling traces by only randomly varying the batch size (from 50 to 400, with steps of 50 traces).

Figure 6 provides the results for the *cnn_architecture* [32] proposed in [9] for the Hamming weight and Identity leakage models (for the HW leakage model, we use the same learning model as for the Identity leakage model, but we set the number of output classes to 9). The framework indicates that increasing the number of profiling traces is not very relevant when possessing an "optimal" profiling model. Indeed, in Fig. 6b, the best results are achieved for 30 000 profiling traces, and adding more profiling traces increases training time and does not improve attack results. In this example, we observe with a real-world dataset that GE< 20 can be achieved with a single attack trace.

The Identity leakage model results from Fig. 6b indicate one more interesting phenomenon, which is, to the best of our knowledge, not before reported in deep learning-based SCA. We can notice for one model setting the behavior called deep double descent [33]. This behavior describes a phenomenon where the test loss first decreases with the increase in the architecture size. Then, the loss starts to increase and finally decreases again. When the loss increases, this is connected with an effect called "sample-wise non-monotonicity". Interestingly, this effect describes a behavior where more training traces damages the test phase's performance. While there is no definitive answer to why this behavior happens, one explanation could be that the model does not have enough capacity to fit the data. Adding more data requires the model to drastically "change" its parameters, improving attack performance.

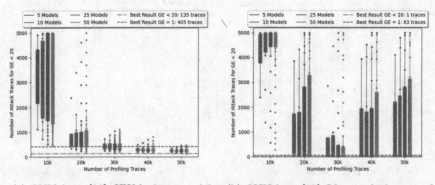

(a) CNN from [32], HW leakage model.   (b) CNN from [32], Identity leakage model.

Fig. 6. Profiled SCA on the ASCAD with fixed keys dataset with CNN architecture from [9].

Figure 7 shows results for *noConv1_ascad_desync_0* [34] proposed in [27]. As this neural network architecture is an optimization built on top of [32], results for the ASCAD fixed key dataset indicate an even smaller minimum number of profiling traces to reach successful results, which is 20 000 profiling traces. Nevertheless, we can also observe the differences in model performance with the Efficient Attacker Framework when selecting different leakage models.

4.4   General Observations

On a general level, while not the core research point in this work, we note that the Identity leakage model requires fewer attack traces to reach GE < 20, which is expected. MLP exhibits better performance than CNN for a smaller number of profiling traces, which is again in line with related works. It is important

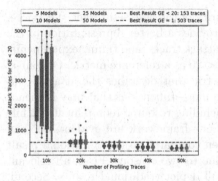
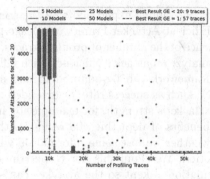

(a) CNN from [34], HW leakage model.   (b) CNN from [34], Identity leakage model.

Fig. 7. Profiled SCA on the ASCAD with fixed keys dataset with CNN architecture from [27].

to observe how the learnability constraint directly influences the required combination of the number of profiling and attack traces to reach a low guessing entropy. Moreover, one can choose a trade-off between profiling traces N and attack traces Q while still performing a successful attack.

While our framework aims to find the minimal number of profiling traces and keep the number of tuning experiments to mount a successful attack as low as possible, we never state what those numbers should be. Indeed, the experiments showcase radically different behaviors for various numbers of profiling and attack traces (coupled with the influence of the number of tuning experiments). Providing actual values makes sense only when the whole experimental environment is considered (datasets, algorithms, environmental settings) and, even more importantly, when one compares experiments on the same targets but with different settings. All our experiments strongly confirm that the number of profiling traces and the number of experiments (complexity) play a paramount role and should be included in proper performance analysis for deep learning-based SCA.

4.5 Advantages of the Efficient Attacker Framework

Usually, an attacker is expected to make use of the maximum possible number of profiling traces to build a model (templates, deep neural networks). Similarly, the number of attack traces tends to be maximized to better estimate the model exploitation capability. In cases when the learning model is inefficient (i.e., unable to fit the existing leakage) and all available side-channel measurements are used, the attacker or evaluator has a limited view of what component has a significant impact on the attack results, which can lead to overestimating the security of the target.

In this case, the reference metric would be the guessing entropy of a single experiment, which says nothing about the influence of the number of measurements and tuning experiments on the security of the assessed target. Therefore, the Efficient Attacker Framework usage provides a better representation of the influence of the number of profiling traces, attack traces, and tuning experiments. We analyze an attack's efficiency with GE < 20 as a reference metric. Of course, the framework can be adapted to any metric that describes the attack's efficiency, such as success rate, or extended to more dimensions that may influence the attacker's strength, for example, by including resource requirements. While the benefits of depicting the results with our framework are evident, one can ask whether we lost some information when compared to the traditional result depiction. We claim this not to be true due to two reasons. First, all relevant information is kept so the attacker can still depict traditional results. Second, once the appropriate performance level is set (e.g., guessing entropy value equal to δ), it is less relevant to observe how that value is reached (as values above the threshold are out of the attacker's reach).

As a common scenario for deep learning side-channel evaluation, our experiments concentrated on the concept of divide-and-conquer strategies for symmetric ciphers. However, the Efficient Attacker Framework is not limited to this scenario, and depending on the threat model of the attack, the framework can be extended, for example, to rank estimation strategies [35] or even to recursive recovering strategies like Extend and Prune (EP) [36]. Instead of using metrics on subkey bytes, an evaluator would choose a rank estimation strategy and depict the number of attack traces to reach a certain estimated rank within the complete keyspace as a performance metric. As in our experiments, this may be evaluated in terms of the number of training traces. Naturally, the Efficient Attacker Framework would allow us to compare different rank estimation strategies. EP techniques are required when estimating models for the entire keyspace is not feasible as for many asymmetric ciphers. While the estimation of key recovery differs, the application of the Efficient Attacker Framework is similar. Depending on the chosen cryptographic primitive, an evaluator could again depict the minimum number of traces in the attack phase, depending on the amount of information (bits or chunks of information).

Some former works also attempted to make the most out of the available information contained within a trace. For instance, soft analytical side-channel analysis [37] aims at leveraging the information collected at different steps in one round (e.g., for AES: `AddRoundKey`, `SubBytes`, `MixColumns`, etc.), and even beyond, from round to round. For such constructive information gathering to occur, the whole secret shall be guessed at once. Belief-propagation algorithms can be used in this respect (to relate all leakage points of interest). However, we notice that such a technique is mostly profitable to exploit as much as possible the online captured side-channel, whereas the scope of our paper is to optimize the usage of the data collected from the learning device.

5   Conclusions

This paper discusses how to evaluate attacks when considering the profiled side-channel analysis. We argue that considering only an unbounded attacker can negatively affect how side-channel analysis is performed while not being realistic. We propose a new framework, denoted as the Efficient Attacker Framework, where we explore the number of measurements and hyperparameter tuning experiments required in the profiling phase such that the attacker is still successful.

We consider our new framework more realistic but also more adept for experimental evaluations since it allows us to compare different results in a more unified way. In particular, our framework will hopefully trigger more research relevant not only for academia but also for evaluation labs. Finally, our framework is relevant beyond profiled side-channel analysis and can be used in any supervised learning setting.

References

1. Mangard, S., Oswald, E., Popp, T.: Power Analysis Attacks: Revealing the Secrets of Smart Cards. Springer, Boston (2006). https://doi.org/10.1007/978-0-387-38162-6. ISBN 0-387-30857-1. http://www.dpabook.org/
2. Schindler, W., Lemke, K., Paar, C.: A stochastic model for differential side channel cryptanalysis. In: Rao, J.R., Sunar, B. (eds.) CHES 2005. LNCS, vol. 3659, pp. 30–46. Springer, Heidelberg (2005). https://doi.org/10.1007/11545262_3
3. Choudary, O., Kuhn, M.G.: Efficient template attacks. In: Francillon, A., Rohatgi, P. (eds.) CARDIS 2013. LNCS, vol. 8419, pp. 253–270. Springer, Cham (2014). https://doi.org/10.1007/978-3-319-08302-5_17
4. Heuser, A., Zohner, M.: Intelligent machine homicide - breaking cryptographic devices using support vector machines. In: Schindler, W., Huss, S.A. (eds.) COSADE 2012. LNCS, vol. 7275, pp. 249–264. Springer, Heidelberg (2012). https://doi.org/10.1007/978-3-642-29912-4_18
5. Lerman, L., Poussier, R., Bontempi, G., Markowitch, O., Standaert, F.-X.: Template attacks vs. machine learning revisited (and the curse of dimensionality in side-channel analysis). In: Mangard, S., Poschmann, A.Y. (eds.) COSADE 2014. LNCS, vol. 9064, pp. 20–33. Springer, Cham (2015). https://doi.org/10.1007/978-3-319-21476-4_2
6. Picek, S., Heuser, A., Jovic, A., Bhasin, S., Regazzoni, F.: The curse of class imbalance and conflicting metrics with machine learning for side-channel evaluations. IACR Trans. Cryptogr. Hardw. Embed. Syst. 2019(1), 209–237 (2019)
7. Cagli, Eleonora, Dumas, Cécile., Prouff, Emmanuel: Convolutional neural networks with data augmentation against jitter-based countermeasures. In: Fischer, Wieland, Homma, Naofumi (eds.) CHES 2017. LNCS, vol. 10529, pp. 45–68. Springer, Cham (2017). https://doi.org/10.1007/978-3-319-66787-4_3
8. Kim, J., Picek, S., Heuser, A., Bhasin, S., Hanjalic, A.: Make some noise. unleashing the power of convolutional neural networks for profiled side-channel analysis. IACR Trans. Cryptogr. Hardware Embed. Syst. 2019(3), 148–179 (2019)
9. Zaid, G., Bossuet, L., Habrard, A., Venelli, A.: Methodology for efficient CNN architectures in profiling attacks. IACR Trans. Cryptogr. Hardw. Embed. Syst. 2020(1), 1–36 (2019)
10. Wu, L., Perin, G., Picek, S.: I choose you: automated hyperparameter tuning for deep learning-based side-channel analysis. Cryptology ePrint Archive, Report 2020/1293 (2020). https://eprint.iacr.org/2020/1293

11. Rijsdijk, J., Wu, L., Perin, G., Picek, S.: Reinforcement learning for hyperparameter tuning in deep learning-based side-channel analysis. IACR Trans. Cryptogr. Hardw. Embed. Syst. **2021**(3), 677–707 (2021)

12. Bhasin, S., Chattopadhyay, A., Heuser, A., Jap, D., Picek, S., Shrivastwa, R.R.: Mind the portability: a warriors guide through realistic profiled side-channel analysis. In: 27th Annual Network and Distributed System Security Symposium, NDSS 2020, San Diego, California, USA, 23–26 February 2020. The Internet Society (2020)

13. Standaert, F.-X., Malkin, T.G., Yung, M.: A unified framework for the analysis of side-channel key recovery attacks. In: Joux, A. (ed.) EUROCRYPT 2009. LNCS, vol. 5479, pp. 443–461. Springer, Heidelberg (2009). https://doi.org/10.1007/978-3-642-01001-9_26

14. Whitnall, C., Oswald, E.: A fair evaluation framework for comparing side-channel distinguishers. J. Cryptogr. Eng. **1**(2), 145–160 (2011)

15. Whitnall, C., Oswald, E.: A comprehensive evaluation of mutual information analysis using a fair evaluation framework. In: Rogaway, P. (ed.) CRYPTO 2011. LNCS, vol. 6841, pp. 316–334. Springer, Heidelberg (2011). https://doi.org/10.1007/978-3-642-22792-9_18

16. Guilley, S., Heuser, A., Rioul, O.: A key to success. In: Biryukov, A., Goyal, V. (eds.) INDOCRYPT 2015. LNCS, vol. 9462, pp. 270–290. Springer, Cham (2015). https://doi.org/10.1007/978-3-319-26617-6_15

17. Duc, A., Faust, S., Standaert, F.-X.: Making masking security proofs concrete. In: Oswald, E., Fischlin, M. (eds.) EUROCRYPT 2015. LNCS, vol. 9056, pp. 401–429. Springer, Heidelberg (2015). https://doi.org/10.1007/978-3-662-46800-5_16

18. Bronchain, O., Hendrickx, J.M., Massart, C., Olshevsky, A., Standaert, F.-X.: Leakage certification revisited: bounding model errors in side-channel security evaluations. In: Boldyreva, A., Micciancio, D. (eds.) CRYPTO 2019. LNCS, vol. 11692, pp. 713–737. Springer, Cham (2019). https://doi.org/10.1007/978-3-030-26948-7_25

19. Witten, I.H., Frank, E.: Data Mining: Practical Machine Learning Tools and Techniques. Morgan Kaufmann Series in Data Management Systems, 2nd edn. Morgan Kaufmann Publishers Inc., San Francisco (2005)

20. publication 140–3, N.F.F.I.P.S.: Security Requirements for Cryptographic Modules (Draft, Revised), vol. 63 (2009). http://csrc.nist.gov/groups/ST/FIPS140_3/. Accessed 09 Nov 2009

21. ISO/IEC JTC 1/SC 27 IT Security Techniques: ISO/IEC 17825:2016 Information technology - Security techniques - Testing methods for the mitigation of non-invasive attack classes against cryptographic modules, January 2016. https://www.iso.org/standard/60612.html

22. ISO/IEC JTC 1/SC 27 IT Security techniques: ISO/IEC 15408-1:2009 Information technology - Security techniques - Evaluation criteria for IT security - Part 1: Introduction and general model, January 2014. https://www.iso.org/standard/50341.html

23. Common Criteria: Supporting Document Mandatory Technical Document Application of Attack Potential to Smartcards (2013). https://www.commoncriteriaportal.org/files/supdocs/CCDB-2013-05-002.pdf

24. Heuser, A., Kasper, M., Schindler, W., Stöttinger, M.: A new difference method for side-channel analysis with high-dimensional leakage models. In: Dunkelman, O. (ed.) CT-RSA 2012. LNCS, vol. 7178, pp. 365–382. Springer, Heidelberg (2012). https://doi.org/10.1007/978-3-642-27954-6_23

25. Cao, Y., Zhou, Y., Yu, Z.: On the negative effects of trend noise and its applications in side-channel cryptanalysis. Chin. J. Electron. **23**, 366–370 (2014)
26. TELECOM ParisTech SEN Research Group: DPA Contest, 1st edn (2008–2009). http://www.DPAcontest.org/
27. Wouters, L., Arribas, V., Gierlichs, B., Preneel, B.: Revisiting a methodology for efficient CNN architectures in profiling attacks. IACR Trans. Cryptogr. Hardw. Embed. Syst. **2020**(3), 147–168 (2020)
28. Veyrat-Charvillon, N., Gérard, B., Renauld, M., Standaert, F.-X.: An optimal key enumeration algorithm and its application to side-channel attacks. In: Knudsen, L.R., Wu, H. (eds.) SAC 2012. LNCS, vol. 7707, pp. 390–406. Springer, Heidelberg (2013). https://doi.org/10.1007/978-3-642-35999-6_25
29. Common Criteria Management Board: Common Methodology for Information Technology Security Evaluation Evaluation methodology, Version 3.1, Revision 4, CCMB-2012-09-004, September 2012. https://www.commoncriteriaportal.org/files/ccfiles/CEMV3.1R4.pdf
30. Benadjila, R., Prouff, E., Strullu, R., Cagli, E., Dumas, C.: Deep learning for side-channel analysis and introduction to ASCAD database. J. Cryptogr. Eng. **10**(2), 163–188 (2019). https://doi.org/10.1007/s13389-019-00220-8
31. Perin, G., Chmielewski, L., Picek, S.: Strength in numbers: improving generalization with ensembles in machine learning-based profiled side-channel analysis. IACR Trans. Cryptogr. Hardw. Embed. Syst. **2020**(4), 337–364 (2020)
32. Zaid, G., Bossuet, L., Habrard, A., Venelli, A.: Methodology for efficient CNN-architectures in SCA. https://github.com/gabzai/Methodology-for-efficient-CNN-architectures-in-SCA/blob/master/ASCAD/N0
33. Nakkiran, P., Kaplun, G., Bansal, Y., Yang, T., Barak, B., Sutskever, I.: Deep double descent: where bigger models and more data hurt (2019)
34. Wouters, L., Arribas, V., Gierlichs, B., Preneel, B.: Revisiting a methodology for efficient CNN architectures in profiling attacks (2020). https://github.com/KULeuven-COSIC/TCHES20V3_CNN_SCA/blob/master/src/models.py. Accessed 20 June 2021
35. Veyrat-Charvillon, N., Gérard, B., Standaert, F.-X.: Security evaluations beyond computing power. In: Johansson, T., Nguyen, P.Q. (eds.) EUROCRYPT 2013. LNCS, vol. 7881, pp. 126–141. Springer, Heidelberg (2013). https://doi.org/10.1007/978-3-642-38348-9_8
36. Chari, S., Rao, J.R., Rohatgi, P.: Template attacks. In: Kaliski, B.S., Koç, K., Paar, C. (eds.) CHES 2002. LNCS, vol. 2523, pp. 13–28. Springer, Heidelberg (2003). https://doi.org/10.1007/3-540-36400-5_3
37. Veyrat-Charvillon, N., Gérard, B., Standaert, F.-X.: Soft analytical side-channel attacks. In: Sarkar, P., Iwata, T. (eds.) ASIACRYPT 2014. LNCS, vol. 8873, pp. 282–296. Springer, Heidelberg (2014). https://doi.org/10.1007/978-3-662-45611-8_15

Towards a Better Understanding of Side-Channel Analysis Measurements Setups

Davide Bellizia, Balazs Udvarhelyi[(✉)], and François-Xavier Standaert

UCLouvain, ICTEAM/ELEN/Crypto Group, Belgium, UK
balazs.udvarhelyi@uclouvain.be

Abstract. The evaluation of side-channel measurement setups and the impact they can have on physical security evaluations is a surprisingly under-discussed topic. In this paper, we initiate a comprehensive study of such setups for embedded software and hardware (FPGA) implementations. We systematically investigate a design space including the choice of the probing method, the clock frequency of the device under test, its supply voltage and the sampling rate of the adversary's oscilloscope. Our results quantify the impact (i.e., the risk of security over-estimations) that suboptimal setups can cause and lead to easy-to-use guidelines for security evaluators. Despite some of our conclusions are device-dependent, we argue that the proposed methodology and some of the proposed guidelines are of general interest and could be applied to other setups.

Keywords: Probing techniques · Frequency and voltage scaling · Sampling rate · Signal-to-noise ratio · Perceived information

1 Introduction

The design of a measurement setup is the first step in the evaluation of a cryptographic implementation against side-channel analysis. Due to its physical nature, this step inherently carries hard to quantify risks of security overstatements. Noisy setups may indeed lead evaluators to conclude that the measurements are less informative than they actually are, and this gap will then be increased in case a countermeasure aiming at noise amplification, like masking [7,13] or shuffling [15,29], is implemented. Surprisingly, and despite papers focused on practical side-channel attacks usually describe how they optimized their setups, especially when targeting challenging real-world devices [3,21], very few works are dedicated to the systematic evaluation of measurement setups and the impact of their optimization on security evaluations. Besides, and to the best of our knowledge, the most advanced (published) investigations of this topic were performed in specific settings such as the exploitation of static leakages, as recently investigated by Moos et al. [19], or the evaluation of physical effects such as couplings to reduce a masked implementation's security order [10,11,16]. But

V. Grosso and T. Pöppelmann (Eds.): CARDIS 2021, LNCS 13173, pp. 64–79, 2022.
https://doi.org/10.1007/978-3-030-97348-3_4

when it comes to the the impact of measurement setups on the noise level in the context of (standard) attacks exploiting the dynamic part of the leakage, the only works we are aware of are the one of Guilley et al. which puts forward the Signal-to-Noise Ratio (SNR) as a meaningful metric to quantify the quality of side-channel acquisitions [14], and the one of Merino del Pozo and Standaert that discusses the impact of different setups in the context of leakage detection [22]. In this respect, and despite these references are important first steps in specifying relevant comparison metrics and highlighting the existence of an interesting design space, they are still have a limited scope: [14] estimates its proposed (univariate) metric for a single measurement setup while [22] compares different analog amplifiers and filters for a single probing method.

Recognizing that the design space of measurement setups is broader than investigated in these previous works, this paper aims at analyzing four important parameters of actual measurement setups. Namely, our goal is to discuss and evaluate the impact of the probing method used in the setups, the clock frequency of the Device Under Test (DUT), its supply voltage and the sampling rate of the oscilloscope used to collect the measurements. We therefore study these parameters systematically for two DUTs: a software (ARM Cortex) target and a hardware (Xilinx FPGA) one. We additionally evaluate the effect of these different parameters for both univariate evaluation metrics like the SNR and multivariate evaluation metrics like the Perceived Information (PI).

We then use our investigations to extract useful observations regarding how to select the parameters of our design space. While most of these observations are admittedly present (implicitly or explicitly) in former experimental works, we hope their compilation for two different devices and the quantitative analysis of the losses a poor measurement setup may imply for security evaluators (which may reach orders of magnitude) make a useful consolidating effort.

2   Background

We will use Mangard's SNR [17] to evaluate the quality of first-order and univariate leakages, as suggested by Guilley et al., and the PI metric analyzed in [6] to evaluate the quality of higher-order or multivariate leakages. For the latter we profile Gaussian templates in a linear subspace. We next recall these different evaluation metrics and detail the profiling tools used in our analyzes.

2.1   Mangard's SNR

Introduced in the context of side-channel analysis by Mangard, the SNR intuitively captures the data-dependent signal as the variance of the mean traces and the noise as the mean of the variance traces, for each time sample [17]. As a result, for a target intermediate variable y, it is defined as the ratio:

$$\hat{\mathrm{SNR}} = \frac{\hat{\mathrm{Var}}_y\left(\hat{\mathrm{E}}_i\left(l_i^y\right)\right)}{\hat{\mathrm{E}}_y\left(\hat{\mathrm{Var}}_i\left(l_i^y\right)\right)}, \tag{1}$$

where $\hat{\mathrm{Var}}$ and $\hat{\mathrm{E}}$ are the sample variance and the sample mean estimated on $l_i^y \in \mathcal{L}$, which represents the i-th side-channel observation generated by a target variable y. It must be pointed out that the noise in Mangard's definition is the result of two contributions. First, physical noise is due to physical phenomena (e.g., thermal noise, flicker noise) and electrical conditions (e.g., impedance mismatch, unwanted coupling with unrelated equipment). Second, algorithmic noise is due to the presence of operations that are independent of the target ones and are processed in parallel to them (i.e., at the same time). As argued by Guilley et al., it is a good metric for assessing the quality of side-channel measurements to be exploited by first-order univariate attacks [14], since it can be related to the complexity of popular attacks such as the Correlation Power Analysis (CPA) and (univariate Gaussian) Template Attacks (TA) [5,8,18].

2.2 Subspace Based Gaussian Templates

Gaussian template attacks are a standard method to exploit multivariate leakages [8]. We combine them with a dimensionality reduction step in order to reduce the possibly high number of informative dimensions d of the leakage traces to a lower value $d' < d$. The profiling consists of an estimation, using n leakage traces l, of the parameters μ_x, Σ_x and W of a Probability Density Function (PDF) of the form:

$$\tilde{\mathrm{m}}_n(l|x) = \frac{1}{\sqrt{(2\pi)^{d'} \cdot |\Sigma_x|}} \cdot \exp^{\frac{1}{2}(Wl-\mu_x)\Sigma_x(Wl-\mu_x)'}, \tag{2}$$

where x is the value of the profiled variable, μ_x the mean vector of length d', Σ_x the covariance matrix of size $d' \times d'$ and W is the projection matrix of size $d' \times d$. This projection matrix is determined thanks to Linear Discriminant Analysis (LDA) [25]. LDA aims to find the subspace that maximizes the inter-class variance (i.e., the signal of Mangard's SNR) and minimizes the intra-class variance (i.e., the noise of Mangard's SNR). In practice, we applied this dimensionality reduction to all the samples with sufficient SNR (which d ranging from 30 to 500 depending on the cases) and usually kept a dozen dimensions for d'. Next, in the online attack phase, the likelihood of x is obtained by applying Bayes' law to the leakage models estimated beforehand such that:

$$\tilde{\mathrm{m}}_n(x|l) = \frac{\tilde{\mathrm{m}}_n(l|x)}{\sum_{x^* \in \mathcal{X} } \tilde{\mathrm{m}}_n(l|x^*)}. \tag{3}$$

The estimated PDF and the likelihood of the profiled variable can then be used to calculate the amount of information contained in the leakages.

2.3 Information Theoretic Metrics and Bounds

For higher-order or multivariate attacks, the SNR metric is not directly applicable and a more general information theoretic metric has to be used. In the context of side-channel attacks, the Mutual Information (MI) is the most frequently considered candidate [26]. It generalizes the SNR in the sense that it can be related to the complexity of worst-case higher-order & multivariate attacks [9,12] (and it is essentially equivalent to the SNR in the first-order univariate case [18]). However, as recently discussed in [6], estimating the MI is in general a hard problem. Known estimators are biased and distribution-dependent. Perfect estimations would therefore require the exact knowledge of the leakage distribution. As a workaround, they proposed the use of the previously introduced PI metric, which represents the amount of information that can be extracted from a device thanks to an the adversary's model, possibly biased due to estimation and assumption errors. For a target secret variable X with leakage variable L, and denoting the leakage model $\tilde{m}_n(l|x)$ as described in the previous section, the PI is expressed as:

$$\hat{PI}_n(X; L) = H(K) + \sum_{x \in \mathcal{X}} p(x) \sum_{l \in \mathcal{L}} p(l|x) \cdot \log_2(\tilde{m}_n(x|l)), \quad (4)$$

. with $H(X)$ the Shannon entropy of the variable $S \in \mathcal{S}$. The PI is a lower bound to the worst-case MI and equality holds in case the adversary's model is perfect. It can be viewed as the amount of information extrated by the best practical attack tried by an evaluator. Concretely, the PI is usually estimated with k-fold cross-validation and we used $k = 10$ in our following experiments.

3   Setup Model and Design Space

We now introduce our model and design space for measurement setups, alongside with the two devices we have adopted to conduct our investigations.

3.1   Setup Model

The setup model is illustrated in Fig. 1. Its goal is to highlight important parameters for the informativeness of the leakages such as the probing method, the DUT's parameters and the Digital Storage Oscilloscope (DSO)'s parameters. As reported in [27], the choice of those components and how they interact with each other impact sensibly on the final outcome of the practical side-channel security evaluation of a leaking implementation. A bit more precisely, the current absorbed by the DUT is first monitored by a probe, which has the role to convert the current signal into a voltage signal. This signal can then be amplified using a preamplifier stage in order to increase its magnitude, to mitigate noise in the measurements and to improve electrical characteristics for the following blocks. At the end of the so-called measurement chain, a DSO samples and quantizes the analog voltage signal, converting it in a digital representation. Usually, the sampling operation is handled following a specific timing, that exploits a trigger signal in order to synchronize different measurements.[1] The precise design space that we will consider for each block of the model will be detailed later.

---

[1] The availability of a good trigger may raise additional challenges [4].

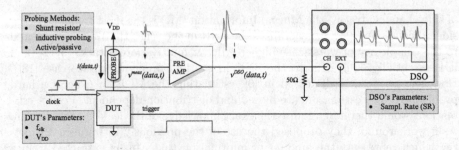

Fig. 1. Measurement setup model for power analysis evaluation.

We note that our investigations do not consider the question of filtering, which we view as an orthogonal one, since it can be performed after the measurements took place in order to compensate a too noisy setup.

3.2 Platforms

In our investigations, we have used two devices in order to cover both hardware and software implementations of cryptographic algorithms. This choice is motivated by the expected differences between the two types of targets. For example, hardware implementations generally allow better controlling the design aspects (from the level of parallelism to low-level implementation choices) while software implementations are usually more general purpose and serial.

Hardware DUT. Our target hardware DUT is a Xilinx Spartan-6 LX75 FPGA, mounted on a Sakura-G board, implementing an AES-128 processor with a 32-bit architecture. It is illustrated in Fig. 2. In order to provide synchronization between measurements, we generate a trigger signal on one of the IO pins of the FPGA, rising to logical '1' one cycle before the starting of the encryption and set back to '0' one cycle after the end of the AES encryption. We used the integrated measurement point for our measurements.

Software DUT. Our target software implementation is running on a Cortex-M0 MCU from the STM32F0308 Discovery board. Small modifications were performed on the board. Namely, we added a crystal oscillator to provide a stable clock source for the measurements and decoupling capacitors were desoldered. The MCU is running tiny-AES [2], an open source AES-128 implementation. We used the same trigger methodology as for the hardware DUT. Our measurements were performed on the dedicated current measuring point for the MCU.

3.3 Design Space

We explored our design space and DUTs by testing the following parameters:

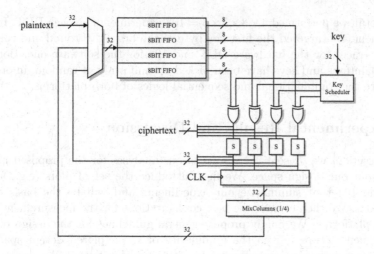

Fig. 2. Architecture of the 32-bit AES encryption co-processor.

Regarding the probing methodology, we used both a $2\,\Omega$ resistor in series with the power supply voltage and an inductive probe (the Tektronix CT-1, which gives a transresistance of $5\,\text{mV/mA}$ in the frequency range $25\,\text{kHz–1}\,\text{GHz}$ [1]). When using the CT-1 current probe, the shunt resistor was short-circuited. We optionally used a preamplifier, namely a R&S HZ16 [24] providing a gain of $20\,\text{dB}$ with a noise figure of $4.5\,\text{dB}$, in the frequency range $100\,\text{kHz–3}\,\text{GHz}$.[2]

Next, the DUT's clock frequency is an important macroscopic feature of a side-channel trace, since it usually reflects the frequency spectrum where leakage can be found. We chose three clock frequency values ($1\,\text{MHz}$, $6\,\text{MHz}$ and $24\,\text{MHz}$) for the hardware DUT and three clock frequencies ($4\,\text{MHz}$, $24\,\text{MHz}$ and $48\,\text{MHz}$) for the software DUT. Note that $48\,\text{MHz}$ is the maximal clock frequency of the device. Those sets of values were chosen to observe the impact of the clock frequency on the shape and distinguishability of the leakage cycles.

Similarly, we chose three power supply voltage ($0.8\,\text{V}$, $1.2\,\text{V}$ and $1.4\,\text{V}$) for the hardware DUT and three power supplies ($2.6\,\text{V}$, $3.0\,\text{V}$ and $3.6\,\text{V}$) for the software DUT. Those sets of values were chosen in order to observe the impact of working at nominal supply voltage vs. in minimum and maximum corner cases.

Finally, we used a Picoscope 6424E providing a vertical resolution of 12 bits and running at three different sampling rates as DSO. We chose sampling rates values according to the clock frequency of the given DUT, to analyze the impact of the collected number of samples per clock cycles (which impacts the acquisition bandwidth and memory requirements). Precisely, we set the sampling rate of the DSO at approximately $\times 1$, $\times 5$, $\times 25$ the chosen DUT's clock frequency. We note that the sampling rate of our DSO is not an integer multiple to the DUT's clock frequency as it may induce correlated noise in the measurements.

---

[2] The on-board Sakura amplifier was not used for consistency with the software setup.

In total, we performed $4 \times 3 \times 3 \times 3 = 108$ experiments on each DUT. In each experiment, we targeted the first key byte of the first AES round and collected 4×10^6 traces for the hardware DUT and 10^5 for the software one. Both the input plaintexts and keys have been picked up uniformly at random, in order to stimulate the combinational and sequential logics of both platforms.

4   Experimental Results and Discussion

In this section, we present the results of our analyses for the proposed metrics throughout our design space. We first introduce the set of plots (e.g., for the SNR and PI) that summarize our experiments and will be the basis of our discussions. We then extract the best configurations for the measurement setup of both platforms. We finally propose general guidelines for the design of good measurement setups. Given the granularity of the explored design space, we organize this discussion according to the setup model in Sect. 3. We also evaluate the relevance of univariate evaluation metrics as predictors of multivariate ones.

Figure 3 shows the highest SNR value we found for each set of parameters for both platforms (in logarithmic scale). We present the results in the form of a matrix where the X-axis contains the different power supply values and sampling speeds, and the Y-axis contains the DUT clock frequencies and probing method used in each experiment. The thick orange lines delimit the probing methods on the X-axis and the sampling speeds on the Y-axis. Darker blue blocks represent setup parameters where the SNR is higher. Figure 4 shows a similar matrix for the PI values obtained after LDA, in order to evaluate the impact of setup choices from a multivariate attack perspective.

A bit more in detail, the SNRs in Fig. 3 were calculated on the whole leakage trace and the maximum value was then taken. In the hardware case, as shown in Fig. 3a, the best SNR is obtained using the CT-1 current probe combined with the amplifier, setting the DUT to the slowest clock speed and lowest power supply value, and sampling at the highest rate. In the software case, as shown in Fig. 3b, the differences are more subtle and many sets of parameters give a peak SNR value close to the best one. The latter is obtained using the resistor combined with the amplifier, setting the DUT to the highest clock speed and sampling at lowest rate (contrary to the hardware case) while still using the lowest power supply value (like in the hardware case).

Regarding our multivariate analysis, we calculated the PI for each set of parameters. Concretely, for each experiment independently, we first pre-selected samples based on the SNR traces, keeping the ones above the noise floor for profiling. We then built Gaussian templates combined with LDA as presented in Sect. 2.2. We next analyzed the impact of the d' parameter, trying $d' = 1$ up to 25 for the hardware platform and 50 for the software one. We finally kept the d' leading to the highest PI, which is reported in Fig. 4.

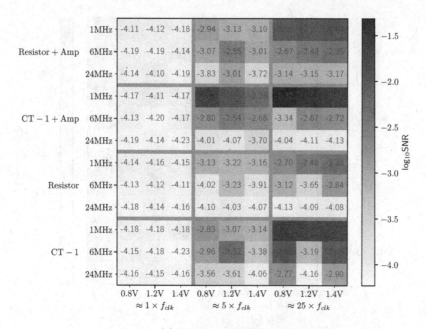

(a) Hardware DUT.

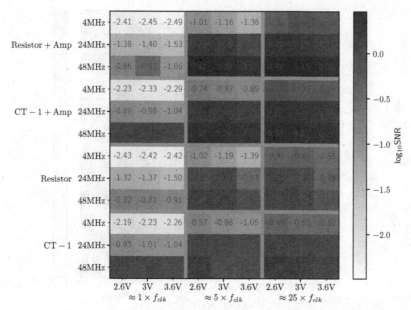

(b) Software DUT.

Fig. 3. Peak SNR values observed for the hardware (a) and software (b) DUTs.

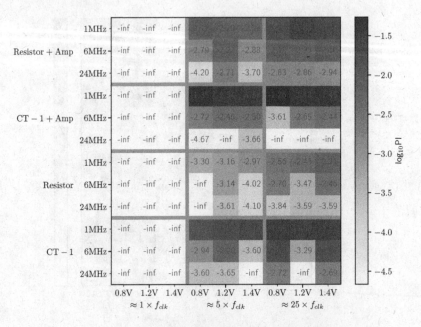

(a) Hardware DUT.

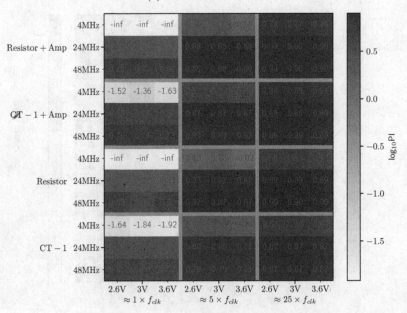

(b) Software DUT.

Fig. 4. Peak PI values observed for the hardware (a) and software (b) DUTs.

For the hardware platform's results reported in Fig. 4a, we observe that the experiment leading to the highest PI is obtained with the same set of parameters that leads to the highest SNR in Fig. 3a. Generally speaking, comparing the two metrics, the PI follows the same trend as the SNR in this case.[3] For the software platform's results reported in Fig. 4b, we see that the effect of the probing method and the power supply voltage are negligible, which is different from the univariate SNR analysis of Fig. 3b. By contrast, observations regarding the clock frequency and sampling rate remain similar as in the univariate case. We also note that our highest PI value is 7.96 for an 8-bit bus.

As a complement, Fig. 5 depicts exemplary SNR and leakage traces for both platforms, corresponding to the best cases in Fig. 3. The SNR traces are in the upper subplots and mean leakage traces in the lower subplots.

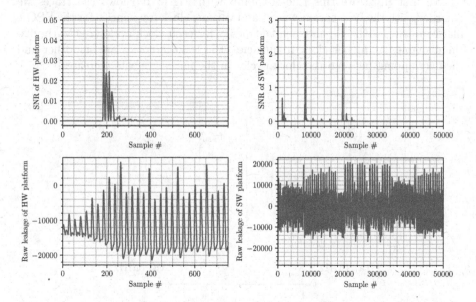

Fig. 5. Exemplary SNR and leakage traces: hardware (left) and software (right).

These experimental investigations lead to the following observations:

Probe. The choice of a probe was more critical for the hardware platform than the software one in our experiments. In the hardware case, the inductive probe gave better results than the resistor. A plausible explanation is that the CT-1 interferes less with the side-channel signal and is intrinsically less noisy than a shunt resistor. So as long as the target leakage is covered by the probe's bandwidth, it seems to be a good choice. In the software case, both the inductive probe

---

[3] The experiments where the $\log_{10}$ PI is -inf correspond to a negative PI, indicating the no information could be extracted from the estimated model.

and the resistor gave good results, presumably due to the easier-to-exploit measurements (reflected by the higher SNR and PI values). As for the use of the amplifier, it does not show a significant impact as in most of our design space, the signal that we sample is within the vertical range of our DSO.

We posit that the observation regarding the inductive (CT-1) probe could change if targeting higher clock frequencies, and the observation regarding the amplifier could change if targeting more advanced technologies or a side-channel signal with lower amplitude (e.g., an electromagnetic one).

Clock Frequency. This parameter is in general important for side-channel analysis. Whenever it can be controlled by the adversary, both our hardware and software results suggest the same rule-of-thumb: *"use the highest available clock frequency such that independent clock cycles are easy to distinguish"*.

We first illustrate this rule-of-thumb with Fig. 6. It shows the traces we recorded with the best parameter set and varying clock frequencies for the FPGA platform. At 1 MHz, the independent peaks for each clock cycle are clearly distinguishable. At higher clock frequencies, the leakage traces are smoother and the overlapping between the clock cycles in the measurements increases.

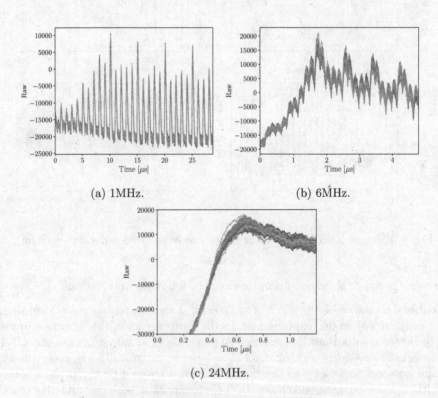

(a) 1MHz.

(b) 6MHz.

(c) 24MHz.

Fig. 6. Clock frequency effect on the hardware setup.

We next turn to the software case study to explain the first part of the rule-of-thumb (i.e., why it is not advisable to reduce the clock frequency unconditionally). In this respect, we first note that for this software DUT, the clock cycles were clearly distinguishable even for the maximum clock frequency (so the second part of the rule-of-thumb was fulfilled). In this case, the best SNR and PI values are observed for higher clock frequencies. We explain this effect by observing that all the samples in a clock cycle are not equally informative. During an MCU clock cycle, most of the dynamic power is contained right after the rising edge of the clock as the effect of the registers changing state. The leakage from the remaining of the clock cycle is mostly due to static power and is usually less informative [20,23]. Therefore, the interest of decreasing the clock frequency can become detrimental when conditioned on a sampling frequency.

More precisely, and as illustrated in Fig. 7, decreasing the clock frequency can lead the collected samples (represented by red diamonds in the figure) to correspond mostly to the static part of the leakage, and to miss the information of the dynamic part (represented by the green rectangles of the figures). Overall, this can lead to a collection of samples that is less informative: the univariate SNR can be lower by missing the most informative sample and the multivariate PI can be lower by cumulatively covering less relevant samples.

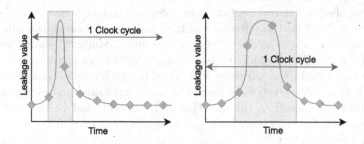

Fig. 7. Sampling with different DUT clock frequencies.

$\mathbf{V_{DD}}$. Despite less definitive than the clock frequency, the supply voltage also affects the shape of the leakage traces, as it increases the critical path and therefore spreads the information towards more samples. This naturally causes the multivariate PI to be improved when lowering the supply voltage below the nominal one. Interestingly, we also observed that for both targets and most sets of other parameters, decreasing V_{DD} is also beneficial to the univariate SNR.

A plausible reason for this observation is that both devices are based on CMOS technology (even though from different technology nodes and manufacturers) which generally exhibits smoother transient current when V_{DD} is lower than nominal, due to reduced transconductance of digital cells. This can reduce both the signal and, here more dominantly, the noise of the leakage.

We note that this observation is admittedly technology-dependent: see [28] for a report on several technology nodes. It is also not unconditional: as reported in the same paper, the output noise of a digital cell in subthreshold regime (that corresponds to extremely low V_{DD} values) is not minimal, as transistors exhibit higher resistance and thus contribute more to increase the noise level. So overall, our conclusion regarding the V_{DD} parameter is that reducing it below the nominal value can have marginal interest, especially for multivariate attacks, but is not expected to lead to significant gain/loss factors.

Sampling Rate. This parameter is especially critical for the cost of the attacks as it affects the memory requirements to store the leakage measurements.

On the one hand, its selection is related to the clock frequency: as in general when quantizing signals, the sampling rate should at least be chosen larger than the Nyquist frequency. This requirement was confirmed in our experiments, and showed to be more critical (resp., less critical) in the hardware case (resp., software case). This is presumably due to the lower (resp., larger) amount of less (resp., more) informative samples of the harware (resp., software) case.

On the other hand, in the context of side-channel analysis, a natural question is whether increasing the sampling rate significantly beyond the Nyquist frequency can be useful. Namely, can it lead to more powerful multivariate attacks? By testing a sampling frequency of ×1, ×5 and ×25 the clock frequency, we observed that collecting more samples helps only to a limited extent. In particular, both for the software and the hardware platforms, the gains when moving from ×1 to ×5 the clock frequency are more significant than when moving from ×5 to ×25 the clock frequency, again with more incentive to increase the sampling rate in the hardware case than in the software case. A plausible reason for this difference is once more the more condensed and noisy nature of the hardware leakage (i.e., the fact that it is concentrated in less cycles with more algorithmic noise, rather than spread over more cycles in software).

Univariate vs Multivariate Evaluations. Eventually, our results indicate that whether the SNR is a good predictor of the PI is quite case-dependent.

If the SNR traces present a single peak or a set of peaks that are close to each other (e.g., within one cycle), they usually indicate correlated leakage coming from a single operation. In this case, which typically corresponds to our hardware experiments (see the left part of Fig. 5), a good univariate SNR will generally be a good indicator of a good multivariate PI. Multivariate attacks will always be more powerful but the SNR can serve as a first-order comparison metric.

By contrast, if the SNR traces contain multiple peaks separated by several clock cycles, they rather indicate independent leakage coming from different operations. In this case, which typically corresponds to our software experiments (see the right part of Fig. 5), multivariate attacks are expected to be significantly more powerful than univariate ones. So the direct estimation of the multivariate PI is in general a better (i.e., more conclusive) evaluation strategy.

5   Conclusions

This study aims at evaluating the risk of over-estimating the physical security of an implementation due inadequate parameter choices when configuring a measurement setup. We focus on four main parameters: the probing method, the clock frequency, the power supply voltage and the sampling rate. We apply our methodology to an embedded software and a hardware FPGA implementation of the AES-128 block cipher. It leads to 108 experiments for each DUT, that we analyze by means of univariate and multivariate evaluation metrics, namely the SNR and the PI. Our findings show that the losses due to a bad selection of parameters can be significant and lead to a strong over-estimations of an implementation's security level. We also use our experiments in order to consolidate general intuitions and recommendations regarding the good choice of parameters and to discuss their device and architecture dependencies.

Acknowledgments. François-Xavier Standaert is a senior research associate of the Belgian Fund for Scientific Research (F.R.S.-FNRS). This work has been funded in parts by the European Union through the ERC project SWORD (724725).

References

1. Accurrent probes - ct1, ct2, ct6 data sheet. https://download.tek.com/manual/070795702web.pdf
2. Tinyaes in c. https://github.com/kokke/tiny-AES-c
3. Balasch, J., Gierlichs, B., Reparaz, O., Verbauwhede, I.: DPA, bitslicing and masking at 1 GHz. In: Güneysu, T., Handschuh, H. (eds.) CHES 2015. LNCS, vol. 9293, pp. 599–619. Springer, Heidelberg (2015). https://doi.org/10.1007/978-3-662-48324-4_30
4. Beckers, A., Balasch, J., Gierlichs, B., Verbauwhede, I.: Design and implementation of a waveform-matching based triggering system. In: Standaert, F.-X., Oswald, E. (eds.) COSADE 2016. LNCS, vol. 9689, pp. 184–198. Springer, Cham (2016). https://doi.org/10.1007/978-3-319-43283-0_11
5. Brier, E., Clavier, C., Olivier, F.: Correlation power analysis with a leakage model. In: Joye, M., Quisquater, J.-J. (eds.) CHES 2004. LNCS, vol. 3156, pp. 16–29. Springer, Heidelberg (2004). https://doi.org/10.1007/978-3-540-28632-5_2
6. Bronchain, O., Hendrickx, J.M., Massart, C., Olshevsky, A., Standaert, F.-X.: Leakage certification revisited: bounding model errors in side-channel security evaluations. In: Boldyreva, A., Micciancio, D. (eds.) CRYPTO 2019. LNCS, vol. 11692, pp. 713–737. Springer, Cham (2019). https://doi.org/10.1007/978-3-030-26948-7_25
7. Chari, S., Jutla, C.S., Rao, J.R., Rohatgi, P.: Towards Sound Approaches to Counteract Power-Analysis Attacks. In: Wiener, M. (ed.) CRYPTO 1999. LNCS, vol. 1666, pp. 398–412. Springer, Heidelberg (1999). https://doi.org/10.1007/3-540-48405-1_26
8. Chari, S., Rao, J.R., Rohatgi, P.: Template attacks. In: CHES. Lecture Notes in Computer Science, vol. 2523, pp. 13–28. Springer, Redwood city (2002)
9. de Chérisey, E., Guilley, S., Rioul, O., Piantanida, P.: Best information is most successful mutual information and success rate in side-channel analysis. IACR Trans. Cryptogr. Hardw. Embed. Syst. **2019**(2), 49–79 (2019)

10. De Cnudde, T., Bilgin, B., Gierlichs, B., Nikov, V., Nikova, S., Rijmen, V.: Does coupling affect the security of masked implementations? In: Guilley, S. (ed.) COSADE 2017. LNCS, vol. 10348, pp. 1–18. Springer, Cham (2017). https://doi.org/10.1007/978-3-319-64647-3_1

11. Cnudde, T.D., Ender, M., Moradi, A.: Hardware masking, revisited. IACR Trans. Cryptogr. Hardw. Embed. Syst. **2018**(2), 123–148 (2018)

12. Duc, A., Faust, S., Standaert, F.-X.: Making masking security proofs concrete. In: Oswald, E., Fischlin, M. (eds.) EUROCRYPT 2015. LNCS, vol. 9056, pp. 401–429. Springer, Heidelberg (2015). https://doi.org/10.1007/978-3-662-46800-5_16

13. Goubin, L., Patarin, J.: DES and differential power analysis (the duplication method). In: Koç, Ç.K., Paar, C. (eds.) CHES 1999. LNCS, vol. 1717, pp. 158–172. Springer, Heidelberg (1999). https://doi.org/10.1007/3-540-48059-5_15

14. Guilley, S., Maghrebi, H., Souissi, Y., Sauvage, L., Danger, J.L.: Quantifying the quality of side-channel acquisitions. In: COSADE 2011. pp. 16–28 (2011)

15. Herbst, C., Oswald, E., Mangard, S.: An AES smart card implementation resistant to power analysis attacks. In: Zhou, J., Yung, M., Bao, F. (eds.) ACNS 2006. LNCS, vol. 3989, pp. 239–252. Springer, Heidelberg (2006). https://doi.org/10.1007/11767480_16

16. Levi, I., Bellizia, D., Standaert, F.: Reducing a masked implementation's effective security order with setup manipulations and an explanation based on externally-amplified couplings. IACR Trans. Cryptogr. Hardw. Embed. Syst. **2019**(2), 293–317 (2019)

17. Mangard, S.: Hardware countermeasures against DPA – a statistical analysis of their effectiveness. In: Okamoto, T. (ed.) CT-RSA 2004. LNCS, vol. 2964, pp. 222–235. Springer, Heidelberg (2004). https://doi.org/10.1007/978-3-540-24660-2_18

18. Mangard, S., Oswald, E., Standaert, F.: One for all - all for one: unifying standard differential power analysis attacks. IET Inf. Secur. **5**(2), 100–110 (2011)

19. Moos, T., Moradi, A., Richter, B.: Static power side-channel analysis - an investigation of measurement factors. IEEE Trans. Very Large Scale Integr. Syst. **28**(2), 376–389 (2020)

20. Moradi, A.: Side-channel leakage through static power. In: Batina, L., Robshaw, M. (eds.) CHES 2014. LNCS, vol. 8731, pp. 562–579. Springer, Heidelberg (2014). https://doi.org/10.1007/978-3-662-44709-3_31

21. Moradi, A., Barenghi, A., Kasper, T., Paar, C.: On the vulnerability of FPGA bitstream encryption against power analysis attacks: extracting keys from xilinx virtex-ii fpgas. In: ACM Conference on Computer and Communications Security, pp. 111–124. ACM (2011)

22. Merino del Pozo, S., Standaert, F.-X.: Getting the most out of leakage detection. In: Guilley, S. (ed.) COSADE 2017. LNCS, vol. 10348, pp. 264–281. Springer, Cham (2017). https://doi.org/10.1007/978-3-319-64647-3_16

23. Pozo, S.M.D., Standaert, F., Kamel, D., Moradi, A.: Side-channel attacks from static power: when should we care? In: DATE, pp. 145–150. ACM (2015)

24. Schwarz, R.: R&s hz-15, r&s hz-17 probe sets, r&s hz-16 preamplifier. https://scdn.rohde-schwarz.com/ur/pws/dl_downloads/dl_common_library/dl_brochures_and_datasheets/pdf_1/service_support_30/HZ-15_16_17_bro_en_5213-6687-12_v0100.pdf

25. Standaert, F.-X., Archambeau, C.: Using subspace-based template attacks to compare and combine power and electromagnetic information leakages. In: Oswald, E., Rohatgi, P. (eds.) CHES 2008. LNCS, vol. 5154, pp. 411–425. Springer, Heidelberg (2008). https://doi.org/10.1007/978-3-540-85053-3_26

26. Standaert, F.-X., Malkin, T.G., Yung, M.: A unified framework for the analysis of side-channel key recovery attacks. In: Joux, A. (ed.) EUROCRYPT 2009. LNCS, vol. 5479, pp. 443–461. Springer, Heidelberg (2009). https://doi.org/10.1007/978-3-642-01001-9_26

27. for Standardization, I.O.: It security techniques - test tool requirements and test tool calibration methods for use in testing non-invasive attack mitigation techniques in cryptographic modules - part 1: Test tools and techniques (Geneva (CH) 2019), iSO/IEC 20082-1

28. Veirano, F., Silveira, F., Navinery, L.: Is intrinsic noise a limiting factor for sub-threshold digital logic in nanoscale CMOS? In: 2015 International Workshop on CMOS Variability (VARI), pp. 45–50 (2015)

29. Veyrat-Charvillon, N., Medwed, M., Kerckhof, S., Standaert, F.-X.: Shuffling against side-channel attacks: a comprehensive study with cautionary note. In: Wang, X., Sako, K. (eds.) ASIACRYPT 2012. LNCS, vol. 7658, pp. 740–757. Springer, Heidelberg (2012). https://doi.org/10.1007/978-3-642-34961-4_44

A Tale of Two Boards: On the Influence of Microarchitecture on Side-Channel Leakage

Vipul Arora[1,2], Ileana Buhan[3], Guilherme Perin[2], and Stjepan Picek[2(✉)]

[1] Riscure B.V, Delft, The Netherlands
[2] Delft University of Technology, Delft, The Netherlands
[3] Radboud University, Nijmegen, The Netherlands

Abstract. Advances in cryptography have enabled the features of confidentiality, security, and integrity on small embedded devices such as IoT devices. While mathematically strong, the platform on which an algorithm is implemented plays a significant role in the security of the final product. Side-channel attacks exploit the variations in the system's physical characteristics to obtain information about the sensitive data. In our scenario, a software implementation of a cryptographic algorithm is flashed on devices from different manufactures with the same instruction set configured for identical execution. To analyze the influence of the microarchitecture on side-channel leakage, we acquire thirty-two sets of power traces from four physical devices. While we notice minor differences in the leakage behavior for different physical boards from the same manufacturer, our results confirm that the difference in microarchitecture implementations of the same core will leak different side-channel information. We also show that TVLA leakage prediction should be treated with caution as it is sensitive to both false positives and negatives.

Keywords: Microarchitecture · Side-channel leakage · TVLA

1 Introduction

The question we ask in this work is both simple and practically relevant for an embedded system developer assigned to implement an existing cryptographic algorithm on a microcontroller. The developer is free to choose any microcontroller meeting the project's functional requirements, e.g., ARM Cortex M0, a popular choice in the IoT industry. Our developer has several options for a *given core* from the diverse SoC range offered by different manufacturers.

Devices supporting a similar instruction set architecture (ISA) vary in design depending on the implementation choices. The ISA represents an abstraction of the underlying hardware implementation, known as *the microarchitecture* [9]. Figure 1 shows the relation between the ISA and the microarchitecture. The ability to separate the ISA design from the microarchitecture was a significant step in the development of modern computing, granting functional compatibility

© Springer Nature Switzerland AG 2022
V. Grosso and T. Pöppelmann (Eds.): CARDIS 2021, LNCS 13173, pp. 80–96, 2022.
https://doi.org/10.1007/978-3-030-97348-3_5

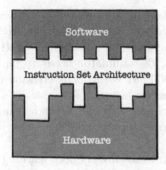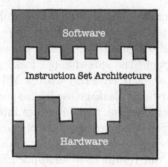

Fig. 1. We refer to the ISA implementation as the *microarchitecture*, which is manufacturer-specific and considered a trade secret. The illustration is inspired by [13].

while allowing for flexibility in the implementation. As the choices made during the ISA implementation significantly impact the final product's performance, the microarchitecture implementation is considered a trade secret, and details are typically not available in the public domain.

All other things being equal, our developer would like to choose the microarchitecture implementation, which minimizes the side-channel leakage. Concretely, the question relevant to our embedded system developer is:

> *Given the choice between two implementations of the same core, how significant is the difference in side-channel leakage?*

This study selected two devices designed with an ARM Cortex M0 core from the same family, the same ISA, and different vendors. To detect the source of differences between different implementations, we took special care to synchronize the traces between two devices for identical execution. We labeled the time samples in the trace with the executed instruction to identify and explain, where possible, the source of difference.

Contributions. We present a methodology for comparing software implementations across devices with the same instruction set and comment on the influence of microarchitecture implementation on side-channel leaks. We compare the manufacturing variability between different physical devices from the same manufacturer. To reveal the effects of the microarchitecture implementation, we compare devices from different manufacturers. We contrast the accuracy of leakage detection techniques with the "real" leaks obtained by profiling for the evaluation. We show that leakage detection techniques are prone to false positives and false negatives, and their results should be treated with caution.

2 Related Works

The results presented in this paper have a wider application than the practical relevance for our embedded system engineer. First, to the area of side-channel leakage simulators, which face the problem of portability across devices. For example, both ELMO [10] and [11], were created specifically for an ARM Cortex M0 STM32F0 (30R8T6) device. If the microarchitecture implementation significantly impacts the side-channel leakage, the simulator needs to be retrained when the target is an ARM Cortex M0 NRFf51 board. The creation of sophisticated gray-boxed leakage models required for accurate side-channel simulators requires including microarchitecture information. While we know that reverse-engineering the microarchitecture of commercial processors is possible [4,10], the effort is intensive.

Second, our results have an application to the area of deep learning for SCA, where training and attacking across different physical boards using the same model is possible but requires a special training procedure [3]. Golder et al. extended the previous work and explored the cross-device perspective for a large number of devices (3) [5]. Van der Valk et al. aimed to analyze the portability problem from the AI explainability perspective and discussed the overspecialization phenomenon. Bhasin et al. showed that portability makes the deep learning attacks more difficult as the deep learning algorithms will easily overfit [1]. To prevent this, the authors proposed the Multiple Device Model approach. Overspecialization denotes the situation when a machine learning attack does not overfit when using the test set from the same device (as when not considering portability), but it overfits when attacking a different device [14]. Wu et al. provide a workaround for the Multiple Device Model where ablation can reduce the overfitting effect [15]. Zhang et al. investigated the difficulty of profiling attacks when considering homogeneous (same devices) and heterogeneous settings (different devices) [16]. Another challenge for profiled attacks is that the collection of side-channel traces becomes less reliable after a long period. Consequently, certain trend noise must be added to the side-channel traces due to temperature and environmental conditions evolution over time. Heuser et al. characterized this effect and proved that trend noise drastically impedes SCA [7]. Similar findings are confirmed by Cao et al. [2].

3   Background

ARM Cortex M0. The Cortex M0 is a 32-bit RISC processor developed by ARM that implements version v6M of the ARM instruction set [8]. It is one of the most widely used embedded devices due to an efficient instruction set and affordable development costs with comprehensive development tools and support. The Cortex M0 has a Harvard architecture with both 16-bit (THUMB) and 32-bit instructions and a 32-bit data path. It does not include a data cache or memory management unit (MMU) but comes with a prefetch buffer. The ARM6 has 37 registers, consisting of thirty-one 32-bit general-purpose registers and six additional status registers. The instruction set determines the functional capabilities of a processor by specifying the list of all supported instructions.

Test Vector Leakage Assessment (TVLA) [6] is one of the most popular leakage detection methods due to its simplicity and relative effectiveness. It is based on statistical hypothesis tests and comes in two flavours: *specific* and *non-specific*. The 'fixed-vs-random' is the most common nonspecific test and compares a set of traces acquired with a fixed plaintext with another set of traces acquired with random plaintext. In the case of a specific test, the traces are divided according to a known intermediate value tested for leakage. Welch's two-sample t-test for equality of means is applied for all trace samples in both cases. A difference between two sets larger than a given threshold is taken as evidence for the presence of a leak.

Key Rank Estimate is a commonly used metric in SCA for assessing the performance of an attack. It is performed in a known key scenario and returns the rank of the correct key candidate in the sorted score vector of all key candidates. The key ran estimate is related to the success rate curve [12], which shows the evolution of the correct key candidate as more traces are added. There are two differences compared to the success rate: first, key ranking is performed on a fixed set of traces, whereas the success rate is performed on a variable set of traces to capture the evolution of the correct key candidate; second, key ranking can be performed for all samples in the trace, whereas the success rate is typically shown for one sample. The result of the key rank estimate is affected by the number of traces used for analysis. If leaks are present, key rank converges towards the first position as more traces are added.

4   Experimental Setup

Target Devices. We selected for this study two ARM Cortex-M0 cores as comprehensive literature is available, and the Cortex M0 has found wide application in embedded and IoT devices:

1. STM32 Discovery is a development board from ST Microelectronics for the STM320f051 device, which consists of an on-board MCU interface enabling easy flashing and debugging using STLink over USB. The development board also offers a PPI port that connects a current probe to measure the current consumption. On inspection of the STM32 board's schematic, we observe that the MCU interface and the target device share the same power source. The target MCU is powered by an external 3V3 supply from the current measurement port using the USB port. The coupling capacitors attached to the power pins of the target MCU are removed; they act as a low pass filter on the input power supply to the target MCU. We used two STM32 boards for our experiments, referring to them as STM_A and STM_B.
2. NRFf51 is an SoC designed for Bluetooth Low Energy applications based on Cortex M0 running at 16 MHz. The NRFf51 development kit also offers a current measurement port, and we found no coupling capacitors to the power line circuitry. The target MCU is already isolated from the interface MCU when the board is powered externally using 3V3, so no hardware modifications are required. We used two NRFf51 boards for our experiments, referring to them as NRF_A and NRF_B.

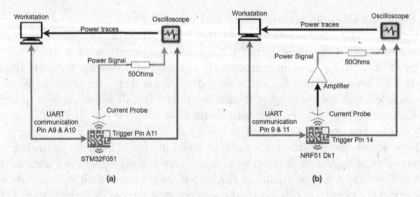

Fig. 2. Acquisition setup for (a) STM32 and (b) NRFf51 boards. Pin A9 and A10 are used on STM32, and pin 9 and pin 11 are used on NRFf51board for UART Rx and Tx, respectively. For connecting the trigger signal, we use pin A11 for the STM32and pin A14 for the NRFf51 boards. For both, the signal from the current probe is attached to the oscilloscope through a 50Ω impedance. For the NRFf51 board, the signal from the current probe is passed through a signal amplifier.

Measurement Setup. Throughout this paper, we maintain the same experimental setup, shown Fig. 2. We use Riscure's Inspector SCA toolchain [1] for
acquisition and signal processing. Furthermore, we use a Picoscope 3000 and a
Riscure-CP189 current probe. An important requirement for our setup is that
both boards execute the same instructions in sync. Since the two boards have a
different startup script for configuration and execution, we took special care to
ensure the code between the triggers is identical for both targets. The same compiler was used to generate the binary files, and we compared the disassembled
code on both boards to verify that the execution was identical. For a consistent
toolchain, the software projects for both devices were created and compiled using
Kiel Vision 5. An unmasked implementation of AES-128[2] was flashed on both
target boards. The execution sequence is:

1. On boot/reset, a startup code runs on both target devices, which sets the
   system and peripheral clocks. While the NRFf51 device works at a fixed clock
   speed of 16 Mhz, the STM32 device supports operation over a wide clock frequency. The startup code sets the clock frequency to 16 MHz.
2. Core and UART drivers are initialized.
3. System tick interrupt is disabled.
4. Control enters the main function, AES object with a preset key is initialized.
5. Enter an infinite loop, repeat the steps below:
   (a) Receive 16 bytes of data over UART.
   (b) Set *trigger pin low*, which signals the oscilloscope to start recording.
   (c) 16 bytes of data are encrypted.
   (d) Encrypted ciphertext is returned over UART.

---

[1] https://www.riscure.com/security-tools/inspector-sca.
[2] https://github.com/ARMmbed/mbedtls.

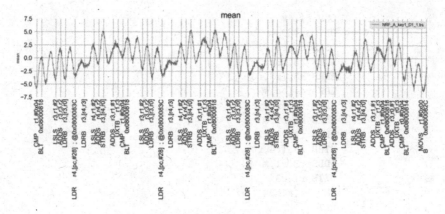

Fig. 3. An example of labeled traces.

Synchronization of Traces. To provide an accurate analysis of the observed effects, we want to align the traces with clock cycle accuracy. We compared the accuracy of the trigger signal from the oscilloscope to the recorded traces to find the level of drift. Using the disassembly of C code, the assembly code line that sets the trigger pin low is found to have exact timing. We use the number of cycles it takes the program flow to enter the encrypt function, and we use it to identify the start of the encrypt function in the recorded traces.

Adding Instruction Labels. We used the ARM process simulator in Keil MDK version 5[3] to record the execution trace of instructions. The tool outputs a CSV file with disassembly code and the execution time for each instruction. We use the execution trace information to link the instruction labels to their power trace segments. An example of the results of combining power traces with instruction labels obtained from the execution trace is shown in Fig. 3. The example presents the acquired power trace immediately after acquisition and up until add_round_key operation on the first four bytes. Unless otherwise mentioned, for the rest of the experiments we use the power trace corresponding to the Listing 1.1. To confirm the correctness of the labeling, we also visually verified that repeated instruction sequences show a similar power consumption.

Trace Sets. We collected a total of 32 trace sets, 2500 traces each, from the four physical boards (STM$_A$, STM$_B$, NRF$_A$, NRF$_B$) available. Half of the traces are provided with a fixed 16-byte plaintext, and half have 16-byte random plaintext. We used two different keys, key_1 and key_2, for the encryption and two different values for the fixed input D_1 and D_2. As the TVLA methodology [6] specifies performing a repetition to verify the results, the trace sets are labeled by 1 or 2, representing two repetitions. Figure 4 shows an overview of the collected traces.

---

[3] https://www2.keil.com/mdk5/docs.

```
1    CMP r1, #0x04
2    BLT 0x08000818
3    LSLS r3,r1,#2
4    ADDS r3,r3,r2
5    LDRB r3,[r3,r0]
6    LDR r4,[pc,#28] : @0x0800083C
7    LDRB r3,[r4,r3]
8    LSLS r4,r1,#1
9    ADDS r4,r4,r2
10   STRB r3,[r4,r0]
11   ADDS r3,r1,#1
12   UXTB r1,r3
13   CMP r1,#0x04
14   BLT 0x08000818
15   LSLS r3, r1,#2
16   ADDS r3,r3,r2
17   LDRB r3,[r3,r0]
18   LDR r4, [pc,#28]: @0x0800083C
19   LDRB r3,[r4,r3]
20   LSLS r4,r1,#1
21   ADDS r4,r4,r2
22   STRB r3,[r4,r0]
23   ADDS r3,r1,#1
```

Listing 1: Code sequence captured during the experiments.

5   A Closer Look at the Implementation

The raw traces from the STM32 and NRFf51 board are shown in Fig. 5. A quick visual comparison confirms that the power consumption for the two devices differs significantly. The operations performed are based on repetitive patterns that can be distinctly identified for both devices.

S-box Leakage. To understand how the devices are leaking, we isolate the samples corresponding to the S-box computation in round one, as shown in Fig. 5. We profile the targets using the Hamming Weight (HW) leakage model. We select all 16 bytes of the S-box and correlate the intermediate values with the selected samples. We rank the probability of leak for all the possible key-byte combinations. With this approach, we relate observable leaks at each time sample index with the probability of the correct key byte leaking to an attacker. The results are shown in Fig. 6.

For the STM32 device, Fig. 6 (top), we observe that key data leaks strongly while the subsequent byte is loaded, which seems evidence for data-overwrite leaks from registers. A small section of leaks is observed again when a key element from the same group is operated upon. This can relate to how key data is stored in subsequent memory locations, and memory access loads more than 1-byte data on the bus. This effect can be due to 4-byte memory access in Cortex M0;

	STM Board			NRF Board		
	Fixed set-1	Fixed set-2		Fixed set-1	Fixed set-2	
Board A	STM_A_key1_D1_1 STM_A_key1_D1_2	STM_A_key1_D2_1 STM_A_key1_D2_2	Key 1	NRF_A_key1_D1_1 NRF_A_key1_D1_2	NRF_A_key1_D2_1 NRF_A_key1_D2_2	
	STM_A_key2_D1_1 STM_A_key2_D1_2	STM_A_key2_D2_1 STM_A_key2_D2_2	Key 2	NRF_A_key2_D1_1 NRF_A_key2_D1_2	NRF_A_key2_D2_1 NRF_A_key2_D2_2	
Board B	STM_B_key1_D1_1 STM_B_key1_D1_2	STM_B_key1_D2_1 STM_B_key1_D2_2	Key 1	NRF_B_key1_D1_1 NRF_B_key1_D1_2	NRF_A_key1_D2_1 NRF_A_key1_D2_2	
	STM_B_key2_D1_1 STM_B_key2_D1_2	STM_B_key2_D2_1 STM_B_key2_D2_2	Key 2	NRF_B_key2_D1_1 NRF_B_key2_D1_2	NRF_B_key2_D2_1 NRF_B_key2_D2_2	

Fig. 4. Overview trace sets. The nomenclature is class_board_key_data_repetition. For example, a trace set with the name NRF_B_key2_D1_1 means it was collected from NRF$_B$ board, key K_2 is used for encryption, D_1 is provided as fixed input, and 1 is the repetition cycle.

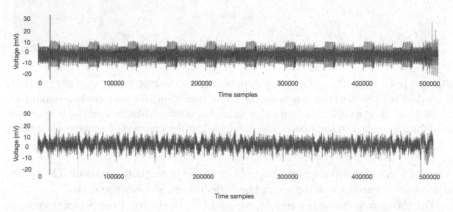

Fig. 5. The raw power trace for the STM$_A$ device (top) and NRF$_A$ device (bottom). The highlighted section marks the 1st round of the S-box operation on the first byte of data. The selection starts at index 14 910 and has a length 1 235 samples. This section of trace has been used for the evaluation in Sects. 6 and 7.

the old key bytes are also sent on the bus due to a word size of 4 bytes. (i.e. we observe leak of k[0][0] when operations are performed on k[0][1], leak of k[0][0], k[0][1] when operation are performed on k[0][2]; similarly We observe leak of k[0][0], k[0][1], k[0][2] when operation are performed on k[0][3]).

Similarly, the results for the NRFf51 device are presented in Fig. 6 (bottom). We observe that the correct key intermediate is leaking consistently after the first time it is read from memory, and key data is leaking when operations are performed on byte data stored in subsequent memory locations. Memory access read 4 bytes of consecutive data from the provided memory address. Comparing the leaks across the two devices, we note that data-overwrite leaks are observed at similar trace sections. The key bytes start to leak subsequent to the STR instructions and leak while the next byte data is loaded by LDR instructions. We surmise that the contrasting behavior results from the difference in microarchitecture implementation. The NRFf51 device is a low power board; memory access

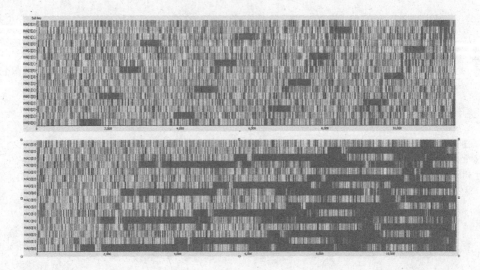

Fig. 6. (To be viewed in colors.) Key rank results for the STM32 (top) and NRFf51 (bottom) devices. The selection captures the s-box operation. We perform key ranking on all 16 bytes in round 1. The red color indicates strong leaks, where the correct key candidate is ranked in the first position, whereas other colors represents weak leaks.

consumes significant power and impacts dynamic power consumption. The choice of memory technology will impact the leaks observed from the board.

For the remainder of the report, we select the leaks from the S-box operation on 1 byte of data (Byte 1). To maintain uniformity in the analysis, the same trace section will be used for all comparisons.

6   The Influence of Manufacturing Variability

Manufactured silicon chips have variations due to the raw material used or variations in the manufacturing process. Non-uniform etc.hing can introduce inconsistencies in transistors' depletion layer, which will affect the leakage current generated on switching. Inconsistencies are spread out across peripherals at the microarchitecture level, which means that each physical device will have its power fingerprint resulting from the accumulation of these effects.

This section explores the manufacturing differences between boards from the same manufacturer, namely, the differences in side-channel leaks from STM_A vs. STM_B, and NRF_A vs. NRF_B. These results are useful for putting in perspective the results obtained in Sect. 7. The devices are prepared with similar hardware modifications and flashed with the same binary, keeping the key and input data parameters identical, as described in Sect. 5.

The result of the TVLA test for both STM_A and STM_B, Fig. 7 (a), shows a similar shape for the leakage. Additionally, the repetition of the test (with different inputs and keys) shown with a dotted line confirms these results. Key rank

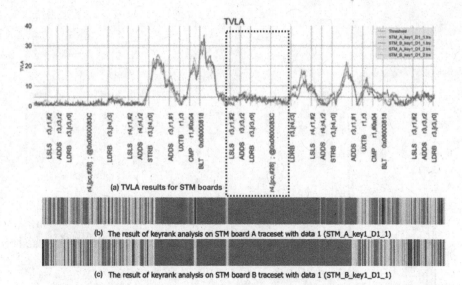

(a) TVLA results for STM boards

(b) The result of keyrank analysis on STM board A traceset with data 1 (STM_A_key1_D1_1)

(c) The result of keyrank analysis on STM board B traceset with data 1 (STM_B_key1_D1_1)

Fig. 7. (To be viewed in color.) Results of data leakage comparison for STM_A and STM_B. From the top: (a) TVLA traces, (b) key rank results for STM_A, (c) key rank results for STM_B. The red rectangle indicates the area of the trace where TVLA shows false negative (profiling indicates leakage).

results in Figs. 7 (b) and (c) show leaks over a wider section of power traces for both devices compared to the results predicted by TVLA. Key rank results for the STM_A device show leaks at the beginning of the trace, a behavior not seen in the key ranking results for the STM_B device. These leaks are probably caused by manufacturing defects in STM_A. Gaps in leakage are observed for both boards during the execution of UXTB and BLT instructions, which can be sourced from effects in the physical layer. We observe gaps in the results of key rank analysis during the ADDS and the BLT instruction, which is consistent for both boards. We could attribute this effect to operations being implemented at the hardware level, which mask the leakage of key data at those locations.

The TVLA results shown in Fig. 8 (a) indicate a very similar trend for both NRFf51 boards. Key rank analysis results for the two boards are shown in Fig. 8 (c) and (d). While we note a slight variation between the leakage NRF_A and NRF_B, the overall trend is similar. However, we note a significant difference between the leakage predicted by TVLA, which indicates both false positive and false negative leakage.

To summarize, we confirm that the manufacturing process may create slight differences between the leaks in the different physical devices we examined, but the overall trend seems consistent. Based on the experimental results, we conclude that there are significant differences between the leakage predicted by TVLA and the ground truth as indicated by profiling the targets.

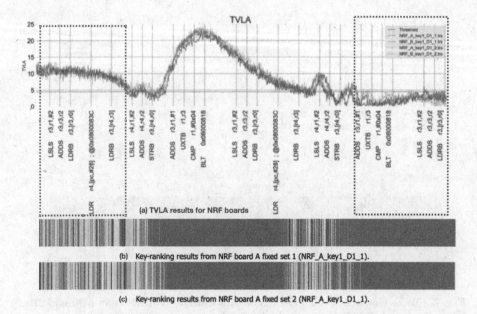

(a) TVLA results for NRF boards

(b)   Key-ranking results from NRF board A fixed set 1 (NRF_A_key1_D1_1).

(c)   Key-ranking results from NRF board A fixed set 2 (NRF_A_key1_D1_1).

Fig. 8. (To be viewed in color.) Results of data leakage comparison for NRF$_A$ and NRF$_B$. From the top: (a) TVLA traces, (b) key rank for NRF$_A$, (c) key rank for NRF$_B$. The blue rectangle indicates the area of the trace where TVLA shows false positive (leakage while profiling indicates no leakage). The red rectangle indicates the area of the trace, where TVLA shows false negative (no leakage while profiling clearly indicates leakage).

7   The Influence of Microarchitectural Implementation

The ARM Cortex-M0 microprocessor has a three-stage pipeline, which means there can be up to three instructions implemented in the fetch, decode, and execute stages of the pipeline. Memory access greatly impacts the dynamic power, so the effect of memory instructions is significant and can be diffused to be visible while other instructions are executed. Furthermore, while we know the instruction executed at every clock cycle, we note that the power trace consists of a *cumulative effect* from all pipeline stages of the processor.

When porting code to a device with a similar hardware architecture, the grouping of instructions in pipeline stages will probably be also similar. However, the magnitude/contribution of leaks from different pipeline stages may vary for different devices. Additionally, as microarchitectural implementation choices are not public, the best we can do for describing the difference in side-channel leakage between the STM32 and NRFf51 boards is a plausible explanation.

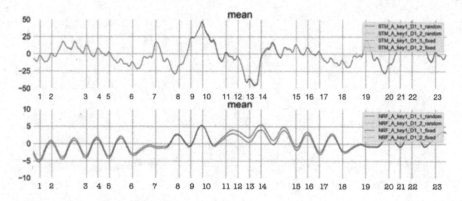

Fig. 9. Fixed vs. random mean trace plot for STM32 (top) and NRFf51 (bottom). The y-axis shows the power consumption, and the x-axis represents time. The numbers on the x-axis are the instruction being executed, see Listing 1.1.

7.1 Power Profiles

Mean Traces. Fixed vs. random mean plots comparing the two devices are presented in Fig. 9. The power traces from STM32 devices have a higher power consumption than the traces obtained from the NRFf51 device, as evident from the scale of the y-axis. STM32 is designed for general-purpose IoT applications, whereas the NRFf51 is a low energy device with a current consumption of 2mA. The low power of the NRFf51 device makes it more sensitive to noise.

Comparing the mean trace plots from both devices, we observe the fixed vs. random lines deviating at the same power trace sections. In Fig. 9, this is visible in the difference between the red (random set) and blue (fixed set) lines for both plots. The deviations reveal sections of code with a dynamic power component. If the underlying data is changed in the code section, we will observe fluctuations in the specific section of power traces. We repeated the experiments with a different value for the input data to verify that the observations were not incidental. We distinguish between the two repetitions by presenting results with a solid and a dotted line in the power profile comparison plots. Repeating artifacts are observed for LDR (labeled 6 and 18) and STRB (labeled 10 and 22) instructions in power trace, confirming the correct labeling of traces with instructions. In the case of the NRFf51 devices, the effects of individual instructions are not as prominent and are difficult to distinguish visually.

From the mean plots of fixed (blue) vs. random (red) execution for both the device, we observe both the sets exhibit a similar trend though they differ along certain sections of the traces. In Fig. 9 (top), we notice that the deviation between the random and fixed sets is visible only following the STRB r3,[r4,r0] (labeled 10) instruction until the BLT branch (labeled 14). In Fig. 9 (bottom), we can distinctly see the execution trace of fixed as well as random sets. The interesting observation is that the distance between the mean of two sets increases substantially after the STRB r3,[r4,r0] (labeled 10) instruction and then slowly

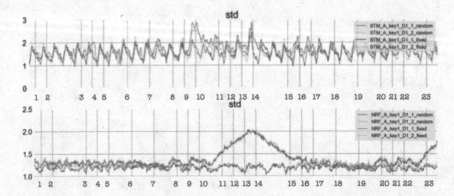

Fig. 10. Fixed vs. random standard deviation trace plot for STM32 (top) and NRFf51 (bottom). The y-axis shows the power consumption, and the x-axis represents time. The numbers on the x-axis are the instruction being executed, see Listing 1.1.

decreases up until the BLT instruction (labeled 14). From the results in the previous section, we know that these are the locations where leaks are observed. The software implementation seems to show evidence of data overwrite leaks at similar sections across devices of both classes.

Standard Deviation. The operands influence the power consumption due to the toggling of bits when new data is loaded. An increase in the standard deviation of the random set is observed where the power consumption depends on the underlying data. The standard deviation of the fixed set provides us with a base level for executing a set of operations with constant data.

Standard deviation plots in Fig. 10 show that the standard deviation for the fixed set consistently varies for every clock cycle. This behavior is consistent for the fixed sets for all boards and repetitions. The increase in standard deviation for the random sets provides evidence of leaks, and interestingly these are observed at similar trace sections for both the STM32 and NRFf51 devices. For the STM32 traces, the deviation in random vs. fixed plot occurs near the ADDS r4,[r4,r2] (labeled 9), STRB r3,[r4,r0] (labeled 9) and BLT 0 × 08000818 (labeled 14) instructions where variance of random set is visibly higher in comparison to the fixed set. In the case of NRFf51 boards, the variance of a random set is higher compared to the fixed set for all sections of the trace. Following the execution of the STRB r3,[r4,r0] instruction (labeled 10), the variance of random set increases until the CMP r1,#0 × 04 instruction (labeled 13) where it peaks and goes down until LSLS r3,r1,#2 instruction (labeled 15) where the operation on next byte starts.

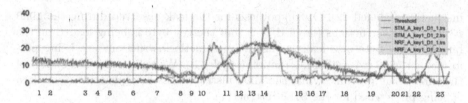

Fig. 11. TVLA results for the STM$_A$ and NRF$_A$ devices. The numbers on the x-axis are the instructions being executed, see Listing 1.1.

7.2   Data Leakage

TVLA Results. Fig. 11 shows the TVLA results for the STM$_A$ (red line) and the NRF$_A$(blue line) devices. A green line represents the threshold value of 4.5. The plot shows that the side-channel leaks for the two devices differ significantly. For the STM$_A$, the TVLA value rises above the 4.5 threshold at STRB r3,[r4,r0] instruction, goes down at UXTB r1, r3 instruction and rises again covering CMP r1,#0 × 04(labeled 13) and BLT 0 × 08000818 (labeled 14) instructions. For the NRF$_A$ device, the TVLA results show leakage for almost all instructions (labeled 1–21). However, as seen in the previous section, the TVLA results need to be considered with caution.

Key Rank Analysis results have been added as a transparent layer over the TVLA for both boards in Fig. 12.

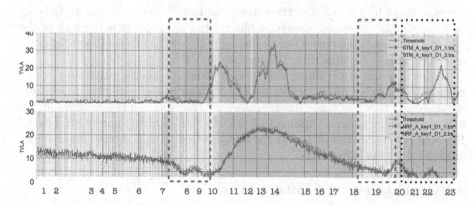

Fig. 12. (To be viewed in colors.) Overlay of the key rank estimate on the TVLA results for STM$_A$ device(top) and NRF$_A$ device (bottom). Red regions represent the index locations where the correct key is ranked first. The rectangles highlight differences in leakage between the two boards. The numbers on the x-axis are the instruction being executed, see Listing 1.1.

For the STM$_A$ device, the correct key data starts leaking Fig. 12 (top) from the LDRB r3, [r4,r3] instruction (labeled 7) until the STRB r3,[r4,r0]

instruction (labeled 22). Our hypothesis for the leak observed during the LDRB
r3,[r4,r3] instructions (labeled 7) is that the key byte is being loaded on the
bus. The key byte also leaks while the arithmetic instructions are being performed, at ADDS r4,r4,r2 instruction (labeled 9). We believe this is an effect of
the three-stage pipeline: while the ADDS instruction is being executed the data
is being pre-fetched for the STRB instruction.

We see that the correct key byte continues to leak in the subsequent instructions even though no operations are performed directly on the key data. In the
analyzed s-box implementation, the loop operates on 4 bytes, four times to oper-
ate on a total of 16 bytes of data; the check for the loop occurs at CMP r1,#0 × 04
instruction(labeled 13). The check compares the relative value of R1 to #0 × 04
and branches to the next instruction if the R1 value is less than 4.

The subsequent instructions LSLS and ADDS compute the relative index from
which the next key data is to be loaded by the LDRB instruction, which is when
the leak of key data stops. We find this to be an interesting behavior since the
data stops leaking when the data in the memory bus-A is overwritten by new
data. We do not have an explanation for the gaps in the resulting leaks for the
STRB (labeled 10) and UXTB (labeled 12).

Figure 12 (bottom) shows the key rank analysis for the NRF_A device. The
correct key byte starts leaking at STRB, r3,[r4,r0] instruction (labeled 10),
and leaks until LDR r4,[pc,#28] instruction (labeled 18). The leaks observed
in the NRF_A device seem to have a strong effect on the dynamic power, and its
effects seem diffused, showing up while other instructions are being executed.
We can infer that the correct key byte is on the bus after the STRB instruction
(labeled 10), which leaks over the subsequent instructions as the data is being
overwritten. An interesting behavior observed in NRF_Aboards is the leak of the
first key byte when the operations are being performed on the next byte of data,
due to register overwrites from LDR instruction.

To summarize, we confirm that the influence of microarchitecture implementation has a significant effect on the leakage behavior of the two boards
we analyzed. The results for the NRF_A device differ from the key rank results on
STM_A device showing an additional leak of arithmetic (LSLS) instruction (labeled
15). The results for the STM_A and the NRF_A devices show a similar trend subsequent to the STRB instruction.

8   Conclusions and Future Work

Our results show that while the power traces collected from the boards of the
two manufacturers have very different visual profiles, some instruction sequences
leak in the same way, which can be explained by the similar pipeline executions
of instructions for both cores. To answer whether the microarchitecture impacts
side-channel leakage, we first investigate the influence of manufacturing variation. While we observe differences between physical boards, the trend for side-
channel leakage for the two boards we investigated is similar. When comparing
the side-channel leak between different chips, we see clear evidence of leakage
behavior that we attribute to microarchitecture implementation differences.

In terms of the impact on the design of side-channel simulators, our results show that the existence of a generic simulator, e.g., for an ARM-Cortex M0, is improbable. Differences in microarchitecture, such as differences in memory implementation or other functional optimizations, require that a simulator predicting side-channel leakage be trained for different silicon implementations. For the portability of templates between different core implementations, we extrapolate that the differences in microarchitecture will be a deciding factor.

We compared TVLA, probably the first choice of leakage assessment technique, with the leakage obtained by profiling. Despite its simplicity and based on the differences observed in our results, we would caution our embedded system developer against using TVLA alone to determine leakage behavior and suggest using key ranking as a more robust, albeit more effort-intensive technique.

References

1. Bhasin, S., Chattopadhyay, A., Heuser, A., Jap, D., Picek, S., Shrivastwa, R.R.: Mind the portability: a warriors guide through realistic profiled side-channel analysis. In: 27th Annual Network and Distributed System Security Symposium, NDSS 2020, San Diego, California, USA, 23–26 February 2020. The Internet Society (2020). https://www.ndss-symposium.org/ndss2020/
2. Cao, Y., Zhou, Y., Yu, Z.: On the negative effects of trend noise and its applications in side-channel cryptanalysis. IACR Cryptology ePrint Arch **2013**, 102 (2013). http://eprint.iacr.org/2013/102
3. Das, D., Golder, A., Danial, J., Ghosh, S., Raychowdhury, A., Sen, S.: X-deepsca: Cross-device deep learning side channel attack. In: 2019 56th ACM/IEEE Design Automation Conference (DAC), pp. 1–6 (2019)
4. Gao, S., Oswald, E., Page, D.: Reverse engineering the micro-architectural leakage features of a commercial processor. Cryptology ePrint Archive, Report 2021/794 (2021). https://eprint.iacr.org/2021/794
5. Golder, A., Das, D., Danial, J., Ghosh, S., Sen, S., Raychowdhury, A.: Practical approaches toward deep-learning-based cross-device power side-channel attack. IEEE Trans. Very Large Scale Integr. (VLSI) Syst. 27(12), 2720–2733 (2019). https://doi.org/10.1109/TVLSI.2019.2926324
6. Goodwill, G., Jun, J., P.Rohatgi: A testing methodology for side channel resistance validation. In: NIST Non-invasive Attack Testing Workshop, vol. 7, pp. 115–136 (2018)
7. Heuser, A., Kasper, M., Schindler, W., Stöttinger, M.: A new difference method for side-channel analysis with high-dimensional leakage models. In: Dunkelman, O. (ed.) CT-RSA 2012. LNCS, vol. 7178, pp. 365–382. Springer, Heidelberg (2012). https://doi.org/10.1007/978-3-642-27954-6_23
8. Limited, A.: Arm v6-m architecture reference manual. Tech. rep., ARM Limited (ARM DDI 0419E (ID070218) 2018)
9. Marshall, B., Page, D., Webb, J.: Miracle: Micro-architectural leakage evaluation. Cryptology ePrint Archive, Report 2021/261 (2021). https://eprint.iacr.org/2021/261
10. McCann, D., Oswald, E., Whitnall, C.: Towards practical tools for side channel aware software engineering: 'grey box' modelling for instruction leakages. In: USENIX Security Symposium, pp. 199–216 (2017)

11. Shelton, M.A., Samwel, N., Batina, L., Regazzoni, F., Wagner, M., Yarom, Y.: Rosita: Towards automatic elimination of power-analysis leakage in ciphers. In: NDSS (2021)

12. Standaert, François-Xavier., Malkin, Tal G.., Yung, Moti: A unified framework for the analysis of side-channel key recovery attacks. In: Joux, Antoine (ed.) EUROCRYPT 2009. LNCS, vol. 5479, pp. 443–461. Springer, Heidelberg (2009). https://doi.org/10.1007/978-3-642-01001-9_26

13. Stokes, J.: Inside the Machine. No startch press/ars technica library, An illustrated Introduction to Microprocessors and Computer Architecture (2007)

14. van der Valk, D., Picek, S., Bhasin, S.: Kilroy was here: the first step towards explainability of neural networks in profiled side-channel analysis. In: Bertoni, G.M., Regazzoni, F. (eds.) Constructive Side-Channel Analysis and Secure Design, pp. 175–199. Springer International Publishing, Cham (2021)

15. Wu, L., Won, Y.S., Jap, D., Perin, G., Bhasin, S., Picek, S.: Explain some noise: Ablation analysis for deep learning-based physical side-channel analysis. Cryptology ePrint Archive, Report 2021/717 (2021). https://eprint.iacr.org/2021/717

16. Zhang, F., et al.: From homogeneous to heterogeneous: Leveraging deep learning based power analysis across devices. In: 2020 57th ACM/IEEE Design Automation Conference (DAC), pp. 1–6 (2020). https://doi.org/10.1109/DAC18072.2020.9218693

Complete Practical Side-Channel-Assisted Reverse Engineering of AES-Like Ciphers

Andrea Caforio[1], Fatih Balli[1,2], and Subhadeep Banik[1(✉)]

[1] LASEC, Ecole Polytechnique Fédérale de Lausanne, Lausanne, Switzerland
{andrea.caforio,subhadeep.banik}@epfl.ch
[2] CSEM, Neuchtel, Switzerland
fatih.balli@csem.ch

Abstract. Public knowledge about the structure of a cryptographic system is a standard assumption in the literature and algorithms are expected to guarantee security in a setting where only the encryption key is kept secret. Nevertheless, undisclosed proprietary cryptographic algorithms still find widespread use in applications both in the civil and military domains. Even though side-channel-based reverse engineering attacks that recover the hidden components of custom cryptosystems have been demonstrated for a wide range of constructions, the complete and practical reverse engineering of AES-128-like ciphers remains unattempted.

In this work, we close this gap and propose the first practical reverse engineering of AES-128-like custom ciphers, i.e., algorithms that deploy undisclosed SubBytes, ShiftRows and MixColumns functions. By performing a side-channel-assisted differential power analysis, we show that the amount of traces required to fully recover the undisclosed components are relatively small, hence the possibility of a side-channel attack remains as a practical threat. The results apply to both 8-bit and 32-bit architectures and were validated on two common microcontroller platforms.

1 Introduction

Over the past few years, the field of side-channel-assisted cryptanalysis has evolved into an intricate spectrum. In this spectrum, the trace, which is the signal collected by the adversary during the execution of a cryptographic operation, can stem from various sources, such as the electromagnetic emission, the power consumption, or even the sound noise generated by the victim device [4,13,19]. Furthermore, there are many available techniques to analyze the collected traces with the goal of recovering the secret key [7,13,15].

Kerckhoffs's principle states that any cryptosystem should be secure even if everything about the system, except the key, is public knowledge. This concept is widely embraced by cryptographers, however *security through obscurity* remains as a tempting path to follow in industry. Undisclosed proprietary cryptographic algorithms are still used in civil applications, e.g., GSM or Pay-TV systems, and in diplomatic or military domains. Even though *security through obscurity* is far

V. Grosso and T. Pöppelmann (Eds.): CARDIS 2021, LNCS 13173, pp. 97–117, 2022.
https://doi.org/10.1007/978-3-030-97348-3_6

from ideal and generally discouraged by cryptographers, from the implementation layer perspective, it is considered as an extra layer of protection against all types of attacks, including that of side-channels. In particular, one idea that we consider in this paper is to implement a custom version of a popular scheme, e.g., AES, by replacing the inner layer of operations without publicly disclosing these modifications. Obviously, the idea is that extrapolating conclusions from side-channel observations becomes significantly harder when the construction in question is not fully disclosed. Therefore, the adversary would need to collect larger amount of traces. This is exactly the approach taken by the Danish enterprise *Dencrypt* whose communication devices ship with a customized AES implementation with secret S-boxes based on the *Dynamic Encryption* proposal [12].

The first known use of side channels to reverse-engineer (SCARE) hidden structures was the case of the A3/8 algorithm used in GSM [17]. This attack reveals the contents of one of the two substitution tables, which are intended to be kept secret, used for authentication and key agreement in GSM. This was later improved by Clavier in an attack that fully recovers both tables [8]. In a related work, Clavier et al. [9] presented a theoretical reverse engineering of AES-like secret ciphers, which shared the same core structure of AES-128, but used secret SubBytes, ShiftRows and MixColumns functions instead. Developed independently around the same time, Rivain and Roche [21] proposed a generic reverse engineering attack which applies to a general class of undisclosed substitution-permutation ciphers, showing that this line of attack works beyond the AES constructions.

Note that none of the previous works demonstrate the mentioned attacks in practice, but instead their results are only based on theoretical simulations. More specifically, they all rely on the assumption that some side-channel observations can be made that allows the attacker to distinguish whether intermediate values of an algorithm are equal at different points during the computation. However, these works neither back up the assumption through an experimental setup, nor present a practical full-recovery attack. It is thus important to determine the efficacy of side-channel reverse engineering on real-world platforms. The first practical attack was presented by Jap and Bhasin [11]. The authors tried to recover the 256 entries of a secret 8-bit S-box implemented on an Atmel AT-mega328P microprocessor mounted on Arduino UNO board and succeeded in recovering 159 out of 256 entries. However, a practical side-channel-assisted reverse engineering attack that recovers the full description of an AES-128-like cipher remains an open problem.

Contributions. In this paper, we demonstrate the first practical side-channel-assisted reverse engineering procedure for the full description of unprotected AES-128-like ciphers that deploy undisclosed SubBytes, ShiftRows and MixColumns functions. A precise definition of such a cipher will be given shortly. Our attacks follow the side-channel-assisted differential plaintext methodology (SCADPA) pioneered by Breier et al. [6] and subsequently extended by Bhasin et al. [5], whose work enhances differential power analysis [13] with tools from conventional differential cryptanalysis. Specifically, the complete recovery routine proceeds in four consecutive steps as detailed in Table 1. This work thus closes the open question of whether such an attack is feasible, and more so on the cost of performing such attack. We validate our recovery routines on both 8-bit and 32-bit systems, namely the 8-bit ATXMEGA128D4 and 32-bit STM32F303 architectures that find wide use in the industry.

Table 1. Complexity (the number of traces) of our proposed AES-128-like side-channel-assisted reverse engineering algorithms. The parameter α denotes the required number of repetitions in order to get a stable average in the extracted power traces. On our testing equipment, $\alpha \approx 10$ was sufficient for effectively de-noising the traces.

Recovery	Platforms	Complexity	Reference
Encryption key	8-bit, 32-bit	$\alpha \times 2^9$	Sect. 2.3
Partial ShiftRows	8-bit, 32-bit	$\alpha \times 32$	Sect. 3.1
255 MixColumns candidates	8-bit, 32-bit	$\alpha \times 2^{20}$	Sect. 3.2
Full SubBytes, ShiftRows, MixColumns	8-bit, 32-bit	$\alpha \times 2^{18}$	Sect. 3.3

Outline. We review some preliminary material concerning side-channel-assisted reverse engineering attacks in Sect. 2. Section 3 details our procedures that recover the complete description of hidden components within AES-128-like ciphers. Ultimately, the paper is concluded in Sect. 4.

2 Preliminaries

We commence the preliminaries with a precise definition of an AES-128-like cipher and then proceed with a review of the power consumption model in microcontrollers.

Definition 1 (AES-like cipher). *Denote by* AES* *an* AES-128-*like SPN cipher over the Rijndael finite field of the form*

$$\text{AES}^* : \mathbb{F}_{256}^{4 \times 4} \times \mathbb{F}_{256}^{4 \times 4} \mapsto \mathbb{F}_{256}^{4 \times 4}$$
$$(p, k) \mapsto y,$$

for some plaintext p and key k. The round function consists of a round key addition layer AK, *a byte-wise substitution layer* SB *defined by a lookup table* $T : \mathbb{F}_{256} \mapsto \mathbb{F}_{256}$, *a byte permutation layer* PB *over* $\mathbb{F}_{256}^{4 \times 4}$ *that shuffles the state bytes according to some permutation* $\Pi \in S_{16}$ *(where S_n is the permutation group over n elements) and a linear diffusion layer* MC *that multiplies the state by a circulant matrix $M \in \mathbb{F}_{256}^{4 \times 4}$ such that*

$$M = \begin{bmatrix} a & b & c & d \\ d & a & b & c \\ c & d & a & b \\ b & c & d & a \end{bmatrix}, \tag{1}$$

where $a, b, c, d \in \mathbb{F}_{256} \setminus \{0\}$. *Without loss of generality, the round key generation is assumed to be achieved via the regular* AES-128 *key scheduling function* KS *using T as the substitution table instead of the Rijndael S-box. Finally, the sequence of operations is the same as the original* AES-128 *algorithm, i.e.,*

$$
\begin{aligned}
&\underline{\mathsf{AES}^*(p, k):} \\
&1:\ \mathsf{AK}(p, k) \\
&2:\ \textbf{for}\ i \leftarrow 1;\ i < 10;\ i \leftarrow i + 1\ \textbf{do} \\
&3:\qquad \mathsf{KS}(k),\ \mathsf{SB}(p),\ \mathsf{PB}(p),\ \mathsf{MC}(p),\ \mathsf{AK}(p, k) \\
&4:\ \mathsf{KS}(k),\ \mathsf{SB}(p),\ \mathsf{PB}(p),\ \mathsf{AK}(p, k)
\end{aligned}
$$

In the following, we adopt the standard column-major notation to denote the individual bytes of the state as per Definition 2.

Definition 2 (Notation). *Let $b_{i, F(j)} \in \mathbb{F}_{256}$ be the value of the i-th state byte after the computational layer $F \in \{\mathsf{AK}, \mathsf{SB}, \mathsf{PB}, \mathsf{MC}\}$ in the j-th round function for $0 \leq i \leq 15$ and $0 \leq j \leq 10$. Analogously, let $c_{i, F(j)} \in \mathbb{F}_{256}^4$ be the value of the i-th state column for $0 \leq i \leq 3$. A graphical depiction of this notation is given in Fig. 1.*

For the experiments we conducted in the paper, on both 8-bit and 32-bit microcontrollers, the AES* algorithm is implemented in a straightforward constant-time and byte-wise manner in which each state byte is computed individually in all layers of the round function. SB and PB are realized via standard lookup tables. The field multiplication steps that are part of MC are computed with a generic Galois field multiplication routine. This type of AES-128 implementation is common for 8-bit central processing units with limited memory. In 32-bit environments, a more compact T-table implementation is sometimes also deployed that combines the substitution and diffusion layers through lookup tables. We remark that for the remainder we are mostly interested in the computation of round key additions and the byte substitutions, hence our attacks are irrespective of the actual choice of implementation for the PB and MC operations. See Fig. 2 for a generic set of byte-wise instructions that implement the AK and SB layers. Note that certain implementations also merge the AK and SB layers, however in many publicly available implementations, like OpenSSL, AVR-crypto-lib and the masked secAES proposal, these layers are separated [1–3].

2.1   Setup

The reverse engineering procedures proposed in this work have been validated on existing platforms. In particular, we utilized the following two microcontrollers:

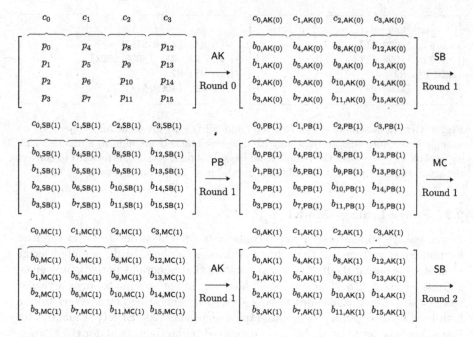

Fig. 1. Byte and column notations for the first two rounds. The notation scheme progresses similarly for later rounds.

- **ATXMEGA128D4.** An 8-bit microcontroller featuring a 2-stage-pipelined AVR processing unit. It offers 128 KB of flash memory and can be clocked at a maximum frequency of 32 MHz.
- **STM32F303.** A 32-bit microcontroller featuring a 3-stage-pipelined ARM Cortex-M4 processing unit. It offers 256 KB of flash memory and can be clocked at a maximum frequency of 72 MHz.

The two target microcontrollers are mounted on a ChipWhisperer CW308 board [18] that clocks them at a frequency of 7.37 MHz. Power traces are captured via the ChipWhisperer CW1173 board through a 10-bit 105 MS/s ADC. A key aspect of this setup, is that power traces are captured synchronously with the target clock, in other words, four samples per clock cycles are obtained at a frequency of roughly 30 MHz. Synchronous sampling, in contrast to asynchronous sampling performed by ordinary oscilloscopes, reduces the number of samples that are required for precise measurements and thus accelerates attacks that necessitate the processing of a large number of traces. This is reflected in the fact that taking an average over $\alpha \approx 10$ repetitions of an experiment was sufficient to effectively de-noise the power traces and attain a stable average.

```
; Round key addition
LD R1, [ADDR PT]
LD R2, [ADDR KEY]
XOR R1, R2
ST R1, [ADDR PT]
```

```
; Byte substitution
LD R1, [ADDR STATE]
ADD R2, R1, [ADDR SBOX]
LD R3, R2
ST R3, [ADDR STATE]
```

Fig. 2. Generic assembly of the AK (left) and ŞB (right) layers in AES* operating on a single byte. Note that statements within square brackets are akin to a function call, e.g., [ADDR PT] computes the plaintext address. It should be straightforward to convert the given snippets to valid assembly for any 8-bit or 32-bit architecture.

2.2 Power Leakage Model

Power leakage simulators for micro-controllers have been developed in the past for numerous systems. In the context of leakage models, SILK (simple leakage simulator) is one of the first power simulators that generates power traces given a C file as input [22]. The simulator, however, is not specific to any particular architecture. Reparaz also described a simulator generating power traces from a high-level C description of a cryptographic algorithm [20]. ELMO (Emulator for Power Leakage for Cortex M0) was introduced by McCann et al. for the Cortex-M0 and M4 processor families [16] whose program takes as input a compiled binary object file. Le Corre et al. proposed the first leakage simulator MAPS (Micro-Architectural Power Simulator) for the ARM Cortex-M3 Processors [10]. This work accounts for the the inter-instruction dependency of the power consumption by utilizing a more refined micro-architectural model of the target processor. Specifically, it models all pipeline registers and validates these models through simulations with an HDL description of the target micro-architecture.

There are two common cases of dynamic power consumption that we exploit, as they correlate with the intermediate values computed in the processor's core:

1. Register-type instructions typically read two values from the register file, compute an arithmetic or logical operation on them, and eventually store the result back in a register. This naturally causes the value stored in the destination register to be updated. Let us use $R1 \leftarrow R2 \oplus R3$ as an example register-type instruction XOR, and denote the value of R1 before and after the execution of the XOR by a and b respectively. Then, some portion of the dynamic power consumption depends on the amount of bits that needs to be flipped when R1 goes through the transition $a \rightarrow b$. Therefore, in the collected power trace, if we focus on the special point in time that corresponds to this instruction's execution, we can find the correlation between the Hamming weight of $a \oplus b$, i.e., $H(a \oplus b)$, and the consumed power. This was referred to as Hamming-distance model by Mangard et al. [14].
2. Memory-type instructions either bring a value from the memory into a register, or store a register value in a specified memory location. These operations cause the memory bus to be driven with the data to be stored (the bus is usually pre-charged to a value that is either all zero or all one logic values). Let

us use [ADDR PT] ← R1 as an example of memory-type instruction, where [ADDR PT] denotes the address of the plaintext byte in the memory. Then, the execution of the store instruction causes a dynamic power consumption that correlates with the amount of logic one values in R1, if the bus is initially pre-charged to all zeroes. In other words, $H(R1)$ correlates with the measured power value at particular point in time that corresponds to the store instruction. This was referred to as Hamming-weight model by Mangard et al. [14].

As our main motivation in this paper is not to investigate the relationship between the power consumption and the intermediate values, but rather use the established model as an abstract tool, this intuition will suffice for the remainder.

Definition 3 (Power Trace). *Let* $\mathrm{Exp}(b_{i,F(j)})$ *be an experiment that obtains a power trace from the computation of the value* $b_{i,F(j)}$, *i.e., the* i-*th state byte of the* j-*th round during the computational layer* F *for* $i \in [0,15]$, $j \in [1,10]$ *and* $F \in \{\mathsf{AK}, \mathsf{SB}, \mathsf{PB}, \mathsf{MC}\}$. *Since computing any particular layer* F *is typically carried out by multiple instructions, let us denote by* $E(b_{i,F(j)})$ *the power signal recorded during the computation of byte* $b_{i,F(j)}$, *e.g., at the moment it is placed on an initially reset bus. Similarly, we define* $\overline{E}(b_{i,F(j)})$ *as the averaged power signal over multiple runs.*[1]

An experimental observation is that $\overline{E}(b_{i,\mathsf{AK}(j)}) > \overline{E}(b'_{i,\mathsf{AK}(j)})$ if and only if $H(b_{i,\mathsf{AK}(j)}) > H(b'_{i,\mathsf{AK}(j)})$ for a large enough number of repetitions where $H(b_{i,F(j)})$ is the Hamming weight of the i-th state byte of the j-th round after the layer F. This follows from the Hamming weight model of power consumption. Analogously, $\overline{E}(b_{i,\mathsf{SB}(j)}) > \overline{E}(b'_{i,\mathsf{SB}(j)})$ if and only if $H(b_{i,\mathsf{SB}(j)}) > H(b'_{i,\mathsf{SB}(j)})$. This observation is validated in Fig. 3 for $\mathsf{AK}(0)$ and $\mathsf{SB}(1)$ on our custom AES^* implementation but can also be observed on most byte-based implementations on both 8-bit and 32-bit architectures.

2.3   Key Recovery

Naturally, the first step of reverse-engineering an undisclosed AES^* structure involves recovering the encryption key. This is a straightforward procedure as it is directly possible to target the whitening key addition before the first round function, meaning that we measure the power trace $\overline{E}(b_{i,\mathsf{AK}(0)})$ for each state byte. We have $b_{i,\mathsf{AK}(0)} = p_i + k_i$, consequently if $\overline{E}(b_{i,\mathsf{AK}(0)}) < \overline{E}(b'_{i,\mathsf{AK}(0)})$ for all $b'_{i,\mathsf{AK}(0)} \in \mathbb{F}_{256} \setminus \{b_{i,\mathsf{AK}(0)}\}$, then $b_{i,\mathsf{AK}(0)} = 0$, or in other words, $p_i = k_i$. The key recovery algorithm thus tests whether a plaintext p_i yields $H(b_{i,\mathsf{AK}(0)}) = 0$. The entire key recovery routine for one byte is given in Algorithm 1. We remark that Algorithm 1 can be modified into a procedure that recovers the Hamming weight of $b_{i,\mathsf{AK}(0)}$ and $b_{i,\mathsf{SB}(1)}$ with identical complexity by simply counting how many traces exhibit a higher, lower and equal power consumption as shown in Algorithm 2. This property will be useful in Sect. 3.2 and Sect. 3.3.

---

[1] For the remainder of this text, we assume that a signal $\overline{E}(b_{i,F(j)})$ corresponds to a plaintext p, while $\overline{E}(b'_{i,F(j)})$ refers to p'.

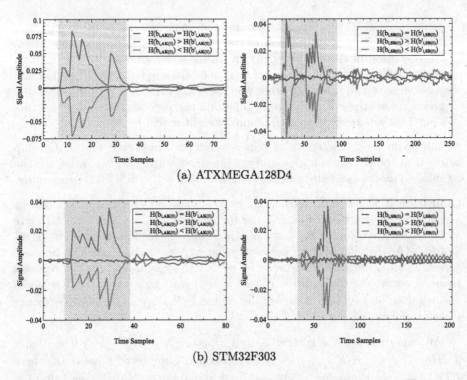

(a) ATXMEGA128D4

(b) STM32F303

Fig. 3. Differential power traces $\overline{E}(b_{i,\mathsf{AK}(0)}) - \overline{E}(b'_{i,\mathsf{AK}(0)})$ and $\overline{E}(b_{i,\mathsf{SB}(1)}) - \overline{E}(b'_{i,\mathsf{SB}(1)})$ corresponding to different Hamming weight distances on 8-bit ATXMEGA128D4 and 32-bit STM32F303 architectures.

The lookup table L in Algorithm 2 is related to the distribution of the Hamming weight of a random variable over $\mathbb{F}_{256}$, which was mentioned in [14, Table 4.1], where $L^{-1}(i) = \sum_{b \in \mathbb{F}_{256}} 1_{H(b) > H(i)} - \sum_{b \in \mathbb{F}_{256}} 1_{H(b) < H(i)}$. For any byte $b \in \mathbb{F}_{256}$, it essentially counts the difference of the number of $b' \in \mathbb{F}_{256} \setminus \{b\}$ for which $\overline{E}(b) > \overline{E}(b')$ and $\overline{E}(b) < \overline{E}(b')$. Since $\overline{E}$ is correlated with the Hamming weight, the method faithfully recovers $H(b)$ using L if the power traces are adequately de-noised. A slightly modified version of Algorithm 1 can be used to uniquely identify $b_{i,\mathsf{AK}(0)}$, $b_{i,\mathsf{SB}(1)}$ such that their Hamming weight is either zero or eight. As $t_{\min}$ already represents the byte whose Hamming weight is zero. Similarly, $t_{\max} = \arg\max J$ is equal to the byte with Hamming weight eight.

Parallelization. Due to the fact that it takes around $\alpha \times 2^8$ traces to recover a single key byte using Algorithm 1, it should take $\alpha \times 2^{12}$ for the complete 16-byte key. However, it is possible to parallelize the key recovery procedure for multiple key bytes at once. The idea is to have an index set $I \subset [0, 15]$, and query the 2^8 plaintexts $p_{i,j} = i$, $\forall j \in I$ and $p_{i,j} = 0$, $\forall j \notin I$, instead of a singleton j (here $p_{i,j}$ implies the j-th byte of the i-th plaintext for $i \in [0, 255]$). The key recovery algorithm again tests whether a plaintext $p_{i,j}$ yields $H(b_{i,\mathsf{AK}(j)}) = 0$ for some $j \in I$. We have observed that if I does not contain consecutive indices

---

Algorithm 1. Recover i-th Key Byte

    ▷ Choose a plaintext p and initialize an empty array J of size 256.

1: $p \in \mathbb{F}_{256}^{4 \times 4}$, $J \leftarrow \{\cdot\}$

2: **for** $t \in \mathbb{F}_{256}$ **do**

    ▷ Replace i-th byte of p with t, encrypt p and obtain a stable power trace.

3:     $p_i \leftarrow t$, $e \leftarrow \overline{E}(b_{i,\mathsf{AK}(0)})$, $J(t) \leftarrow e$

4: $t_{\min} = \arg\min J$

5: **return** $t_{\min}$

---

then the power peaks corresponding to the round key addition are reasonably spaced apart in the time axis, allowing for efficient identification of the j-th peak only by visual inspection. As a consequence, if we repeat the process for $I = \{0, 2, 4, \ldots, 14\}$ and then $\{1, 3, 5, \ldots, 15\}$ we can recover the entire key in two runs.

Complexity. Since by parallelization we recover eight key bytes using $\alpha \times 2^8$ traces, we need $\alpha \times 2^9$ traces for the complete key.

The reader will note that it is possible to further accelerate the proposed key recovery procedure by utilizing bit-wise differentials. Let $p = 0$ be the all-zero plaintext with corresponding power trace for the first byte after the key addition $\overline{E}(b_{0,\mathsf{AK}(0)})$. Similarly, let $p' = p + (1 \ll j)$ for $j \in [0, 7]$ be the plaintext where all bits are set to zero except the j-th bit of the first plaintext byte with respective power trace $\overline{E}(b'_{0,\mathsf{AK}(0)})$. Clearly, if $\overline{E}(b_{0,\mathsf{AK}(0)}) < \overline{E}(b'_{0,\mathsf{AK}(0)})$, then the j-th bit of k_0 is zero. On the other hand, an inequality $\overline{E}(b_{0,\mathsf{AK}(0)}) > \overline{E}(b'_{0,\mathsf{AK}(0)})$ indicates that that the j-th bit of k_0 is equal to one. Repeating this for all j yields the full key byte k_0 in $\alpha \times 2^3$ encryptions, which again can be parallelized in an analogous fashion as done before with Algorithm 1 in order to recover multiple key bytes in a single iteration.

Algorithm 2. Recover Hamming Weight $H(b)$ for $b \in \{b_{i,\mathsf{AK}(0)}, b_{i,\mathsf{SB}(1)}\}$

    ▷ Initialize a lookup table L and choose a plaintext p for which we want to calculate either $H(b_{i,\mathsf{AK}(0)})$ or $H(b_{i,\mathsf{SB}(1)})$.

1: $L \leftarrow \{\ 255 : 0,\ 246 : 1,\ 210 : 2,\ 126 : 3,\ 0 : 4,\ -126 : 5$

       $-210 : 6,\ -246 : 7,\ -255 : 8\ \}$

2: $p \in \mathbb{F}_{256}^{4 \times 4}$, $e \leftarrow \overline{E}(b)$, $h \leftarrow 0$

3: **for** $t \in \mathbb{F}_{256}$ **do**

    ▷ Replace the i-th byte of p with t and extract the averaged power trace. Count how many t have a larger/smaller Hamming weight.

4:     $p_i \leftarrow t$, $e' \leftarrow \overline{E}(b)$

5:     **if** $e' < e$ **then** $h \leftarrow h - 1$.

6:     **else if** $e' > e$ **then** $h \leftarrow h + 1$.

7: Find h_0 in the set $\{255, 246, 210, 126, 0, -126, -210, -246, -255\}$ such that $|h - h_0|$ is minimized.

8: **return** $L(h_0)$

---

3   Reverse-Engineering AES-Like Ciphers

Having established the preliminaries, we proceed with our recovery algorithms for the byte permutation PB, the matrix M of the diffusion layer MC and ultimately the lookup table T of the nonlinear substitution layer.

3.1   Partial Π Recovery

The key recovery algorithm exploited the correlation between the Hamming distance of two values and their respective power consumption. This connection implies that any differential introduced in the plaintext that is diffusing through the rounds of the cipher incurs either a power spike or drop at specific points. The utilization of this phenomenon in attacks is a relatively recent addition to the large assortment of side-channel assisted cryptanalytic attacks and was first introduced by Breier et al. with an attack on PRESENT[6]. The detection of differentially active bytes and columns lays the groundwork for our algorithms that recover Π in the byte permutation layer PB, M as part of the linear diffusion layer MC and the S-box T in the substitution layer.

Definition 4 (Differential Activity). *Denote by $\delta_{i,F(j)} \in \{\square, \blacksquare\}$ an indicator that signals whether a state byte is differentially active (with $\blacksquare$ representing an active byte). Analogously, let $\Delta_{i,F(j)} \in \{\square, \blacksquare\}$ be an indicator for differentially active columns.*

A direct approach that uniquely recovers Π consists in injecting a difference in a single plaintext byte $p_i + p'_i = d$ such that $\delta_{j,\text{PB}(1)} = \blacksquare$ is observable in the differential power trace $\overline{E}(b_{j,\text{PB}(1)}) - \overline{E}(b'_{j,\text{PB}(1)})$ at some byte position $j \in \{0, \ldots, 15\}$. However, this method might not be reliable in certain implementations for the following reasons:

1. Depending on the implementation, the PB and MC operations may be combined together so that a distinct region in the trace segregating the PB layer may not be deducible.
2. Even if the PB region is clearly separated, any particular implementation may swap bytes in a specific order depending on the algebraic description of Π.
3. The active position i may be a fixed point of Π, due to which no operation the i-th byte in the PB operation is necessary.

Instead, we will observe the peaks in the differential traces during round key addition $\overline{E}(b_{i,\text{AK}(1)}) - \overline{E}(b'_{i,\text{AK}(1)})$ of the first round or the substitution layer of the second round $\overline{E}(b_{i,\text{SB}(2)}) - \overline{E}(b'_{i,\text{SB}(2)})$. If the permutation function Π is such that i-th byte is mapped to the j-th column (for any $0 \leq j \leq 3$), i.e., $\Pi(i) \in \{4j, 4j+1, 4j+2, 4j+3\}$ then after the first round MC, the j-th column becomes active, which shows up as a sequence of four spikes after the second round substitution layer in the differential trace. The relative order in the time axis of these peaks tells us the value of j such that $4j \leq \Pi(i) \leq 4j + 3$, for each i. In other words, we are able to deduce which column each byte is mapped to after the PB operation. The diffusion of a single active plaintext byte into an active column $\Delta_{j,\text{AK}(1)} = \blacksquare$ is shown in Fig. 4. Furthermore, the experimental detection of an active column on actual hardware is given in the plots of Fig. 5.

At this point, we do not yet have the precise description of Π but only the the column to which each byte is mapped. The full permutation is recovered alongside the diffusion matrix M and the S-box T in the following sections.

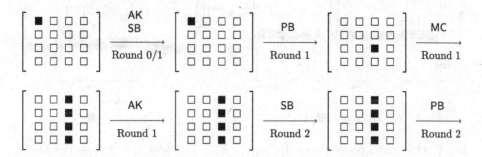

Fig. 4. Diffusion of a single active byte during the initial computational layers with $\Pi(0) = 10$. $\delta_{l,\text{AK}(1)} = \blacksquare$ and $\delta_{l,\text{SB}(2)} = \blacksquare$ for $8 \leq l \leq 11$ are observable as four spikes in the differential power trace (see Fig. 5), i.e., $\overline{E}(b_{l,\text{AK}(1)})$ - $\overline{E}(b'_{l,\text{AK}(1)})$ and $\overline{E}(b_{l,\text{SB}(2)})$ - $\overline{E}(b'_{l,\text{SB}(2)})$.

Complexity. Recovering Π up to column permutations exhibits a worst-case complexity of $\alpha \times 32$ traces, i.e., two averaged power traces are required for each state byte.

3.2 Finding 255 Candidates for M

Given the unknown matrix from (1), we proceed in multiple steps with differentials on the certain specific locations after the substitution layer of the first round. More specifically, we are interested in plaintext differentials that diffuse to two active bytes after the PB operation of the first round, e.g., $\delta_{0,\text{PB}(1)} = \blacksquare$, $\delta_{1,\text{PB}(1)} = \blacksquare$, $\delta_{2,\text{PB}(1)} = \square$, $\delta_{3,\text{PB}(1)} = \square$. With some probability, such a difference leads to three active bytes in the first state column after the MC layer of the first round, e.g., $\delta_{0,\text{MC}(1)} = \square$, $\delta_{1,\text{MC}(1)} = \blacksquare$, $\delta_{2,\text{MC}(1)} = \blacksquare$, $\delta_{3,\text{MC}(1)} = \blacksquare$. In the following, let d_0, d_1, d_2, d_3 denote the four differentials in the first column after the PB layer of the first round, i.e.,

$$d_0 = b_{0,\text{PB}(1)} + b'_{0,\text{PB}(1)}, \quad d_1 = b_{1,\text{PB}(1)} + b'_{1,\text{PB}(1)},$$
$$d_2 = b_{2,\text{PB}(1)} + b'_{2,\text{PB}(1)}, \quad d_3 = b_{3,\text{PB}(1)} + b'_{3,\text{PB}(1)}.$$

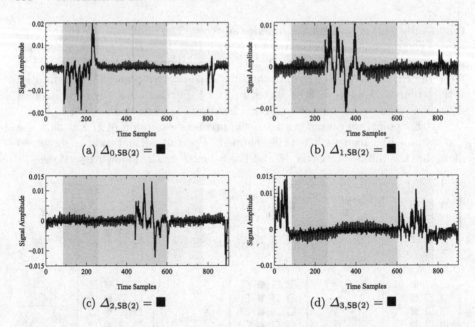

Fig. 5. Differential power traces $\overline{E}(b_{i,\mathsf{SB}(2)})$ - $\overline{E}(b'_{i,\mathsf{SB}(2)})$ for $0 \le i \le 15$ on the 32-bit STM32F303 platform for different active state columns. The color coding indicates the time frame during which a state column is computed (blue for the first and yellow for the fourth column). The plots for the ATXMEGA128D4 architecture are given in the appendix.

In order to detect whether two active bytes in the first column activate three bytes after the multiplication by M, we can check the differential power traces $\overline{E}(b_{i,\mathsf{AK}(1)}) - \overline{E}(b'_{i,\mathsf{AK}(1)})$ or $\overline{E}(b_{i,\mathsf{SB}(2)}) - \overline{E}(b'_{i,\mathsf{SB}(2)})$ for $0 \le i \le 3$ for the occurrence of spikes and drops. It is important to remark that since we only know to which column a byte is shifted during PB it is not possible to infer which two bytes are actually active in the first column. Let u_i be such that $\Pi(u_i) = i, \forall i \in [0,15]$, i.e., $u_{4i}, u_{4i+1}, u_{4i+2}, u_{4i+3}$ are the bytes in the state that get mapped to the i-th column after the first round PB. We have already determined the values of u_0, u_1, u_2, u_3 up to a permutation of the 4 elements. As such, this means we have narrowed down the exact values of u_i for $i = 0 \rightarrow 3$ to a set of $4! = 24$ candidates.

Now assume that we lock one of the 24 possible choices of the four-tuple of indices u_0, u_1, u_2, u_3 and proceed in the following way:

1. Fix plaintext bytes $p_{u_2} = p'_{u_2}$, $p_{u_3} = p'_{u_3}$ to some values in $\mathbb{F}_{256}$.
2. Use Algorithm 2 to find plaintext bytes p_{u_0}, p_{u_1} for which $H(b_{u_0,\mathsf{SB}(1)}) = 0$ and $H(b_{u_1,\mathsf{SB}(1)}) = 0$.
3. Similarly, find p'_{u_0} that yields $H(b'_{u_0,\mathsf{SB}(1)}) = 8$, which gives us a differential $d_0 = 255$.

4. Subsequently, iterate over all $p'_{u_1} \in \mathbb{F}_{256} \setminus \{p_{u_1}\}$ and check whether $\delta_{0,\mathsf{MC}(1)} = \square$. This can be done by checking for the absence of any peaks in the differential power traces $\overline{E}(b_{i,\mathsf{AK}(1)}) - \overline{E}(b'_{i,\mathsf{AK}(1)})$ or $\overline{E}(b_{i,\mathsf{SB}(2)}) - \overline{E}(b'_{i,\mathsf{SB}(2)})$.

5. Such an occurrence only happens for a single p'_{u_1} for which we then calculate the Hamming weight $H(b'_{u_1,\mathsf{SB}(1)}) = H(d_1) = H(x_1) = w_1$.

Consequently, we have $d_0 = 255$, $d_1 = x_1$, $d_2 = 0$, $d_3 = 0$, which corresponds to the relation

$$255a + x_1 b = 0 \;\rightarrow\; 255a = x_1 b.$$

By appropriately choosing different differentials d_0, d_1, d_2, d_3, it is possible to infer more relations for the same choice of indices u_0, u_1, u_2, u_3 as shown in Table 2.

Table 2. Ten choices of differentials d_0, d_1, d_2, d_3 to obtain relations between the x_i and the unknown M coefficients. Note that only the Hamming weight of the x_i, i.e., $H(x_i) = w_i$ are known but not their actual values. A graphical schematic of the first four steps is given in Fig. 6.

Step	d_0	d_1	d_2	d_3	$\delta_{i,\mathsf{MC}(1)} = \square$	Relation	
1	255	x_1	0	0	$i = 0$	$255a = x_1 b$	(2)
2	x_2	255	0	0	$i = 0$	$255b = x_2 a$	(3)
3	255	x_3	0	0	$i = 1$	$255d = x_3 a$	(4)
4	x_4	255	0	0	$i = 1$	$255a = x_4 d$	(5)
5	255	x_5	0	0	$i = 2$	$255c = x_5 d$	(6)
6	x_6	255	0	0	$i = 2$	$255d = x_6 c$	(7)
7	255	x_7	0	0	$i = 3$	$255b = x_7 c$	(8)
8	x_8	255	0	0	$i = 3$	$255c = x_8 b$	(9)
9	255	0	x_9	0	$i = 0$	$255c = x_9 a$	(10)
10	x_{10}	0	255	0	$i = 0$	$255a = x_{10} c$	(11)

The ten inferred relations from the side-channel observations can be combined with each other to yield a set of filter equations as listed in Table 3.

It is possible to computationally verify that, given the filters from Table 3 alongside the set of recovered Hamming weights $H(x_i) = w_i$, there will always be a unique solution for all x_i whenever the indices u_0, u_1, u_2, u_3 are correctly guessed. In particular, filtering out wrong x_i proceeds in the following loop:

1. Select a set of ten bytes $b_1, \ldots, b_{10}$ with $b_i \in \mathbb{F}_{256}$ such that $H(b_i) = w_i$.
2. If the selected set satisfies the filter equations in Table 3, then retain them as the solution for the x_i and return. Otherwise, repeat from the first step.

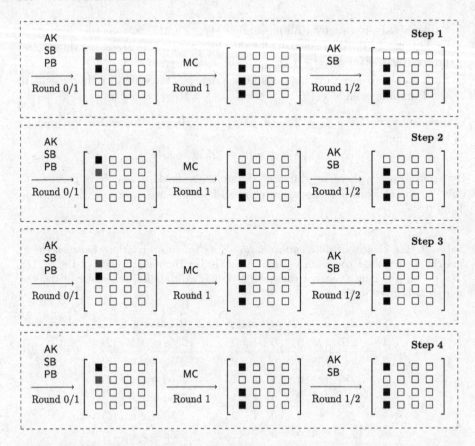

Fig. 6. First four steps of the linear diffusion layer recovery. Red squares indicate differentials of value 255. (Color figure online)

From here we can get $2^8 - 1$ solutions for M as follows: we freely choose a to be any non-zero byte. Then b, c, d are obtained from above as $b = 255^{-1} \cdot x_2 \cdot a$, $c = 255^{-1} \cdot x_9 \cdot a$ and $d = 255^{-1} \cdot x_3 \cdot a$. For the 23 incorrect initial guesses the situation is slightly more complicated. For exactly 20 other incorrect guesses the above algorithm returns no solution which implies that our guess was incorrect. However, for the remaining three guesses in which the starting u_0, u_1, u_2, u_3 are rotations of the correct guess, the algorithm also yields a unique solution. The remaining solutions in the latter cases are row rotated versions of M in the opposite direction. To understand why this happens, let Π_t be the 4×4 permutation matrix that rotates a column vector by t locations for $0 \leq t \leq 3$ in some direction. Let $c_{i,\mathsf{PB}(1)}$ be the i-th column after PB of the first round. Note that if M is a circulant matrix, then $M \cdot \Pi_t^{-1}$ is also a circulant matrix, in which the rows of M are rotated t locations in the opposite direction. Since $M \cdot c_{i,\mathsf{PB}(1)} = \left(M \cdot \Pi_t^{-1} \right) \cdot \left(\Pi_t \cdot c_{i,\mathsf{PB}(1)} \right)$, this explains that any starting guess of

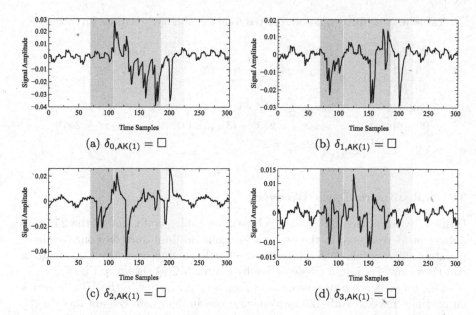

Fig. 7. Differential power traces $\overline{E}(b_{i,\mathsf{AK}(1)})$ - $\overline{E}(b'_{i,\mathsf{AK}(1)})$ for $0 \leq i \leq 3$ on the 8-bit ATXMEGA128D4 platform with a single inactive byte in the first column. The color coding indicates the four key additions of the first column (blue for the first and yellow for the fourth). The plots for the STM32F303 architecture are given in the appendix. (Color figure online)

u_0, u_1, u_2, u_3 that is a rotation of the correct guess also yields a set of solutions for the matrix M that is a row-rotated version of the correct matrix.

The next question is then how to recover t and Π_t? The answer is, it is not necessary, because it is straightforward to see that for any value of t, it yields an algebraically equivalent block cipher. We repeat the above algorithm to for the three other columns of the state, i.e., all possible guesses of $U_i = [u_{4i}, u_{4i+1}, u_{4i+2}, u_{4i+3}] \in [4i, 4i+3]$ for $1 \leq i \leq 3$. For each column we get four rotationally equivalent initial guesses that yield solutions for M. We first select the guesses for the four sets of initial guesses U_i that yield the same set of $2^8 - 1$ solutions for M up to multiplication by the free variable a.

Complexity. Identifying plaintext bytes p_{u_0}, p_{u_1} and p_{u_2} that facilitate the zero images $H(b_{u_0,\mathsf{SB}(1)}) = 0$, $H(b_{u_1,\mathsf{SB}(1)}) = 0$ and $H(b_{u_2,\mathsf{SB}(1)}) = 0$ using Algorithm 1 requires $3 \times \alpha \times 2^8$ traces as it only needs to be done in the first and ninth step. Similarly, it requires $3 \times \alpha \times 2^8$ to find plaintext bytes that yield $d_i = 255$. In the worst case, it takes $10 \times \alpha \times 2^8$ traces to find the occurrence of an inactive byte in the first column in each step and ultimately another $10 \times \alpha \times 2^8$ encryptions to find the x_i. Hence, the ten steps have a cumulative worst-case complexity of $26 \times \alpha \times 2^8$ traces. Finally, the whole procedure is repeated 4×24 times for each state column and each choice of u_0, u_1, u_2, u_3, yielding a total worst-case complexity of $4 \times 24 \times 26 \times \alpha \times 2^8 \approx \alpha \times 2^{20}$ traces.

Table 3. Nine filter equations derived from the obtained relations in Table 2.

Combination	Filter	Combination	Filter
(2), (3)	$x_1 x_2 = 255^2$	(4), (5)	$x_3 x_4 = 255^2$
(6), (7)	$x_5 x_6 = 255^2$	(8), (9)	$x_7 x_8 = 255^2$
(10), (11)	$x_9 x_{10} = 255^2$	(2), (8), (10)	$x_1 x_7 x_9 = 255^3$
(3), (9), (11)	$x_2 x_8 x_{10} = 255^3$	(3), (5), (7), (9)	$x_1 x_3 x_5 x_7 = 255^4$
(4), (6), (8), (10)	$x_2 x_4 x_6 x_8 = 255^4$	–	–

3.3   Substitution Layer Recovery

Ultimately, to recover the hidden substitution table, we fix one of the 255 candidates of M recovered in the previous section and limit ourselves once again to plaintext differentials that diffuse onto a single column after the PB operation and then converge into a single active byte after MC as shown in Fig. 8.

This convergence property was a cornerstone of the See-in-the-Middle attack on partially masked AES-128 implementations in [5] where the authors experimentally verified that it occurs with probability 2^{-22} and thus necessitates on average $2^{11.5}$ encryptions. Mathematically, a convergence onto the first byte of the column only happens when the differential output of the substitution layer is of the following form:

$$
\begin{aligned}
b_{0,\mathrm{SB}(1)} + b'_{0,\mathrm{SB}(1)} &= T(p_0 + k_0) + T(p_0 + k_0 + d_0) = e\lambda, \\
b_{1,\mathrm{SB}(1)} + b'_{1,\mathrm{SB}(1)} &= T(p_1 + k_1) + T(p_1 + k_1 + d_1) = f\lambda, \\
b_{2,\mathrm{SB}(1)} + b'_{2,\mathrm{SB}(1)} &= T(p_2 + k_2) + T(p_2 + k_2 + d_2) = g\lambda, \\
b_{3,\mathrm{SB}(1)} + b'_{3,\mathrm{SB}(1)} &= T(p_3 + k_3) + T(p_3 + k_3 + d_3) = h\lambda,
\end{aligned}
\tag{2}
$$

for all non-zero $\lambda \in \mathbb{F}_{256}$ and a four-tuple of differentials $d_0, d_1, d_2, d_3 \in \mathbb{F}_{256}$ where the parameters $e, f, g, h \in \mathbb{F}_{256}$ stem from the inverse of M, i.e.,

$$
M^{-1} = \begin{bmatrix} e & f & g & h \\ h & e & f & g \\ g & h & e & f \\ f & g & h & e \end{bmatrix}.
$$

The first step of our recovery procedure involves simplifying (2) by finding a four-tuple of plaintext bytes p_0, p_1, p_2, p_3 such that $T(p_i + k_i) = 0$, which yields

$$
\begin{aligned}
T(p_0 + k_0 + d_0) &= e\lambda, \quad T(p_1 + k_1 + d_1) = f\lambda, \\
T(p_2 + k_2 + d_2) &= g\lambda, \quad T(p_3 + k_3 + d_3) = h\lambda.
\end{aligned}
\tag{3}
$$

Subsequently, we look for the occurrence of a convergence by varying the differentials d_0, d_1, d_2, d_3 and observing the differential power traces $\overline{E}(b_{i,\mathrm{AK}(2)})-$

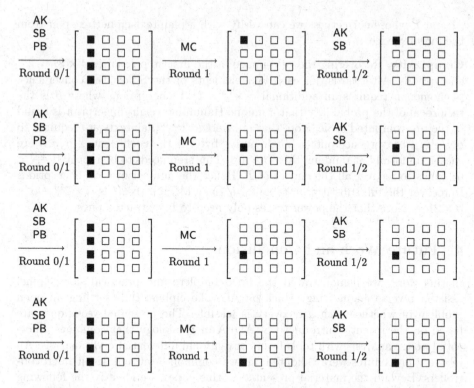

Fig. 8. Convergence of a differentially active column into a single active byte in the same column. On average, roughly $2^{11.5}$ encryptions are required for the convergence to occur.

$\overline{E}(b'_{i,\mathsf{AK}(2)})$ or $\overline{E}(b_{i,\mathsf{SB}(2)}) - \overline{E}(b'_{i,\mathsf{SB}(2)})$. Once found, the Hamming weight of the substitution box outputs is recovered, i.e.,

$$H(T(p_0 + k_0 + d_0)) = w_0,\ H(T(p_1 + k_1 + d_1)) = w_1,$$
$$H(T(p_2 + k_2 + d_2)) = w_2,\ H(T(p_3 + k_3 + d_3)) = w_3.$$

Since at this point p_i, k_i, d_i are known, the task boils down to filling up the 256 entries of T by some method to convert the weights w_i recovered above into actual values. However, the actual values are related by (3) which can be leveraged as follows: we pre-compute a lookup table L whose λ-th entry is the tuple $L[\lambda] = [H(e\lambda), H(h\lambda), H(g\lambda), H(f\lambda)]$ for all $0 < \lambda < 256$ and infer the value of λ if $L[\lambda] = [w_0, w_1, w_2, w_3]$ for some table entry. For random values of e, f, g, h, through computer simulations we have found that more than 200 entries of L are unique. If the fingerprint $[w_0, w_1, w_2, w_3]$ is a unique entry in the table, we recover four substitution table elements. Otherwise, we can repeat the procedure for a different differential. We were able to recover all entries within a few repetitions of the above procedure. Note that there are 255 candidates for M and for each one a lookup table is created yielding a potential solution for

M and T whose correctness we can verify with a plaintext-ciphertext pair from the target device.

Complexity. Recovering the zero-image in the first step requires $4 \times 2^8 = 2^{10}$ encryptions. Afterwards, for each four elements of the S-box, the convergence phenomenon requires an additional $\alpha \times \beta \times 2^{11.5}$ encryptions where β is the reciprocal of the probability that a unique Hamming weight fingerprint is found in the pre-computed table. Note that on average $2^{11.5}$ plaintexts are required to observe a convergence onto a single active byte. If the coefficients e, f, g, h are chosen uniformly at random, then $\beta \approx 1.3$. This step needs to be repeated $\frac{256}{4} = 64$ times to recover all the entries of T. Hence the number of total encryptions to recover the full substitution table for a given MC matrix M is $\alpha \times 2^{10} + \alpha \times \beta \times 2^{17.5}$. Note that the power traces only need to be extracted once.

4   Future Work and Conclusion

In this work, we demonstrated the first complete and practical side-channel assisted reverse engineering attack on AES-like ciphers thus settling an open problem of whether such a recovery is feasible. The presented techniques are based on the recently introduced SCADPA methodology that combines differential power analysis with tools from conventional differential cryptanalysis. All recovery procedures were validated on two common 8-bit and 32-bit microcontrollers. Beyond the material presented in this paper, we identify the following set of open problems:

- **Non-Circulant MixColumns.** The recovery of the 255 MixColumns matrix candidates in Sect. 3.2 relies on the fact that M is circulant. One could also imagine an attack that is applicable to invertible non-circulant matrices in $\mathbb{F}_{256}^{4 \times 4}$ as was the assumption in [9].
- **Protected Implementations.** Our recovery procedures apply to unprotected byte-wise implementations, however masking and shuffling are common side-channel countermeasures that attempt to prevent deductions from power measurements and thus also complicate any reverse engineering efforts.
- **T-Table Implementations.** The S-box recovery routine of Sect. 3.3 relies on the assumption that the Hamming weight of substituted bytes after the SB layer is recoverable via Algorithm 2. This may not be the case anymore in T-table implementations that merge the S-box with the MixColumns layer in a set of lookup tables.

Acknowledgements. We wish to thank Thomas Roche for helping us improve this paper. Fatih Balli and Subhadeep Banik are supported by the Swiss National Science Foundation (SNSF) through the Ambizione Grant PZ00P2_179921.

A Supplementary Plots

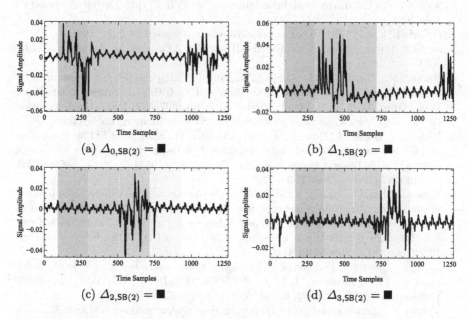

Fig. 9. Differential power traces $\overline{E}(b_{l,\mathrm{SB}(0)})$ - $\overline{E}(b'_{l,\mathrm{SB}(0)})$ on the 8-bit ATXMEGA128D4 platform for different active state columns.

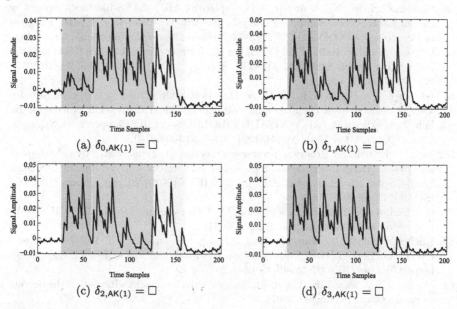

Fig. 10. Differential power traces $\overline{E}(b_{i,\mathrm{AK}(1)})$ - $\overline{E}(b'_{i,\mathrm{AK}(1)})$ for $0 \leq i \leq 3$ on the 32-bit STM32F303 platform with a single inactive byte in the first column.

References

1. AVR-Crypto-Lib. https://wiki.das-labor.org/w/AVR-Crypto-Lib/en. Accessed 03 July 2021
2. OpenSSL. https://github.com/openssl/openssl. Accessed 03 July 2021
3. secAES. https://github.com/ANSSI-FR/secAES-ATmega8515. Accessed 03 July 2021
4. Backes, M., Dürmuth, M., Gerling, S., Pinkal, M., Sporleder, C.: Acoustic side-channel attacks on printers. In: Proceedings of 19th USENIX Security Symposium, Washington, DC, USA, 11–13 August 2010, pp. 307–322. USENIX Association (2010). http://www.usenix.org/events/sec10/tech/full_papers/Backes.pdf
5. Bhasin, S., Breier, J., Hou, X., Jap, D., Poussier, R., Sim, S.M.: SITM: see-in-the-middle side-channel assisted middle round differential cryptanalysis on SPN block ciphers. IACR Trans. Cryptogr. Hardw. Embed. Syst. 95–122 (2020). https://doi.org/10.13154/tches.v2020.i1.95-122
6. Breier, J., Jap, D., Bhasin, S.: SCADPA: side-channel assisted differential-plaintext attack on bit permutation based ciphers. In: Madsen, J., Coskun, A.K. (eds.) 2018 Design, Automation & Test in Europe Conference & Exhibition, DATE 2018, Dresden, Germany, 19–23 March 2018, pp. 1129–1134. IEEE (2018). https://doi.org/10.23919/DATE.2018.8342180
7. Brier, E., Clavier, C., Olivier, F.: Correlation power analysis with a leakage model. In: Joye, M., Quisquater, J.-J. (eds.) CHES 2004. LNCS, vol. 3156, pp. 16–29. Springer, Heidelberg (2004). https://doi.org/10.1007/978-3-540-28632-5_2
8. Clavier, C.: An improved SCARE cryptanalysis against a secret A3/A8 GSM algorithm. In: McDaniel, P., Gupta, S.K. (eds.) ICISS 2007. LNCS, vol. 4812, pp. 143–155. Springer, Heidelberg (2007). https://doi.org/10.1007/978-3-540-77086-2_11
9. Clavier, C., Isorez, Q., Wurcker, A.: Complete SCARE of AES-like block ciphers by chosen plaintext collision power analysis. In: Paul, G., Vaudenay, S. (eds.) Progress in Cryptology - INDOCRYPT 2013–14th International Conference on Cryptology in India, Mumbai, India, 7–10 December 2013. Proceedings. Lecture Notes in Computer Science, vol. 8250, pp. 116–135. Springer (2013). https://doi.org/10.1007/978-3-319-03515-4_8
10. Le Corre, Y., Großschädl, J., Dinu, D.: Micro-architectural power simulator for leakage assessment of cryptographic software on ARM Cortex-M3 processors. In: Fan, J., Gierlichs, B. (eds.) COSADE 2018. LNCS, vol. 10815, pp. 82–98. Springer, Cham (2018). https://doi.org/10.1007/978-3-319-89641-0_5
11. Jap, D., Bhasin, S.: Practical reverse engineering of secret sboxes by side-channel analysis. In: IEEE International Symposium on Circuits and Systems, ISCAS 2020, Sevilla, Spain, 10–21 October 2020, pp. 1–5. IEEE (2020). https://doi.org/10.1109/ISCAS45731.2020.9180848
12. Knudsen, L.R.: Dynamic encryption. J. Cyber Secur. Mobil. 357–370 (2014). https://doi.org/10.13052/jcsm2245-1439.341
13. Kocher, P., Jaffe, J., Jun, B.: Differential power analysis. In: Wiener, M. (ed.) CRYPTO 1999. LNCS, vol. 1666, pp. 388–397. Springer, Heidelberg (1999). https://doi.org/10.1007/3-540-48405-1_25
14. Mangard, S., Oswald, E., Popp, T.: Power Analysis Attacks - Revealing the Secrets of Smart Cards. Springer (2007)
15. Mayer-Sommer, R.: Smartly analyzing the simplicity and the power of simple power analysis on smartcards. In: Koç, Ç.K., Paar, C. (eds.) CHES 2000. LNCS, vol. 1965, pp. 78–92. Springer, Heidelberg (2000). https://doi.org/10.1007/3-540-44499-8_6

16. McCann, D., Oswald, E., Whitnall, C.: Towards practical tools for side channel aware software engineering: 'grey box' modelling for instruction leakages. In: Kirda, E., Ristenpart, T. (eds.) 26th USENIX Security Symposium, USENIX Security 2017, Vancouver, BC, Canada, 16–18 August 2017, pp. 199–216. USENIX Association (2017). https://www.usenix.org/conference/usenixsecurity17/technical-sessions/presentation/mccann

17. Novak, R.: Side-channel attack on substitution blocks. In: Zhou, J., Yung, M., Han, Y. (eds.) ACNS 2003. LNCS, vol. 2846, pp. 307–318. Springer, Heidelberg (2003). https://doi.org/10.1007/978-3-540-45203-4_24

18. O'Flynn, C., Chen, Z.D.: ChipWhisperer: an open-source platform for hardware embedded security research. In: Prouff, E. (ed.) COSADE 2014. LNCS, vol. 8622, pp. 243–260. Springer, Cham (2014). https://doi.org/10.1007/978-3-319-10175-0_17

19. Quisquater, J.-J., Samyde, D.: ElectroMagnetic analysis (EMA): measures and counter-measures for smart cards. In: Attali, I., Jensen, T. (eds.) E-smart 2001. LNCS, vol. 2140, pp. 200–210. Springer, Heidelberg (2001). https://doi.org/10.1007/3-540-45418-7_17

20. Reparaz, O.: Detecting flawed masking schemes with leakage detection tests. In: Peyrin, T. (ed.) FSE 2016. LNCS, vol. 9783, pp. 204–222. Springer, Heidelberg (2016). https://doi.org/10.1007/978-3-662-52993-5_11

21. Rivain, M., Roche, T.: SCARE of secret ciphers with SPN structures. In: Sako, K., Sarkar, P. (eds.) ASIACRYPT 2013. LNCS, vol. 8269, pp. 526–544. Springer, Heidelberg (2013). https://doi.org/10.1007/978-3-642-42033-7_27

22. Veshchikov, N.: SILK: high level of abstraction leakage simulator for side channel analysis. In: Preda, M.D., McDonald, J.T. (eds.) Proceedings of the 4th Program Protection and Reverse Engineering Workshop, PPREW@ACSAC 2014, New Orleans, LA, USA, 9 December 2014, pp. 3:1–3:11. ACM (2014). https://doi.org/10.1145/2689702.2689706

Fault Attacks

Fast Calibration of Fault Injection Equipment with Hyperparameter Optimization Techniques

Vincent Werner[1,2(✉)], Laurent Maingault[1], and Marie-Laure Potet[2]

[1] Univ. Grenoble Alpes, CEA, LETI, DSYS, CESTI, 38000 Grenoble, France
{vincent.werner,laurent.maingault}@cea.fr
[2] Univ. Grenoble Alpes, CNRS, VERIMAG, 38000 Grenoble, France
{vincent.werner,marie-laure.potet}@univ-grenoble-alpes.fr

Abstract. Although fault injection is a powerful technique to exploit implementation weaknesses, this is not without limitations. An important preliminary step, based on rigorous calibration of the fault injection equipment, greatly affects the exploitability and repeatability of injected faults. The equipment parameter space is usually explored with random search, grid search, and more recently with the help of metaheuristic algorithms. In this article, we apply, for the first time, two recent hyperparameter optimization techniques to fault injection. We evaluate these optimization techniques on three different 32-bit microcontrollers, and find better glitch waveforms than with metaheuristic algorithms. In addition, we propose a two-stage optimization strategy under black-box conditions to reduce the dimensionality of the parameter space and speed up the equipment calibration. Finally, we apply this approach to bypass the code read protection of a built-in bootloader faster than with genetic algorithms.

Keywords: Fault injection · Voltage glitch · Parameter optimization

1 Introduction

Fault injection is a powerful technique to bypass security features of embedded systems, such as code protection mechanisms [8,15,26]. Using electrical glitches [2], focused light [31], electromagnetic pulses [13] or even nanofocused X-rays [1], one can locally perturb the chip environment to alter its behavior and gain access to critical information. Although fault injection can lead to impressive results, this is not without limitation. One of the biggest challenges is the calibration of fault injection equipment. Each fault injection equipment has multiple specific parameters that must be adjusted precisely, such as the positions x, y, z of an

This work is supported by the French National Research Agency in the framework of the "Investissements d'avenir" program (ANR-15-IDEX-02 and ANR-10-AIRT-05).

V. Grosso and T. Pöppelmann (Eds.): CARDIS 2021, LNCS 13173, pp. 121–138, 2022.
https://doi.org/10.1007/978-3-030-97348-3_7

electromagnetic probe tip. This preliminary calibration step is required in order to find exploitable and repeatable faults.

The parameter space is often too large to be entirely covered manually during time-constrained security evaluation. The most commonly-used methods to explore the parameter space are Grid Search (GS) and Random Search (RS). GS is a semi-exhaustive search on a predetermined and progressively refined range of values. Although GS is effective with small parameter space, this technique is inefficient to explore a high dimensional parameter space, as the number of evaluated configurations increases exponentially with the number of parameters considered. Even though RS is slightly better than GS for exploring large parameter space [6], both GS and RS select next configurations to evaluate independently of the previous results, thus, many evaluations are wasted on poorly-performing configurations.

Several approaches have been proposed to reduce the time spent on the equipment calibration, using more complex optimization techniques, such as metaheuristic algorithms. However, genetic and memetic algorithms are inherently chaotic and can suffer from premature convergence [19]. Accordingly, Bayesian and Bandit Optimization techniques are typically preferred over metaheuristic algorithms to optimize hard combinatorial problem solvers [16] or machine learning models [20]. To the best of our knowledge, such techniques have not been considered for fault injection yet. Therefore, in this article, we propose applying two efficient hyperparameter optimization techniques, so as to simplify and speed up the calibration of a fault injection equipment for a given target microcontroller. In addition, we also propose an optimization strategy to reduce the dimensionality of the parameter space in order to speed up even more the equipment calibration. To sum up, our contribution is threefold:

- We apply for the first time two hyperparameter optimization techniques, *Successive Halving Algorithm* (SHA) and *Sequential Model-based Algorithm Configuration* (SMAC), to find the best settings and induce repeatable and exploitable faults with our voltage fault injection (VFI) setup, on three different 32-bit microcontrollers.
- We propose breaking down the optimization problem into two stages, so as to simplify but also to speed up the equipment calibration; first, 1) during the *Calibration stage*, we focus on fault injection parameters only, using *fault characterization tests*, which are small programs running on the target device, designed to maximize fault propagation, and then, once the best configurations are identified, 2) during the *Exploitation stage*, we find the fault injection timing to exploit vulnerabilities on the target application.
- Using this strategy and SMAC, we successfully bypass the code protection mechanism of a built-in bootloader. Moreover, SMAC reduces the equipment calibration time by half compared to *Genetic Algorithm* (GA).

The outline of the rest of the article is as follows. After an overview of the related work to overcome the limitations of GS and RS in Sect. 2, we comprehensively explain our fault injection optimization strategy in Sect. 3. In Sect. 4, we detail SHA and SMAC optimization techniques, which are used for equipment calibration. In Sect. 5, to evaluate the performance of these optimization techniques, we calibrate our VFI setup for three different microcontrollers using SHA, SMAC, GA and RS. Finally, in Sect. 6, we apply our fault injection strategy using SMAC to bypass a read protection mechanism on a 32-bit microcontroller faster than with GA.

2   Related Work

Parameter optimization has recently gained in popularity in the fault injection community. Different approaches have been proposed to speed up the equipment calibration step. When possible, reducing the parameter space by identifying the regions of interest helps considerably. For example, using a scanning electron microscope, Courbon et al. [12] find the most sensitive areas of the die to focus with Laser Fault Injection (LFI). Similarly, Schellenberg et al. [30] measure the optical beam induced current, as imaging technique, in order to localize flip-flops of an hardware AES accelerator. Madau et al. [23] propose to acquire EM emission traces, so as to detect EM hotspots and reduce the parameter space of EM Fault Injection (EMFI) equipment. Finally, to reduce the dimensionality of the problem, Carpi et al. [10] split the optimization problem into two stages, one focusing on voltage parameters and the other one on proper timing. Note that Picek et al. [28] also mention this approach, without further evaluating this idea.

Another way to find the best settings faster is to use better optimization algorithms than RS or GS. GA is a popular metaheuristic algorithm based on the evolutionary theory, which has been applied to EMFI [24] but also VFI [8,10,28] to find the best configurations. Picek et al. [27] use Memetic algorithm, which is an extension of the traditional GA with a local search technique, also to explore more efficiently the VFI parameter space. More recently, Wu et al. [35] have proposed a characterization method for LFI setups based on deep learning to tune the pulse width and the power of the laser.

Table 1. Comparison of the related work according to the optimization technique, the dimension reduction of the parameter space, and the fault injection technique.

Related work	Optimization technique	Dimension reduction	FI technique
Our contribution	Bandit optimization	✓	VFI
	Bayesian optimization		
[27]	Memetic algorithm	✗	VFI
[24]	Genetic algorithm	✗	EMFI
[8,28]	Genetic algorithm	✗	VFI
[10]	Genetic algorithm	✓	VFI
[35]	Deep learning	✗	LFI
[23]	Grid search	✓	EMFI
[12,30]	Grid search	✓	LFI

Nevertheless, the main limitation of metaheuristic algorithms is the introduction of additional hyperparameters that must be configured, such as the size of the population, the mutation rate, or the fitness function. Moreover, depending on the optimization problem, metaheuristic algorithms can suffer from premature convergence. Similarly, finding the right number of hidden layers and neurons of the deep neural network is tedious.

More efficient optimization techniques have been proposed over the past decade, such as Bayesian optimization or Bandit optimization. Although already used for hyperparameter optimization of machine learning algorithms, these techniques have never been applied to fault injection. Accordingly, we propose for the first time to apply SMAC (Bayesian optimization) and SHA (Bandit optimization) to improve the calibration of fault injection equipment. Moreover, we also reduce the dimensionality of the parameter space by splitting the optimization in two stages, but unlike [10], we decide to use fault characterization tests to find the best configurations.

3   Fault Injection Optimization Approach

In this section, we detail our general approach for fault injection optimization. This strategy aims to reduce the time spent on searching for the best equipment settings, by reducing the dimensionality of the parameter space. Speeding up the parameter space exploration is particularly important as security evaluations are often time-constrained.

3.1   Common Approach

The most common strategy to optimize fault injection consists to calibrate the fault injection equipment directly with the target application. But for large applications, identifying the critical sections, that can potentially lead to vulnerabilities, is tedious, therefore, it is nearly impossible during a black-box, time-constrained, security evaluation to find the right equipment settings and the right timing to inject the fault. In addition, the lack of feedback for some application further complicates the equipment calibration [33], and significantly increases the amount of work required.

3.2   Our Approach

In an effort to tackle these issues, we propose reducing the dimensionality of the parameter space by breaking down the problem of fault injection optimization into two stages, so as to simplify and speed up the parameter space exploration. First, 1) the *Calibration stage* optimizes the equipment calibration independently of the target application, using fault characterization tests and then, 2) the *Exploitation stage* finds the right timing to inject a fault in order to exploit a vulnerability on the target application. Figure 1 presents our fault injection optimization strategy.

Fault Probability. During the calibration stage, *only faults resulting in a faulty output are considered as effective*, while faults resulting in a crash, a timeout or a normal output are not taken into account. The *fault probability* is used as a metric to compare performance between configurations. The *fault probability* of a configuration is given by $\frac{\#\{\text{faulty results}\}}{\#\{\text{fault injected}\}}$ for this configuration.

Fault Characterization Test. The *fault characterization test*, is not the target application itself, but rather a series of instructions, arranged in such a way as to maximize the number of effective faults on the target microcontroller, in order to quickly find the settings with the highest fault probability. Fault characterization tests have been already applied to highlight fault effects on various microcontrollers with different fault injection techniques [4,11,14,25,29,32,34]. The main advantage of using a fault characterization test is that we can completely ignore the injection timing during the optimization of our setup for the target microcontroller, which helps the exploration of the parameter space. In addition, a characterization test is often smaller than the target application, reducing the time required in the long run. Furthermore, a fault characterization test simplifies the equipment calibration by giving instant feedback on the effectiveness of the fault injection parameters, in comparison with an equipment calibration directly with black-box applications [33].

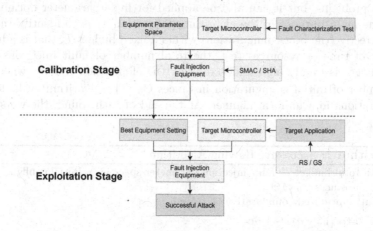

Fig. 1. Overview of our fault injection optimization strategy.

Optimization Techniques. We use different optimization techniques for each step of our approach. During the *calibration stage*, we use hyperparameter optimization techniques such as SMAC or SHA, to quickly explore the equipment parameter space, way faster than with GS or RS (due to the curse of dimensionality [5]). Then, once the best settings are identified, the right timing to inject the fault can be found with a simple random/grid search on the target application during the *exploitation stage*.

4   Hyperparameter Optimization Techniques

In this section, we comprehensively explain the two hyperparameter optimization techniques, SHA and SMAC, which are used to improve the convergence speed towards the best fault injection settings during the *calibration stage*.

4.1   Parameter Space and Equipment Configuration

The parameter space Θ depends on the fault injection technique and the setup used. For example, our VFI setup has 9 free parameters defining the glitch waveform (8 voltage levels and the glitch duration, more detailed information is provided in Sect. 5.2, Fig. 2). Each configuration $\theta \in \Theta$ describes how to adjust each parameter of the given fault injection equipment (e.g. the positions x, y, z of an electromagnetic probe tip). Depending on the number of equipment configurations possible within the parameter space, and the target microcontroller, the complexity of the search will vary. SHA or SMAC can significantly help to reduce the time spent identifying configurations that induce exploitable faults.

4.2   Successive Halving Algorithm

SHA has been originally proposed by Karnin et al.[18] to solve multi-armed bandits problems, but it can also be applied for hyperparameter optimization [36]. The main purpose of the algorithm (Algorithm 1) is to identify the best arm correctly (the best configuration) within a fixed budget T, that is a limited amount of time or resources (e.g. the total number of fault injections). The total budget is evenly allocated across $\log_2(n)$ elimination rounds, where n is the number of initial configuration instances $\vec{\Theta}_0$. The algorithm evaluates the configurations in a uniform manner. At the end of each round, the worst ones

---

Algorithm 1: Successive Halving Algorithm

Input: Total budget T, fault injection parameter space Θ, n initial configuration instances $\vec{\Theta}_0 \subset \Theta$

Output: Optimized configuration $\theta_{inc} \in \vec{\Theta}_{\lceil \log_2(n) \rceil}$

for $r = 0$ **to** $\lceil \log_2(n) \rceil - 1$ **do**

$\quad t_r \leftarrow \left\lfloor \dfrac{T}{|\vec{\Theta}_r| \lceil \log_2(n) \rceil} \right\rfloor$;

$\quad$**foreach** $\theta_i \in \vec{\Theta}_r$ **do**

$\qquad$ Test t_r times each configuration θ_i;

$\qquad$ Compute the empirical mean $\mu_{r,i}$ of θ_i;

$\quad k_r \leftarrow \lceil |\vec{\Theta}_r|/2 \rceil$;

$\quad$/* Keep the k_r^{th} best θ_i with the largest $\mu_{r,i}$ */

$\quad \vec{\Theta}_{r+1} \leftarrow \texttt{BestKthConfigurations}(\vec{\Theta}_r, k_r)$;

return $\theta_{inc} \in \vec{\Theta}_{\lceil \log_2(n) \rceil}$;

---

are eliminated. Then, on each successive round, the remaining configurations are evaluated twice as much as the previous round, and the process repeats until only one remains.

The main concern is, for a fixed budget T, whether to consider many configurations (large n) with smaller number of trials for each (t_r); or a small number of configurations (small n) with larger number of trials for each (t_r). A solution, proposed by Aziz [3], is to take a budget $T = n \log_2(n)$, resulting in an aggressive selection of configurations after just a single shot $(\Rightarrow t_r = 1)$ in the first round. Although only a conjecture has been presented to give an upper bound on the simple regret, the particular parameterization $T = n \log_2(n)$ of the Algorithm 1 is better empirically than more complex solutions, also based on SHA, such as HyperBand [20].

4.3 Sequential Model-Based Algorithm Configuration

SMAC, proposed by Hutter et al. [16], is a general framework for Sequential Model-Based Optimization (SMBO), also known as Bayesian Optimization. SMAC has been successfully applied for hyperparameter optimization of hard combinatorial problem solvers and various machine learning algorithms. Contrary to classical Bayesian-based approaches, SMAC supports all types of parameters, including continuous, discrete, categorical, but can also handle non-deterministic processes which is a key feature to optimize fault injection parameters. In Sect. 4, we will see that SMAC outperforms common approaches used to optimize the fault injection equipment. In the following, we explain the SMAC algorithm in detail.

Sequential Model-Based Optimization. Unlike previous approaches, SMBO keeps track of past results to fit iteratively a probabilistic model, in order to select the next fault injection configurations which could potentially maximize the number of effective faults on the target microcontroller.

SMBO, as detailed in Algorithm 2, is structured around two key components, a probabilistic model and a selection function, also called the surrogate model and the acquisition function respectively. The probabilistic model $\mathcal{M}$ is fitted (FitModel) to previous results $\mathbf{R} = \{(\theta_1, o_1), ..., (\theta_n, o_n)\}$ where θ_i is a possible configuration of the fault injection equipment, and o_i is the observed fault probability with configuration θ_i. The model aims to predict the fault probability o_{i+1} of a new configuration θ_{i+1} to determine if θ_{i+1} is worth being evaluated. The new configurations $\vec{\Theta}_{new}$ are selected from the fault injection parameter space Θ by the acquisition function (SelectConfigurations) which keeps balance between *exploitation* (sampling where the model predicts the highest fault probability) and *exploration* (sampling where the model has no prior distribution). On top of that, SMBO adds an intensification mechanism (Intensify), which determines 1) the budget allocated for each configuration θ_i and 2) the best known configuration so far θ_{inc} [16].

SMAC uses Random Forests (RF) as a surrogate model instead of more commonly-used Gaussian process models, which explains how SMAC supports

---

Algorithm 2: Sequential Model-Based Optimization

Input: Total budget T, fault injection parameter space Θ, initial configuration
        instances $\vec{\Theta}_{init} \subset \Theta$
Output: Optimized parameter configuration θ_{inc}
$\mathbf{R}, \theta_{inc} \leftarrow \text{Initialize}(\vec{\Theta}_{init})$;
repeat
 | /* Fit the model $\mathcal{M}$ based on results $\mathbf{R}$ */
 | $\mathcal{M} \leftarrow \text{FitModel}(\mathbf{R})$;
 | /* Select promising configurations $\vec{\Theta}_{new}$ */
 | $\vec{\Theta}_{new} \leftarrow \text{SelectConfigurations}(\mathcal{M}, \Theta)$;
 | /* Find the best configuration θ_{inc} */
 | $\mathbf{R}, \theta_{inc} \leftarrow \text{Intensify}(\theta_{inc}, \vec{\Theta}_{new})$;
until *total budget T is exhausted*;
return θ_{inc};

---

discrete and categorical parameters. RF [9] is an ensemble method that grows many individual decision trees, which together, can be used to solve both classification and regression problems. For the latter, decision trees take continuous values (e.g. fault probability) rather than class labels at their leaves (also called *regression trees*). SMAC estimates the performance (fault probability) mean μ_θ and variance σ_θ^2 for a new configuration θ by computing the empirical mean and variance of the individual regression trees prediction of the RF. By default, and to maintain a low computational cost, SMAC builds $B = 10$ regression trees with a maximum depth of 20. Each tree is grown to the largest extent possible, based on a training set of n results sampled at random with replacement from the previous results $\mathbf{R}$ (also called *bagging*). Then, at each node, m features (e.g. fault injection parameters) are randomly selected from the initial features, and the one minimizing the reduced squared sum loss among the training set is chosen to split the node.

Finally, the acquisition function of SMAC is based on Expected Improvement (EI), which is used to quantify how much a new configuration θ should improve performance (fault probability) over our current optimum θ_{inc}. Formally, the improvement $I(\theta) = \max(f(\theta_{inc}) - f(\theta), 0)$ compares the performance between the new configuration θ with the best known configuration so far θ_{inc}. As the objective function f is unknown, EI is computed instead using the posterior distribution of θ given the predictive mean μ_θ and variance σ_θ^2 obtained with RF and the empirical mean performance $f_{\theta_{inc}}$ of the best configuration seen so far [16,17]. Next, the new configurations which yield to the highest expected improvement are selected and evaluated.

Initial Configuration Instances. One main limitation of SMAC is that initial conditions can greatly affect the convergence speed, thus we propose our additional two-step procedure to select the initial configuration instances to better calibrate a given fault injection equipment. Without at least one configuration in $\vec{\Theta}_{init}$ which induces an effective fault, SMAC struggles to identify the best settings. This procedure ensures that we do not start SMAC without at least one working configuration.

- *Pure exploration*: configurations $\theta \in \Theta$ are sampled at random and tested until 1) at least k_{min} configurations that generate an effective fault have been found, **and** 2) n_{min} faults have been injected. By default, $k_{min} = 1$ and $n_{min} = 1000$.
- *Mutation*: the set $\vec{\Theta}_{init}$ of initial configuration instances includes at least the k_{min} configurations identified during the pure exploration step, **and** additional configurations generated with a gaussian mutation operator [7] using the configurations found so far, so as to reach $|\vec{\Theta}_{init}| = k_{init}$ configurations. By default, $k_{init} = 100$.

Based on the target microcontroller, k_{min}, n_{min} and k_{init} can be adjusted. For example, SMAC may struggle with some secure microcontrollers. Extending the pure exploration phase (i.e. $k_{min} > 1$ and $n_{min} > 1000$) can significantly help SMAC in early stages, especially when only a few configurations induce effective faults.

5   Equipment Calibration with Different Microcontrollers

In this section, we optimize our VFI setup for three different 32-bit microcontrollers, using SMAC, SHA, GA and RS. In these experiments, SMAC outperforms other optimization techniques and consistently identifies the best settings for our VFI setup. First, we present the target microcontrollers and general information about the experiments. Then, we detail our VFI setup and the parameter space associated. Afterwards, we compare the performance (fault probability and convergence speed) of SMAC and SHA with more commonly-used techniques, such as GA and RS.

5.1   Target Microcontrollers

We have selected three different 32-bit microcontrollers, based on different Cortex-M cores. The die of these microcontrollers are different, thus, they will not react the same way to voltage fault injections. Therefore, the best settings for our VFI setup will be different for each microcontroller. The selected microcontrollers are:

- μ**C-M0** is a Cortex M0+ running at 24 Mhz, based on the ARMv6-M architecture with 2 stages pipeline.
- μ**C-M3** is a mainstream microcontroller based on the Cortex M3 running at 24Mhz, which implements the ARMv7-M architecture with 3 stages pipeline.
- μ**C-M4** is ultra-low-power microcontroller based on the Cortex M4, running at 72Mhz. The core is based on the ARMv7E-M architecture with 3 stages pipeline and branch speculation.

5.2 Setup

General Information. During the *Calibration Stage* (Fig. 1), we use the fault characterization test detailed in Table 2. This test has been designed to maximize the propagation of bit-set or bit-reset on the fetched instruction, but also instruction skips (not detailed in this study). For each optimization technique (SMAC, SHA, GA and RS), we inject 50,000 faults ($\approx$ 6 h). For SMAC, we use the Python library SMACv3 [21], and more precisely the class `SMAC4HPO`. For SHA, GA and RS, we do not use an external library.

For SHA, as described in Sect. 3, we use the parameterization $T = n \log_2(n)$, with $n = 4096$. For GA, each individual of the population represents a valid configuration of the fault injection equipment considered. We train a population of 50 individuals over 200 generations, where each individual is tested five times. In addition, we use a gaussian mutation operator [7], a roulette-wheel selection via stochastic acceptance [22] and the fitness of an individual is given by its fault probability. For RS, we evaluate 10,000 configurations, where each configuration is tested five times. In the following, we detail our VFI setup and its associated parameter space.

Table 2. Instruction Corruption (IC) Test for the ARMv7-M instruction set, as well as the initial values of registers.

Instruction Corruption (IC) Test		

adds r2, #1
 subs r7, #ff
 adds r2, #1
 subs r7, #ff } Repeat n times		

R0	0x00000000	R1	0x11111111
R2	0x22222222	R3	0x33333333
R4	0x44444444	R5	0x55555555
R6	0x66666666	R7	0x77777777

Voltage Fault Injection Setup. Our VFI setup is similar to the Bozzato et al. [8] test bench. We use a custom 30 MSps Digital-to-Analog Converter (DAC) to generate arbitrary glitch waveforms instead of an external arbitrary waveform generator. The DAC is a simple R-2R ladder with 8-bit resolution, which converts digital input byte into analog output voltage. The glitch waveform, sent to the DAC, is generated with a function that takes a set of 8 instantaneous voltage levels, that are then interpolated with cubic interpolation on a grid, up to 2048-by-256, that depends on the waveform size requested. This setup is cheap ($\approx$ 100\$) and yet offers great versatility to adapt to different targets with the ability to generate a large spectrum of glitch waveforms ([8]).

However, the versatility comes at a price, as the parameter space of our VFI setup, presented in Fig. 2, is larger than those of more commonly-used VFI setups. Indeed, most of the time, only two parameters are used (glitch duration and glitch amplitude), while our setup has 9 free parameters (8 voltage levels and the glitch duration). Therefore, our VFI setup is a good candidate to evaluate the relevance of SMAC and SHA optimization techniques.

| | | Parameter | |
		$x_0...x_7$	$duration$
Digital	Range	$[\![80, 180]\!]$	$[\![8, 128]\!]$
Digital	Resolution	8-bit	8-bit
Analog	Range	$[0.6, 5.1]$	$[0.2, 3.2]$
Analog	Unit	V	µs

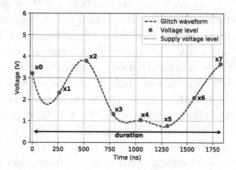

Fig. 2. VFI parameter space, $\approx 10^{18}$ configurations. The glitch waveform is defined with 8 voltage levels ($x_0...x_7$) and the duration.

5.3 Experimental Protocol

The results of the fault injection optimization with SMAC, SHA, GA and RS are heterogeneous. While SMAC and SHA, by design, return a single configuration (the best found), RS and GA return several configurations. Indeed, SMAC and SHA progressively increase the number of test to better approximate the fault probability in order to select the best configuration whereas RS and GA always evaluate each configuration the same number of times, thus several configurations can end up with the same fault probability. Accordingly, to fairly compare the fault probability evolution over time of the configuration(s) found with SMAC, SHA, GA and RS, several considerations have to be taken into account:

- *SMAC*: by design, with SMAC, the best configuration known so far is updated during runtime execution, thus no post-processing required.
- *RS*: unlike SMAC, post-processing is required for RS. Every 5000 fault injections, we inject 1000 more faults to evaluate the fault probability of the best configuration(s) found so far.
- *GA*: The same post-processing as RS is required.
- *SHA*: We evaluate the average fault probability at each halving of the remaining configurations.

For each microcontroller considered, we optimize our VFI setup using SMAC, SHA, GA and RS and we compare the fault probability evolution over time of the configuration(s) found. The best optimization technique is the one that finds the configuration with the highest fault probability, within a minimum number of fault injections.

5.4 Results

The results of the experiments are summarized in Fig. 3 and Table 3. In the Fig. 3, we compare the evolution of fault probability over 50,000 fault injections, to visually determine the convergence speed of each optimization technique (fast or slow). Table 3 presents the fault probability of the best settings found with each technique.

For each microcontroller, SMAC is significantly faster than other optimization techniques. In particular, in less than 10,000 fault injections, SMAC systematically identifies configurations with higher fault probability than GA, RS and SHA. Therefore, SMAC can be used to calibrate an equipment faster than more commonly-used optimization techniques, hence saving valuable time during security evaluations. On the other hand, SHA slowly converges towards the best configuration. However, at the end, after 50,000 fault injections, SHA finds the configuration with the best fault probability for μC-M0 and μC-M3.

By design, SHA uses all the allocated budget T, and removes iteratively the worst configurations at each round, which explains the slow convergence speed, in comparison with other optimization techniques. Nevertheless, we find that SHA wastes many evaluations on poorly-performing configurations during the first rounds, in particular with μC-M0. Our additional procedure for SMAC, described in Sect. 4.3 could also help SHA to select the initial configuration instances $\vec{\Theta}_0$, so as to reduce the time spent on poorly-performing configurations. Although we have not evaluated SMAC or SHA with other fault injection techniques, we believe that these optimization techniques can be easily adapt-

Table 3. Performance comparison between optimization techniques.

		SMAC	SHA	GA	RS
μC-M0	Max fault probability	0.52	**0.53**	0.49	0.49
	Convergence speed	**Fast**	Slow	**Fast**	Slow
μC-M3	Max fault probability	0.77	**0.81**	0.52	0.24
	Convergence speed	**Fast**	Slow	Slow	Slow
μC-M4	Max fault probability	**0.95**	0.79	0.81	0.71
	Convergence speed	**Fast**	Slow	**Fast**	Slow

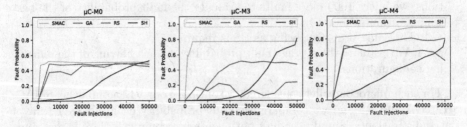

Fig. 3. Evolution of fault probability over 50,000 fault injections, according to SMAC, GA, SHA and RS, with VFI

able to EMFI or LFI. Regarding the results, SMAC is more efficient than GA, RS, and SHA, in particular to quickly calibrate fault injection equipment for a given microcontroller. In the following, we will show that SMAC can also be used to exploit vulnerabilities faster than GA.

6   SMAC to Bypass a Code Protection Mechanism

In this section, we apply our two-stage strategy with SMAC to bypass a code protection mechanism, with VFI, on a 32-bit microcontroller. The presented attack is a known attack [8] which downgrades the security level of the target, so as to extract the firmware. We will show that SMAC is better than GA at identifying the best settings within a limited number of fault injections, and therefore that SMAC can save valuable time during security evaluations.

6.1   STM32F103RB

The microcontroller STM32F103RB is a 32-bit ARM Cortex-M3 core operating at 24 MHz. The preprogrammed bootloader offers code protection mechanisms to prevent any read or write operations from the bootloader on the user flash memory. In practical terms, once the read protection (RDP) is enabled, the bootloader returns a negative response (NACK) when a Read Memory command is issued. To disable RDP, the flash must be completely erased.

Attack. The known attack [8] to bypass the read protection mechanism consists in injecting a fault during the Read Memory command. Indeed, when the bootloader receives the Read Memory command, it checks the RDP value and returns the ACK or the NACK byte, depending on whether RDP is disabled or

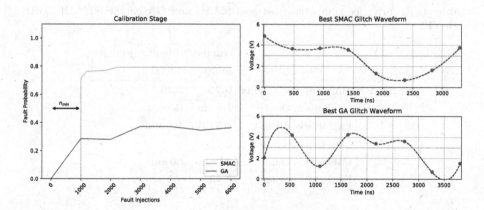

Fig. 4. Evolution of fault probability over 6000 fault injections, according to SMAC and GA, on the STM32F103RB; and the best glitch waveforms found with SMAC and GA during the calibration stage.

enabled, respectively. By injecting a fault during the RDP checking phase, an attacker can deceive the read protection mechanism and retrieve the content of the selected memory block.

Calibration Stage. In order to find the best settings for our VFI equipment to glitch the STM32F103RB, we will use SMAC and GA, and compare the fault probability evolution. For both SMAC and GA, we perform the *calibration stage* with 6000 fault injections (24 generations for GA) during ≈ 15min, with the fault characterization test in Table 2, and with the default parameters. Figure 4 presents the fault probability evolution over time of the best configuration(s) found with SMAC and GA. We have arbitrarily chosen a small number of fault injections during the *calibration stage*, so as to show that SMAC is definitely faster at identifying the best settings than more commonly-used optimization techniques, such as GA. Not only does SMAC converge faster than GA, but SMAC also identifies configurations twice as efficient as those found with GA (Table 4).

Exploitation Stage. We compare the average of the elapsed time to perform the attack to bypass RDP (*exploitation stage*) with SMAC and GA, using the best glitch waveforms found during the *calibration stage*. The attack is easily achieved with the best configuration found with SMAC, *on average in less than 5 minutes*. On contrary, with the best configurations found with GA, we have not been able to bypass the read protection mechanism of the STM32F103RB. This shows that with only 6,000 fault injections during the *calibration stage*, GA clearly underperforms SMAC. Figure 5 presents the oscilloscope traces of the attack to bypass RDP on the STM32F103RB, using the best glitch waveform found with SMAC.

Table 4. Performance comparison between SMAC and GA on the STM32F103RB with VFI.

		Number of fault injections	
		6000	12000
SMAC	Max fault probability	**0.79**	0.79
	Calibration time	15 min	30 min
	Exploitation time	**<5 min**	<5 min
GA	Max fault probability	0.37	0.55
	Calibration time	15 min	30 min
	Exploitation time	N/A	<5 min

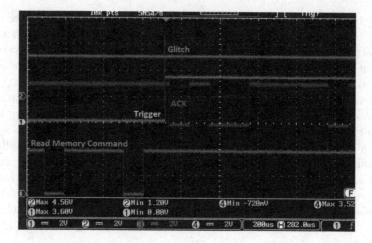

Fig. 5. Oscilloscope traces of the glitch attack to bypass RDP on the STM32F103RB.

Note that with a larger number of fault injections during the calibration stage, it is also possible to bypass RDP using GA. For example, with twice as many fault injections during the calibration stage (i.e. 12,000 instead of 6,000), GA identifies equipment settings that can successfully glitch the STM32F103RB and bypass the code protection mechanism (Table 4). But even after 12.000 fault injections, the configurations identified with GA have a lower fault probability than with SMAC.

7 Conclusion

Fault injection requires a preliminary step of equipment calibration in order to find exploitable and repeatable faults. In this article, we have proposed applying state-of-the-art optimization techniques, already used for machine learning and other hard combinatorial problems, to fault injection. Bayesian Optimization (SMAC) and Bandit Optimization (SHA) are used to identify the best equipment configurations which maximize exploitable faults on a target microcontroller. While SHA is a simple algorithm, easily adaptable to fault injection and yet offers decent performance, SMAC is arguably the most interesting optimization technique, finding better equipment configurations faster than metaheuristic algorithms.

In addition, to simplify and speed up the equipment calibration, we have proposed splitting fault injection optimization into two stages, *the calibration stage* and *the exploitation stage*. We optimize fault injection parameters independently of the target application with a fault characterization test and then, once the best configurations are identified, we find fault injection timings to exploit vulnerabilities on the target application. With SMAC and this strategy, we successfully bypass a code protection mechanism of the STM32F103RB bootloader. In particular, the calibration stage with SMAC is twice as fast as with

GA. Furthermore, SMAC and SHA have systematically identified better configurations than metaheuristic algorithms, and although it has not been studied in this article, finding configurations with high fault probability is even more important when multi-fault injections are necessary, as inducing more repeatable faults greatly help in carrying out complex multi-fault attacks.

As future work, it will be interesting to apply other promising optimization techniques such as HyperBand (Bandit Optimization) or Tree-structured Parzen Estimator (Bayesian Optimization). Moreover, we will investigate the applications of hyperparameter optimization techniques to find exploitable faults with other fault injection techniques, such as LFI or EMFI. Finally, our ongoing research is focused on direct applications of fault injection optimization with SMAC or SHA on secure microcontrollers. For example, we believe that we can find exotic waveforms with SMAC that can bypass voltage glitch attack detectors.

References

1. Anceau, S., Bleuet, P., Clédière, J., Maingault, L., Rainard, J., Tucoulou, R.: Nanofocused X-ray beam to reprogram secure circuits. In: Fischer, W., Homma, N. (eds.) CHES 2017. LNCS, vol. 10529, pp. 175–188. Springer, Cham (2017). https://doi.org/10.1007/978-3-319-66787-4_9

2. Aumüller, C., Bier, P., Fischer, W., Hofreiter, P., Seifert, J.-P.: Fault attacks on RSA with CRT: concrete results and practical countermeasures. In: Kaliski, B.S., Koç, K., Paar, C. (eds.) CHES 2002. LNCS, vol. 2523, pp. 260–275. Springer, Heidelberg (2003). https://doi.org/10.1007/3-540-36400-5_20

3. Aziz, M.: On Multi-Armed Bandits Theory and Applications. PhD thesis, Ph. D. Thesis, Northeastern University, Boston, MA, USA (2019)

4. Balasch, J., Gierlichs, B., Verbauwhede, I.: An in-depth and black-box characterization of the effects of clock glitches on 8-bit mcus. In: 2011 Workshop on Fault Diagnosis and Tolerance in Cryptography, pp. 105–114. IEEE (2011)

5. Bellman, R.E.: Adaptive Control Processes. Princeton University Press, Princeton (1861)

6. Bergstra, J., Bengio, Y.: Random search for hyper-parameter optimization. J. Mach. Learn. Res. 13(2), 281–305 (2012)

7. Beyer, H.-G., Schwefel, H.-P.: Evolution strategies-a comprehensive introduction. Natural Comput. 1(1), 3–52 (2002)

8. Bozzato, C., Focardi, R., Palmarini, F.: Shaping the glitch: optimizing voltage fault injection attacks. IACR Trans. Cryptogr. Hard. Embed. Syst. 199–224, 2019 (2019)

9. Breiman, L.: Random forests. Mach. Learn. 45(1), 5–32 (2001)

10. Carpi, R.B., Picek, S., Batina, L., Menarini, F., Jakobovic, D., Golub, M.: Glitch it if you can: parameter search strategies for successful fault injection. In: Francillon, A., Rohatgi, P. (eds.) CARDIS 2013. LNCS, vol. 8419, pp. 236–252. Springer, Cham (2014). https://doi.org/10.1007/978-3-319-08302-5_16

11. Colombier, B., Menu, A., Dutertre, J.-M., Moëllic, P.-A., Rigaud, J.-B., Danger, J.-L.: Laser-induced single-bit faults in flash memory: instructions corruption on a 32-bit microcontroller. IACR Cryptol. ePrint Arch. 2018, 1042 (2018)

12. Courbon, F., Loubet-Moundi, P., Fournier, J.J.A., Tria, A.: Increasing the efficiency of laser fault injections using fast gate level reverse engineering. In: 2014 IEEE International Symposium on Hardware-Oriented Security and Trust (HOST), pp. 60–63. IEEE (2014)
13. Dehbaoui, A., Dutertre, J.M., Robisson, B., Tria, A.: Electromagnetic transient faults injection on a hardware and a software implementations of AES. In: 2012 Workshop on Fault Diagnosis and Tolerance in Cryptography, pp. 7–15. IEEE (2012)
14. Dureuil, L., Potet, M.-L., de Choudens, P., Dumas, C., Clédière, J.: From code review to fault injection attacks: filling the gap using fault model inference. In: Homma, N., Medwed, M. (eds.) CARDIS 2015. LNCS, vol. 9514, pp. 107–124. Springer, Cham (2016). https://doi.org/10.1007/978-3-319-31271-2_7
15. Gerlinsky, C.: Breaking code read protection on the nxp lpc-family microcontrollers (2017)
16. Hutter, F., Hoos, H.H., Leyton-Brown, K.: Sequential model-based optimization for general algorithm configuration. In: Coello, C.A.C. (ed.) LION 2011. LNCS, vol. 6683, pp. 507–523. Springer, Heidelberg (2011). https://doi.org/10.1007/978-3-642-25566-3_40
17. Hutter, F., Hoos, H.H., Leyton-Brown, K., Murphy, K.P.: An experimental investigation of model-based parameter optimisation: spo and beyond. In: Proceedings of the 11th Annual conference on Genetic and evolutionary computation, pp. 271–278 (2009)
18. Karnin, Z., Koren, T., Somekh, O.: Almost optimal exploration in multi-armed bandits. In: International Conference on Machine Learning, pp. 1238–1246. PMLR (2013)
19. Katoch, S., Chauhan, S.S., Kumar, V.: A review on genetic algorithm: past, present, and future. Multimedia Tools Appl. **80**, 1–36 (2020)
20. Li, L., Jamieson, K., DeSalvo, G., Rostamizadeh, A., Talwalkar, A.: Hyperband: a novel bandit-based approach to hyperparameter optimization. J. Mach. Learn. Res. **18**(1), 6765–6816 (2017)
21. Lindauer, M., Eggensperger, K., Feurer, M., Falkner, S., Biedenkapp, A., Hutter, F.: Smac v3: algorithm configuration in python (2017). https://github.com/automl/SMAC3
22. Lipowski, A., Lipowska, D.: Roulette-wheel selection via stochastic acceptance. Physica A Stat. Mech. Appl. **391**(6), 2193–2196 (2012)
23. Madau, M., Agoyan, M., Maurine, P.: An EM fault injection susceptibility criterion and its application to the localization of hotspots. In: Eisenbarth, T., Teglia, Y. (eds.) CARDIS 2017. LNCS, vol. 10728, pp. 180–195. Springer, Cham (2018). https://doi.org/10.1007/978-3-319-75208-2_11
24. Maldini, A., Samwel, N., Picek, S., Batina, L.: Optimizing electromagnetic fault injection with genetic algorithms. In: Breier, J., Hou, X., Bhasin, S. (eds.) Automated Methods in Cryptographic Fault Analysis, pp. 281–300. Springer, Cham (2019). https://doi.org/10.1007/978-3-030-11333-9_13
25. Moro, N., Dehbaoui, A., Heydemann, K., Robisson, B., Encrenaz, E.: Electromagnetic fault injection: towards a fault model on a 32-bit microcontroller. In: 2013 Workshop on Fault Diagnosis and Tolerance in Cryptography, pp. 77–88. IEEE (2013)
26. Obermaier, J., Tatschner, S.: Shedding too much light on a microcontroller's firmware protection. In: 11th {USENIX} Workshop on Offensive Technologies ({WOOT} 2017) (2017)

27. Picek, S., Batina, L., Buzing, P., Jakobovic, D.: Fault injection with a new flavor: memetic algorithms make a difference. In: Mangard, S., Poschmann, A.Y. (eds.) COSADE 2014. LNCS, vol. 9064, pp. 159–173. Springer, Cham (2015). https://doi.org/10.1007/978-3-319-21476-4_11

28. Picek, S., Batina, L., Jakobović, D., Carpi, R.B.: Evolving genetic algorithms for fault injection attacks. In: 2014 37th International Convention on Information and Communication Technology, Electronics and Microelectronics (MIPRO), pp. 1106–1111. IEEE (2014)

29. Riviere, L., Najm, Z., Rauzy, P., Danger, J. L., Bringer, J., Sauvage, L.: High precision fault injections on the instruction cache of armv7-m architectures. In: 2015 IEEE International Symposium on Hardware Oriented Security and Trust (HOST), pp. 62–67. IEEE (2015)

30. Schellenberg, Markus F., et al.: On the complexity reduction of laser fault injection campaigns using obic measurements. In: 2015 Workshop on Fault Diagnosis and Tolerance in Cryptography (FDTC), pp. 14–27. IEEE (2015)

31. Skorobogatov, S.P., Anderson, R.J.: Optical fault induction attacks. In: Kaliski, B.S., Koç, K., Paar, C. (eds.) CHES 2002. LNCS, vol. 2523, pp. 2–12. Springer, Heidelberg (2003). https://doi.org/10.1007/3-540-36400-5_2

32. Trouchkine, T., Bouffard, G., Clédière, J.: Fault injection characterization on modern CPUs. In: Laurent, M., Giannetsos, T. (eds.) WISTP 2019. LNCS, vol. 12024, pp. 123–138. Springer, Cham (2020). https://doi.org/10.1007/978-3-030-41702-4_8

33. Van den Herrewegen, J., Oswald, D., Garcia, F.D., Temeiza, Q.: Fill your boots: Enhanced embedded bootloader exploits via fault injection and binary analysis. IACR Trans. Cryptogr. Hardw. Embed. Syst. **56–81**, 2021 (2021)

34. Werner, V., Maingault, L., Potet, M.-L.: An end-to-end approach for multi-fault attack vulnerability assessment. In: 2020 Workshop on Fault Detection and Tolerance in Cryptography (FDTC), pp. 10–17. IEEE (2020)

35. Wu, L., Ribera, G., Beringuier-Boher, N., Picek, S.: A fast characterization method for semi-invasive fault injection attacks. In: Jarecki, S. (ed.) CT-RSA 2020. LNCS, vol. 12006, pp. 146–170. Springer, Cham (2020). https://doi.org/10.1007/978-3-030-40186-3_8

36. Yang, L., Shami, A.: On hyperparameter optimization of machine learning algorithms: theory and practice. Neurocomputing **415**, 295–316 (2020)

Laboratory X-rays Operando Single Bit Attacks on Flash Memory Cells

Laurent Maingault[1], Stéphanie Anceau[1(✉)], Manuel Sulmont[1], Luc Salvo[2],
Jessy Clediere[1], Pierre Lhuissier[2], Emrick Beliard[1], and Jean Luc Rainard[1]

[1] CEA-Leti, 17 Avenue Des Martyrs, 38054 Grenoble, France
stephanie.anceau@cea.fr

[2] Université Grenoble Alpes, CNRS, UMR5266, Grenoble INP, Laboratoire SIMaP,
38000 Grenoble, France

Abstract. The need to increase the level of digital security standards requires a
sustained research effort on new means of perturbations likely to disturb the processing of integrated circuits. X-rays modification is a powerful semi-permanent
fault injection technique with a high spatial accuracy, which allows an adversary
to modify efficiently secret data from an electronic device. Experimental results
demonstrate that several semi-permanent bit erase faults can be injected in code
and data with corrupting flash memory, even with an X-rays spot from an X-rays
laboratory source of less than 10 μm in diameter. This is the order of magnitude
of 15 memory cells with a process node of 350 nm in the presented experiments.
The article also presents the specificity of performing an X-rays attack without
the need of a synchrotron-focused beam, as presented in CHES 2017 [1].

Keywords: X-rays · Physical attacks · Cybersecurity

1 Introduction

The possibility of using visible and IR light to perform attack on integrated circuit was
revealed by Skorobogatov and Anderson [2]. The physical phenomena have been studied and explained by the failure-analysis community [3–6]. Laser light can be synchro-
nized and focused in order to induce transient and persistent faults. During the security-
evaluation practice, these attacks may give powerful results. In order to further investigate the wavelength spectrum of perturbations, it is proposed here to study the effects
of ionizing radiation like X-rays. Compare to fault perturbations induced in a circuit by
a laser light, where the spot size is few microns, X-rays beam allows to obtain a spot
size down to 50 nm using synchrotron source and down to 400 nm in laboratory nano
sources. This is therefore more suitable to modify one single transistor for the most
advanced technology mode. It is physically possible to modify one single bit transistor
with the X-rays and the limitation is only coming from the way used to focus the beam.
Security countermeasures can be deactivated in the flash block memory or the registers in the glue logic for example. The second advantage of X-rays is their potential to

© Springer Nature Switzerland AG 2022
V. Grosso and T. Pöppelmann (Eds.): CARDIS 2021, LNCS 13173, pp. 139–150, 2022.
https://doi.org/10.1007/978-3-030-97348-3_8

penetrate deeply through materials and induced semi-permanent faults on flash memory cells and NMOS transistors. The X-rays beam can penetrate through the plastic or ceramic package, through the front side active shield of the circuit or the backside die paddle. This semi-permanent perturbation of the X-rays is completely reversible with a simple heat treatment in a classical oven and no physical modification is visible after the X-rays perturbations. X-rays interaction with electronic circuits has been analyzed [7–22], but its use for security evaluation has been mainly restricted to die and package imaging or occasional perturbation with no practical success [23, 24] before the single bit semi-permanent fault injections performed at the European synchrotron facility in Grenoble [1].

Since the late 90s, the flash memory cells are known to be vulnerable to the cyber attacks of secure integrated circuits. However, significant improvements have been done to secure electronic devices: The stored data, that often contains critical secret keys, is indeed now ciphered and scrambled in the flash memory blocks. Nowadays it is difficult to reread the flash memory content for the actual technology node. It is therefore interesting to develop another method for the modification of the memory content. This document demonstrates the feasibility of semi-permanent X-rays modifications of localized several flash memory cells using backside and frontside attack with laboratory X-rays source. For the purpose of this article, we chose to attack ATmega128P devices. Despite its large technology node compared to standard devices in the cybersecurity field, it is a perfect demonstrator of an attack feasibility. Furthermore, the availability in DIP packages allows to easily decapsulate the target device and, even if the device is damaged by the X-rays fault injection, it can easily be replaced. We will first present the methods to prepare the circuit for X-rays attacks, the methodology of an attack with a laboratory X-rays source and the results obtained using both backside and frontside attack.

2 Materials and Methods

2.1 Preparation of Integrated Circuit ATmega128P for X-rays Attack

In this work, we target an 8-bit AVR microcontroller, the Atmel ATmega128P. It has 128 kB of flash memory, 4 kB of EEPROM and 4 kB of RAM. The technology node is 350 nm and the 128 kB flash memory block is visible on the right part of Fig. 1.

Fig. 1. ATmega128P integrated circuit after package removal.

The backside of the chip's package together with the copper paddle was removed using a cheap ASAP milling machine. The metal connections of the package are returned to the opposite side: each connection is brazed to strengthen the connection in order to avoid any breakdown during multiple manipulations (Fig. 2).

Fig. 2. ATmega128P device sample without preparation (left picture). The ASAP milling machine for the device backside thinning is used and the ATmega128P device backside pads are returned and milled (right picture).

The device protection shown in Fig. 2 relies on four steps::

i.   Deposition of 20 μm thickness W over 300 μm diameter on the flash memory.
ii. Drilling of a 10 μm diameter hole into the W layer.
iii. A square Pb foil (1 cm × 1 cm) with thickness of 300 μm is drilled to make a hole of 250 μm.
iv. The Pb foil is placed over the W deposit in order to protect the circuit and keep the 10 μm hole visible.

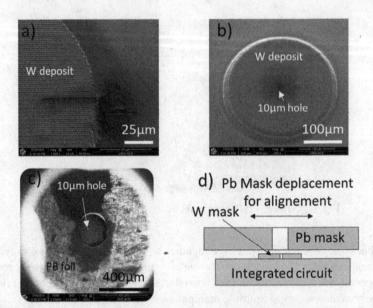

Fig. 3. (a) Thickness measurement of the W mask deposited on the ATmega128P device backside surface. (b) 10 μm diameter hole visible on the same W mask used for the X-rays focalization. (c) Lead mask shown on the circuit. (d) Principle of Pb mask alignment

Step (i) is performed with a V400 Focused Ion Beam (FIB). We put the sample on the right part of on a sample holder inside the FIB vacuum chamber. The sample holder is custom made and its dimensions are optimized for the following experimentation. First, the backside memory block is localized thanks to an in-situ infrared camera. Then gas is injected for the circle deposition of tungsten thickness of 20 μm localized in the center of the memory block on the backside surface of the device. The precise positioning in the center of the memory block is possible thanks to the piezoelectric XY table with a movement precision of 0.2 μm. The thickness of the deposited tungsten layer is measured with a quick etching of a single line on the border of the tungsten deposition layer. The sample is then tilted to an angle of 45° inside the FIB vacuum chamber. The diameter of the W deposit is 300 μm. We check the diameter and the thickness value of the tungsten (W) mask and the result is visible on the left picture of the Fig. 3.

Step (ii) is also performed in the V400 FIB using a 65 nA current without any gas. 2 h are required to make a hole of 10 μm diameter and 20 μm thickness in the W deposit. The hole can be seen in Fig. 3 (b).

Step (iii) the Pb foil is drilled with a 200 μm drill bit using a conventional tabletop drilling machine.

Step (iv) The Pb foil is superposed on the Tungsten (W) mask under the inversed optical microscope on the backside sample surface. For that, the sample is fixed under the microscope with several stickers. Then the Pb foil is positioned slowly and we check that there is a good superposition of the two masks. Then we use a transparent UV light polymerization glue in order to fix the Pb foil in the right position. The viscosity of the UV sticker is correct for the border fixation of the Pb foil on the backside device surface at the right position. We still check with the microscope that the Pb foil does not move under the microscope during the glue polymerization. The result of the Pb and W foil superposition is visible in Fig. 3 (c).

2.2 X-rays Source Laboratory

We used an Hamamatsu nano-tube with Lab6 and Mo target. Operating condition was 40 kV with 1.9 W in large spot configuration (meaning a focus of the spot of around 2 μm). Imaging is done with a Varian flat panel allowing to easily see the W hole made with the FIB. The experimental setup, the principle of attack on the sample and a radiograph of the system are shown in Fig. 4. Bright pixels in a very small area are visible and correspond to the position of the 10 μm diameter of W mask hole on the surface of the ATmega128P backside device (see arrow). The shape around the W mask corresponds to the PCB soldering X-rays picture in transmission on the dedicated electronic card.

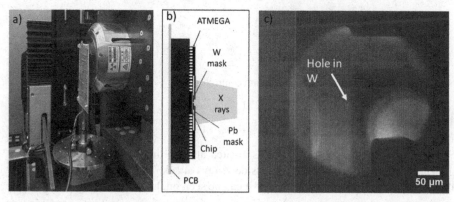

Fig. 4. (a) Experimental setup of the X-rays source laboratory experiment. The ATmega128P sample electronic PCB mounted near the nano X-rays source. (b) Transmission image of the component with the 10 μm hole can be seen in (c).

2.3 Operando Analysis of ATmega128P Device During X-rays Exposure

Two interfaces have been made for the frontside and the backside of the device in order to use a PC with a USB port for the functionality exploitation of the ATmega128P device. Python programs have been developed for the CESTI laboratory in order to write and read the flash memory block of the ATmega128P device. We used PyQt5 for the GUI, numpy and matplotlib for data treatment and image visualization and library Ftd2xx to communicate with the Atmega circuit. This program detects the faulted errors during the reading sequence and allows the visualization of the faults during the experiment. It is possible to follow in operando the fault that are created. Figure 5 presents the program interface. The first window on the left allows connecting to the circuit, program the flash and read it. The log windows indicates at each pass the number of faulted bits and the last window is an image of the faulted memory cells.

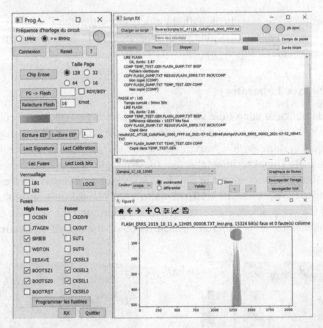

Fig. 5. Interface of the program controlling the operando experiment

3 Results and Discussion

Figure 6 presents the number of faults created at each time as well as some images showing the fault location during backside X-rays attack. The first faults are observed after 520 s and two bits were faulted as it can be seen on the image shown in Fig. 6.

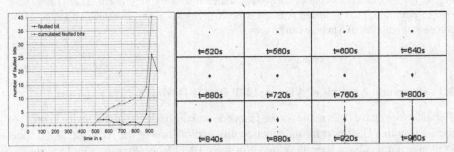

Fig. 6. Number of faulted transistors with various X-rays exposure duration and visualization of the faulted transistors.

The first part of the faulted results (before 880 s) correspond to the floating gate transistor erasing: electrons are evacuated from the floating gate to the substrate as shown on the left of Fig. 7. The second part of the faulted results appears at 880 s where columns start to be faulted. This type of fault transistors correspond to the semi-permanent conduction of the NMOS transistors. These transistors correspond to the NMOS access transistors of each memory cell and the permanent conduction of the NMOS transistor. The ionization of the oxide layer between the NMOS transistor generates positive charge at the interface with the substrate. This induces electron leakage in the substrate channel at the interface as shown on the two figures on the right of Fig. 7. These erase and conduct phenomena are well explained in the aerospace applications studies in which radiation naturally occurs and prevents chips from functioning properly. All these extensive effect studies are used for the protection of the devices in the space environment [7–22]. The so-called semi-permanent effect is based on the fact that a simple one-hour heat annealing treatment at 150 °C allows recovering the previous device functional behavior [1]. However, if the X-rays irradiation lasts too long it will be impossible to retrieve the initial behavior.

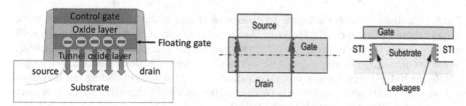

Fig. 7. Erased memory cell mechanism illustration (left image) and permanent conductivity mechanism of the NMOS access transistor illustration (right images) [ref pour le images?]

The functionality of the flash memory block is presented on Fig. 8. On the left, it is possible to see the erased cells faulted results and on the right, the NMOS access transistor faulted result. The evolution of the corruption with time exposure is shown on Fig. 8. After 520 s, the memory cells in the W mask hole are corrupted and the floating gates of the memory cell transistors are emptied thanks to the photoemission of carriers stored in the floating gates. This result is visible during the reading of the corresponding line of the corrupted memory cells. After 880 s, the access to any line of the exposed array is corrupted due to these NMOS transistors that are conductive, even if the corresponding line is not selected. This is due to charge trappings in insulating layers, inducing Vt shifts in NMOS transistors. If we stop the X-rays irradiation between 520 s and 880 s, the programed memory cells will remain in the erased state during the next writing operation.

The flash block memory cells are programed with alternating 1s and 0s for each memory cell side by side we have programmed the flash memory block with 5555 logic values. It is clearly possible to stop the experiment after the first part of the faulted results (i.e. before 880 s) in order to keep only the erased memory cell faults and performed an exploitable security attack. Figure 9 presents longitudinal and transverse cross sections allowing to measure the size of the block cell which is approximately (1.3 μm × 3.5 μm). Figure 9 also presents a schematic of the memory cell blocks indicating that sixteen floating gate transistors could be irradiated in the 10 μm diameter hole. Only half of the sixteen floating gates are full of electrons and thus will be faulted, which means eight floating gate transistors. During the experiment, seven floating gate transistors were

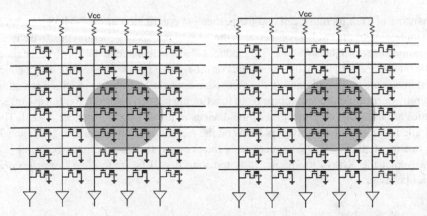

Fig. 8. The figure presents the logical representation of part of the flash memory block in the X-rays exposed area (red circle). The logical functionality of part of the flash block memory cells is visible during the X-rays irradiation. The two parts of the attack process are clearly visible: on the left picture, the floating gates of the memory cells are in an erased state and on the right picture, the NMOS access transistors are conductive. The state of the fault floating gate transistors and the fault NMOS access transistor is conductive; the red arrows represent each fault memory cell and each fault transistor. (Color figure online)

faulted (see Fig. 6). This difference may be due to the fact that the tungsten hole might be slightly smaller or not exactly in the position shown in Fig. 9.

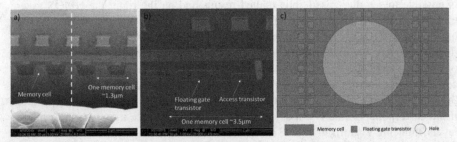

Fig. 9. (a) Frontside perpendicular FIB cross section and SEM pictures of the flash block memory cells of the ATMEGA128P device. (b) Transverse cross section (dashed white line of (a)). (c) Schematic of the memory cell blocks with the W hole.

4 Towards Simple Single Bit Attacks with Laboratory X-rays Source

The principle of using W mask to perform X-rays attack on backside integrated circuits has been clearly validated in the previous section. We therefore tried to simplify the sample preparation and explored the availability of performing frontside attack. Knowing the flash zone position, a lead film (10 mm height × 20 mm width × 50 μm thickness) was glued on the frontside of the component to protect the surrounding electronic components. We choose to start with a lead film, easier to manipulate and cut than W plate and to limit the FIB use to the drilling of holes. Different square holes with edge length ranging from 5 μm to 10 μm were drilled directly in the Pb film with the FIB with a 65 nA current during 3 h. The main advantage of this procedure is that we avoid several tricky steps of the sample preparation procedure presented in the previous section: there is no need to return the metal legs connecting the component to the boardconnection as necessary in backside attack, to use ASAP machining neither to align Pb film with W deposit and hole as explained earlier. Furthermore, we also simplified the X-rays attack: in this case, we do not use a Mo target, which is not a classical target, but a W target that is available in common X-rays sources. The X-rays attack conditions were similar: 40 kV, 1.9 W with large spot size of around 2 μm focalization. Figure 10 (**a**) presents the sample with the Pb lead directly glued on the front side with carbon tape. Figure 10 (**b, c**) presents FIB images of the holes performed in the flash and a X transmission image of the device mounted in the X-rays source, showing holes in white.

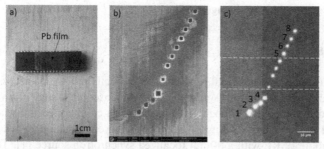

Fig. 10. (a) Frontside component with Pb film of 50 μm thickness protecting the circuit in the middle. (b) FIB images of the series of hole made in the Pb film. (c) X-rays transmission image of the component showing holes.

Figure 11 presents the images of the faulted bits with various X-rays exposure durations. The first fault appears in less than one hour (at 2960 s) and it is a single bit fault (see red arrows on Fig. 11). Other faults appear with time in the different holes. It is interesting to note that in each hole we start by a single bit fault as indicated by red arrows. The second bit fault in each hole is generally coming after 60 s to 120 s after the first fault. This could let time to switch off the X-rays in order to perform only single bit attack, keeping only the single erased memory cell fault and perform an exploitable attack. However, it would be better to reduce the size of the holes and thus only attack one transistor. It can be seen from the last image of Fig. 11 that some holes are not presenting faults when compared to Fig. 10: only eight holes present faults. This is due to the 5555 programming of the flash where 128 columns are set to 1 and 128 columns are set to 0 alternatively. Only columns set to 1 can be changed to 0 and produce a fault. This explains why four holes in between the white dashed lines of Fig. 10 are not producing faults.

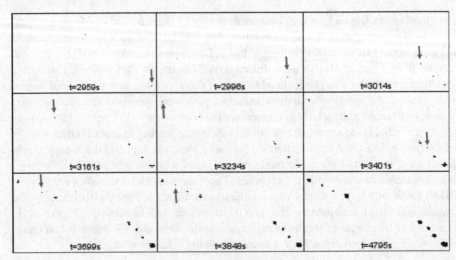

Fig. 11. Images of the faulted bits with time during front side X-rays attacks of Atmega: red arrow indicates the single bit fault. (Color figure online)

5   Conclusion

It is possible to attack only several flash memory block cells and NMOS access transistors with a simple X-rays laboratory source. The seven erased cells may allow a program change stored in the memory block or to deactivate a countermeasure when this one needs a flash memory cell reading. This work is the continuation of what has been done in Grenoble ESRF with a 50 nm focalized synchrotron source [1]. The fact that we do not need a synchrotron and that a conventional W target X-rays source can be used for managing such an attack is a very interesting feature. Furthermore, we show that it is possible to perform frontside attacks with a quite simple sample preparation to protect the circuit. We show that single-bit attacks can be done but we need to reduce the size of the holes in order not to fault other transistors around. It is interesting to note that the Pb film with hole down to μm size can be prepared with FIB and then put in front of the components (not glued on it) to perform random single-bit attacks in the flash memory. This limits drastically the use of the FIB to perform attacks: indeed, this removable protective film can be reused to attack other components with different technology node. The 350 nm technology of the Atmega128 is a proof of concept and the aim is to perform such attacks on more advanced technology nodes.

Acknowledgements. This work was carried out in the framework of the MITIX project funded by ANR Project.

References

1. Anceau, S., Bleuet, P., Clédière, J., Maingault, L., Rainard, J.-L., Tucoulou, R.: Nanofocused x-ray beam to reprogram secure circuits. In: Fischer, W., Homma, N. (eds.) CHES 2017.

LNCS, vol. 10529, pp. 175–188. Springer, Cham (2017). https://doi.org/10.1007/978-3-319-66787-4_9

2. Skorobogatov, S.P., Anderson, R.J.: Optical fault induction attacks. In: Kaliski, B.S., Koç, Ç.K., Paar, C. (eds.) CHES 2002. LNCS, vol. 2523, pp. 2–12. Springer, Heidelberg (2003). https://doi.org/10.1007/3-540-36400-5_2

3. Habing, D.H.: The use of lasers to simulate radiation-induced transients in semiconductor devices and circuits. IEEE Trans. Nucl. Sci. **12**, 99–100 (1965)

4. Henley F.J.: Logic failure analysis of CMOS VLSI using a laser probe. In: Reliability Physics Symposium, 22nd Annual, pp. 69–75 (1984)

5. Burns D., Pronobis M., Eldering C., Hillman R.: Reliability/design assessment by internal-node timing-margin analysis using laser photocurrent injection. In: 22nd Annual Proceedings on Reliability Physics 1984, pp. 76–82. IEEE (1984)

6. Hériveaux, L., Clédière, J., Anceau, S.: Electrical modeling of the effect of photoelectric laser fault injection on bulk CMOS design. ISTFA. In: 39th International Symposium for Testing and Failure Analysis (2013)

7. Micheloni R., Crippa L., Marelli A.: Inside NAND Flash Memories, pp. 537–571. Springer, New York (2010). https://doi.org/10.1007/978-90-481-9431-5

8. Oldham, T.R., McLean, F.B.: Total ionizing dose effects in MOS oxides and devices. IEEE Trans. Nucl. Sci. **50**, 483–499 (2003)

9. Oldham T.R.: Ionizing Radiation Effect in MOS Oxides. Advances in Solid State Electronics and Technology (ASSET) Series, World Scientific, Singapore (1999)

10. Soucarros, M., Clediere, J., Dumas, C., Elbaz-Vincent, P.: Fault analysis and evaluation of a true random number generator embedded in a processor. J. Electron. Test. **29**, 367–381 (2013)

11. Ma, T.P., Dressendorfer, P.V.: Lonizing Radiation Effects in MOS Devices and Circuits. Wiley, New York (1989)

12. Shaneyfelt, M.R., Schwank, J.R., Fleetwood, D.M., Winokur, P.S., Hughes, K.L., Sexton, F.W.: Field dependence of interface trap buildup in polysilicon and metal gate MOS devices. IEEE Trans. Nucl. Sci. **37**(6), 1632 (1990)

13. Caywood, J., Prickett, B.: Radiation-induced soft errors and floating gate memories. In: Proceedings of 21st Annual Reliability Physics Symposium, pp. 167–172 (1983)

14. Snyder, E., McWhorter, P., Dellin, T., Sweetman, J.: Radiation response of floating gate EEPROM memory cells. IEEE Trans. Nucl. Sci. **36**, 2131–2139 (1989)

15. McNulty, P., Yow, S., Scheick, L., Abdel-Kader, W.: Charge removal from FGMOS floating gates. IEEE Trans. Nucl. Sci. **49**, 3016–3021 (2002)

16. Cellere, G., Paccagnella, A., Visconti, A., Bonanomi, M.: Lonizing radiation effects on floating gates. Appl. Phys. Lett. **85**, 485–487 (2004)

17. Cellere, G., Paccagnella, A., Visconti, A., Bonanomi, M., Caprara, P., Lora, S.: A model for TID effects on floating gate memory cells. IEEE Trans. Nucl. Sci. **51**, 3753–3758 (2004)

18. Cellere, G., Paccagnella, A., Lora, S., Pozza, A., Tao, G., Scarpa, A.: Charge loss after 60Co irradiation of ash arrays. IEEE Trans. Nucl. Sci. **51**, 2912–2916 (2004)

19. Wang, J., et al.: Total ionizing dose effects on flash-based field programmable gate array. IEEE Trans. Nucl. Sci. **51**, 3759–3766 (2004)

20. Wang J., Kuganesan G., Charest N., Cronquist B.: Biased-irradiation characteristics of the floating gate switch in FPGA. In Proc. IEEE Radiation Effects Data Workshop, pp. 101–104, Jul. 2006

21. Cellere, G., et al.: Total ionizing dose effects in NOR and NAND ash memories. IEEE Trans. Nucl. Sci. **54**, 1066–1070 (2007)

22. Nguyen D.N., Lee C.I., Johnston A.H.: Total ionizing dose effects on flash memories. In: IEEE Radiation Effect Data Workshop, p. 100 (1998)
23. Gerardin, S., et al.: Radiation effects in flash memories. IEEE Trans. Nucl. Sci. **60**(3), 1953–1969 (2013)
24. Bar-El H., Choukri H., Naccache D., Tunstall M., Whelan C.: The Sorcerer's Apprentice Guide to Fault Attacks. IACR Cryptology ePrint Archive (2004)

Multi-Spot Laser Fault Injection Setup: New Possibilities for Fault Injection Attacks

Brice Colombier[1]([✉]) [iD], Paul Grandamme[2], Julien Vernay[2], Émilie Chanavat[2], Lilian Bossuet[2] [iD], Lucie de Laulanié[3], and Bruno Chassagne[3]

[1] Université Grenoble Alpes, CNRS, Grenoble INP Institute of Engineering Université Grenoble Alpes, TIMA, 38000 Grenoble, France
`brice.colombier@grenoble-inp.fr`
[2] Université Lyon, UJM-Saint-Etienne, CNRS, Laboratoire Hubert Curien UMR 5516, 42023 Saint-Étienne, France
`{paul.grandamme,julien.vernay,lilian.bossuet}@univ-st-etienne.fr,`
`emilie.chanavat@etu.univ-st-etienne.fr`
[3] ALPhANOV Centre Technologique Optique et Lasers Institut d'Optique d'Aquitaine, 33400 Talence, France
`{lucie.bon,bruno.chassagne}@alphanov.com`

Abstract. Fault injection attacks rely on experimental techniques to inject one or several faults into a device during operation. Among these techniques, laser fault injection is known as a powerful one, thanks to its unmatched spatial and temporal precision. So far though, the overwhelming majority of published laser fault injection attacks were performed with only one laser spot. In this article, we present a new multi-spot laser fault injection setup. After a description of the optical system, we highlight its new capabilities against the limitations of existing single-spot laser fault injection setups. We then discuss some intrinsic limitations that this setup has, making it not equivalent to running multiple single-spot setups simultaneously on the same target. We then provide experimental evidence of faults performed with two and four spots which are unfeasible with a single-spot laser fault injection setup. This paves the way for new fault attacks on security and cryptography algorithms that exploit this new type of fault.

Keywords: Fault attacks · Laser fault injection · Multi-spot

1 Introduction

Faults induced in electronic systems by natural events, such as radiations, had been well studied for several decades by research in the safety domain. However, it was not until the article by Boneh *et al.* in 1997 that their importance with regards to security was acknowledged [7]. In that article, authors show how to take advantage of hardware faults to break cryptography algorithms. Since then,

© Springer Nature Switzerland AG 2022
V. Grosso and T. Pöppelmann (Eds.): CARDIS 2021, LNCS 13173, pp. 151–166, 2022.
https://doi.org/10.1007/978-3-030-97348-3_9

fault injection attacks have become a field of research in their own right [5]. In this setting, faults are injected *intentionally* to carry out the attack.

In order to induce a fault in an electronic system, an attacker has several tools to choose from [4]. We refer to the first category as *global* fault injection techniques: it is not possible to target a specific element of the system under attack. Among those techniques, we find voltages glitches [3] clock glitches [2] or heating [14]. The second category of fault injection techniques are *local*: they allow an attacker to target a specific feature of the device under attack. These techniques usually exploit radiations, either electromagnetic [16], optical [23] or in the form of X-rays [1].

In this article, we focus on optical fault injection. In particular, we deal with multi-spot laser fault injection setups. Compared with existing single-spot setups, multi-spot setups have the ability to inject multiple faults. This allows new types of faults to be performed, which are out of reach of single-spot setups, effectively extending the possible fault model. However, multi-spot laser fault injection setups also have some intrinsic limitations, due to the physical arrangement of optical elements. This constraint must be taken into account in the fault model. Finally, this extended fault model could be exploited to mount new attacks on security algorithms.

1.1   Contributions

This article makes the following contributions:

- We describe the different components of the optical apparatus used by the multi-spot laser fault injection setup,
- We show the possibilities of this new setup when compared to a single-spot laser fault injection setup,
- We highlight the limitations of a multi-spot laser fault injection setup, showing how mechanical and optical constraints lead to the fact that a multi-spot laser fault injection setup is not equivalent to multiple single-spot laser fault injection setups,
- We verify the capabilities of the setup by performing fault injection on characterisation codes. We experimentally perform two example faults, involving two and four laser spots respectively, that are impossible to achieve with a single-spot laser fault injection setup.

1.2   Outline

This article is organised as follows. Section 2 provides an overview of related work on laser fault injection. Section 3 describes the limitations of a single-spot laser fault injection setup with respect to the data corruption fault model. Section 4 presents the multi-spot laser fault injection, its capabilities as well as its intrinsic limitations. Section 5 provides experimental evidence for two new faults that can only be performed with a multi-spot laser fault injection setup. Finally, we conclude the article in Sect. 6.

2   Related Work

Laser fault injection was first described in the context of hardware security by Skorobogatov and Anderson [23]. However, the action of photons on silicon devices was already known before. It was exploited to simulate the effect of ion beams and evaluate the reliability of integrated circuits [8].

As detailed in [20], when a laser shot passes through silicon, electron-hole pairs are created. If an electric field exists in the region, then these charges drift in opposite directions, inducing an electric current. This in turn may have an effect on the transistors, depending on their logic state before the laser shot. The exact sensitive areas of the transistors, which depend on the data handled, are detailed in [20]. Another important point is that, for the laser beam to penetrate deep enough in silicon and reach the active areas of the transistors, its wavelength must be in the infrared region, where silicon is transparent. Thus an infrared laser whose wavelength is in the micrometer range is commonly used for this purpose [11,17,20].

While access to the die is granted in the context of wafer-level testing, this is not the case for physical attacks. Thus the device under attack must first be decapsulated [5]. This can be done by chemical and mechanical means to dissolve the package and provide physical access to the die. An optional step of mechanical polishing can also be taken to thin the die, reducing absorption of the laser beam before it reaches the active areas of the transistors.

Pioneer work in laser fault injection was carried out on integrated circuits manufactured at micrometer-scale technology nodes. In [23], the target is a 6-transistor SRAM cell that has $20\,\mu m$ on each side. This is of the same order of magnitude as the size of the laser spot used in this work, which had a diameter of $10\,\mu m$ approximately. As technology nodes shrunk, the ability to perform precise laser fault injection was questioned. However, later work performed at the 90, 45 and 28nm technology nodes showed that single bit faults are still within reach, by fine tuning the laser power [12,21]. The correlation between the number of faulty bits and the laser power was explicitly established in [12]. A complex System-on-Chip was eventually attacked with this technique [24] and single-bit faults were observed in this case as well. Therefore, even though the features at a given technology nodes are far smaller than the laser spot size, laser fault injection remains a technique of choice for precise fault injection attacks.

Although the effect of multiple faults performed by laser fault injection was modeled at the register-transfer level in [19], no experiments were performed in this work. There are very few articles in the literature that claim to perform an attack using a multi-spot laser fault injection setup [6,22,25]. The first one [22] performs the same fault on two branches of an AES hardware implementation on an FPGA protected by redundancy, so the fault cannot be corrected. However, as noted by the authors, the attack relies on a very precise placement of the target elements, making it hard to reproduce on a real target design. The second one gives an overview of two certification processes followed by secure products, and describes the various tools which are used to perform the security evaluation [6]. The multi-spot laser fault injection setup is said to be capable of defeating protected implementations, by shining one laser spot on the target while others are used to disable the hardware redundancy and cross-check verification. No further practical details were provided though. Finally, in [25], even though a two-spot setup is used, the fault models considered are described at the software level. Therefore, a lot of faults obtained cannot be explained and are referred to as "Fatal Errors": for instance, the target chip is not responding. Other valid faults are mostly classified as multiple instructions skip. Eventually, some faults are still left unexplained.

In this article, we chose instead to characterize the possibilities of a multi-spot laser fault injection setup with fault models that are fully explained and reproducible. For this reason, we focus on fault models that deal with data corruption in basic memory elements.

2.1 Fault Model Considered

We restrict our study here to works where clear evidence of data corruption by laser fault injection has been produced, either in the form of bit-set, bit-resets or bit-flips. In this regard, while previous work focused on memory elements like SRAM cells [20,21] or D-flip flops [10] a recent line of work deals with NOR Flash memory architecture instead [11,13,15,17]. The associated fault model is single or dual-bit bit-set. The photoelectric effect is still the root cause of the fault, and its effect on the NOR Flash architecture is detailed in [11,17].

In other works, the occurrence of multi-bit faults was dependent on the physical layout of memory elements: a matrix of D flip-flops in a custom ASIC design in [12] and processor registers in [24]. Conversely, when performing laser fault injection in NOR Flash memory, it is not the individual memory elements that are faulty but the read-out circuitry. Data stored in the Flash memory remains unaffected by the fault. This makes the laser positioning much easier, since the bit-lines of the read-out circuitry are shared among memory bits. More precisely, bits of index i share the jth bit-line such that $i \equiv j \mod n$ where n is the width of data read from the Flash memory, usually 32 bits. Thus, traversing the memory lengthwise allows to fault the individual bits and their index is directly related to the position of the laser spot in the memory Flash length, as depicted in Fig. 1. On our target device, which we will describe in more details in Sect. 4, the Flash memory has a length of $1500\,\mu m$, so individual bits can be targeted by making steps as large as $1500/32 \simeq 45\,\mu m$. This is feasible manually with the joystick provided with most laser fault injection stations. We insist that we obtain the same perfect repeatability observed in [11,17].

As experimentally demonstrated in [17], the results can be easily ported to a different target as long as it comes with NOR Flash memory. This is actually a very common feature in embedded systems where NOR Flash memory is used as EEPROM[1] to store the configuration of the microcontroller. For all these reasons, we chose to use this fault model to illustrate the possibilities of the multi-spot laser fault injection setup.

---

[1] Electrically-Erasable Programmable Read-Only Memory.

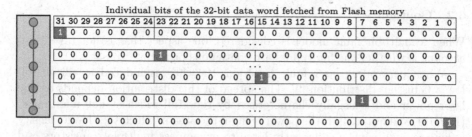

Fig. 1. Effect of the laser spot moving lengthwise over the flash memory on all-zero 32-bit data (0x00000000) fetched from the flash memory

3 Limitations of Single-Spot Laser Fault Injection Setups

Before introducing the multi-spot laser fault injection setup, it is important to identify the limitations of existing single-spot laser fault injection setups. To this end, we start by reviewing existing fault models for data corruption and identify two limitations in the way they are currently described.

3.1 Existing Fault Models for Data Corruption

We place ourselves here in the framework of fault injection attacks targeting data corruption. This choice brings us to a low level of abstraction, where we deal directly with data fetched from the Flash memory. If such data are instructions, then this could for example lead to the processor executing corrupted instructions, inducing another fault model, such as instruction skip, which is described at a higher level of abstraction. However, here, we consider the lowest possible level of abstraction to remain as general as possible.

The fault models dealing with data corruption capture quite well three aspects of the fault. The first one is the *direction* of the fault. Since we are dealing with binary data here, the different directions of the fault are: set (the data is forced to 1), reset (the data is forced to 0) or flip (the data is flipped from 0 to 1 or from 1 to 0).

The second one is the *cardinality* of the fault, that is, how many bits are affected by the fault. For instance the fault can have the following cardinalities: single-bit (one bit is faulty), multi-bit (multiple bits are faulty) or byte (eight bits are faulty).

The third one is the *repeatability* of the fault, that is, what is the probability that the fault occurs given a set of experimental fault injection parameters.

These existing characteristics of the data corruption fault models fail to capture two features of the fault, which are especially significant for the multi-spot laser fault injection setup. The first one is the contiguity of the fault and the second one is the time dimension of the fault model.

3.2 Contiguity

When a multi-bit fault model is considered, one aspect that is not taken into account is whether the faulty bits are contiguous or not.

When performing laser fault injection, the charges induced in silicon follow a Gaussian distribution [9]. The spread of this distribution depends on the laser power and is usually characterised by the "full-width at half-maximum" (FWHM) value [12,24]. If the power is high, the area in which the charge density is high enough can be sufficiently large to encompass multiple transistors and induce a fault on multiple bits [12].

Based on this observation, one could argue that non-contiguous bits could be targeted by having multiple zones in the laser beam where the power is high enough. To achieve this, an SLM (Spatial Light Modulator), a DMD (Digital Micromirror Device), or a DOE (Diffractive Optical Element) can be used, that allows to split the incoming laser beam into multiple laser beams to target the device under attack. While these solutions may seem attractive, since they require only one laser source, the optical elements involved are complex and expensive. Moreover, the laser spots which are eventually focused on the device under attack are not fully independent, either spatially or temporally. In addition, the initial power is split among the beams, is dependent on their final shape and is hard to control. Therefore, these solutions make it very challenging to perform laser fault injection on non-contiguous bits with a single laser source in a controlled manner.

Another possibility to fault non-contiguous bits is to exploit the layout of target elements. For instance, if memory elements are organised in a grid shape, then injecting a fault on one side of the grid could lead to fault non-contiguous bits of the data. However, in this case, the fault model is layout-dependent, which obviously incurs a loss of generality.

Therefore, the first limitation of a single-spot laser fault injection setup is its inability to inject non-contiguous faults in general, as summarised in Fig. 2.

31	30	29	28	27	26	25	24	23	22	21	20	19	18	17	16	15	14	13	12	11	10	9	8	7	6	5	4	3	2	1	0
0	0	0	0	0	0	0	0	0	0	0	0	0	0	0	1	1	0	0	0	0	0	0	0	0	0	0	0	0	0	0	0

(a) Contiguous multi-bit fault: feasible with a single-spot setup

31	30	29	28	27	26	25	24	23	22	21	20	19	18	17	16	15	14	13	12	11	10	9	8	7	6	5	4	3	2	1	0
0	0	0	0	0	0	0	0	0	0	0	0	0	1	0	0	0	0	1	0	0	0	0	0	0	0	0	0	0	0	0	0

(b) Non-contiguous multi-bit fault: not feasible with a single-spot setup, but feasible with a multi-spot setup

Fig. 2. Feasibility of contiguous and non-contiguous multi-bit faults with a single-spot laser fault injection setup

3.3   Time Dimension

Another aspect which is not captured by existing fault models is the ability to perform two faults at different locations, but close in time. Indeed, with a single-spot laser fault injection setup, doing so requires to turn the laser off, move the target and turn the laser on again. On some setups, the objective lenses move while the target remains fixed, but the reasoning is identical. Indeed, the mechanical system can only be operated so fast. This should be contrasted with the clock frequencies at which the usual targets are operating, ranging from tens of megahertz to a few gigahertz [24].

If the time interval between the two intended faults is too small, then it is simply not possible to perform this type of fault with a single-spot laser fault injection setup. Let Δ_t be the time interval between the two faults, v_{max} the maximum linear speed of the mechanical setup and $d_{targets}$ the distance between the two target features on the die. Then, for this type of fault to be feasible, we need the relation given in Eq. (1) to hold.

$$\Delta_t > \frac{d_{targets}}{v_{max}} \tag{1}$$

To simplify, we consider that the mechanical system always operates at full speed. In reality, the acceleration and deceleration phases are often sinusoidal to prevent abrupt changes in speed that could misalign the elements. With a realistic maximum linear speed of 20 mm/s and assuming that the features are distant of 10 % of a die that has 2 mm on each side, then the minimum time interval $\Delta_{t_{min}}$ between the two faults is given in Eq. (2).

$$\Delta_{t_{min}} = \frac{d_{targets}}{v_{max}} = \frac{2 \times \frac{10}{100}}{20} = 0.01\,s \tag{2}$$

Considering a rather slow device running at only 10 MHz, that is, with a clock period of 100 ns, then $\Delta_{t_{min}}$ is equal to 10^5 clock periods. This imposes a very hard constraint on the time interval between target instructions in a program if an attacker wants to perform multiple faults during its execution. These considerations are summarised in Fig. 3.

Another critical aspect of having to move the target between two faults is the difficulty to synchronise these two faults together. Indeed, while the laser shots are very precise and synchronised with a trigger sent to the laser sources, the mechanical system cannot be synchronised precisely, adding a non-deterministic delay before the positioning is correct and the second laser shot can be made. Therefore, synchronising the two faults requires two triggers. This adds another constraint to the attack scenario.

As we will show in the next section, a multi-spot laser fault injection setup frees us from these constraints. It allows to perform multiple faults that are arbitrarily close in time without requiring multiple triggers.

31	30	29	28	27	26	25	24	23	22	21	20	19	18	17	16	15	14	13	12	11	10	9	8	7	6	5	4	3	2	1	0
0	0	0	0	0	0	0	0	0	0	0	0	0	0	0	**1**	0	0	0	0	0	0	0	0	0	0	0	0	0	0	0	0

$$\downarrow\ t < \Delta_t$$

0	0	0	0	0	0	0	0	0	0	0	0	0	0	0	**1**	0	0	0	0	0	0	0	0	0	0	0	0	0	0	0	0

(a) Consecutive faults on the same bit: feasible with a single-spot setup

31	30	29	28	27	26	25	24	23	22	21	20	19	18	17	16	15	14	13	12	11	10	9	8	7	6	5	4	3	2	1	0
0	0	0	0	0	0	0	0	0	0	0	0	0	0	0	**1**	0	0	0	0	0	0	0	0	0	0	0	0	0	0	0	0

$$\downarrow\ t < \Delta_t$$

0	0	0	0	0	0	0	0	0	0	0	0	0	0	0	0	0	0	0	0	0	0	0	0	**1**	0	0	0	0	0	0	0

(b) Consecutive faults on different bits: not feasible with a single-spot setup, but feasible with a multi-spot setup

Fig. 3. Feasibility of consecutive faults with a single-spot laser fault injection setup on a 16-bit data word

4 Four-spot Laser Fault Injection Setup

4.1 Setup Description

Figure 4 shows the four-spot laser fault injection setup[2] used in the experiments.

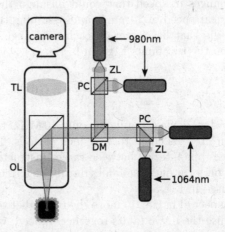

Fig. 4. Schematic of the four-spot laser fault injection setup (DM: dichroic mirror, PC: polarization beam splitter cube, OL: objective lens, TL: tube lens, ZL: zoom lenses).

Four monomode laser sources are integrated, two with a wavelength of 980 nm and two with a wavelength of 1064 nm. Monomode sources can be focused to smaller spots than multimode ones, allowing smaller features on the die to be

---

[2] QLMS by ALPhANOV: https://www.alphanov.com/actualites/alphanov-concu-un-banc-laser-quatre-spots-pour-linjection-de-fautes-sur-circuits.

targeted. The two laser sources of same wavelength are linearly polarized but perpendicular. They are combined by the polarization beam splitter cubes (PC) which are reflective for one direction of polarization and transmissive for the other one. The dichroic mirror then spectrally combines the laser beams of different wavelengths, reflecting the beam at 980 nm since it is reflective for this wavelength and tranmitting the beam at 1064 nm since it is transmissive for this wavelength. These are eventually focused on the die through the same objective lens (OL). Different objective lenses are available, namely x2.5, x20 and x50.

4.2   Capabilities

Each laser source is independent and can be moved across the focal plane in the optical field of view of the objective lens, allowing laser spots on the die to be positioned independently. Moreover, each laser source is triggered independently, allowing faults to be as close in time as required by the target application. The trigger signal may also be shared between multiple laser sources to perform simultaneous faults on distinct target elements.

4.3   Limitations

While the capabilities described above make it look like the four-spot laser fault injection setup is equivalent to four single-spot laser fault injection setups, this is in fact not the case. Indeed, since all laser beams must go through the same objective lens, the distance between the laser spots on the die is limited by the field of view of the objective. This distance between the spots depends on the magnification of the objective lens, which also affects the minimal laser spot diameter, as shown in Table 1.

Table 1. Field of view and minimal spot diameter for different objective lenses

Magnification	Field of view	Minimal spot diameter
x2.5	4 mm	25 μm
x20	500 μm	2.2 μm
x50	200 μm	1.3 μm

For instance, with a x20 magnification, the laser spots cannot be more than 500 μm apart from one another. Therefore, if the targets elements on the die are further apart than this limit, they cannot be targeted at the same time. Doing so would require to move the target, which as detailed above is unrealistic in most attack scenarios. In addition, with this magnification, the laser spot cannot have a diameter smaller than 2.2 μm. As mentioned before, this is not an obstacle when aiming for single-bit faults, since we can tune the laser power so that only a smaller area has a charge density high enough to cause a fault.

Another aspect relative to the laser spot positions is the fact that, when moved away from the center of the field of view, they gradually lose power, as shown in Fig. 5. While barely visible for x2.5 and x20 objective lenses, this effect is very strong for the x50 objective lens. Indeed, in this setting, if a laser spot is positioned on the edge of the field of view, then almost no optical power reaches the die. This turned out not to be an issue in the following experiments, since we used the x20 objective lens only.

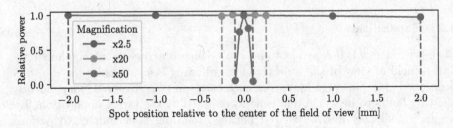

Fig. 5. Relative power of laser for different spot positions in the field of view of different objective lenses

5   Two Examples of New Possible Faults

5.1   Experimental Setup

Full Experimental Setup. The hardware target communicates with a PC over a serial interface. It generates a trigger signal, sent to a function generator, which generates the four distinct control signals for the laser sources. This is shown in Fig. 6a. A picture of the Flash memory area of the microcontroller is shown in Fig. 6b while Fig. 6c shows four laser spots over the Flash memory.

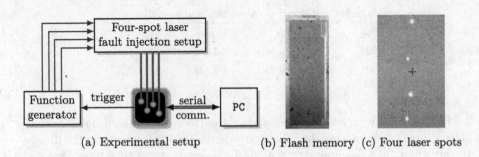

(a) Experimental setup   (b) Flash memory (c) Four laser spots

Fig. 6. Four-spot laser fault injection in flash memory

Hardware Target. The hardware target we perform the experiments on is a 32-bit microcontroller, integrated on a custom target board for the ChipWhisperer platform [18] to allow for backside access. The microcontroller embeds an ARM Cortex-M3 core and comes with 128 kB of integrated Flash memory. It runs at a frequency of 7.4 MHz, as dictated by the ChipWhisperer platform.

Laser Fault Injection Setup Parameters. After characterisation, following the method detailed in [17], we set the laser power to 1.5 W to obtain single-bit faults on data fetched from Flash memory, with one laser spot only, a 980 nm laser source and the x20 objective lens. The duration of the laser pulse was set to 135 ns, which is the clock period of the microcontroller. We observed that, on this hardware target, the laser spot must be moved in steps of 45 μm to perform a transient fault on the individual bits of data fetched from the Flash memory.

5.2   First Characterisation Code

The goal of this first code is to validate the possibility to perform simultaneous non-contiguous faults. For that, we target a MOV instruction that loads an 8-bit value in a register, as shown in Fig. 7a where 0x00 is loaded in R0. We raise a trigger signal before the target instruction and lower it after, before reading back the content of the R0 register.

This source code is compiled using the Thumb instruction set without any optimisation. Figure 7b shows how this instruction is encoded. We aim for the imm8 part of the instruction and want to load 0x55 instead of 0x00, to demonstrate the ability to perform four simultaneous non-contiguous bit-sets.

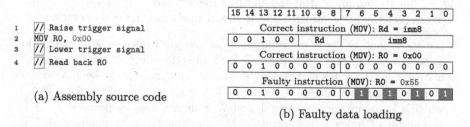

```
1   // Raise trigger signal
2   MOV R0, 0x00
3   // Lower trigger signal
4   // Read back R0
```

(a) Assembly source code

(b) Faulty data loading

Fig. 7. Characterisation code for four simultaneous faults on non-contiguous bits

Experimental Results. We started the experiment with only one laser spot, with the experimental parameters given above. We gradually increased the delay up to 1113 ns where a single-bit fault was observed. We then positioned the three other spots with a distance of 90 μm between them, since there is a step of 45μm between individual bits. We had to lower their individual power to approximately 750 mW, otherwise the chip crashed and was not responding anymore. Finally, we succeeded to store the value 0x55 in R0.

5.3   Second Characterisation Code

The second fault consists in targeting two instructions which are close, but perform the fault on different bits. To this end, we use the characterisation code shown in Fig. 8a.

```
1    #define N_ITER 1000
2    void charac_func(void) {
3        volatile uint32_t ref_count = 0;
4        uint32_t results[2] = {0, 0};
5        uint32_t XOR, ADD = 0;
6        trigger_high();
7        for (volatile uint32_t iter = 1;
8             iter <= N_ITER;
9             iter++)
10       {
11           ref_count++;
12           XOR = iter ^ iter;
13           ADD = iter + iter;
14           results[1] += (XOR == ADD);
15       }
16       results[0] = N_ITER - ref_count;
17       trigger_low();
18       // Read back results
19   }
```

(a) C source code with target instructions pointed by arrows

15	14	13	12	11	10	9	8	7	6	5	4	3	2	1	0

Correct instruction (ADD): Rdn = Rdn + imm8

| 0 | 0 | 1 | 1 | 0 | Rdn | | | imm8 | | | | | | | |

Correct instruction (ADD): Rdn = Rdn + 1

| 0 | 0 | 1 | 1 | 0 | Rdn | | | 0 | 0 | 0 | 0 | 0 | 0 | 0 | 1 |

Faulty instruction (ADD): Rdn = Rdn + 5

| 0 | 0 | 1 | 1 | 0 | Rdn | | | 0 | 0 | 0 | 0 | 0 | 1 | 0 | 1 |

(b) Faulty loop increment

15	14	13	12	11	10	9	8	7	6	5	4	3	2	1	0

Correct instruction (EORS): Rdn = Rdn ⊕ Rm

| 0 | 1 | 0 | 0 | 0 | 0 | 0 | 0 | 0 | 1 | Rm | | | Rdn | | |

Faulty instruction (ADCS): Rdn = Rdn + Rm

| 0 | 1 | 0 | 0 | 0 | 0 | 0 | 1 | 0 | 1 | Rm | | | Rdn | | |

(c) Faulty exclusive-OR operation

Fig. 8. Characterisation code for two faults close in time on different bits

Again here, we raise a trigger signal at the beginning of the execution (see Fig. 8a, line 6) and lower it at the end (see Fig. 8a, line 17)

We target the instructions associated with the following two operations:

- the increment of the loop counter. This compiles into an ADD instruction as shown in Fig. 8b. We perform a fault injection on the imm8 part of the instruction. More specifically, we modify the increment to make it N instead of 1. We assume a single-bit bit-set fault model, so N is of the form $2^i + 1$, where i is an integer between 1 and 7. This requires to perform a bit-set on the bit of index i. For example, the increment can be changed to 5 by performing a bit-set on the bit of index 2, as shown in Fig. 8b.
- an exclusive-OR in the body of the loop. This compiles into an EORS instruction as shown in Fig. 8c. We perform a fault injection on the opcode, turning the EORS instruction into an ADCS instruction, to perform an addition with carry instead. This requires to perform a bit-set on the 8th bit.

The experimental results are stored in an array of two elements. The first one stores the difference between the original and the actual number of times the body of the *for* loop has been executed. The second one stores the number of times the exclusive-OR operation has been turned into an addition. This way, we isolate the two faults and are able to observe their respective influences.

Experimental Results. We performed different experiments by changing the increment of the loop counter to different values, while faulting the EORS instruction in the body of the *for* loop at the same time. As specified above, the hardware target sends only one trigger signal. From there on, in order for the fault injection to be successful, the main challenge is to find the correct parameters for the two control signals of the two laser sources. To this end, four parameters must be tuned on the function generator:

- the initial delay for the first laser source t_{init_1}. This is the delay between raising of the trigger signal and executing the first instruction to fault.
- the initial delay for the second laser source t_{init_2}. This is the delay between raising of the trigger signal and executing the second instruction to fault.
- the period t_{lasers} which is the time it takes to execute the body of the *for* loop once. Note that both control signals have the same period.
- the duty cycle α which defines how long every laser shot should last. Since we want each laser to fault one instruction per execution of the body of the *for* loop, the duty cycle must be set accordingly.

The first step is to tune the two initial delays. This is done by increasing these delays one after the other while monitoring the result values. As soon as one fault is observed, the initial delay is found. We obtain the following values: $t_{init_1} = 2070\,ns$ and $t_{init_2} = 3825\,ns$. The second step is to tune the period of the control signals. This is done by producing only two pulses and increasing the period until two faults are observed. We obtain the following value: $t_{lasers} = 5535\,ns$. This corresponds to 41 clock periods ($5535 = 41 \times 135$) given that our target has a clock period of 135 ns. Therefore, executing the body of the *for* loop takes 41 clock cycles. Finally, we set the duty cycle to $\alpha = \frac{1}{41} \simeq 2.4\,\%$ to target one clock cycle out of the 41 of the body of the *for* loop.

These four settings are shown in Fig. 9, where the actual fault performed by each laser shot is shown as well. Using this settings, we were able to change the loop increment to 5 instead of 1 and alter the exclusive-OR operation in the body of the loop to turn it into an addition.

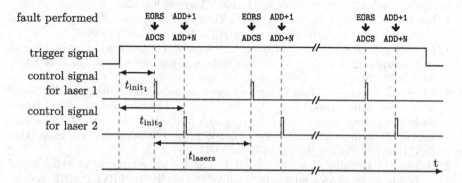

Fig. 9. Timing of signals used to control the fault injection setup

6   Conclusion

In this article, we highlighted the limitations of single-spot laser fault injection setups, which are not considered by previously considered fault models. We then presented a new four-spot laser fault injection setup that can overcome these limitations. With experiments on two characterisation codes, we showed that two new types of fault are feasible with this setup: four simultaneous non-contiguous faults and two faults very close in time on different bits. Having identified this extension of the data corruption fault model, feasible by laser fault injection, future works could focus on applying this to new attacks on security algorithms.

Acknowledgement. This work was carried out in the framework of the FUIAAP22 Project PILAS supported by Bpifrance. This work is supported by the French National Research Agency in the framework of the "Investissements d'avenir" program "ANR-15-IDEX-02" and the LabEx PERSYVAL "ANR-11-LABX-0025-01". This work is supported by INS2I in the framework of the PANTACOUR project.

The authors would also like to thank Jean-Max Dutertre from EMSE for providing them with a backside-opened device suitable for laser fault injection.

References

1. Anceau, S., Bleuet, P., Clédière, J., Maingault, L., Rainard, J., Tucoulou, R.: Nanofocused x-ray beam to reprogram secure circuits. In: Fischer, W., Homma, N. (eds.) CHES 2017. LNCS, vol. 10529, pp. 175–188. Springer, Cham (2017). https://doi.org/10.1007/978-3-319-66787-4_9
2. Anderson, R., Kuhn, M.: Low cost attacks on tamper resistant devices. In: Christianson, B., Crispo, B., Lomas, M., Roe, M. (eds.) Security Protocols 1997. LNCS, vol. 1361, pp. 125–136. Springer, Heidelberg (1998). https://doi.org/10.1007/BFb0028165
3. Aumüller, C., Bier, P., Fischer, W., Hofreiter, P., Seifert, J.-P.: Fault attacks on RSA with CRT: concrete results and practical countermeasures. In: Kaliski, B.S., Koç, K., Paar, C. (eds.) CHES 2002. LNCS, vol. 2523, pp. 260–275. Springer, Heidelberg (2003). https://doi.org/10.1007/3-540-36400-5_20
4. Bar-El, H., Choukri, H., Naccache, D., Tunstall, M., Whelan, C.: The sorcerer's apprentice guide to fault attacks. Proc. IEEE **94**(2), 370–382 (2006)
5. Barenghi, A., Breveglieri, L., Koren, I., Naccache, D.: Fault injection attacks on cryptographic devices: theory, practice, and countermeasures. Proc. IEEE **100**(11), 3056–3076 (2012)
6. Bhasin, S., Lomné, V., Tobich, K.: An industrial outlook on challenges of hardware security in digital economy. In: Ali, S.S., Danger, J., Eisenbarth, T. (eds.) International Conference on Security, Privacy, and Applied Cryptography Engineering. Lecture Notes in Computer Science, vol. 10662, pp. 1–9. Springer, Goa, India (Dec (2017). https://doi.org/10.1007/978-3-319-71501-8_1
7. Boneh, D., DeMillo, R.A., Lipton, R.J.: On the importance of checking cryptographic protocols for faults. In: Fumy, W. (ed.) EUROCRYPT 1997. LNCS, vol. 1233, pp. 37–51. Springer, Heidelberg (1997). https://doi.org/10.1007/3-540-69053-0_4

8. Buchner, S., et al.: Pulsed laser-induced SEU in integrated circuits: a practical method for hardness assurance testing. IEEE Trans. Nucl. Sci. **37**(6), 1825–1831 (1990)

9. Buchner, S., Knudson, A.R., Kang, K., Campbell, A.: Charge collection from focussed picosecond laser pulses. IEEE Trans. Nucl. Sci. **35**(6), 1517–1522 (1988)

10. Champeix, C., Borrel, N., Dutertre, J., Robisson, B., Lisart, M., Sarafianos, A.: SEU sensitivity and modeling using pico-second pulsed laser stimulation of a D flip-flop in 40 nm CMOS technology. In: International Symposium on Defect and Fault Tolerance in VLSI and Nanotechnology Systems, pp. 177–182. IEEE Computer Society, Amherst, MA, USA, October 2015

11. Colombier, B., Menu, A., Dutertre, J.M., Moëllic, P.A., Rigaud, J.B., Danger, J.L.: Laser-induced single-bit faults in flash memory: instructions corruption on a 32-bit microcontroller. In: IEEE International Symposium on Hardware Oriented Security and Trust, pp. 1–10. McLean, VA, USA, May 2019

12. Dutertre, J.M., et al.: Laser fault injection at the CMOS 28 nm technology node: an analysis of the fault model. In: Workshop on Fault Diagnosis and Tolerance in Cryptography, pp. 1–6. IEEE Computer Society, Amsterdam, The Netherlands, September 2018

13. Garb, K., Obermaier, J.: Temporary laser fault injection into flash memory: calibration, enhanced attacks, and countermeasures. In: International Symposium on On-Line Testing and Robust System Design, pp. 1–7. IEEE, Napoli, Italy, July 2020

14. Hutter, M., Schmidt, J.-M.: The temperature side channel and heating fault attacks. In: Francillon, A., Rohatgi, P. (eds.) CARDIS 2013. LNCS, vol. 8419, pp. 219–235. Springer, Cham (2014). https://doi.org/10.1007/978-3-319-08302-5_15

15. Kumar, D.S.V., Beckers, A., Balasch, J., Gierlichs, B., Verbauwhede, I.: An in-depth and black-box characterization of the effects of laser pulses on ATmega328P. In: Bilgin, B., Fischer, J.-B. (eds.) CARDIS 2018. LNCS, vol. 11389, pp. 156–170. Springer, Cham (2019). https://doi.org/10.1007/978-3-030-15462-2_11

16. Maurine, P.: Techniques for EM fault injection: equipments and experimental results. In: Bertoni, G., Gierlichs, B. (eds.) Workshop on Fault Diagnosis and Tolerance in Cryptography, pp. 3–4. IEEE Computer Society, Leuven, Belgium, September 2012

17. Menu, A., Dutertre, J.M., Rigaud, J.B., Colombier, B., Moëllic, P.A., Danger, J.L.: Single-bit laser fault model in NOR flash memories: analysis and exploitation. In: Workshop on Fault Diagnosis and Tolerance in Cryptography, pp. 41–48. IEEE, Milan, Italy, September 2020

18. O'Flynn, C., Chen, Z.D.: ChipWhisperer: an open-source platform for hardware embedded security research. In: Prouff, E. (ed.) COSADE 2014. LNCS, vol. 8622, pp. 243–260. Springer, Cham (2014). https://doi.org/10.1007/978-3-319-10175-0_17

19. Papadimitriou, A., Hély, D., Beroulle, V., Maistri, P., Leveugle, R.: A multiple fault injection methodology based on cone partitioning towards RTL modeling of laser attacks. In: Fettweis, G.P., Nebel, W. (eds.) Design, Automation & Test in Europe Conference & Exhibition, pp. 1–4. European Design and Automation Association, Dresden, Germany, March 2014

20. Roscian, C., Sarafianos, A., Dutertre, J., Tria, A.: Fault model analysis of laser-induced faults in SRAM memory cells. In: Fischer, W., Schmidt, J. (eds.) Workshop on Fault Diagnosis and Tolerance in Cryptography, pp. 89–98. IEEE Computer Society, Los Alamitos, CA, USA, August 2013

21. Selmke, B., Brummer, S., Heyszl, J., Sigl, G.: Precise laser fault injections into 90 nm and 45 nm SRAM-cells. In: Homma, N., Medwed, M. (eds.) CARDIS 2015. LNCS, vol. 9514, pp. 193–205. Springer, Cham (2016). https://doi.org/10.1007/978-3-319-31271-2_12

22. Selmke, B., Heyszl, J., Sigl, G.: Attack on a DFA protected AES by simultaneous laser fault injections. In: Workshop on Fault Diagnosis and Tolerance in Cryptography, pp. 36–46. IEEE Computer Society, Santa Barbara, CA, USA, August 2016

23. Skorobogatov, S.P., Anderson, R.J.: Optical fault induction attacks. In: Kaliski, B.S., Koç, K., Paar, C. (eds.) CHES 2002. LNCS, vol. 2523, pp. 2–12. Springer, Heidelberg (2003). https://doi.org/10.1007/3-540-36400-5_2

24. Vasselle, A., Thiebeauld, H., Maouhoub, Q., Morisset, A., Ermeneux, S.: Laser-induced fault injection on smartphone bypassing the secure boot-extended version. IEEE Trans. Comput. **69**(10), 1449–1459 (2020)

25. Werner, V., Maingault, L., Potet, M.: An end-to-end approach for multi-fault attack vulnerability assessment. In: Workshop on Fault Diagnosis and Tolerance in Cryptography, pp. 10–17. IEEE, Milan, Italy, September 2020

Public-Key Cryptography

In-depth Analysis of Side-Channel Countermeasures for CRYSTALS-Kyber Message Encoding on ARM Cortex-M4

Hauke Malte Steffen⬤, Lucie Johanna Kogelheide$^{(\boxtimes)}$⬤,
and Timo Bartkewitz⬤

Division for Hardware Evaluation, TÜV Informationstechnik GmbH,
TÜV NORD Group, Essen, Germany
{h.steffen,l.kogelheide,t.bartkewitz}@tuvit.de

Abstract. A variety of post-quantum cryptographic schemes are currently undergoing standardization in the National Institute of Standards and Technology's post-quantum cryptography standardization process. It is well known from classical cryptography that actual implementations of cryptographic schemes can be attacked by exploiting side-channels, e.g. timing behavior, power consumption or emanation in the electromagnetic field. Although several of the reference implementations currently in the third and final standardization round are – to some extent – implemented in a timing-constant fashion, resistance against other side-channels is not taken into account yet.

Implementing sufficient countermeasures, however, is challenging. We therefore exemplarily examine CRYSTALS-Kyber, which is a lattice-based key encapsulation mechanism currently considered as a candidate for standardization. By analyzing the power consumption side-channel during message encoding we develop four more and compare six different implementations with an increasing degree of countermeasures. We show that introducing randomization countermeasures is crucial as all examined implementations aiming at reducing the leakage by minimizing the Hamming distance of the processed intermediate values only are vulnerable against single-trace attacks when implemented on an ARM Cortex-M4.

Keywords: Post-quantum cryptography · NIST competition · Message encoding · CRYSTALS-Kyber · Side-channel analysis

1 Introduction

Quantum computers have been a merely theoretical construction for many decades. However, during the last years significant progress has been made and increasingly large quantum computers have been built [14,15]. A cryptographically relevant quantum computer threatens today's most wide-spread asymmetric cryptographic schemes, namely Rivest-Shamir-Adleman (RSA) and Elliptic Curve Cryptography (ECC). These schemes rely on either the integer

© Springer Nature Switzerland AG 2022
V. Grosso and T. Pöppelmann (Eds.): CARDIS 2021, LNCS 13173, pp. 169–188, 2022.
https://doi.org/10.1007/978-3-030-97348-3_10

factorization problem or the discrete logarithm problem which a quantum computer can efficiently solve using Shor's algorithm [30]. For industries with products in the field for a long time (e.g. automotive) or data that might be valuable even decades from now (e.g. health data) the transition to quantum resistant cryptographic schemes therefore has to be initiated as soon as possible [19, 20, 29].

The field of Post-Quantum Cryptography (PQC) is based on mathematical problems that are hard to solve for both classical and quantum computers, thereby offering suitable replacement candidates for RSA and ECC. The most prominent standardization effort for PQC is conducted by the National Institute of Standards and Technology (NIST) in their PQC standardization process [23]. The Key Encapsulation Mechanism (KEM) CRYSTALS-Kyber is a third round candidate of the NIST PQC standardization process [22].

Side-channel attacks exploit channels which unintentionally carry data dependent information, e.g. power consumption or timing behavior [8, 12, 16, 17]. By monitoring these channels during execution of a security critical function an attacker might extract secret data. Side-channel attacks thereby do not focus on attacking the algorithm itself but on a potentially insecure implementation. Side-channel attacks also apply to PQC schemes and resistance against side-channel attacks is an evaluation criteria in the third and final round of the NIST PQC standardization process [18].

Simple Power Analysis (SPA) aims at extracting a secret by measuring only one execution of the security relevant function while Differential Power Analysis (DPA) requires an attacker to record a certain number of traces in order to perform an attack. In general, DPA is considered the more powerful attack technique. However, if an SPA does succeed the results are devastating as only a single trace is enough to attack the implementation. Side-channel resistance of the remaining candidates in the NIST PQC standardization process has for example been investigated in [26, 31, 32], with CRYSTALS-Kyber being one of the examined – and vulnerable – candidates. The second round candidate NewHope proved vulnerable against SPA, with the authors suggesting that a nearly identical attack path could also be applied to CRYSTALS-Kyber [1].

To counter SPA and DPA, masked implementations of CRYSTALS-Kyber have been proposed [4, 7, 10]. Masking reduces side-channel leakage by processing data in shares. An attacker can only recompute the original value if she can correctly recover all involved shares. However, in case of a high SPA success rate, conducting an SPA on the involved shares becomes a feasible attack path. Therefore, on top of examining sufficiency of masking schemes themselves [5] it might be necessary to implement additional countermeasures.

This work aims at comparing countermeasures which are applicable on top of a masking approach. CRYSTALS-Kyber hereby is merely chosen as an exemplary PQC scheme, as both publications on side-channel vulnerabilities as well as first suggestions on how to mitigate the threat do exist.

The following chapters are organized as follows: Sect. 2 briefly introduces CRYSTALS-Kyber. Section 3 outlines several attack paths motivating the selection of the message encoding step for the attacks conducted in this work. Section 4 presents the six different implementations which have been examined introducing the subsequently added countermeasures for each of the implementations.

Following the attack path lined out for NewHope in [1], we first evaluate the reference implementation submitted to the third round of the NIST PQC standardization process [2]. The second implementation is based on an approach to reduce the Hamming distance of the leaking values as suggested by Amiet et al. [1]. For the third implementation, we introduce the use of a dummy polynomial aiming at hiding the processing of the involved coefficients. The fourth implementation on top of that balances the look-ups of the involved polynomials. For the fifth implementation, we use randomness to invert the order in which the polynomials are processed. The sixth implementation then fully randomizes the order in which the involved data is processed.

Section 5 contains the experimental results for each of the implementations with all but the last implementation failing to withstand the conducted attacks. Summing up the experimental results, Sect. 6 comes to the conclusion that relatively simple countermeasures are not sufficient to prevent an SPA. Therefore, more sophisticated countermeasures have to be developed to secure PQC not only against SPA but also against the more powerful DPA. We show that randomization countermeasures can reduce the SPA success rate to random guessing, making these countermeasures a potentially beneficial extension even for masked implementations.

2   Background on CRYSTALS-Kyber

Kyber is an IND-CCA2-secure KEM originally published in [6]. To obtain CCA-security, Kyber applies a variant of the Fujisaki-Okamoto (FO) transform [11] to the CPA-secure Public Key Encryption (PKE) scheme Kyber.CPAPKE. In general, KEMs are used by the communicating parties to generate shared keys for symmetric encryption allowing them to establish a secure communication channel. PKE is used to transmit encrypted data between the participants while processing the KEM.

Kyber is parametrized by a set of chosen integers. The security strength of the exchanged symmetric keys is basically determined by n which also defines the ring together with prime number q within this lattice-based scheme.

Algorithm 1 describes the encapsulation of the Kyber KEM scheme. For each execution of the encapsulation, the message m is randomly chosen and hashed by the initiator. Afterwards, m and the hash of the public key pk are hashed into the preliminary key $\bar{K}$ and into the random coins r. Thereafter, pk, m, and r are given to the encryption function of the PKE scheme (line 4, Algorithm 1), which is described in Algorithm 2. The shared key K is derived from the preliminary key $\bar{K}$, and the ciphertext c is sent to the responder. The symmetric primitives $H(\cdot)$, $G(\cdot)$, and $KDF(\cdot)$ are preferably instantiated by SHA3-256, SHA3-512, and SHAKE-256, respectively [3, 21].

The random message m is the only unknown session related variable and has to remain secret while it is incorporated as fresh entropy during the encapsula-

Algorithm 1. KYBER.CCAKEM.Enc(pk): encapsulation [3]

Input: Public key pk
Output: Ciphertext c
Output: Shared key K
1: $m \leftarrow \{0,1\}^{256}$
2: $m \leftarrow \mathrm{H}(m)$
3: $(\bar{K}, r) := \mathrm{G}(m \| \mathrm{H}(pk))$
4: $c := \mathrm{KYBER.CPAPKE.Enc}(pk, m, r)$
5: $K := \mathrm{KDF}(\bar{K} \| \mathrm{H}(c))$
return (c, K)

tion. With knowledge about m, it is possible to reconstruct the encapsulation, and hence compute the shared key K.

During the encryption (line 5, Algorithm 2), m is given to the Decode($\cdot$) function. This processing, also denoted as *message encoding*, only bases on the message itself, potentially leaking information about the message m. Please note that the Decode($\cdot$) function is further discussed in Sect. 4.1 which describes the implementation of the message encoding step for the reference implementation [2].

Algorithm 2. KYBER.CPAPKE.Enc(pk, m, r): encryption [3]

Input: Public key pk
Input: Message m
Input: Random coins r
Output: Ciphertext c
1: $\hat{t} := \mathrm{Decode}(pk)$
2: $\hat{A} := \mathrm{Sample}(pk)$
3: $(\hat{r}, e_1, e_2) := \mathrm{Sample}(r)$
4: $u := \mathrm{NTT}^{-1}(\hat{A}^T \circ \hat{r}) + e_1$
5: $v := \mathrm{NTT}^{-1}(\hat{t}^T \circ \hat{r}) + e_2 + \mathrm{Decompress}(\mathrm{Decode}(m))$
6: $c_1 := \mathrm{Encode}(\mathrm{Compress}(u))$
7: $c_2 := \mathrm{Encode}(\mathrm{Compress}(v))$
return $c = (c_1 \| c_2)$

As a result of the applied FO transform, the decrypted message m' is re-encrypted and compared with the received ciphertext c during the decapsulation, which is described in line 6 of Algorithm 3. Therefore, the message encoding can be targeted at both participating sides of the KEM.

During the CPAPKE decryption, the Decode($\cdot$) function, which is not explicitly described in this section, processes not only the message m but also the secret key sk (see [3]).

Algorithm 3. KYBER.CCAKEM.Dec(sk, c): decapsulation [3]

Input: Secret key sk
Input: Ciphertext c
Output: Shared key K

1: $pk := sk + 12 \cdot k \cdot \frac{n}{8}$
2: $h := sk + 24 \cdot k \cdot \frac{n}{8} + 32$
3: $z := sk + 24 \cdot k \cdot \frac{n}{8} + 64$
4: $m' := $ KYBER.CPAPKE.Dec(sk, c)
5: $(\bar{K}', r') := $ G($m'\|h$)
6: $c' := $ KYBER.CPAPKE.Enc(pk, m', r')
7: **if** $c = c'$ **then**
8:     $K := $ KDF($\bar{K}'\|$H(c))
9: **else**
10:     $K := $ KDF($z\|$H(c))
11: **end if**
return K

3 Side-channel Attack Paths Against CRYSTALS-Kyber

This section aims at categorizing several potential side-channel attack paths allowing for a reconstruction of the shared key. To generate a shared key basically only two non-public variables are involved: the session-bound random message m and a participant's secret key. The random message m is generated during the key encapsulation (Algorithm 1) and transformed into the ciphertext c utilizing the public key. Consequently, if an attacker manages to obtain m, she can easily compute the shared key.

The secret key, by contrast, is utilized within the key decapsulation to recover m or rather m' from c (Algorithm 3). Hence, if an attacker manages to obtain the secret key, she can compute the shared key as well.

Potentially, side-channels might leak sufficient information on these two variables and also, trivially, side-channels might leak sufficient information on the shared key itself during its generation.

Different attack categories can be considered: attack category 1 aims at recovering the message m by attacking the key encapsulation. Attack categories 2 and 3 concentrate on the secret key, and the shared key, respectively. Naturally, attacks on the message (cat. 1) and the shared key (cat. 3) only allow for intercepting a single session and need to be continuously repeated, whereas attacks on the secret key (cat. 2) would allow for intercepting all sessions established with the same secret key. This work focuses on attacks on the message with the attack paths A to E explained in the following paragraph. Category 2 and 3 are not discussed any further throughout this work but, nevertheless, require as much attention as category 1 in order to create a properly secured implementation.

- **Attack Path 1.A** The random message m is freshly generated for each encapsulation call (Algorithm 1, line 1), and thus can be observed only once. Therefore, an SPA with horizontal attacks is feasible. Especially the fetch from a random number source as well as the move from such a source to a dedicated Random-Access Memory (RAM) variable is in the focus of this attack path.

- **Attack Path 1.B** The random message m is fed into the hash function $H(\cdot)$ (Algorithm 1, line 2). Here, m is most likely moved from its dedicated RAM variable to an interface RAM variable of the hash function. The same holds true for the output $H(m)$ that simply replaces m in the remainder of the encapsulation. Additionally, the message treatment, e.g. the message scheduling for SHA3-256, could be exploited. Again, an SPA with horizontal attacks is the method of choice.
- **Attack Path 1.C** This attack path (Algorithm 1, line 3) is similar to path B. With the input of $G(\cdot)$, an attacker might obtain m, whereas the 256 most significant bits of the output $\bar{K}$ of $G(m||H(pk))$ could directly be used to compute the shared key K since the ciphertext c is public. Note that r is not of interest since it can be computed if m is recovered or not required if $\bar{K}$ is recovered. Though, r alone cannot be used as an attack vector.
- **Attack Path 1.D** This attack path is related to the message encoding (Algorithm 1, line 4) utilized within the CPAPKE encryption (Algorithm 2, line 5). We refer to the following section where we elaborate on that process.
- **Attack Path 1.E** This attack path (Algorithm 1, line 5) is likewise similar to path B and C. With the input of $KDF(\cdot)$, an attacker might obtain $\bar{K}$, whereas the output is the shared key K.

Summarizing, each step of the key encapsulation is suitable to recover the shared key if side-channels leak sufficient information.

We decided to concentrate on attack path 1.D for several reasons: on the one hand there are already published works dealing with securing the message encoding [1] and on the other hand the message m is processed in bitwise manner during the message encoding. In contrast, the other attacks paths only allow for observing the target variables while they are moved. It is widely believed in side-channel attacks that the smaller the portion of the target variable the better the exploitability in case side-channels leak sufficient information on that portion. Therefore, attacks on the message encoding are presumably more hazardous.

In order to secure an implementation against side-channel attacks, a variety of countermeasures can be considered. Masked implementations have been proposed, e.g. by Reparaz et al. [28], and Oder et al. [25], with masked encoding functions processing two shares individually. However, in case of a high SPA success rate both shares might be determined by an attacker who can thereby reconstruct the original message. Reparaz et al. [27] also presented an additively homomorphic Ring-Learning-With-Errors masking that does not require a masked encoder and uses an unprotected encoding function. Consequently, in case single-trace SPA attacks apply flawlessly (which we demonstrate in Sect. 5.2), masking in shape of sharing is not effective at all.

4   Message Encoding With Countermeasures

Focusing on the message encoding step (see Sect. 3, attack path 1.D), we implement and attack different countermeasures. The third up to the sixth implementation candidates have been designed and developed through the course of this work. Please note that we do not claim full effectiveness. Our selection of countermeasures shall rather demonstrate how to proceed to minimize side-channel leakage only by modifying the message encoding algorithm without introducing complex masking or hiding schemes. The following approaches are explained in detail in Sect. 4.1 to Sect. 4.6:

1. The message encoding step as implemented in the reference implementation [2] without additional countermeasures against SPA.
2. An implementation of the message encoding according to [1], which aims at reducing the Hamming distance of the leaking values based on a multiplicative approach.
3. A dummy polynomial is included aiming at hiding the processing of the involved coefficients.
4. The preceding approach is improved by balancing the look-ups of the polynomials, leading to a Hamming distance independent of the processed bits.
5. The order of the processed polynomials is randomly inverted for each execution of the encoding, changing the signature of the processed bit in the power side-channel.
6. Additionally, the processed bytes and bits are randomly shuffled for each execution of the encoding.

For all presented implementations, an SPA is carried out aiming at recovering the value of the processed bits by examining a single trace. Within the implementations, the message m, and the prime q are denoted as msg, and KYBER_Q, respectively.

4.1   Message Encoding According to Reference Implementation

Listing 1 presents the reference implementation [2] of the message encoding function as submitted to the third round of the NIST PQC standardization process. It takes a 32-byte message msg as an input and converts it to a polynomial r of degree 256. To this end, the function iterates in a bitwise manner over msg and sets a coefficient of r either to 0 or to the constant (KYBER_Q+1)/2, depending on whether the bit of msg is 0 or 1.

To set the coefficients of the polynomial to the correct value in line 6 of Listing 1, a mask is calculated which is either 0×0000 or 0xFFFF, depending directly on a single bit of msg.

```
1    void poly_frommsg(poly *r, const uint8_t msg[
        KYBER_INDCPA_MSGBYTES]) {
2        unsigned int i,j;
3        int16_t mask;
```

```
4     for(i=0;i<KYBER_N/8;i++) {
5         for(j=0;j<8;j++) {
6             mask = -(int16_t)((msg[i] >> j) & 1);
7             r->coeffs[8*i+j] = mask & ((KYBER_Q+1)/2);
8         }
9     }
10  }
```

Listing 1. CRYSTALS-Kyber – Message Encoding [2]

The two values of the mask have the maximum possible Hamming distance of 16, i.e. all bit positions differ. We assume that this leads to a distinguishable difference in the amount of power consumption when processing the mask, and thus allows for extracting information on the actual secret message as for each bit of msg the value of the mask is evaluated again.

4.2   Message Encoding With Multiplication

Amiet et al. [1] presented an approach to make the attack more difficult by reducing the Hamming distance between the two possible values of the mask. To encode a message, the coefficients of the polynomial are calculated by multiplying the message bit and (KYBER_Q+1)/2. Hence, line 6 and 7 in Listing 1 are replaced by Listing 2. The two possible values for the mask are 0 and 1 reducing the maximum possible Hamming distance from 16 to one.

```
6     mask = ((msg[i] >> j) & 1);
7     r->coeffs[8*i+j] = mask*((KYBER_Q+1)/2);
```

Listing 2. CRYSTALS-Kyber – Message Encoding with multiplication [1]

Decreasing the Hamming distance should result in reduction of the observed leakage, however, an SPA, as described in [1], might still be applicable.

4.3   Message Encoding Using Data Independent Polynomial Generation

To counteract vulnerabilities still present in the previous implementation, we first remove the mask evaluation as it may leak information about the message bit during its storing and loading instructions. Furthermore, information leakage is reduced by generating polynomials in a data independent fashion: additionally to the already provided r, we define a second polynomial r_d which is discarded after the message encoding. We first initialize all coefficients of r and r_d to the constant (KYBER_Q+1)/2. Afterwards, each time a single bit of msg is processed, one coefficient of one of the polynomials is set to zero. If the extracted message bit is zero, the coefficient of the real polynomial r is altered, otherwise the coefficient of the dummy polynomial r_d is altered. The reference implementation is modified by replacing all lines from line 3 onwards in Listing 1 by Listing 3.

```
3     poly r_d;
4     poly *p_r[2] = {r, &r_d};
5     for(i=0;i<KYBER_N;i++) {
6         r->coeffs[i] = (KYBER_Q+1)/2;
7         r_d.coeffs[i] = (KYBER_Q+1)/2;
8     }
9     for(i=0;i<KYBER_N/8;i++) {
10        for(j=0;j<8;j++) {
11            p_r[(msg[i] << (7-j)) >> 7]->coeffs[8*i+j] = 0;
12        }
13    }
```

Listing 3. CRYSTALS-Kyber – Message Encoding using data independent polynomial generation

In contrast to the previous implementations, information leakage should be reduced significantly as the very same operation of setting a polynomial to zero is performed each time independently of the processed value. Remaining leakage could still be caused by determining which polynomial should be used, based on the currently evaluated bit of msg.

4.4 Message Encoding Using Data Independent Polynomial Generation With Balanced Byte Look-Up

We extend the previously introduced approach by balancing the look-ups of the polynomials by covering the extracted message bits with alternating masks. To do so, we initialize a pointer array p_r of size 256 alternately containing both polynomials. Furthermore, we define two mask values with identical Hamming weight for later balancing of the look-ups. Line 4 of Listing 3 is replaced by Listing 4. We remark that the code presented in Listing 4 can be placed outside the message encoding function.

```
4     poly *p_r[256];
5     uint32_t xorMasks[2] = {0xaaaaaaaa, 0x55555555};
6     for(i=0;i<256;i+=2) {
7         p_r[i] = r;
8         p_r[i+1] = &r_d;
9     }
```

Listing 4. CRYSTALS-Kyber – Message Encoding using data independent polynomial generation with balanced byte look-up – Initialization

While processing the bits of msg the index of p_r is calculated as an 8 bit value with Hamming distance independent of the processed bits for each message byte. This corresponds to replacing line 11 in Listing 3 with Listing 5.

```
11    p_r[((xorMasks[j & 1] ^ msg[i]) >> j) & 0xff]->
      coeffs[8*i+j] = 0;
```

Listing 5. CRYSTALS-Kyber – Message Encoding using data independent polynomial generation with balanced byte look-up – Balanced look-up

As a result, potential information leakage depending on the polynomial look-ups should be reduced. Remaining leakage might be caused by the data dependency of the addressed polynomial as well as the evaluated message bit.

4.5   Message Encoding Using Polynomial Randomization

In this section, we present an additional measure to decrease leakage of the polynomial processing. The strategy is to shift the pointer array p_r and the balancing array xorMask by 0 or 1, depending on the most significant bit of the first message byte (MSB). As the message msg is randomly chosen, evaluating the MSB serves as a source of randomness without introducing an additional fetch from a random number generator. To first extend the used arrays, we replace line 4 of Listing 4 by Listing 6.

```
4     poly *p_r[256+1];
5     uint32_t xorMasks[3] = {0xaaaaaaaa,0x55555555,0xaaaaaaaa};
```

Listing 6. CRYSTALS-Kyber – Message Encoding using polynomial randomization – Initialization

In order to randomly invert the polynomial look-ups, the arrays are shifted to the left by adding Listing 7 after line 8 of Listing 3.

```
9      uint32_t b_inv = ((0xaaaa00aa ^ msg[0]) >> 7) & 0xff;
10     for(i=0; i<255;i++) {
11         *(p_r+i) = *(p_r+i+b_inv);
12     }
13     for(i=0; i<2;i++) {
14         *(xorMasks+i) = *(xorMasks+i+b_inv);
15     }.
```

Listing 7. CRYSTALS-Kyber – Message Encoding using polynomial randomization – Inversion by shifting

Compared to the preceding implementation, information leakage should further decrease. But again, processing the polynomials can still cause small differences in the amount of power consumption. We furthermore remark that this implementation introduces a new data dependency based on the most significant bit of the MSB.

4.6   Message Encoding Using Byte and Bit Level Random Ordering

We extend the previous approach by shuffling the order in which the bytes and their bits are processed. Again, the MSB is used as a source of randomness. We define two masking variables i_m, and j_m to shuffle the bytes and their bits. Therefore, line 9 of Listing 7 is replaced by Listing 8.

```
9    uint32_t rand = (0xaaaa00aa ^ msg[0]);
10   uint8_t i_m = rand & 0x1f;
11   uint8_t j_m = (rand >> 5) & 0xff;
12   uint32_t b_inv = (rand >> 7) & 0xff;
```

Listing 8. CRYSTALS-Kyber – Byte and bit level random ordering – Initialization

The shuffling variables i_m, and j_m are added to the loop counters i, and j, respectively while iterating through the bytes and bits of msg by an exclusive-or. Therefore, the order of the bytes is shuffled and the bits of each byte are processed in the same but randomized order. For this, we replace line 9 onwards in Listing 3 by Listing 9.

```
9    uint8_t i_r, j_r;
10   for(i=0;i<KYBER_N/8;i++){
11       i_r = i ^ i_m;
12       for(j=0;j<8;j++){
13           j_r = j ^ j_m;
14           p_r[((xorMasks[(j_r & 1)] ^ msg[i_r]) >> j_r) & 0
     xff]->coeffs[8*i_r+j_r] = 0;
15       }
16   }
```

Listing 9. CRYSTALS-Kyber – Byte and bit level random ordering – Shuffled look-ups

Introducing this level of randomization should significantly reduce the observed leakage. However, the masking variables in Listing 8 themselves become a target of side-channel analysis, potentially requiring additional protection.

5   Experimental Results

This section presents our practical results of the side-channel analysis of Kyber's message encoding, targeting all implementations listed in Sect. 4.1 to Sect. 4.6.

5.1   Measurement Setup

Figure 1 shows the setup targeting the Cortex-M4 processor (@120 MHz) on the FRDM-K22F development board (rev. D) programmed with the MCUXpresso software development kit (11.2.1) to prepare the board for our measurements [24]. Hardware modifications are necessary – all capacitors between the measuring point and the power pins of the Cortex-M4 have been removed – in order not to degrade the power consumption signal. Power traces are recorded utilizing a populated resistor with a Teledyne LeCroy AP033 active differential probe attached to a Teledyne LeCroy HDO9404M. The horizontal resolution of the oscilloscope is set to 0.1 ns, i.e. 10 GS/s sampling rate. A dedicated trigger signal – a signal pulse framing the encoding – is utilized via a general purpose pin. Thus, only minimal alignment (via cross-correlation) is needed.

(a) Teledyne LeCroy oscilloscope   (b) FRDM-K22F development board

Fig. 1. Measurement setup

5.2 Message Encoding According to Reference Implementation

First, the reference implementation according to [2] is targeted, involving processing of a 16 bit mask for the encoding of each bit of the message. An exemplary power trace as well as the analysis results are depicted in Fig. 2.

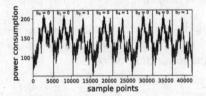
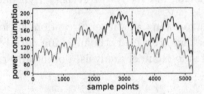

(a) Power consumption while processing one byte

(b) Mean traces for processing 0 (black) and 1 (gray) with the maximum distance marked by the red line

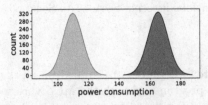
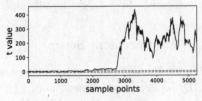

(c) Distribution of power consumption

(d) t-test result

Fig. 2. Side-channel analysis of message encoding according to the reference implementation [2]

Figure 2a depicts the power consumption while processing one byte. Whether a 0 or a 1 is processed results in a clearly distinguishable pattern in the power trace allowing for extraction of the message msg by observation of a single trace with the bare eye. Focusing on processing one bit only, Figure 2b shows the mean traces for the two classes 0 and 1 for a total of 8,000 involved traces. The red vertical line marks the sample for which the difference between the mean traces reaches its maximum. For this sample, all traces are analyzed, resulting in Figure 2c which depicts the means' distributions which we assume to be Gaussian for the two classes 0 and 1. Whereas the means are significantly distinguishable, the variances are very close. Performing a t-test over the whole sample range, with considered noise thresholds according to [9], Figure 2d is obtained. On top of the t-test a single-trace SPA is performed which results in a success rate[1] of 100.0%. The available traces were halved for profiling as well as matching and Points Of Interest (POI) were selected by Sum Of Squared pairwise Tdifferences (SOST) [13].

5.3   Message Encoding with Multiplication

In order to reduce the Hamming distance of the processed internal values, the calculation of the 16 bit mask is replaced by a multiplication operation according to the approach suggested in [1] and outlined in Sect. 4.2. Each bit of the message msg is multiplied with the constant (KYBER_Q+1)/2. Thus, the evaluated mask is either equal to 0 or 1.

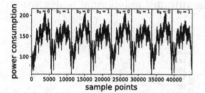

(a) Power consumption while processing one byte

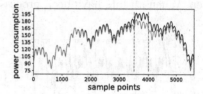

(b) Mean traces for processing 0 (black) and 1 (gray) with the maximum distance located within the red lines

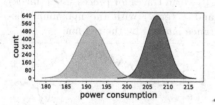

(c) Distribution of power consumption

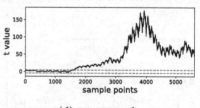

(d) t-test result

Fig. 3. Side-channel analysis of message encoding with multiplicative mask

Figure 3a illustrates a single trace of the power consumption. Though the shape of the trace changed in comparison to Fig. 2a, significant differences can still be observed for the two classes. Thus, a single-trace attack by observation with the bare eye is still possible. The mean traces for processing 0 and 1 are

---

[1] Proportion of correctly classified traces, i.e. $r_s = \frac{\text{Correctly classified traces}}{\text{Number of traces}}$.

shown in Fig. 2b. As for the reference implementation, a total of 8,000 traces is analyzed. Figure 2c depicts the power distribution for the two classes 0 and 1 as extracted from the sample with the highest power consumption within the timeframe marked by the red vertical lines in Fig. 2b. Whilst the two distributions move closer together and the variances are more distinguishable compared to the reference implementation, the overlap is still negligible. This is reflected in the t-test result, depicted in Fig. 2d. The SPA success rate is still 100.0%, despite reduction of Hamming distance by the multiplication approach. Presumably due to the high horizontal oscilloscope resolution, the leakage is fully exploitable leading to a flawless single-trace SPA.

5.4 Message Encoding Using Data Independent Polynomial Generation

As leakage of the mask could be exploited even for a Hamming distance of only one, an alternative approach is examined which does not require a mask (compare Sect. 4.3). Instead, a dummy polynomial is used, and for each bitwise encoding step, a coefficient of either the polynomial r or its dummy counterpart r_d is set to zero. Pointers to the real and the dummy polynomial are stored in a pointer array. Therefore, the same operation is performed for each encoding step. When all bits have been processed, the dummy polynomial is discarded.

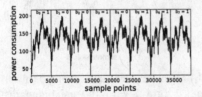

(a) Power consumption while processing one byte

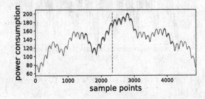

(b) Mean traces for processing 0 (black) and 1 (gray) with the maximum distance marked by the red line

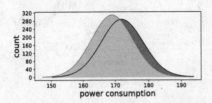

(c) Distribution of power consumption

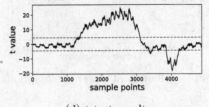

(d) t-test result

Fig. 4. Side-channel analysis of message encoding with data independent polynomial generation

In contrast to the previous measurements, it is indistinguishable to the bare eye whether a 0 or 1 is processed (compare Fig. 4a). Figure 4b depicts the mean traces for processing 0 and 1 with small differences in the mean power consumption still identifiable for the two classes. Figure 4c depicts the distributions of the measured power values for one selected sample for the two classes. The distributions lie closer together and the overlap is strongly increased, however, the variance of the two classes significantly differs. Figure 4d shows the corresponding t-test result which still indicates information leakage. When an SPA is conducted, the success rate noticeably drops to 68.6% compared to the attacks on the previous implementations.

5.5 Message Encoding Using Data Independent Polynomial Generation with Balanced Byte Look-Up

Aiming at further reducing the remaining leakage, the look-ups of the polynomials are balanced, meaning that the selection of whether an operation shall be performed on the real or the dummy polynomial is done with the help of two masking values with identical Hamming weight (compare Sect. 4.4).

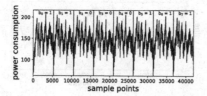

(a) Power consumption while processing one byte

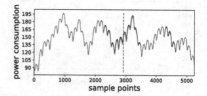

(b) Mean traces for processing 0 (black) and 1 (gray) with the maximum distance marked by the red line

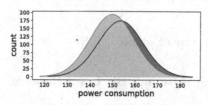

(c) Distribution of power consumption

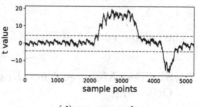

(d) t-test result

Fig. 5. Side-channel analysis of message encoding with data independent polynomial generation with balanced byte look-up

The power trace depicted in Fig. 5a cannot be interpreted by the bare eye only. Comparing the average traces for both classes, subtle differences are still visible (compare Fig. 5b). This results in the two distributions depicted in Fig. 5c not fully overlapping and also differing in their variance. The t-test as presented in Fig. 5d accordingly yields results above the noise threshold. The conducted SPA results in a success rate of 67.9%, nearly as high as the unbalanced implementation shown in the previous section.

5.6   Message Encoding Using Polynomial Randomization

In order to introduce greater variance, the ordering of real and dummy polynomials within the pointer array is randomized for each function call (compare Sect. 4.5). Thereby, leakage caused by accessing the same index values over and over again shall be reduced. However, the distributions in Fig. 6c as well as the t-test results in Fig. 6d indicate that the leakage is only slightly reduced.

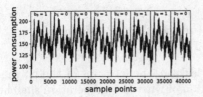

(a) Power consumption while processing one byte

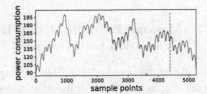

(b) Mean traces for processing 0 (black) and 1 (gray) with the maximum distance marked by the red line

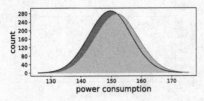

(c) Distribution of power consumption

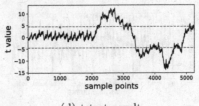

(d) t-test result

Fig. 6. Side-channel analysis of message encoding with polynomial randomization

The conducted SPA still yields a success rate of 64.0%.

5.7   Shuffled Message Encoding Using Byte and Bit Level Random Ordering

The last investigated implementation shuffles the processed message bytes as well as the order in which the bits of each byte are processed (compare Sect. 4.6).

In contrast to the previous tests the number of analyzed traces is increased from 8,000 traces to 80,000 traces. To this end, Fig. 7d shows the t-test result for ten times more traces compared to the previous implementations. Analyzing this larger trace set, the t-test yields results slightly above the noise threshold for a very limited range of samples. When only 8,000 traces are included, the t-test values remain below the noise barrier. The distributions for the two classes as shown in Fig. 7c are indistinguishable from each other.

Performing an SPA, the success rate reduces to 50.1% which corresponds to random guessing.

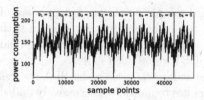

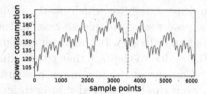

(a) Power consumption while processing one byte

(b) Mean traces for processing 0 (black) and 1 (gray) with the maximum distance marked by the red line

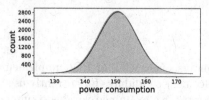

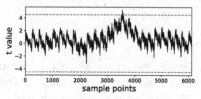

(c) Distribution of power consumption

(d) t-test result

Fig. 7. Side-channel analysis of message encoding with byte and bit level random ordering

5.8 Comparison of Countermeasures

Table 1 summarizes our results of Sect. 5.2 to Sect. 5.7 for the applied t-tests and SPA as well as the required number of clock cycles and the overhead with respect to the reference implementation. Please recall that the implementation with random byte and bit level ordering has been analyzed with a higher number of involved traces compared to all other implementations (80,000 compared to 8,000 traces).

Table 1. Comparison of implementations

	t-test	SPA		Clock cycles (overhead)
Implementation	t_{max}	# POI	Success rate	
Reference implementation[2]	437	1,535	100.0%	11,732
Multiplication[1]	177	796	100.0%	12,500 (1.09×)
Data independent polynomial gen.	24.8	525	68.6%	16,066 (1.42×)
Balanced data independent polynomial gen.	19.6	700	67.9%	19,425 (1.66×)
Polynomial randomization	13.8	1,231	64.0%	26,893 (2.29×)
Byte and bit level random ordering	5.2	1,755	50.1%	29,211 (2.49×)

POIs are selected by means of SOST. The selection of POIs for the SPA is conducted in such a way that only samples are included for which the SOST value reaches at least 20% of the maximum SOST value. A high number of selected POIs therefore corresponds to either an implementation which can be easily attacked (please refer to the row regarding the reference implementation) or an implementation for which nearly all measured sample points are independent of the processed data (please refer to the row regarding the implementation with random ordering). In the latter case many sample points lie above the threshold of 20% due to the fact that the maximum SOST value itself is low.

Comparing the maximum absolute t-test values t_{max} with the SPA success rates, it can be observed that both indicators are reduced for successively added countermeasures. For the last implementation, the t-test values only slightly exceed the noise barrier and the SPA success rate reaches 50.1% which corresponds to random guessing.

6   Conclusion

Achieving resistance against side-channel analysis is crucial for PQC implementations to make PQC schemes suitable replacement candidates for currently used asymmetric cryptographic schemes. In this work, we examined various countermeasures for the CRYSTALS-Kyber message encoding step on an ARM Cortex-M4. For a total of six different implementations, we performed a side-channel analysis targeting the power domain. The amount of leakage is classified using a t-test, then, an SPA is conducted targeting the processing of individual bits.

Masking only is a suitable countermeasure if the success rate for an SPA is lower than 100%. However, for the first two examined implementations, the value of the processed bit can be read from the power trace with the bare eye. Processing this value in a number of shares would not improve side-channel resistance as the shares could be attacked with the same success rate leading to full recovery of the message.

The Cortex-M4 shows significant leakage even for already protected implementations, e.g. accessing a dummy in comparison to the real polynomial still results in exploitable leakage, which leads us to the conclusion that it is a challenging task to implement an algorithm in a side-channel secured fashion on this hardware. The most promising countermeasure which we could identify is full randomization of the order of the processed bits. It is therefore considered beneficial to introduce randomization countermeasures even on top of masked implementations.

The message decoding function is the inverse operation of the examined message encoding. In order to apply the presented randomization approach to the decoding step, however, one byte has to be decoded first to serve as the source of randomness. To minimize leakage at this point in time, the independent polynomial generation countermeasure could be applied.

Furthermore, the same message is encoded twice, first by the initiator and then by the responder during the re-encryption. In combination with the decoding step, the very same message could be attacked up to three times. However, choosing different but static randomization bytes prevents such an attack.

When a randomization approach is selected, fetching and processing random numbers becomes a suitable target for side-channel analysis and has to be implemented in a side-channel secure fashion as well.

References

1. Amiet, D., Curiger, A., Leuenberger, L., Zbinden, P.: Defeating NEWHOPE with a single trace. In: Ding, J., Tillich, J.-P. (eds.) PQCrypto 2020. LNCS, vol. 12100, pp. 189–205. Springer, Cham (2020). https://doi.org/10.1007/978-3-030-44223-1_11
2. Avanzi, R., et al.: NIST Submission Package for round 3 (2020). https://pq-crystals.org/kyber/resources.shtml
3. Avanzi, R., et al.: CRYSTALS - kyber: algorithm specifications and supporting documentation (version 3.01) (2021). https://pq-crystals.org/kyber/data/kyber-specification-round3-20210131.pdf
4. Bache, F., Paglialonga, C., Oder, T., Schneider, T., Güneysu, T.: High-Speed Masking for Polynomial Comparison in Lattice-based KEMs. IACR Trans. Cryptogr. Hardw. Embed. Syst. 2020(3), 483–507 (2020)
5. Bhasin, S., D'Anvers, J.P., Heinz, D., Pöppelmann, T., Beirendonck, M.V.: Attacking and defending masked polynomial comparison for lattice-based cryptography. Cryptology ePrint Archive, Report 2021/104 (2021)
6. Bos, J.W., et al.: CRYSTALS - Kyber: a CCA-secure module-lattice-based KEM. In: 2018 IEEE European Symposium on Security and Privacy, Euro S&P 2018, pp. 353–367. IEEE (2018)
7. Bos, J.W., Gourjon, M., Renes, J., Schneider, T., van Vredendaal, C.: Masking Kyber: first- and higher-order implementations. Cryptology ePrint Archive, Report 2021/483 (2021)
8. Diffie, W., Hellman, M.: New Directions in Cryptography. IEEE Transactions on Information Theory 22(6), 644–654 (2006)
9. Ding, A.A., Zhang, L., Durvaux, F., Standaert, F.-X., Fei, Y.: Towards sound and optimal leakage detection procedure. In: Eisenbarth, T., Teglia, Y. (eds.) CARDIS 2017. LNCS, vol. 10728, pp. 105–122. Springer, Cham (2018). https://doi.org/10.1007/978-3-319-75208-2_7
10. Fritzmann, T., et al.: Masked accelerators and instruction set extensions for post-quantum cryptography. Cryptology ePrint Archive, Report 2021/479 (2021)
11. Fujisaki, E., Okamoto, T.: Secure Integration of Asymmetric and Symmetric Encryption Schemes. In: Wiener, M.J. (ed.) Advances in Cryptology - CRYPTO '99. LNCS, vol. 1666, pp. 537–554. Springer (1999).
12. Gandolfi, K., Mourtel, C., Olivier, F.: Electromagnetic Analysis: Concrete Results. In: Koç, Ç.K., Naccache, D., Paar, C. (eds.) Cryptographic Hardware and Embedded Systems - CHES 2001. pp. 251–261. Springer (2001).
13. Gierlichs, B., Lemke-Rust, K., Paar, C.: Templates vs. Stochastic Methods. In: Goubin, L., Matsui, M. (eds.) Cryptographic Hardware and Embedded Systems - CHES 2006. pp. 15–29. Springer (2006).
14. Google: A Preview of Bristlecone, Google's New Quantum Processor (2018). https://ai.googleblog.com/2018/03/a-preview-of-bristlecone-googles-new.html
15. IBM: IBM's Roadmap For Scaling Quantum Technology (2020). https://www.ibm.com/blogs/research/2020/09/ibm-quantum-roadmap
16. Kocher, Paul, Jaffe, Joshua, Jun, Benjamin: Differential Power Analysis. In: Wiener, Michael (ed.) CRYPTO 1999. LNCS, vol. 1666, pp. 388–397. Springer, Heidelberg (1999). https://doi.org/10.1007/3-540-48405-1_25
17. Kocher, P.C.: Timing Attacks on Implementations of Diffie-Hellman, RSA, DSS, and Other Systems. In: Koblitz, N. (ed.) Advances in Cryptology - CRYPTO '96. pp. 104–113. Springer (1996)

18. Moody, D., et al.: Status Report on the Second Round of the NIST Post-Quantum Cryptography Standardization Process (2020)
19. Mosca, M.: Towards quantum-safe cryptography. In: Mosca, M., Lenhart, G., Pecen, M. (eds.) 1st Quantum-Safe-Crypto Workshop, pp. 39–49. ETSI (2013). https://docbox.etsi.org/Workshop/2013/201309_CRYPTO/e-proceedings_Crypto_2013.pdf
20. Mosca, M.: Cybersecurity in an Era with Quantum Computers: Will We Be Ready? IEEE Secur. Priv. 16(5), 38–41 (2018)
21. National Institute of Standards and Technology: SHA-3 Standard: Permutation-Based Hash and Extendable-Output Functions. Technical Report. Federal Information Processing Standards Publications (FIPS PUBS) 202, U.S. Department of Commerce, Washington, D.C. (2015)
22. National Institute of Standards and Technology: PQC Standardization Process: Third Round Candidate Announcement (2020). https://www.nist.gov/news-events/news/2020/07/pqc-standardization-process-third-round-candidate-announcement
23. NIST: Post Quantum Cryptography - Workshops and Timeline (2021). https://csrc.nist.gov/Projects/post-quantum-cryptography/workshops-and-timeline
24. NXP: FRDM-K22F: NXP Freedom Developement Platform for Kinetis K22 MCUs (2021). https://www.nxp.com/design/development-boards/freedom-development-boards/mcu-boards/nxp-freedom-development-platform-for-kinetis-k22-mcus:FRDM-K22F
25. Oder, T., Schneider, T., Pöppelmann, T., Güneysu, T.: Practical CCA2-secure and masked ring-LWE implementation. IACR Trans. Cryptogr. Hardw. Embed. Syst. **2018**(1), 142–174 (2018)
26. Ravi, P., Roy, S.S., Chattopadhyay, A., Bhasin, S.: Generic Side-channel attacks on CCA-secure lattice-based PKE and KEMs. IACR Trans. Cryptogr. Hardw. Embed. Syst. 2020(3), 307–335 (2020)
27. Reparaz, O., de Clercq, R., Roy, S.S., Vercauteren, F., Verbauwhede, I.: Additively Homomorphic Ring-LWE Masking. In: Takagi, T. (ed.) Post-Quantum Cryptography - PQCrypto 2016. LNCS, vol. 9606, pp. 233–244. Springer (2016).
28. Reparaz, O., Roy, S.S., Vercauteren, F., Verbauwhede, I.: A Masked Ring-LWE Implementation. In: Güneysu, T., Handschuh, H. (eds.) Cryptographic Hardware and Embedded Systems - CHES 2015. LNCS, vol. 9293, pp. 683–702. Springer (2015).
29. Rodriguez-Henriquez, F., Jaques, S., Lochter, M., Mosca, M.: How long can we safely use pre-quantum ECC? (2020). https://eccworkshop.org/2020
30. Shor, P.W.: Polynomial-Time Algorithms for Prime Factorization and Discrete Logarithms on a Quantum Computer. SIAM J. Comput. 26(5), 1484–1509 (1997)
31. Sim, B., et al.: Single-trace attacks on message encoding in lattice-based KEMs. IEEE Access **8**, 183175–183191 (2020)
32. Xu, Z., Pemberton, O., Roy, S.S., Oswald, D.: Magnifying side-channel leakage of lattice-based cryptosystems with chosen ciphertexts: the case study of kyber. Cryptology ePrint Archive, Report 2020/912 (2020)

Hardware Implementations of Pairings at Updated Security Levels

Arthur Lavice[1,2,3]([✉]) [iD], Nadia El Mrabet[1] [iD], Alexandre Berzati[2],
Jean-Baptiste Rigaud[1] [iD], and Julien Proy[2] [iD]

[1] Mines Saint-Etienne, CEA, Leti, Centre CMP, 13541 Gardanne, France
{arthur.lavice,nadia.el-mrabet,jean-baptiste.rigaud}@emse.fr
[2] Thales DIS Design Services SAS, Meyreuil, France
{arthur.lavice,alexandre.berzati,julien.proy}@thalesgroup.com
[3] ARMINES, Paris, France

Abstract. Pairings are cornerstones to several interesting cryptographic protocols including Non-interactive ARgument of Knowledge currently used in Zcash cryptocurrency. The Kim and Barbulescu Number Field Sieve attack has weakened pairing-friendly curves. Most impacted are the famous BN curves which now require an increase of the parameters to provide equivalent security. Recent cost estimations of pairings have recommended switching to other curves, but their selections are no longer clearly straightforward. This paper aims at providing the first hardware-based pairing implementations on the best curve candidates at both 128-bit and 192-bit security levels. The proposed architecture intends to fit both lightweight FPGA and ASIC purposes and the design is prototyped on a Kintex-7 FPGA device. It computes a pairing within 42.7 ms for 128-bit of security and 184.2 ms for 192-bit.

Keywords: Pairings · Lightweight hardware/software implementations · Updated key size · Parallel computation

1 Introduction

Pairings are cryptographic tools whose bilinearity property allows finding efficient solutions to many protocols such as the tripartite Diffie-Hellman key exchange [23] or short signature schemes [9]. It also enables the creation of new protocols such as Identity-Based Encryption [8] or zero knowledge-Succinct Non-interactive ARgument of Knowledge (zk-SNARK) [7] used in Zcash cryptocurrency. A pairing is a bilinear and non-degenerate map $e : \mathbb{G}_1 \times \mathbb{G}_2 \to \mathbb{G}_3$ where $\mathbb{G}_1$ (resp. $\mathbb{G}_2$) is generally taken as a subgroup of an elliptic curve over $E(\mathbb{F}_p)$ (resp. $E(\mathbb{F}_{p^k})$) and $\mathbb{G}_3$ is usually a subgroup of $\mathbb{F}_{p^k}$. $\mathbb{G}_1$, $\mathbb{G}_2$, and $\mathbb{G}_3$ are subgroups of prime order r. Pairing computation strongly depends on curve parameters such as $\rho = \frac{\log_2(p)}{\log_2(r)}$. But pairings friendly elliptic curves are rare and

© Springer Nature Switzerland AG 2022
V. Grosso and T. Pöppelmann (Eds.): CARDIS 2021, LNCS 13173, pp. 189–209, 2022.
https://doi.org/10.1007/978-3-030-97348-3_11

a lot of research has been done to find suitable curves such as BLS [5], BN [6], KSS [24] and DCC [13] curves. A taxonomy of these methodologies is found in [15].

Through numerous arithmetic optimizations, BN curves were found to be the best choice for pairings at the 128-bit security level. But the Kim and Barbulescu attack [27] has improved the discrete logarithm attack against these curves and thus threatens the security of many families of pairings. Since this attack depends on curve parameters, it has reshuffled the field and, BN curves are no longer the best ones. Now, performance time seems to be similar on several other curves at the 128-bit security level. In [4], the authors make an extensive literature review to study actual security of pairings. Their estimations only take into account the complexity of modular multiplications and neglect other operations. This approach may not be sufficient to determine the best curves at the 128-bit security level. Another approach from [18] is to create new pairing-friendly curves resistant to the Kim and Barbulescu attack.

There are many time-efficient software versions of pairings, but their implementations on constrained devices are challenging. Indeed, one pairing computation could take seconds to complete with the 128-bit security level [36] prior to the Kim and Barbulescu attack. Having fast pairing implementations on small devices is essential, for example, to guarantee user-friendly utilization of Zcash currency on a hardware wallet.

Our Contribution. This paper proposes a way to efficiently support emerging curves at both the 128 and the 192-bit security levels. A new formula for squaring over cyclotomic fields $\mathbb{G}_{\phi_2(q)}$ is proposed and is more suitable for curves introduced in [18] than the previous one given in [17]. Our work provides a $time \times area$ efficient lightweight coprocessor with configurable modulo to support multiple curves. This coprocessor enables parallel computation of modular multiplications with additional operations in order to cut down additional costs brought by neglected operations such as modular additions. This paper also presents a hardware-software co-design architecture based on a Microblaze CPU to demonstrate the performance of our coprocessor. The genericity of our design allows us to give the first comparison between hardware implementations of several pairings at updated security levels with the same design. Finally, this paper shows that, following the Kim and Barbulescu attack, the optimal choice of a curve at the 128-bit security level depends on the target platform.

Organization of the Paper. Section 2 provides some mathematical background on pairings as well as a summary of the latest estimations of pairing costs at updated security levels. Section 3 details curve parameters and recalls some arithmetic optimization of the Miller algorithm and the final exponentiation formula for the 3 best candidates at the 128-bit security level and for the best candidate at the 192-bit security level. It also provides a new formula for cyclotomic squaring in $\mathbb{G}_{\phi_2(q^2)}$ (see Eq. 13). In Sect. 4, we present our dedicated hardware implementation used to accelerate operations on the base field and our hardware/software codesign used for pairing implementations. Finally, we summarize our work and discuss future research directions in Sect. 5.

Notation. In this paper, we will use the following notation. $\mathbb{F}_p$: a finite field of prime characteristic p. $\mathbb{F}_{p^k}$: an extension field of degree k of $\mathbb{F}_p$. $\mathbb{G}[r]$: a subgroup of order r of $\mathbb{G}$. e (resp. n): the number of words used to represent numbers in $\mathbb{F}_p$ (resp. $\log_2(p)$). M_q (resp, S_q, A_q, Dbl_q): a multiplication (resp. square, addition, double) in $\mathbb{F}_q$. $Mulx_q$: a multiplication of an element $\mathbb{F}_q$ by x, a *small* constant in $\mathbb{F}_q$.

2 Background on Pairings

The following part gives some background about pairings and their implementations. There are several pairings such as [20,22,34], but constructions of the most efficient ones are similar to the Ate pairing defined below [19].

2.1 Introduction and Definition

Definition 1. *(Ate pairing).* *Let E be an elliptic curve defined over $\mathbb{F}_p$; r be a large prime divisor of $\#E(\mathbb{F}_p)$; t be the trace of E and k be the embedding degree of E with respect to r (k is the smallest integer such that $r|p^k - 1$). Let $\mathbb{G}_1 \subseteq E(\mathbb{F}_p)[r]$, $\mathbb{G}_2 \subseteq E(\mathbb{F}_{p^k})[r]$, $\mathbb{G}_3 = \mathbb{F}_{p^k}[r]$ and $u = t - 1$. The Ate pairing is defined as:*

$$\begin{cases} e : E(\mathbb{F}_p)[r] \times E(\mathbb{F}_{p^k})[r] \to \mathbb{F}_{p^k}[r], \\ (P, Q) \qquad\qquad \longmapsto f_{u,Q}(P)^{\frac{p^k-1}{r}}. \end{cases} \tag{1}$$

The computation of such pairing relies on two distinct steps. First, the function $f_{u,Q}(P)$ is computed with Miller's algorithm (see Algorithm 1) [30]. The complexity of Miller's algorithm depends on the Hamming Weight(HW) and the $\log_2$ of u. To decrease the complexity of Miller's algorithm, the Non-Adjacent Form (NAF) is classically used to represent u. The second part is the so-called final exponentiation. It raises $f_{u,Q}(P)$ at the power of $(p^k - 1)/r$.

2.2 Pairing Optimizations

Pairing implementations are based on different arithmetics presented in Fig. 1. Elliptic curves and extension field arithmetics depend on modular arithmetic which again depends on integer arithmetic. Curve parameters have a direct impact on the complexity of these operations. The three principal optimizations regarding these parameters are cited below:

Embedding Degree k. It is a crucial parameter since it defines the extension fields used during computations. Having k in the form $k = 2^i 3^j$ enables efficient extension field arithmetic with Karatsuba and Toom-Cook formulae [28] and is one prerequisite to using twisted curves during computations [14].

Algorithm 1. Miller's algorithm [30]

Input: $u = (u_{n-1} \ldots u_0)$ NAF decomposition of $t - 1$, $P \in E(\mathbb{F}_p)$ and $Q \in E(\mathbb{F}_{p^k})$
Output: $f_{u,Q}(P) \in \mathbb{F}_{p^k}[r])$

1: $T \leftarrow Q$; $f_1 \leftarrow 1$;
2: **for** $i = n - 2, \ldots, 0$ **do**
3:     $T \leftarrow 2T$; $f_1 \leftarrow f_1^2 \times l_{Q,Q}(P)/v_{2Q}(P)$; Where $l_{Q,Q}$ is the tangent of E at point Q, and v_{2Q} is the vertical line of E at point $[2]Q$.
4:     **if** $u_i = 1$ **then**
5:         $T \leftarrow T + Q$; $f_1 \leftarrow f_1 \times l_{Q,T}(P)/v_{Q+T}(P)$; Where $l_{Q,T}$ is the line (QT), and v_{Q+T} is the vertical line of E at point $Q + T$.
6:     **else if** $u_i = -1$ **then**
7:         $T \leftarrow T + Q$; $f_1 \leftarrow f_1 \times l_{-Q,T}(P)/v_{-Q+T}(P)$;
8:     **end if**
9: **end for**
10: **return** $f_1 = f_{u,Q}(P)$

Twisted Curves. Let E be an elliptic curve defined over $\mathbb{F}_{p^k}$. An elliptic curve $\tilde{E}$ defined over $\mathbb{F}_{p^{k/d}}$ is called a twisted curve of degree d of E if there exists an isomorphism ψ_d from $\tilde{E}$ into E According to the value of k, the potential degrees for a twist are $d = 2, 3, 4$ or 6. Computing Miller's algorithm on the twisted curve also enables avoiding the computation of the denominator when k is a multiple of 2 [29] or 3 [38]. Twist also makes line and tangent evaluations sparse elements of $\mathbb{F}_{p^k}$ (with at least one null coefficient).

Generation of Curves. The generation of pairing-friendly elliptic curves is the most important step because it conditions the use of optimizations cited in this section. A family of pairing-friendly elliptic curves is a mathematical method to create curves with a prescribed embedding degree as in the taxonomy presented in [15]. The characteristic p, the trace t and a large prime factor of r such that $r | \#E(\mathbb{F}_p)$ are given by polynomials evaluated in an integer u. This integer (u) has a significant impact on the complexity of pairings. Hence, it is important to choose an appropriate generator u with low Hamming Weight representation.

3   Selection of Pairing-Friendly Curves and Parameters

3.1   Summary of Estimated Pairings Complexity

The arithmetic required to implement a pairing depends on curve parameters. For this reason, much attention was given to Optimal Ate pairings [34] on BN curves. But parameters that make a curve pairing-friendly also make it vulnerable to the extended tower Number Field Sieve (NFS) attack presented in [27]. As a result, recent security analysis of pairings presented in [3] and [4] have led to new key size requirements. BN curves are the most impacted and are no

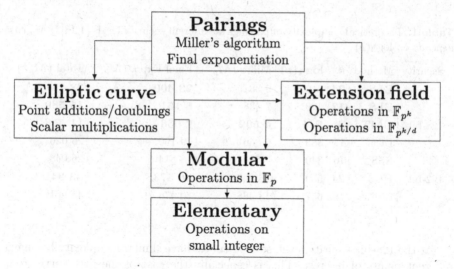

Fig. 1. Required operations for pairings

longer considered as interesting curves for pairings. Recent research has identified more resilient curves against such attacks. To our knowledge, the most promising alternative are curves presented in [18].

In [4] the authors estimate pairings complexity by taking into account only the cost of modular multiplications. They use the compressed squaring formulae given in [25] to estimate the complexity of the final exponentiation of pairings on BLS12, BLS24 and KSS18 [24] curves which admit a twist of degree 6. Compressed squaring is an interesting method since it decreases the number of multiplications but it computes several modular inversions. To compute modular inversions of a number $\alpha \in \mathbb{F}_p$ with the coprocessor presented in Sect. 4, we have to use Fermat's theorem and compute α raised to the power of $p - 2$. Then, the cost of a modular inversion is approximated for naive implementation at the cost of $\lceil 3n/2 \rceil M_p$, which is significant.

Moreover, compressed squaring requires storing several elements in $\mathbb{F}_{p^k}$ [2]. This increases the memory needed by approximately 30% for a slight latency benefit compared to cyclotomic squaring of [17]. We choose to use the formula proposed in [17] in order to target implementation on constrained devices. Table 1 presents the best pairing candidates at the 128-bit and 192-bit security levels according to [4] and [18]. In what follows, we denote by GMT8 the curve presented in [18] with embedding degree $k = 8$.

The complexity of Miller's algorithm is critical when computing the product of pairings in short signatures for example. When computing scalar multiplications on $\mathbb{G}_1$, $\log_2(r)$ and $\log_2(p)$ are crucial parameters; $\log_2(r)$, $\log_2(p)$, the embedding degree k and the degree of the twist d are also important when computing a scalar multiplication on $\mathbb{G}_2$.

Table 1. Theoretical complexity of pairings at different security levels [4,18] *: M_p *cost depends on* $\log_2(p)$

Security	Method	k	$\log_2(p)$	Miller (M_p*)	Final Expo. (M_p*)	Total (M_p*)
128-bit	**BLS**	24	319	9 381	**23 400**	**32 781**
	BLS	12	460	7 438	**8 151**	**15 589**
	GMT	8	**544**	**4 502**	**7 056**	**11 558**
	DCC	15	383	6 836	19 190	26 026
	KSS	16	340	7 534	18 514	26 048
192-bit	**BLS**	24	559	16 368	**36 573**	**52 941**
	KSS	18	657	13 488	30 473	43 961

At the 128-bit security level, several curves have similar complexity but have different points of interest. This is especially the case of the first curve from Table 1 (BLS24) and the second candidate (GMT8). At the 192-bit security level, KSS18 and BLS24 have similar complexity but also similar parameters. KSS18 is a bit less interesting than BLS24 when looking at the complexity of Miller's algorithm, the characteristic p, or the order r. At this security level, BLS24 should be the better choice whatever the target application. Based on these estimations, we choose to implement the two best pairing candidates at the 128-bit security level: BLS24 and GMT8. Since BLS12 is still one of the best candidates, we consider it as the reference curve at the 128-bit security level and implement it. We also provide an implementation of BLS24 at 192-bit security.

In the following section, we present the parameters of the chosen curves and provide some aspects of their implementation.

3.2   Pairing Arithmetic and Implementation Aspects

All the selected curves (BLS12, BLS24, GMT8) have an even embedding degree. In this case, the vertical lines computed in Algorithm 1 are elements of $\mathbb{F}_{p^{k/d}}$ and will be sent to 1 during the final exponentiation. Hence, the computation of denominators v_{2Q} or v_{Q+T} can be omitted during Miller's algorithm.

"High-level" operations such as extension fields or elliptic curve operations can be computed with a succession of modular operations (or operations in the base field: $\mathbb{F}_p$). Searching for a cost-efficient hardware coprocessor to compute these operations is a way to enhance the efficiency of pairing implementations. Moreover, arithmetic used to implement pairings highly depends on the pairing family. Hence, the sequence of modular operations also depends on the curve. To ensure the flexibility of our design, we choose to focus on modular operations to design a hardware accelerator suitable for all curves.

Common Operations: Multiplication and Squaring in $\mathbb{F}_{p^2}$. During pairing computations, most of the operations are computed over the extension field $\mathbb{F}_{p^{k/d}}$. For the selected curves, $\mathbb{F}_{p^{k/d}} = \mathbb{F}_{p^2}$ or $\mathbb{F}_{p^4}$. An element A of $\mathbb{F}_{p^k}$ is a polynomial of degree n, with $0 \leq n \leq k - 1$ and with its coefficient in $\mathbb{F}_p$. Let P be an irreducible polynomial of degree k. Let A and B be two elements of $\mathbb{F}_{p^k}$. The result C of the multiplication of A by B is defined as the Euclidean remainder of the polynomial $A \times B$ by the polynomial P. As previously said, the curves selected in our study all have an embedding degree of $k = 2^i 3^j$. To construct extension fields of these embedding degrees, the classical method is to use extension field towers. For instance, $\mathbb{F}_{p^4}$ can be seen as an extension of degree 2 of $\mathbb{F}_{p^2}$. Algorithm 2 (resp. Algorithm 3) is the standard way to compute a multiplication (resp. a square) in extension fields of degree 2.

Curves Admitting a Twist of Degree 6. BLS curves are defined over $\mathbb{F}_p$ by $E : y^2 = x^3 + b$ and by a parameter $u \in \mathbb{Z}$ such that the parameters p, r, t are evaluations of some polynomials at u ($p = p(u)$, $r = r(u)$, and $t = t(u)$). In our implementations, we select the same parameters as in [4] which are $u = -2^{32} + 2^{28} + 2^{12}$ (resp. $u = -2^{56} - 2^{43} + 2^9 - 2^6$) For BLS24 at 128-bit (resp. 192-bit) security and $u = -2^{77} + 2^{50} + 2^{33}$ for BLS12.

Algorithm 2. Multiplication in $\mathbb{F}_{p^k} = \mathbb{F}_{p^{k/2}}[g], g^2 = v, v \in \mathbb{F}_{p^{k/2}}$	**Algorithm 3.** Square in $\mathbb{F}_{p^k} = \mathbb{F}_{p^{k/2}}[g], g^2 = v, v \in \mathbb{F}_{p^{k/2}}$
Input: $A = a_0 + a_1 g$, $B = b_0 + b_1 g \in \mathbb{F}_{p^k}$ **Output:** $Z \leftarrow AB \in \mathbb{F}_{p^k}$ **Cost:** $3M_{p^{k/2}} + 5A_{p^{k/2}} + 1Mulv_{p^{k/2}}$ **Begin**	**Input:** $A = a_0 + a_1 g \in \mathbb{F}_{p^k}$, **Output:** $Z \leftarrow A^2 \in \mathbb{F}_{p^k}$ **Cost:** $2M_{p^{k/2}} + 4A_{p^{k/2}} + 1Dbl_{p^{k/2}} + 2Mulv_{p^{k/2}}$ **Begin**
1: $t_0 \leftarrow a_0 b_0; \; t_1 \leftarrow a_0 + a_1$	1: $z_0 \leftarrow a_0 a_1; \; t_0 \leftarrow a_0 - a_1;$
2: $z_0 \leftarrow b_0 + b_1; \; z_1 \leftarrow a_1 b_1;$	2: $t_1 \leftarrow a_0 - v a_1; \; t_0 \leftarrow t_0 t_1;$
3: $t_1 \leftarrow t_1 z_0; \; z_0 \leftarrow t_0 - v z_1;$	3: $z_1 \leftarrow 2 z_0; \; z_0 \leftarrow t_0 + (v+1) z_0;$
4: $z_1 \leftarrow t_0 + z_1; \; z_1 \leftarrow z_1 - t_1;$	4: **return** $Z = z_0 + z_1 g;$
5: **return** $Z = z_0 + z_1 g;$	**End**
End	

To our knowledge, the most efficient way to compute Miller's algorithm on these curves is to use mixed affine-projective coordinates along with the line evaluations proposed in [12]. Then the characteristic $p(u)$, the order of the subgroups $r(u)$ and the trace $t(u)$ of E are given by Eq. 2 for BLS12 and by Eq. 3 for BLS24.

$$\begin{cases} r(u) = u^4 - u^2 + 1, \\ p(u) = (u-1)^2 r/3 + u, \qquad (2) \\ t(u) = u + 1. \end{cases} \qquad \begin{cases} r(u) = u^8 - u^4 + 1, \\ p(u) = (u-1)^2 r/3 + u, \qquad (3) \\ t(u) = u + 1. \end{cases}$$

The same extension fields and elliptic curves as in [26] are used for BLS12 (see Eq. 4) at 128-bit security and for BLS24 (see Eq. 5) at 192-bit security. Multiplications and squares over $\mathbb{F}_{p^{12}}$ (resp. $\mathbb{F}_{p^{24}}$) are computed with formulae given in [28] for cubic extension.

$$\begin{cases} \log_2(p) = 461, \\ \log_2(r) = 308, \\ \mathbb{F}_{p^2} \quad = \mathbb{F}_p[i], i^2 = -1, \\ \mathbb{F}_{p^4} \quad = \mathbb{F}_{p^2}[v], v^2 = i + 1, \\ \mathbb{F}_{p^{12}} \quad = \mathbb{F}_{p^2}[g], g^3 = v, \\ E(\mathbb{F}_p) \;\; : \;\; y^2 = x^3 + 4, \\ \tilde{E}(\mathbb{F}_{p^2}) : \;\; y^2 = x^3 + 4(i + 1). \end{cases} \quad (4)$$

$$\begin{cases} \log_2(p) = 559, \\ \log_2(r) = 449, \\ \mathbb{F}_{p^2} \quad = \mathbb{F}_p[i], i^2 = -1, \\ \mathbb{F}_{p^4} \quad = \mathbb{F}_{p^2}[v], v^2 = i + 1, \\ \mathbb{F}_{p^{24}} \quad = \mathbb{F}_{p^4}[g'], g'^6 = v, \\ E(\mathbb{F}_p) \;\; : \;\; y^2 = x^3 + 9, \\ \tilde{E}(\mathbb{F}_{p^4}) : \;\; y^2 = x^3 + 9(-i + 1)v/2. \end{cases} \quad (5)$$

For BLS24 at 128-bit security, g' can not be chosen such that $g'^{12} = i + 1$ as in Eq. 4 because this extension tower does not construct a field. Therefore, we choose to define $\mathbb{F}_{p^{24}}$ and E as described in Eq. 6 to simplify the expression of $\tilde{E}$, and to ease the computation of Miller's algorithm.

$$\begin{cases} \log_2(p) = 318, & \mathbb{F}_{p^{24}} \quad = \mathbb{F}_{p^4}[g'], g'^6 = v, \\ \log_2(r) = 256, & E(\mathbb{F}_p) \;\; : \;\; y^2 = x^3 + 5, \\ \mathbb{F}_{p^2} \quad = \mathbb{F}_p[i], i^2 = -1, & \tilde{E}(\mathbb{F}_{p^4}) : \;\; y^2 = x^3 + 5/v, \\ \mathbb{F}_{p^4} \quad = \mathbb{F}_{p^2}[v], v^2 = i + 3, & \tilde{E}(\mathbb{F}_{p^4}) : \;\; y^2 = x^3 + (-i + 3)v/2. \end{cases} \quad (6)$$

The Case of GMT8. The curves proposed in [18] differ from BLS12 or BLS24 curves as the modulo p and the order of subgroups r can not be represented by polynomials in the variable u. Moreover, This curve admits a twist of degree $d = 4$ and is generated using a variant of the Cocks-Pinch algorithm [11]. In [18], they define $\mathbb{F}_{p^8}$ as $\mathbb{F}_p[g]$ with $g^8 = 5$.

The most efficient formula to compute Miller's algorithm for these kinds of curves is the one proposed in [12] along with the mixed affine-"weight-(1, 2) coordinates." These coordinates represent points of E by $(X : Y : Z)$, which corresponds to the affine point (x, y) where $x = \frac{X}{Z}$ and $y = \frac{Y}{Z^2}$. The parameters of the GMT8 curve at 128-bit security are given in Eq. 7.

$$\begin{cases} r = 0xff0060739e18d7594a978b0ab6ae4ce3d & \log_2(r) = 256, \\ \quad bfd52a9d00197603fffdf0000000101, & \log_2(p) = 544, \\ p = 0xbb9dfd549299f1c803ddd5d7c05e7cc03 & \mathbb{F}_{p^2} \quad = \mathbb{F}_p[v], v^2 = 5, \\ \quad 73d9b1ac15b47aa5aa84626f33e58fe6694 & \mathbb{F}_{p^4} \quad = \mathbb{F}_{p^2}[u], u^2 = v, \quad (7) \\ \quad 3943049031ae4ca1d2719b3a84fa363bcd2 & \mathbb{F}_{p^8} \quad = \mathbb{F}_{p^4}[g], g^2 = u, \\ \quad 539a5cd02c6f4b6b645a58c1085e14411, & E(\mathbb{F}_p) \;\; : \;\; y^2 = x^3 + 2x, \\ t = 2^{64} - 2^{54} + 2^{37} + 2^{32} - 4, & \tilde{E}(\mathbb{F}_{p^2}) : \;\; y^2 = x^3 + 2vx. \end{cases}$$

Summary of Operations Required by Miller's Algorithm. For curves $E : y^2 = x^3 + ax + b$ that admit a sextic or quartic twist, the complexity of Miller's algorithm of the selected curves is given in Table 2. For the sake of simplification, p^k (resp $p^{k/d}$) is denoted q (resp. l). Since a and b are small coefficients, Multiplication by a or b can be computed without modular multiplications. Pairing implementations on BLS12 and BLS24 curves both rely on

$\mathbb{F}_{p^2} = \mathbb{F}_p[i]$ but GMT8 relies on $\mathbb{F}_{p^2} = \mathbb{F}_p[v]$. The formulae used to compute operations on these fields are similar since they only differ in the reduction step (see Algorithm 2 and Algorithm 3).

The dependency between operations required by Miller's algorithm for the selected curves is summarized in Fig. 2, where operations specific to each curve are framed. Modular operations are the common points of selected curves even if the size of the characteristic (p) differs between BLS24, BLS12 and GMT8.

Table 2. The complexity of Miller's step using twist

Operation	Complexity	
Twist	Sextic twist	Quartic twist
Doubling (D)	$k/3.M_p + 3M_l + 5S_l + M_q + S_q$	$k/2.M_p + 3M_l + 6S_l + M_q + S_q + Mula_l$
Mixed add (MA)	$k/3.M_p + 10M_l + 2S_l + M_q + Mulb_l$	$k/2.M_p + 9M_l + 5S_l + M_q$
Miller (total)	$\log_2(u).D + HW(u).MA$	

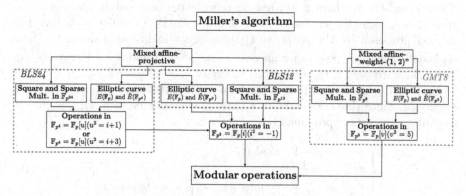

Fig. 2. Operations during Miller's algorithm selected curves

3.3 Implementation of the Final Exponentiation

The second part of a pairing calculation is computing Miller's algorithm result raised to the power of $\frac{p^k - 1}{r}$. This is called the final exponentiation and its complexity depends on different curve parameters. This section presents arithmetic optimizations used to compute this step on selected curves.

Curves Admitting a Twist of Degree 6. The decomposition of the final exponentiation is a well-known optimization of pairings. To our knowledge, the most efficient is proposed in [16] for both BLS12 and BLS24. They used the parametrization of modulo p to provide fast and memory-efficient implementations. For BLS12, the ratio $\frac{p^{12}-1}{r}$ is split into an easy part $(p^6-1)(p^2+1)$, and a hard one $(p^4-p^2+1)/r$. Then, the hard part is also decomposed as:

$(p^4-p^2+1)/r = \lambda_0 + \lambda_1 p + \lambda_2 p^2 + \lambda_3 p^3$ and the λ_i are calculated according to Eq. 8. The same methodology applies for BLS24. The ratio $\frac{p^{24}-1}{r}$ is split into an easy part $(p^{12}-1)(p^4+1)$ and a hard one $(p^8-p^4+1)/r$. Then, the hard part is decomposed into: $(p^8-p^4-1)/r = \lambda_0 + \lambda_1 p + \lambda_2 p^2 + \lambda_3 p^3 + \lambda_4 p^4 + \lambda_5 p^5 + \lambda_6 p^6 + \lambda_7 p^7$ and the λ_i are calculated according to Eq. 9.

$$
\begin{cases}
\lambda_3 = u^2 - 2u + 1, \\
\lambda_2 = \lambda_3 u, \\
\lambda_1 = \lambda_2 u - \lambda_3, \\
\lambda_0 = \lambda_1 u + 3.
\end{cases}
\tag{8}
$$

$$
\begin{cases}
\lambda_7 = u^2 - 2u + 1, & \lambda_3 = \lambda_4 u - \lambda_7, \\
\lambda_6 = \lambda_7 u, & \lambda_2 = \lambda_3 u, \\
\lambda_5 = \lambda_6 u, & \lambda_1 = \lambda_2 u, \\
\lambda_4 = \lambda_5 u, & \lambda_0 = \lambda_1 u + 3.
\end{cases}
\tag{9}
$$

After the easy part of the final exponentiation, all computations are done in cyclotomic subgroups of $\mathbb{F}_{p^k}$. This allows faster squaring formulae as the ones presented in [17].

The Case of GMT8. The curves presented in [18] are defined over a finite field of characteristic p, where p can not be represented as a polynomial evaluated in u. Hence, formulae similar to Eq. 8 or Eq. 9 for BLS are not available. The method proposed by the authors of [18] consists in breaking down the final exponentiation $\frac{p^8-1}{r}$ again into an easy part (p^4-1) and a hard part $(\frac{p^4+1}{r})$. Then, the hard part is represented as in Eq. 10.

Once again, the second part of the final exponentiation is done in cyclotomic subgroups. Since this curve admits a twist of even degree $(d=4)$, a square in this subgroup costs approximately 2 squares in $\mathbb{F}_{p^4}$.

$$
\begin{cases}
t_0 = p + 1 \mod r, \\
c = \frac{p+1-t_0}{r}, \\
\frac{p^4+1}{r} = \frac{(t_0-1)^4+1}{r} + (p + t_0 - 1)(p^2 + (t_0-1)^2)c.
\end{cases}
\tag{10}
$$

Let $\mathbb{F}_{p^8}$ and $\mathbb{F}_{p^4}$ be defined as in Eq. 7 and let $a = a_0 + a_1 g$, with $a \in \mathbb{F}_{p^8}$, $a_0, a_1 \in \mathbb{F}_{p^4}$. A square in $\mathbb{G}_{\phi_2(\mathbb{F}_{p^4})}$ is computed as follows:

$$
a^2 = (a_0^2 + v a_1^2) + 2a_0 a_1 g = a_0^2 + a_1^2 + [(a_0 + a_1)^2 - (a_0^2 + a_1^2)]g.
\tag{11}
$$

Following [17], $a \in \mathbb{G}_{\phi_2(\mathbb{F}_{p^4})} \Rightarrow a_0^2 - v a_1^2 = 1$. Thus, we can replace a_1^2 in the Eq. 11 by $\frac{1-a_0^2}{v}$ and compute a^2 with the following formula:

$$
a^2 = 2a_0^2 - 1 + [(a_0 + b_0)^2 - a_0^2 - (a_0^2 - 1)/v]g.
\tag{12}
$$

If $\frac{1}{v}$ can be computed without a modular inverse, then the cost of the above formula is 2 squares in $\mathbb{F}_{p^4}$ and some additions.

However, this is not the case with the GMT8 curve as $\frac{1}{v} = \frac{v^3}{5}$. We can precompute this value, but it increases the cost of Eq. 11 by at least a multiplication of a $\mathbb{F}_{p^4}$ element by a $\mathbb{F}_p$ element (which costs four M_p). To avoid these multiplications, we propose to replace a_0^2 by $1 + va_1^2$ in Eq. 11. It leads to the following formula which does not require any inversion:

$$a^2 = 2va_1^2 + 1 + [(a_0 + a_1)^2 - 1 - (v + 1)a_1^2]g. \tag{13}$$

Thus, our formula is more suitable to compute squaring in the cyclotomic subgroup for pairing on the GMT8 curve.[1]

Summary of Operations Required by Final Exponentiation. Analogously to the computation of Miller's algorithm, we summarize the different operations required during the final exponentiation in Fig. 3. Basic operations are the same as in Miller's algorithm, but there are other operations such as efficient squaring in the cyclotomic subgroups.

Modular operations form the basis of pairing arithmetic. The following section, presents a lightweight coprocessor suitable to compute pairings on different curves and at different security levels.

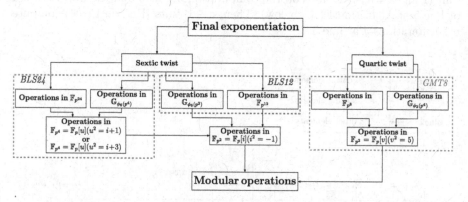

Fig. 3. Operations during final exponentiation on selected curves

4 Hardware Implementation of Pairings

In this section, we present a lightweight coprocessor design to accelerate modular operations and cut down the additional cost brought by neglected operations. This coprocessor will be called the base field unit in the rest of the paper. Then, we propose a hardware/software co-design architecture to compare pairings on different curves at updated security levels.

---

[1] At the time of submitting this article, the proposed formula was new in the literature. However, we later realized that it also appears in the RELIC project [1].

4.1 Base Field Unit

As previously explained, the computation of pairings relies both on elliptic curves and extension fields arithmetic. These arithmetics can be carried out with sequences of operations in the base field $\mathbb{F}_p$ (also called modular operations). The required operations are modular multiplications, reductions, additions, subtractions, doubles, and divisions by 2. These operations are computed with the base field unit. To limit the number of memory accesses, we implement elementary operations on 64-bit integers. Finally, we choose to use single-port RAM to store intermediate values. This memory model is more likely to be suitable for light use because its cost is lower compared to a dual port RAM.

Modular Multiplication. Given its complexity compared to other operations over the base field, modular multiplication is a key operation. The proposed multiplier, described in Fig. 4, is a variant of the systolic architecture proposed in [21]. It computes an alternative form of the Montgomery algorithm [31]: the Multiple Word Radix-2 Montgomery Multiplication (MWR2-MM, see Algorithm [33]). This architecture is composed of e processing elementary units. One unit (PE_0 on Fig. 4) focuses on the computation of line 3 and the first iteration at line 5 of Algorithm 4 (see below). Then, $e - 1$ units (PE_j on Fig. 4) compute other iterations j at line 5.

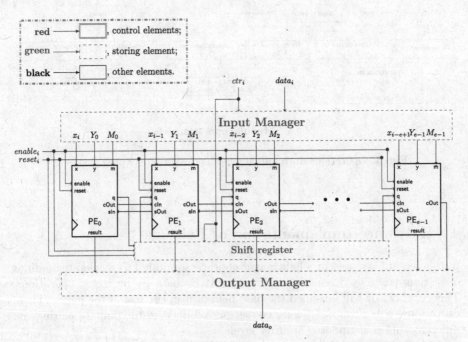

Fig. 4. Hardware design dedicated to compute Modular multiplications

These units compute bitwise and logical operations on 64-bit integers such as shift, addition or xor. Therefore, it does not require any DSP in FPGA implementation. This design offers a good performance area trade-off. It distributes the calculation over several small processing elements. Hence, the size of the modulo has a limited impact on hardware frequency. All modular operations are decomposed into 64-bit additions, subtractions or shifts.

Algorithm 4. MWR2-MM [33]

Input: $X = \sum_{i=0}^{n-1} x_i.2^i$, $Y = \sum_{i=0}^{e-1} Y^{(j)}.2^{(w.j)}$, $p = \sum_{j=0}^{e-1} p^{(j)}.2^{(w.j)}$

Output: $S = \sum_{j=0}^{e-1} S^j.2^{w.j} = X.Y.2^{-n} \mod (n)$ with $0 \leq S \leq 2.p$

Begin

1: $S = 0$
2: **for** $i = 0, ..., n-1$ **do**
3:     $q_i = (x_i.Y_0^{(0)}) \oplus S_0^{(0)}$
4:     $(C^{(1)}, S^{(0)}) = x_i.Y^{(0)} + q_i.p^{(0)} + S^{(0)}$
5:     **for** $j = 1, ..., e$ **do**
6:        $(C^{(j+1)}, S^{(j)}) = C^{(j)} + x_i.Y^{(j)} + q_i.p^{(j)} + S^{(j)}$
7:        $S^{(j-1)} = (S_0^{(j)}, S_{w-1..1}^{j-1})$
8:     **end for**
9:     $S^{(e)} = 0$
10: **end for**
11: **return** S

Additional Operations. The dedicated component presented in Fig. 5 is designed to compute additional operations (addition, subtraction, double, division by 2 and reduction). As for modular multiplications, the modulo is loaded once prior to any computation. It is stored on a cyclic register (**CyclReg** on Fig. 5). Two 64-bit adder-subtractors (**Add** and **Red**) are used. One for the addition (or subtraction) and the other to compute the modular reduction. The two possible results are stored in two dedicated registers **RegAdd** and **RegRed**. These registers allow us to chain operations. Thus, we restrict the quantity of memory access to the minimum: load operands and store the final result. Then, the component **Div** is used to compute divisions by 2. The computation of a modular double is considered as a computation of a special modular addition. In this case, the loading of the operand is faster than in classical addition and this enables computing modular doubles faster than modular additions.

Similarly, the modular division by two is a special subtraction. Our adder computes both $A - 0$ and $A + p$, and then, depending on the parity of A, the results will either be $A/2$ or $(A+p)/2$. Once again, it enables computing modular divisions by two faster than modular subtractions. The number of clock cycles required by each operation in $\mathbb{F}_p$ is expressed in Table 3. The implementation of doubles and divisions by 2 operations allows saving e clock cycles for these operations. Implementation of additional operations (addition, double, ...) has less impact on design performances than the implementation of modular multiplication. However, their costs can not be neglected since they are called about 6 times

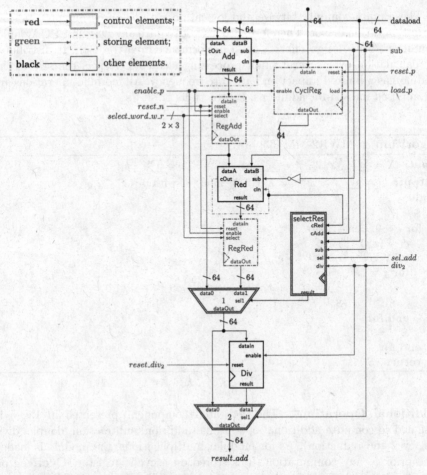

Fig. 5. Hardware design dedicated to compute additional operations

more than multiplications. As an example for GMT8 curves, when $\log_2(p) = 544$ and $e = 9$, the computation time of a modular multiplication is around 18 (resp. 25) times longer than a modular addition (resp. double). Additional operations represent 25% of pairing computation times which is significant.

Table 3. Costs of base field operations

Operation	Number of clock cycles
Modular multiplication	$n + 3\lceil n/64 \rceil + 4$
Modular reduction	$2\lceil n/64 \rceil + 6$
Modular addition/subtraction	$3\lceil n/64 \rceil + 6$
Modular double	$2\lceil n/64 \rceil + 6$
Modular division by 2	$2\lceil n/64 \rceil + 7$

Proposed Hardware/Software Architecture for Prototyping Purposes.
The multiplier and the custom adder are both controlled by a Finite State
Machine (Scheduler in Fig. 6). This scheduler allows loading operands from the
dedicated RAM (CryptoRAM in Fig. 6), launching a modular operation, and saving the final result into the CryptoRAM. The sequence of modular operations
can be fixed for a specific pairing implementation, but we choose to maintain
flexibility in our design and use a CPU instead. It allows implementing different
pairings on the same component. Macro instructions are defined to pilot our
base field unit which is connected to the CPU with an AXI interface (Advanced
eXtensible Interface). This interface is chosen for its compatibility with a wide
variety of processors (including ARM and RISC-V CPUs). To execute complex
operations, the CPU must control the base field unit and the cryptoRAM, again
to load operands, compute selected operations and save the results.

The chosen CPU for prototyping purposes is the MicroBlaze unit provided by Vivado tools. It is based on a 32-bit architecture. However, it can
be easily replaced by any processor. 32-bit instructions of the form: $ins =$
$\{@A, @B, @Z, Code\}$ are used by the CPU to pilot the base field unit. Having
32-bit CPU does not hinder the control of our 64-bit base field unit.

As shown in Fig. 6, instructions are sent by the CPU to the base field
unit through the AXI. A decoder (Ins-decoder) stores addresses of operands
$(@A, @B)$, address of the result $(@Z)$, and selects the base field operation corresponding to $Code$. Then, the Scheduler controls the CryptoRAM and either the
multiplier or the custom adder computes this operation. In this way, a modular
operation can be launched with a single instruction.

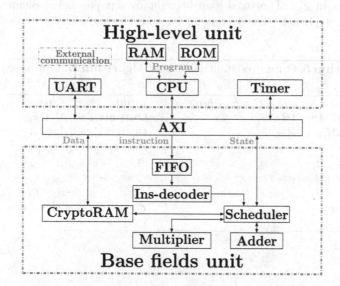

Fig. 6. Proposed hardware/software architecture

Finally, a FIFO stacks several instructions to mask the cost of sending instructions to the base field unit. The CPU can read and write into the CryptoRAM to load operands and to read the result of the computation. Instructions are sent from the CPU to the coprocessor through the AXI as shown in Fig. 6. The CPU also controls a timer to monitor coprocessor computation times and a Universal Asynchronous Receiver Transmitter (UART) component to allow external communication.

Finally, the MicroBlaze CPU runs a software program in C to compute High-level operations. The objective of this design is to minimize the impact of additional operations on implementation performances. Thus, the base field unit is built to be able to launch additional operations while performing modular multiplications.

Common Optimization: Parallelized Multiplication and Square in $\mathbb{F}_{p^2}$. The selected curves all rely on $\mathbb{F}_{p^2} = \mathbb{F}_p[v]$ arithmetic. In Sect. 3, $\mathbb{F}_{p^2} = \mathbb{F}_p[v]$, where v is defined as $v = -1$ for BLS12 and BLS24 curves and $v = 5$ for GMT8 curves. Multiplication by 5 can be computed with two doubles and one addition. Then, multiplications by v can also be parallelized in Algorithm 2 and Algorithm 3. Four additions and one multiplication by v can be computed in parallel during multiplications and three additions, one double and two multiplications by v during squaring.

Additional operations that can be computed in parallel are written with grey letters in Algorithm 5 and Algorithm 6. Optimized multiplications and squares in $\mathbb{F}_{p^2}$ cut the computation time by 10% with our architecture.

We manage to parallelize more additional operations during multiplications and squares in $\mathbb{F}_{p^4}$. The total gain brought by our parallel implementation is approximately 12% for BLS12 and 15% for GMT8 and BLS24 curves.

Algorithm 5. Optimized multiplication in $\mathbb{F}_{p^2} = \mathbb{F}_p[g], g^2 = v, v \in \mathbb{F}_p$

Input: $A = a_0 + a_1 g, B = b_0 + b_1 g \in \mathbb{F}_{p^2}$
Output: $Z \leftarrow AB \in \mathbb{F}_{p^2}$
Cost: $3M_{p^2} + 1A_{p^2}$
Begin

1: $t_0 \leftarrow a_0 b_0$; $t_1 \leftarrow a_0 + a_1$ $z_0 \leftarrow b_0 + b_1$;
2: $z_1 \leftarrow a_1 b_1$; $t_1 \leftarrow t_1 z_0$; $z_0 \leftarrow t_0 - v z_1$;
3: $z_1 \leftarrow t_0 + z_1$; $z_1 \leftarrow t_1 - z_1$;
4: **return** $Z = z_0 + z_1 g$;

End

Algorithm 6. Optimized square in $\mathbb{F}_{p^2} = \mathbb{F}_p[g], g^2 = v, v \in \mathbb{F}_p$

Input: $A = a_0 + a_1 g \in \mathbb{F}_{p^2}$,
Output: $Z \leftarrow A^2 \in \mathbb{F}_{p^2}$
Cost: $2M_p + 1A_p$
Begin

1: $z_0 \leftarrow a_0 a_1$; $t_0 \leftarrow a_0 - a_1$;
2: $t_1 \leftarrow a_0 - v a_1$; $t_0 \leftarrow t_0 t_1$;
3: $z_1 \leftarrow 2 z_0$; $z_0 \leftarrow t_0 + (v+1) z_0$;
4: **return** $Z = z_0 + z_1 g$;

End

Verification and Test. The procedure presented in Fig. 7 is used to ensure the correctness of our implementation. First, we use Magma calculator software [10] as a reference implementation to generate P (resp. Q), a generator of $\mathbb{G}_1$ (resp. $\mathbb{G}_2$). Then, a Python script computes the test vector $\{P, [\alpha]P, Q, [\alpha]Q\}$ with α a random element. Subsequently, our design computes both $e(P, [\alpha]Q)$ and $e([\alpha]P, Q)$. Finally, the CPU sends these two values back to the desktop which checks for the equality of: $e(P, [\alpha]Q) = e([\alpha]P, Q)$. Verifying the pairing bilinearity ensures the correctness of our implementations. This method is used to test our design at each level of the development, from operations on the base field to the entire pairing.

4.2   Implementation Results

The proposed design is coded in VHDL and implemented on a Kintex-7. Our base field unit is packaged into a custom IP and integrated into a System on Chip with a MicroBlaze CPU. The *time × area* metric is chosen to estimate the overall performance of the hardware component. This value gives a complete picture since it does not only take into account the estimated area but also the amount of performance provided. It gives a fairer comparison than the classical one using the equivalent gate metrics. The obtained performances are presented in Table 4 for the old 128-bit and for the updated 128-bit and 192-bit security levels.

In [35], authors build a highly parallel architecture to design a fast and energy-efficient pairing unit for BN curves at the old 128-bit security level. However, their design required thousands of slices and several Digital Signal Processing (DSP) units and would be difficult to fit in lightweight designs.

To our knowledge, the fastest pairing architecture at the old 128-bit security level is the one proposed in [37]. To maximize the benefit of parallelization, the authors use several triple-port RAMs. This memory requires around four times the area required by classical simple-port ones. As a result, this architecture could also barely fit in lightweight designs.

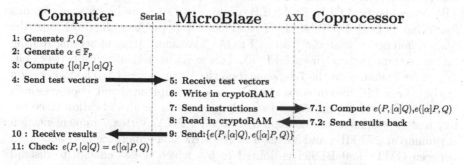

Fig. 7. Procedure for a test sequence with our ALU

Authors in [32] propose a lightweight hardware accelerator for modular multiplication and pilot it with a Cortex A9 CPU to compute pairings on BN curves at the old 128-bit security level. They also demonstrate that adding dedicated hardware to compute operations in the base field can decrease both time and energy required to compute a pairing. Our BLS12-381 implementation has a better *time × area* than previous hardware implementations on BN curves of [32,35].

Table 4. Performances comparison of pairing hardware implementations

Security	Ref.	Curves	Platform	Area (slices)	DSP	Time (ms)	*time × area*
	[37]	BN-254	Virtex-6	5237	64	**0.41**	**2147**
99.7-bit	[35]		Virtex-7	28400	128	3.43	97412
	[32]		Zynq-7020	598	0	134	80132
120.7-bit	This work	BLS12-381	Kintex-7	1006	0	36.14	**36357**
	This work	BLS12-460	**Kintex-7**	1223	0	48.91	59817
			Virtex-7	1235	0	48.91	60404
			Virtex-6	1446	0	65.21	94294
		BLS24-318	**Kintex-7**	**925**	0	64.78	59922
128-bit			Virtex-7	922	0	64.78	**59727**
			Virtex-6	1156	0	86.37	99844
		GMT8-544	**Kintex-7**	1325	0	**42.71**	**56591**
			Virtex-7	1463	0	42.71	62485
			Virtex-6	1654	0	56.94	94195
192-bit	This work	BLS24-518	**Kintex-7**	1325	0	184.23	**244105**

For the sake of fair comparison with future work, we implement our ALU on a Virtex-7 and a Virtex-6 FPGA. These platforms are chosen because they have been widely used in previous work. FPGAs are built with Configurable Logic Blocks (CLB), and 7-series FPGA such as Kintex-7 or Virtex-7, and Virtex-6 FPGA use identical CLB. Each CLB contains two slices and each slice contains four 6-inputs Look Up Table (LUT) and four flip-flops. According to Xilinx, the main difference is that the 7-series FPGAs have more interconnecting routing resources compared to Virtex-6 FPGA. This explains the difference between our design performance on the 7-series and on the Virtex-6 FPGA. The last version of the Xilinx ISE design suite (14.7) is used to implement our coprocessor in Virtex-6. The results presented in Table 4 are given as an indication since the test and development are done on a Kintex-7 FPGA. Virtex-7 implementation is running at 200 MHz and Virtex-6 at 150 MHz. The difference in *time × area* between GMT8 and BLS24 is limited to 5% which is not enough to discard a curve. Furthermore, pairings at actual security levels require a consequent amount of memory. With our implementation, GMT8 requires 5976B, BLS12 7040B and BLS24 9920B respectively. Since memory is often the critical resource in constrained devices, GMT8 may be the appropriate choice at the updated 128-bit security level.

Table 4 also shows that the curve ranking in terms of *time × area*, not only differs from estimations given in [4], but also differs from one platform to another. Therefore, it becomes interesting to choose the curve according to the desired application and platform.

5 Conclusion and Future Work

The Kim and Barbulescu attack created a new paradigm as BN curves are no longer undisputed pairing champions. Authors of [4] and [18] have studied new curves. The consequences are that any dedicated hardware implementation ought to support multiple arithmetics to maximize flexibility. Pairing complexity estimates only take into account the complexity of modular multiplications. This paper shows that neglected operations such as modular additions have also a significant impact on implementation performances since they represent 25% of the overall computation time in our architecture. Based on the best curve candidates for implementations, we presented a flexible hardware architecture to support all of them. The proposed lightweight hardware is designed to accelerate modular operations. It has a reconfigurable modulus which enables the support of different curves and allows parallel computing during multiplication. This improves performance by approximately 15% decreasing the cost of additional operations to consider only multiplications.

To the best of our knowledge, this paper presents the first hardware implementation of pairings at the updated 128-bit and 192-bit security levels as proposed in [4] and in [18]. Moreover, the proposed implementations provide promising performances compared to previous work on lightweight implementations since our *time × area* product is three times better than the one presented in [32]. Our different FPGA porting results also provide evidence that the best curves have similar complexity at the updated 128-bit security level. It shows that there is no optimal choice of pairings at the 128-bit security level. With our architecture, the GMT8 curve seems to provide the best time and *time × area* performances. But it also requires a bigger coprocessor than for BLS24 or BLS12. On the other hand, BLS24 requires much more memory than GMT8. Future work could consider other promising curves such as KSS16, DCC15 or other curves proposed in [18] and evaluate their performance on classical protocols.

References

1. Aranha, D.F., Gouvêa, C.P.L., Markmann, T., Wahby, R.S., Liao, K.: RELIC is an Efficient LIbrary for Cryptography. https://github.com/relic-toolkit/relic
2. Aranha, D.F., Karabina, K., Longa, P., Gebotys, C.H., López, J.: Faster explicit formulas for computing pairings over ordinary curves. In: Paterson, K.G. (ed.) EUROCRYPT 2011. LNCS, vol. 6632, pp. 48–68. Springer, Heidelberg (2011). https://doi.org/10.1007/978-3-642-20465-4_5

3. Barbulescu, R., Duquesne, S.: Updating key size estimations for pairings. J. Cryptol. (2018). https://hal.archives-ouvertes.fr/hal-01534101

4. Barbulescu, R., El Mrabet, N., Ghammam, L.: A taxonomy of pairings, their security, their complexity. IACR Cryptol. ePrint Arch. **2019**, 485 (2019)

5. Barreto, P.S.L.M., Lynn, B., Scott, M.: Constructing elliptic curves with prescribed embedding degrees. In: Cimato, S., Persiano, G., Galdi, C. (eds.) SCN 2002. LNCS, vol. 2576, pp. 257–267. Springer, Heidelberg (2003). https://doi.org/10.1007/3-540-36413-7_19

6. Barreto, P.S.L.M., Naehrig, M.: Pairing-friendly elliptic curves of prime order. In: Preneel, B., Tavares, S. (eds.) SAC 2005. LNCS, vol. 3897, pp. 319–331. Springer, Heidelberg (2006). https://doi.org/10.1007/11693383_22

7. Ben-Sasson, E., Chiesa, A., Tromer, E., Virza, M.: Succinct non-interactive zero knowledge for a von Neumann architecture. In: USENIX Security Symposium, pp. 781–796. USENIX Association (2014)

8. Boneh, D., Franklin, M.: Identity-based encryption from the weil pairing. In: Kilian, J. (ed.) CRYPTO 2001. LNCS, vol. 2139, pp. 213–229. Springer, Heidelberg (2001). https://doi.org/10.1007/3-540-44647-8_13

9. Boneh, D., Lynn, B., Shacham, H.: Short signatures from the weil pairing. In: Boyd, C. (ed.) ASIACRYPT 2001. LNCS, vol. 2248, pp. 514–532. Springer, Heidelberg (2001). https://doi.org/10.1007/3-540-45682-1_30

10. Bosma, W., Cannon, J., Playoust, C.: The Magma algebra system. I. The user language. J. Symb. Comput. **24**(3–4), 235–265 (1997). https://doi.org/10.1006/jsco.1996.0125

11. Cocks, C., Pinch, R.: Identity-based cryptosystems based on the Weil pairing. In: manuscript (2001)

12. Costello, C., Lange, T., Naehrig, M.: Faster pairing computations on curves with high-degree twists. In: Nguyen, P.Q., Pointcheval, D. (eds.) PKC 2010. LNCS, vol. 6056, pp. 224–242. Springer, Heidelberg (2010). https://doi.org/10.1007/978-3-642-13013-7_14

13. Duan, P., Cui, S., Chan, C.: Special polynomial families for generating more suitable elliptic curves for pairing-based cryptosystems. IACR Cryptol. ePrint Arch. **2005**, 342 (2005)

14. El Mrabet, N., Guillermin, N., Ionica, S.: A study of pairing computation for elliptic curves with embedding degree 15. IACR Cryptol. ePrint Arch. **2009**, 370 (2009)

15. Freeman, D., Scott, M., Teske, E.: A taxonomy of pairing-friendly elliptic curves. J. Cryptol. **23**(2), 224–280 (2010)

16. Ghammam, L., Fouotsa, E.: Improving the computation of the optimal Ate pairing for a high security level. J. Appl. Math. Comput. **59** (2018). https://doi.org/10.1007/s12190-018-1167-y

17. Granger, R., Scott, M.: Faster squaring in the cyclotomic subgroup of sixth degree extensions. In: Nguyen, P.Q., Pointcheval, D. (eds.) PKC 2010. LNCS, vol. 6056, pp. 209–223. Springer, Heidelberg (2010). https://doi.org/10.1007/978-3-642-13013-7_13

18. Guillevic, A., Masson, S., Thomé, E.: Cocks-Pinch curves of embedding degrees five to eight and optimal Ate pairing computation. Cryptology ePrint Archive, Report 2019/431 (2019). https://eprint.iacr.org/2019/431

19. Hess, F., Smart, N., Vercauteren, F.: The Eta pairing revisited. Cryptology ePrint Archive, Report 2006/110 (2006). https://eprint.iacr.org/2006/110

20. Hess, F.: Pairing lattices. In: Galbraith, S.D., Paterson, K.G. (eds.) Pairing 2008. LNCS, vol. 5209, pp. 18–38. Springer, Heidelberg (2008). https://doi.org/10.1007/978-3-540-85538-5_2

21. Huang, M., Gaj, K., El-Ghazawi, T.: New hardware architectures for Montgomery modular multiplication algorithm. IEEE Trans. Comput. **60**(7), 923–936 (2011). https://doi.org/10.1109/TC.2010.247
22. John, T.: Duality theorems in Galois cohomology over number fields. In: International Congress of Mathematicians Stockholm 1962, Djursholm (1963)
23. Joux, A.: A one round protocol for tripartite diffie-hellman. In: ANTS-IV: Proceedings of the 4th International Symposium on Algorithmic Number Theory, London, UK, p. 385394 (2000)
24. Kachisa, E.J., Schaefer, E.F., Scott, M.: Constructing brezing-weng pairing-friendly elliptic curves using elements in the cyclotomic field. In: Galbraith, S.D., Paterson, K.G. (eds.) Pairing 2008. LNCS, vol. 5209, pp. 126–135. Springer, Heidelberg (2008). https://doi.org/10.1007/978-3-540-85538-5_9
25. Karabina, K.: Squaring in cyclotomic subgroups. Cryptology ePrint Archive, Report 2010/542 (2010). https://eprint.iacr.org/2010/542
26. Khandaker, M.A.-A., Nanjo, Y., Ghammam, L., Duquesne, S., Nogami, Y., Kodera, Y.: Efficient optimal ate pairing at 128-bit security level. In: Patra, A., Smart, N.P. (eds.) INDOCRYPT 2017. LNCS, vol. 10698, pp. 186–205. Springer, Cham (2017). https://doi.org/10.1007/978-3-319-71667-1_10
27. Kim, T., Barbulescu, R.: Extended tower number field sieve: a new complexity for the medium prime case. In: Robshaw, M., Katz, J. (eds.) CRYPTO 2016. LNCS, vol. 9814, pp. 543–571. Springer, Heidelberg (2016). https://doi.org/10.1007/978-3-662-53018-4_20
28. Knuth, D.E.: The Art of Computer Programming, Volume 1 (3rd Ed.): Fundamental Algorithms. Addison Wesley Longman Publishing Co., Inc., USA (1997)
29. Koblitz, N., Menezes, A.: Pairing-based cryptography at high security levels. In: Smart, N.P. (ed.) Cryptography and Coding 2005. LNCS, vol. 3796, pp. 13–36. Springer, Heidelberg (2005). https://doi.org/10.1007/11586821_2
30. Miller, V.S.: The weil pairing, and its efficient calculation. J. Cryptol. **17**(4), 235–261 (2004). https://doi.org/10.1007/s00145-004-0315-8
31. Montgomery, P.L.: Modular multiplication without trial division. Math. Comput. **44**(170), 519–521 (1985)
32. Salman, A., Diehl, W., Kaps, J.: A light-weight hardware/software co-design for pairing-based cryptography with low power and energy consumption. In: FPT, pp. 235–238. IEEE (2017)
33. Tenca, A., Koc, C.: A scalable architecture for Montgomery multiplication. In: Proceedings of First International Workshop Cryptographic Hardware and Embedded Systems (CHES 1999), pp. 94–108 (01 1999)
34. Vercauteren, F.: Optimal pairings. IEEE Trans. Inf. Theory **56**(1), 455–461 (2010). https://doi.org/10.1109/TIT.2009.2034881
35. Wang, A.T., Guo, B.W., Wei, C.J.: Highly-parallel hardware implementation of optimal Ate pairing over Barreto-Naehrig curves. Integration **64**, 13–21 (2019)
36. Xiong, X., Wong, D.S., Deng, X.: Tinypairing: a fast and lightweight pairing-based cryptographic library for wireless sensor networks. In: WCNC, pp. 1–6. IEEE (2010)
37. Yao, G.X., Fan, J., Cheung, R.C.C., Verbauwhede, I.: Faster pairing coprocessor architecture. In: Abdalla, M., Lange, T. (eds.) Pairing 2012. LNCS, vol. 7708, pp. 160–176. Springer, Heidelberg (2013). https://doi.org/10.1007/978-3-642-36334-4_10
38. Zhang, X., Lin, D.: Analysis of optimum pairing products at high security levels. In: Galbraith, S., Nandi, M. (eds.) INDOCRYPT 2012. LNCS, vol. 7668, pp. 412–430. Springer, Heidelberg (2012). https://doi.org/10.1007/978-3-642-34931-7_24

A Hard Crystal - Implementing Dilithium on Reconfigurable Hardware

Georg Land[1,2]([⊠]) [iD], Pascal Sasdrich[1] [iD], and Tim Güneysu[1,2] [iD]

[1] Ruhr University Bochum, Horst Görtz Institute for IT Security, Bochum, Germany
{georg.land,pascal.sasdrich,tim.guneysu}@rub.de
[2] DFKI GmbH, Cyber-Physical Systems, Bremen, Germany

Abstract. CRYSTALS-Dilithium as a lattice-based digital signature scheme has been selected as a finalist in the Post-Quantum Cryptography (PQC) standardization process of NIST. As part of this selection, a variety of software implementations have been evaluated regarding their performance and memory requirements for platforms like x86 or ARM Cortex-M4. In this work, we present a first set of Field-Programmable Gate Array (FPGA) implementations for the low-end Xilinx Artix-7 platform, evaluating the peculiarities of the scheme in hardware, reflecting all available round-3 parameter sets. As a key component in our analysis, we present results for a specifically adapted Number-Theoretic Transform (NTT) core for the Dilithium cryptosystem, optimizing this component for an optimal Look-Up Table (LUT) and Flip-Flop (FF) utilization by efficient use of special purpose Digital Signal Processors (DSPs). Presenting our results, we aim to shed further light on the performance of lattice-based cryptography in low-cost and high-throughput configurations and their respective potential use-cases in practice.

Keywords: FPGA · Dilithium · PQC

1 Introduction

In the light of continuous progress and advancement on the development of quantum computers, security of existing public-key cryptographic schemes starts to crumble [12]. While most existing and currently deployed schemes rely on the hardness of *integer factorization* or computing *discrete logarithms*, broken by Shor's quantum algorithm [15], given that an attacker has access to a large-scale quantum computer, a call for the design, proposal, and standardization of new post-quantum secure schemes for Key Encapsulation Mechanism (KEM) and digital signatures has been initiated by the United States National Institute for Standards and Technology (NIST) in 2017 [10].

After two competitive rounds of thorough scrutiny and examination, NIST announced the seven finalists from the initial field of 69 candidates in 2020 which still have to undergo further evaluation in a third and final round. Moreover, the

© Springer Nature Switzerland AG 2022
V. Grosso and T. Pöppelmann (Eds.): CARDIS 2021, LNCS 13173, pp. 210–230, 2022.
https://doi.org/10.1007/978-3-030-97348-3_12

seven finalists can be categorized into the four key establishment schemes, Classic McEliece, Kyber, NTRU, and Saber as well as the three digital signature schemes Dilithium, Falcon, and Rainbow.

Interestingly, five out of the seven remaining finalists are using hard lattice problems as fundamental security assumption. Along with Falcon [7], Dilithium [5] is one of the two remaining lattice-based digital signature schemes, while Rainbow is based on multivariate cryptography instead. Further, Dilithium and Kyber are part of the Cryptographic Suite for Algebraic Lattices (CRYSTALS) using structured lattices to allow fast arithmetic and enable compact key, ciphertext and signature sizes. More precisely, the underlying polynomial ring enables efficient polynomial multiplication leveraging the Number-Theoretic Transform (NTT).

While literature is rich in efficient and optimized implementations on lattice-based KEMs, to date, lattice-based digital signature schemes are mostly neglected. In particular, efficient implementation of lattice-based signature schemes in reconfigurable hardware urgently needs to be investigated in order to guide and support the selection of the future post-quantum cryptography standards. In this regard, we are only aware of a two existing hardware implementations of Dilithium [13,16], while several optimized software implementations, e.g., targeting AVX2 [4] or Cortex-M4 [8] architectures, have been presented recently. Further, even though the design in [13] has been implemented on a high-performance Virtex-7 Field-Programmable Gate Array (FPGA), it does not exploit important features of modern reconfigurable hardware architectures efficiently. For this, we present a novel set of efficient and compact FPGA implementations specifically targeting a low-end Xilinx Artix-7 series through evaluating the peculiarities of the Dilithium digital signature scheme for efficient and clever mapping into modern FPGA features and components[1].

Contribution. For this, our contribution can be summarized as follows:

- An optimized NTT component making extensive use of Digital Signal Processors (DSPs) is presented to exploit peculiarities and features of modern low-end FPGAs. We were able to synthesize our NTT implementation for a frequency of 311 MHz, resulting in a latency of 1.7 μs, which is, to the best of our knowledge, the fastest NTT implementation for comparable parameters in Artix-7 FPGAs.
- Our Dilithium core is compact and self-contained, providing functionalities for key generation, signature generation, signature verification, precomputation, arbitrary-length message digesting, and packing and unpacking keys and signatures.
- For Dilithium-III, our core uses 30k Look-Up Tables (LUTs), 11k Flip-Flops (FFs), 45 DSPs and 23 Block-RAMs (BRAMs) with $f_{max} = 142$ MHz. For key generation, our core is capable of performing 4290 OP/s, for signature generation 1351 OP/s and for signature verification 11751 OP/s.

---

[1] Our implementation is publicly available at https://github.com/Chair-for-Security-Engineering/dilithium-artix7.

- Additionally, we report area and speed results for individual stand-alone cores, supporting either only key generation, signature generation, or verification. These smaller cores still support the necessary unpacking, packing, digesting, and precomputation operations.
- For Dilithium-III, our keygen-only core is capable of performing 7250 OP/s. The sign-only core performs 1560 OP/s and the verify-only core 16137 OP/s.

Related Work. Many lattice-based schemes have been proposed in recent years and there is a wide variety of implementations in hardware. The first implementation of a lattice-based signature scheme was proposed by Güneysu et al. [9] in 2012. Pöppelmann et al.extend this work in [11]. Soni et al. present an implementation of the second-round parameter set of Dilithium targeting Artix-7 FPGAs [16]. However, they use a High Level Synthesis (HLS) approach resulting in a rather large design. Another implementation of the second-round parameter set of Dilithium is provided by Ricci et al., which targets the high-end Virtex-7 platform [13]. Most notably, their design achieves a high throughput for signature generation. Other post-quantum secure signature schemes that have been implemented in reconfigurable hardware include Rainbow [6], SPHINCS [1] and XMSS [17]. Furthermore, efficient implementation of the NTT in hardware has been researched very well. Roy et al. presented an efficient design that uses two merged NTT layers [14]. Banerjee et al. presented an Application-Specific Integrated Circuit (ASIC) design of the NTT that can be used to accelerate multiple schemes [2]. Finally, Zhang et al. present a way to integrate the post-processing of the inverse transformation into the main computation resulting in a low-complexity implementation [19].

2   Preliminaries

2.1   Notation

Throughout this work, we will use and assume the following notation. Let n and q be two integers, such that $n = 256$ and $q = 2^{23} - 2^{13} + 1$. Further, let $\mathcal{R}_q$ be a polynomial ring with $\mathcal{R}_q = \mathbb{Z}_q[X]/(X^n + 1)$. In addition, let us denote vectors in bold lower-case letters, e.g., $\mathbf{v}$, while matrices are denoted in bold upper-case letters, e.g., $\mathbf{A}$. Polynomials in NTT domain are indicated by a hat.

Additionally, for an integer s, we denote $s[a : b]$, where $a > b$, as the bit slice of s bounded by the offsets a, b counting from LSB to MSB, for example for $s = 6$ we have $s[2 : 1] = 11_2 = 3$.

2.2   Number-Theoretic Transform

The NTT, as used in Dilithium, can be seen as a discrete Fourier transform over polynomials in $\mathcal{R}_q$, where the complex arithmetic is replaced by the modular arithmetic of the polynomial coefficients. Since the ring structure enables negative wrapped convolution, we can use an n-point NTT for fast polynomial multiplication by transforming both factor polynomials to the NTT domain, multiplying coefficient-wise in NTT domain, and then applying the inverse transform to the result to obtain the final product polynomial.

2.3   CRYSTALS-Dilithium

In July 2020, NIST announced the 7 finalist and 8 alternate candidates for the Post-Quantum Cryptography (PQC) standardization competition, with both schemes of the CRYSTALS suite being selected as finalist for their respective categories. In particular the digital signature scheme Dilithium has undergone a thorough scrutiny during the competition process and since then reached version 3.1 [5], while most recently some major changes and updates for the various security parameter sets have been presented.

In general, the Dilithium digital signature scheme has been designed to adopt simple and secure design principles, in particular substituting discrete Gaussian sampling in favor of uniform sampling. In addition, all remaining fundamental operations have been carefully chosen such that they easily can be performed in constant time. Aiming at long-term security, the different security levels and parameters have been chosen conservatively while endeavoring to minimize the combined size of public key and signatures. Eventually, the modular construction of Dilithium favors efficient and highly optimized implementations across all security levels and parameter sets as the main operations rely on SHAKE-128 or SHAKE-256 and the multiplication in the polynomial ring $\mathcal{R}_q$, regardless of the security level. Instead, higher or lower security is only achieved through addition or reduction in the number of operations performed in $\mathcal{R}_q$.

Further, as a digital signature scheme, Dilithium provides the following three core methods for *key generation*, *signature generation*, and *signature verification*.

Key Generation. For key generation, the respective algorithm generates a $k \times l$ matrix $\mathbf{A}$ such that each entry in the matrix is a polynomial of the ring $\mathcal{R}_q$. Using randomly sampled vectors $\mathbf{s}_1$ and $\mathbf{s}_2$, with polynomials in $\mathcal{R}_q$ where each coefficient is in $[-\eta, \eta]$, the second part of the public key is generated as $\mathbf{t} = \mathbf{A}\mathbf{s}_1 + \mathbf{s}_2$, performing all algebraic operations over $\mathcal{R}_q$. To keep the public key size small, the matrix $\mathbf{A}$ is replaced by a seed ρ which generates $\mathbf{A}$ deterministically, which is a widespread technique in lattice-based cryptography. Additionally, to further decrease the size of the public key, the lower d bits of each coefficient in $\mathbf{t}$ are placed in the secret key rather than the public key.

Signature Generation. The fundamental operation of Dilithium is the generation of digital signatures. For this, the signing algorithm chooses a masking vector $\mathbf{y}$ with coefficients from $[-\gamma_1, \gamma_1)$ in order to compute $\mathbf{w} = \mathbf{A}\mathbf{y}$ and rounds the result such that $\mathbf{w} = \mathbf{w}_1 \cdot 2\gamma_2 + \mathbf{w}_0$, where each coefficient in $\mathbf{w}_0$ is less than or equal to γ_2. The challenge c, a polynomial in $\mathcal{R}_q$ with coefficents from $\{-1, 1\}$ at τ random positions and all other coefficients being 0, is sampled by hashing the message and $\mathbf{w}_1$ and is used to generate the potential signature $\mathbf{z} = \mathbf{y} + c\mathbf{s}_1$.

Using rejection sampling, leakage of the secret key is prevented, at the penalty of repeating the signature generation process if the signature fails the security and correctness checks. Additionally, since for the verification t is needed but only the upper 10 bits of t are contained in the public key, the signer needs to compute the vector of carry bits ("hints") h that result from the unknown part in t during the verification computation. Finally, if a z is found that passes the checks, the signature is returned as (c, z, h).

Signature Verification. For signature verification, $Az - ct$ is rounded analogously to the signing procedure and the resulting *higher-order* bits are set to be w'_1. Since the lower bits of each coefficient in t are not contained in the public key, the verifier makes use of the hints h to perform this operation. Following this, the challenge c is recomputed from the message and w'_1 and compared to the one provided in the signature. Also, z is checked to have a valid norm (i.e., whether each coefficient has the maximum value as checked during signature generation).

Parameter Sets. With introduction of version 3.1 of the Dilithium algorithm specification, the list of supported security parameter sets has been adjusted for the three NIST security levels II, III, and V. Since the operations in $\mathcal{R}_q$ do not change for the different parameter sets, the performance-critical dimensions of A are adjusted, resulting in an increased or reduced number of operations, depending on the targeted security level.

Compared to round 2, the following adjustments have been proposed:

- d is decreased from 14 to 13.
- τ is now different for each parameter set rather than 60 for all, resulting in a slight speed-up for the lower parameter sets.
- γ_1 is now a power of two, which simplifies sampling y significantly.
- $\eta = 2$ for security levels II and V and $\eta = 4$ for security level III, rather than different ηs for each parameter set.
- $\gamma_2 = (q - 1)/88$ for security level II. Both other security levels keep $\gamma_2 = (q - 1)/32$.

3   Design Considerations

Modern FPGA generations are equipped with a multitude of general purpose logic. However, for certain applications, highly optimized special purpose components such as very compact and optimized DSP cores are provided, offering efficient and fast integer arithmetic operations, or BRAMs, offering compact true dual-port memory banks for easy storage of larger amounts of data. Given this, our primary design goal was to reduce the footprint of our architecture in terms of general purpose components such as LUTs and FFs, as these components usually are the limiting factor in larger systems. Additionally, we design all operations such that there is no timing dependency on secret values.

3.1 Arithmetic

As a first step, we opted to implement the basic arithmetic using DSP modules for fast and efficient coefficient-level computations. DSP blocks are abundantly available on latest FPGA devices but in general applications rarely used. More precisely, we exploit several special features of modern Xilinx DSP blocks, including:

Runtime Reconfiguration. During design and synthesis time, the DSP can be configured to provide different functionalities during runtime. Based on this, we configured some of our instantiated DSP modules to provide multiple different arithmetic operations, allowing to re-use the same DSP for different operations, hence resulting in a highly integrated and optimized design with respect to area and utilization.

Pre-addition. Besides fast integer multiplication, each DSP unit is equipped with a pre-adder stage, allowing to merge multiple arithmetic operations within a single DSP.

Single Instruction Multiple Data. Although each DSP unit can perform up to 48-bit wide additions, we opted to use DSP cores in a Single Instruction Multiple Data (SIMD) fashion, allowing to perform two 24-bit additions or subtractions instead, perfectly fitting the constrains of underlying arithmetic operations in the polynomial ring.

Number-Theoretic Transform. On a high level, we follow the design ideas from [19], especially including the inverse NTT without post-processing. However, by applying the aforementioned DSP features to our NTT design, our implementation achieves a low latency despite processing relatively big coefficients. In contrast to known NTT architectures, which usually utilize DSPs only for a low-latency multiplication and perform any other arithmetic with general-purpose logic, our novel approach of leveraging the full capabilities of DSPs results in a low latency for any involved arithmetic. This approach fits the requirements for implementing Butterfly Units (BFUs) particularly well, as during the forward NTT, e.g., $a + b\omega$ is computed, which can be mapped to DSP functionality *without* additional arithmetic logic. Also, even though this operation is not useful for our inverse NTT, we still can re-use the exact same DSPs by reconfiguring them at runtime at the cost of additional control logic.

3.2 Memory

Besides efficient arithmetic, a specific memory architecture and layout is required to store and load coefficients and polynomials efficiently during arithmetic operations. Given the design considerations for our arithmetic modules including the NTT unit, we identified the following two design constraints for our memory architecture:

1. Given the NTT architecture, the design would benefit from reading and writing up to four coefficients simultaneously. For this, we decided to use four simple dual port BRAMs to store polynomials. More precisely, we use four parallel 18K BRAM instances for this, each of them holding up to 512 coefficients. This means, since for a single polynomial only 64 coefficients are stored per BRAM, we can fill the four 18K BRAM units with up to eight full polynomials.

2. The memory layout has to be adjusted such that the number of read and write conflicts are minimized. In particular, the layout has to ensure that the coefficients of the polynomials are distributed among the BRAMs such that we always can read or write data during the arithmetic operations without stalling due to memory access conflicts. This can be achieved as follows: For a polynomial's coefficient aX^i, the coefficient is placed in memory $bankaddr$ (Eq. 1) at address $addr$ (Eq. 2) [19, Sec. 3.1].

$$bankaddr = i[7:6] + i[5:4] + i[3:2] + i[1:0] \bmod 4 \tag{1}$$
$$addr = i[7:2] \tag{2}$$

Our design needs to hold $k \cdot l + 2l + 6k + 1$ polynomials in total. It is possible to reduce this memory footprint significantly by sampling single polynomials of $\hat{\mathbf{A}}$ just in time. However, we opt to expand $\hat{\mathbf{A}}$ once and store it for further computations. This has the advantage that introducing a pre-processing operation enables signing multiple messages (or verifying multiple signatures) under the same key without the necessity of re-sampling $\hat{\mathbf{A}}$.

Since $\mathbf{z}$ and $\mathbf{y}$ are never accessed simultaneously, we only plan with l polynomials for both together. Additionally, $\mathbf{s}_1$ takes storage for l polynomials. c occupies storage for one polynomial. Four of the six polynomial vectors of size k are $\mathbf{s}_2, \mathbf{t}_0, \mathbf{t}_1, \mathbf{w}$. The remaining $2k$ polynomials are used as temporary storage, for example during MakeHint.

Given that we can store up to 8 polynomials using four BRAM units, the total number of BRAM instances is governed by the security level. In particular, we need storage for 49 polynomials for level II, 77 polynomials for level III, and 119 polynomials for level V. We were able to identify efficient memory mappings for each parameter set, such that it only requires $\lceil 4(kl + 2l + 6k + 1)/8 \rceil$ 18K BRAM primitives. We did so by iteratively searching through possible memory mappings in a randomized way and checking whether the requirements are met. The memory mapping enables the following operations in a pipelined or parallel fashion:

- During matrix-vector multiplication, the vector elements are transformed sequentially to NTT domain. Upon completion of the transformation, the multiply-accumulate module updates the resulting vector elements through coefficient-wise multiplication with the $\hat{\mathbf{A}}$ polynomials.

- In pre-computations for signature generation and verification, the matrix $\hat{\mathbf{A}}$ is expanded and in parallel, NTTs of $\mathbf{s_1}$, $\mathbf{s_2}$, $\mathbf{t_0}$ and $\mathbf{t_1}$ can be performed.
- During verification, the norm check of $\mathbf{z}$ can be performed in parallel to sampling c.
- Since, at the end of key generation, $\mathbf{s_1}$ is part of the secret key, during matrix-vector multiplication, $\mathbf{s_1}$ is transformed to NTT domain for fast multiplication. To avoid the necessity of performing an inverse NTT, $\mathbf{s_1}$ is stored in two locations simultaneously during sampling, after which one can be transformed and the other location is used as result.

3.3   Functionality

In order to provide an integrated and self-contained core for generation and verification of digital signatures based on the Dilithium scheme, our architecture needs to support the full set of the following operations:

KeyGen Generation of a key from a given seed.

Sign$_{pre}$ Expansion of $\hat{\mathbf{A}}$ and pre-computation of $\hat{s}_1$, $\hat{s}_2$, and $\hat{t}_0$.

Sign Signature computation.

Verify$_{pre}$ Expansion of $\hat{\mathbf{A}}$ and pre-computation of $\hat{t}_1$.

Verify Signature verification.

Digest$_{msg}$ Hashing of arbitrary-length messages along with tr (of the public key).

Store Storing and unpacking public keys, secret keys, signatures, or seeds.

Load Packing and sending public keys, secret keys, or signatures.

Additionally, we provide individual cores which only support either key generation, signature generation, or verification. Besides featuring only a subset of the operations, these smaller cores also come with a lower BRAM usage since some polynomials are only required for a subset of operations. An overview which operation is supported by each single-task core can be found in Table 1.

Table 1. Operation support matrix for single-task cores

	KeyGen	Sign$_{pre}$	Sign	Verify$_{pre}$	Verify	Digest$_{msg}$	Store	Load
KeyGen-only	✓	✗	✗	✗	✗	✗	Seed	Keys
Sign-only	✗	✓	✓	✗	✗	✓	k_{priv}	Sign.
Verify-only	✗	✗	✗	✓	✓	✓	k_{pub}	

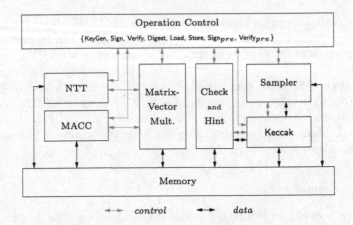

Fig. 1. Dilithium high-level architecture

4   Implementation on Reconfigurable Hardware

In this section, we outline the basic architecture of our comprehensive Dilithium architecture. In particular, our construction exploits special purpose units and features of an Artix-7 FPGA (XC7A100T).

4.1   Architectural Details

The high-level architecture of our implementation is shown in Fig. 1. All basic arithmetic operations are performed by the *NTT, Multiply-Accumulate (MACC)*, and *Matrix-Vector Multiplication* units. However, even though the matrix-vector multiplication serves as master and control unit for the NTT and MACC cores, both sub-cores must be accessible from the global operation control unit as well to provide auxiliary support for additional arithmetic operations. Besides, the check units directly access polynomials in the memory for norm checking and provide the check result to the operation control module. The *Sampler* module controls and accesses the *Keccak* hash core in order to buffer the hash output before writing the uniformly generated random samples to memory. However, the Keccak-based hash core is also accessible from the operation control unit, mostly required for random seed expansion. Finally, the *hint* modules control read and write access to the hint registers in the memory unit. Further, as already highlighted in Sect. 3, the memory unit consists of several BRAMs for the intermediate polynomials, two 512-bit registers to store ρ' and μ as well as some additional 256-bit registers for ρ, $\tilde{c}$, tr, K, and the seed for the key generation.

Number-Theoretic Transform. As already mentioned in Sect. 3, our NTT implementation follows the design principles of [19]. However, we pre-multiply the stored twiddle factors for the inverse transform by a factor of 2^{-1} in order to avoid the additional logic for mutliplying one coefficient by 2^{-1} in the BFU.

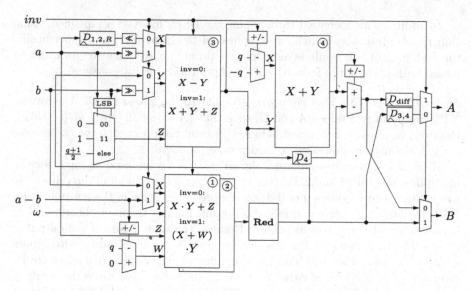

Fig. 2. Architecture of the BFU. DSPs are numbered, D_i are shift registers that compensate for the DSPs or the reduction as given in their respective index. D_{diff} compensates for the difference of cycle counts between $D_{1,2,R}$ and $D_{3,4}$

From an implementation perspective, we modify several details: First, as already mentioned we utilize DSPs for all arithmetic operations in order to achieve a low area footprint and a high frequency. Second, we make use of the *true* dual-port capabilities of the BRAM modules, enabling our design to read two twiddle factors simultaneously in the lowest NTT layer and thus still allowing processing four coefficients at the same time.

At the core of the NTT, we instantiate two independent BFUs, as depicted in Fig. 2. More precisely, each BFU receives two unsigned 23-bit coefficients, an unsigned 23-bit twiddle factor, and the *signed* 24-bit value $a - b$. Note, however, that this value can be computed for both BFUs simultaneously using a single DSP in SIMD mode.

Forward Number-Theoretic Transform. In general, the butterfly configuration for the forward NTT computes two values A and B such that $(A, B) := (a + b \cdot \omega, a - b \cdot \omega)$, given that ω denotes the pre-computed twiddle factor. For this, we use the DSPs 1 and 2 to compute $a + b\omega$. More precisely, we need to combine two DSPs for this operation since each DSP itself can only perform signed 25×18-bit multiplications. However, when combining DSPs for larger multiplications, we can leverage a dedicated low-latency cascade path. After multiplication, the resulting product is reduced to a representative in $[0, q)$ and already provides the first part of the forward NTT computation. Further, subtracting the first part from $2a$ and adding or subtracting q (depending on the sign of the subtraction result), we obtain the second part of the forward NTT output.

In addition, for increased throughput, the BFUs have been pipelined, using shift register instances to delay the input a of the third DSP. More specifically, the first part of the result is also delayed through a shift register in order to return both parts of the forward NTT computation simultaneously.

Inverse Number-Theoretic Transform. Similar to the forward NTT, the inverse NTT computes two values A and B, such that $(A, B) := (2^{-1}(a+b), (a-b)\omega)$. However, as already mentioned before, this time the operand ω for the inverse NTT is already pre-processed to incorporate the factor 2^{-1}.

Here, ω and the pre-computed, signed value $a - b$ are used as input for the multiplication DSPs 1 and 2. Further, depending on the sign bit of the value $a-b$, we choose between adding q or 0 using the pre-adder stage of the multiplication DSPs to obtain a positive multiplication result. Finally, the multiplication result is then reduced and serves as output. Besides, the second part of the output is designed to be $2^{-1}(a+b)$. For this, we use DSP 3 as 3-input adder with inputs $\lfloor a/2 \rfloor$, $\lfloor b/2 \rfloor$ and either 1 (if both least signification bits (LSBs) of a and b are 1), or $(q+1)/2$ (if the LSB of either a or b is 1), or 0 otherwise. Since the result of this operation might be greater or equal to q, we use the fourth DSP to subtract q from the result. The second part of the BFU output is then chosen between the output of DSPs 3 and 4.

Multiply-Accumulate. The second arithmetic core is used to perform *multiply-accumulate* operations. More specifically, this core is designed to perform four computations per clock cycle in parallel in order to make full use of the available memory bandwidth. It consists of eight DSPs and four reduction modules. Each two DSPs perform one of the following operation, while the result then is fed into the reduction module.

$a \cdot b + c$: The first DSP performs the multiplication of a with the lower 17 bits of b and the addition. The second DSP multiplies a with the remaining upper bits of b and updates the first result to the final 46 bit value that is then fed into the reduction module.

$a + b$: The first DSP computes the sum, while the second one subtracts q. Eventually, the result of the second DSP is selected if it is non-negative, else the result of the first DSP is selected.

$b - a$: The first DSP computes the subtraction, while the second one adds q. Eventually, the result of the first DSP is selected as output if it is positive, else the output of the second DSP is selected.

Note that for operations without multiplication, the reduction module can be bypassed, resulting in a lower latency. Again, this module is fully pipelined, allowing to process an entire polynomial within 64 cycles (in addition to the initial pipeline length).

Matrix-Vector Multiplication. This module controls both the NTT module and the MACC module to (1) transform the polynomials in the input vector into NTT domain and (2) perform a matrix-vector multiplication with $\hat{\mathbf{A}}$. The resulting polynomial vector is then in NTT representation as well.

First, the first input polynomial is transformed by the NTT module. Then, while the second input polynomial is transformed, the point-wise multiplication between each polynomial from the first column in $\hat{\mathbf{A}}$ and the first, already transformed input polynomial is carried out consecutively using the MACC module. The resulting polynomials are stored in the result vector polynomial storage. Note that the point-wise multiplications take $k \cdot 64 + 14$ cycles[2], while one NTT takes 533 cycles. When both operations are finished, the NTT module transforms the third input polynomial and in parallel, the second, already transformed input polynomial is multiplied point-wise with each polynomial from the second column in $\hat{\mathbf{A}}$ and added to the intermediate result from the first k MACC operations. The resulting polynomials again are stored back to the result vector polynomial storage.

This procedure is repeated until all l input polynomials are transformed. Afterwards, the resulting k polynomials are updated to the final result using the MACC module. With this, a whole matrix-vector multiplication is carried out in $k \cdot 512 + 23 + k \cdot 64 + 14$ cycles[3].

Modular Reduction. In our implementation, we need a total of six reduction module instantiations: While each BFU module contains a single reduction module, the MACC module contains four reduction modules. For the modular reduction of a 46-bit value s, we recursively exploit the relation $2^{23} \equiv 2^{13} - 1 \bmod q$ in a similar way as in [19].

$$s[45:0] \equiv 2^{23}s[45:23] + s[22:0] \equiv 2^{13}s[45:23] - s[45:23] + s[22:0]$$
$$\equiv 2^{23}s[45:33] + 2^{13}s[32:23] - s[45:23] + z$$
$$\equiv 2^{13}\left(s[45:33] + s[32:23]\right) - \left(s[45:33] + s[45:23]\right) + z$$
$$\equiv 2^{23}s[45:43] + 2^{13}\left(s[42:33] + s[32:23]\right) - \left(s[45:33] + s[45:23]\right) + z$$
$$\equiv 2^{13}\left(s[45:43] + s[42:33] + s[32:23]\right) - \left(s[45:43] + s[45:33] + s[45:23]\right) + z$$
$$\equiv 2^{13}x - y + z \equiv 2^{23}x[11:10] + 2^{13}x[9:0] - y + z$$
$$\equiv 2^{13}\left(x[11:10] + x[9:0]\right) - \left(y + x[11:10]\right) + z \bmod q$$

The result of our reduction can still be greater than 2^{23} so that we could repeat the substitution once again at the expense of additional depth and delay in the arithmetic computation. However, we observe that the result of the reduction at this point is already within the interval $(-\mathbf{q}, 2\mathbf{q})$[4]. For this, we can simply

---

[2] 14 is the initial pipeline length.

[3] The NTTs can be pipelined as well and thus, 23 is the initial pipeline length.

[4] Since in our implementation all coefficients are stored in the standard representation $[0, q)$, this reduction also works for results of computations $ab + c$, since $(\mathbf{q} - 1)^2 + (\mathbf{q} - 1) < 2^{46}$.

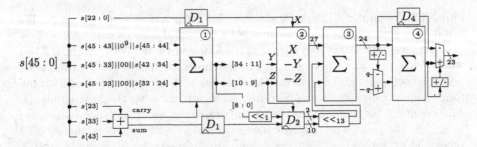

Fig. 3. Architecture of the modular reduction. DSPs are numbered, D_i are shift registers that compensate for the DSPs as given in their respective index. At the output multiplexer, the sign bit is discarded, which decreases the bit width to 23.

add **q** to a negative result or subtract **q** if the result is positive. Eventually, delaying the reduced result, as well as given the sum or subtraction with **q**, the final result is determined by selecting the non-negative value out of both.

In practice, we use four DSPs and one small addition implemented in general-purpose logic to perform the modular reduction. The first DSP computes x and y by using a Kronecker substitution-like approach: The lower bits compute x and the higher bits compute y. However, as the computation does not fit entirely into the pre-adder stage, we need to add the least-significant bit of x using general-purpose logic outside the DSP and delay the resulting bit, while the carry is fed into the DSP as well. Thus, DSP 1 is used as a fully pipelined 4-input adder with a latency of four clock cycles. Note, however, that for recent Ultrascale FPGAs, the witdh of pre-adder stage within the DSPs increased, which would allow to improve this reduction and give up the general-purpose addition.

Further, the second DSP computes $z + x[11 : 10] - y$. The result is fed into DSP 3 via a low-latency path, where $(x[11 : 10] + x[9 : 0]) \cdot 2^{13}$ are added to the previous result. Note that $x[11 : 10]$ corresponds to the output bits 10 and 9, and $x[9 : 1]$ correspond to the output bits 8 to 0 from DSP 1. $x[0]$ has been computed separately before DSP 1 and is delayed accordingly. The fourth and final DSP is connected to the third one via a low-latency path and adds **q** if the result of the third DSP is negative or subtracts **q** otherwise. Eventually, only the positive result is selected as output.

Keccak. A fundamental part of Dilithium is the application of SHAKE-128 and SHAKE-256, both as hash function or as Extendable-Output Function (XOF). More precisely, both functions use the same Keccak permutation with the same state size of 1500 bits but a different rate r, which either is 1344 bits for SHAKE-128 or 1088 bits for SHAKE-256. Thus, our implementation features a single Keccak core that performs the permutation in 24 cycles (i.e., using a single cycle per round).

For data input and output we decided to implement 32-bit buses. During I/O operations, the Keccak module rotates the internal state for $r = 1344$ on a 32-bit basis, while simultaneously the input is added (exclusive-or) to the rotation feedback. Note that this behavior can also be used to compute SHAKE-256, i.e., by just using an unaltered feedback for the last $8 = (1344 - 1088)/32$ words.

Sampling. Dilithium requires several sampling algorithms that use the output of SHAKE. Unfortunately, none of the sampling algorithms is aligned to work on 32-bit words. We solved this problem using buffers with a length of the *least common multiple* of 32 and the desired output bit width. This enables converting a stream of 32-bit words to a stream of words with the desired output bit width.

Sampling the challenge c involves the Fisher-Yates shuffle. We implement this using a shift register with runtime-variable depth that contains all offsets of the non-zero coefficients and their sign bit. Once a random offset is found in rejection sampling, we *rotate* through the shift register and compare the stored offsets with the newly sampled one. If they are equal, we replace the old one with the current rejection threshold (keeping the sign bit), which essentially performs the swap. Then we increase the register depth and shift in the newly sampled offset with the corresponding sign bit. Finally, the polynomial is written to the BRAM.

Rounding. Implementing the Power2Round operation in hardware is very efficient, since during the computation of $\mathbf{t}$, we simply split the result into the upper 10 bits and the lower 13 bits, stored into different polynomial memories. However, since the $\mathbf{t_0}$ coefficients are interpreted as signed integers and our main paradigm is to store coefficients always as standard representatives, we need to add $\mathbf{q}$ if the most signification bit (MSB) is 1. Due to the structure of the operation, this is efficient with a LUT-based adder, which allows to avoid the additional usage of a DSP.

We implement the HighBits operation as a simple behavioral description of a range look-up depending on the input coefficient, which is efficient since for $\gamma_2 = (q-1)/32$, since there are only 16 different possible output values and only the 15 MSB of a coefficient contribute to the result. For $\gamma_2 = (q-1)/88$, there are only 44 different outputs and only the 13 MSB of a coefficient contribute to the result.

Checking the low bits of $\mathbf{w} - c\mathbf{s_2}$, however, involves the MACC module in subtraction mode. Again, we implement a simple look-up that returns HighBits times $2\gamma_2$ – which is efficient for the same reasons as explained above – and we subtract the result from the coefficient to obtain the low bits and check their norm without storing them.

Hint. We store the hint in two registers, i.e., one storing the 1's offsets and the other one storing the k polynomial boundaries in the same format as specified for the packed signatures. For the MakeHint operation, we have $\mathbf{w} - c\mathbf{s_2}$ and $\mathbf{w} - c\mathbf{s_2} + c\mathbf{t_0}$ stored separately such that both can be read simultaneously. Eventually, we look up both HighBits and if differing, a new offset is shifted in. Further, for the UseHint operation, the hint module looks up the HighBits for each coefficient, i.e., both for h=0 and h=1. Then, selecting the correct one, the value is shifted into a buffer register for sampling (as described before) and absorbed to compute the value $\tilde{c}$, which ultimately is compared to the value of the signature during verification.

Memory Access. In-place NTTs as deployed in our implementation usually require polynomials to be re-orderd according to a bit-reversal permutation. Our NTT with two BFUs requires reading and writing four coefficients simultaneously, which is ensured by distributing the coefficients according to Eqs. 1 and 2. However, this also ensures that four coefficients with position $br(i), br(i+1), br(i+2), br(i+3)$ (with $4|i$) are placed in different memories. As a consequence, we can access polynomials either in bit-reversed order or in normal order, which eliminates the necessity of an explicit re-ordering operation. Our implementation makes use of this either by sampling polynomials in bit-reversed order or by accessing polynomials in bit-reversed order during NTT.

Single-Task Cores. In order to instantiate single-task cores that only support a subset of operations which are sufficient to perform either key generation, signing, or verification (see Table 1), we adjust the opcode decoder in our top level module and delete all unnecessary module instantiations. Furthermore, we adjust the load module such that only values that are generated by the respective single-task core can be packed and loaded. Similarly, we adjust the store module such that only values can be unpacked and stored that are necessary for the respoective single-task core. Thus, by applying slight changes to three files, a set of single-task cores is generated. Note that in order to adjust the security level, a single-line change is sufficient. Additionally, we generate memory mappings for each single-task core that exclude all polynomials which are not used in the respective core, resulting in a lower BRAM usage.

4.2   Utilization and Performance Results

This section provides area utilization and performance results obtained after Place-and-Route (PnR) on a Xilinx XC7A100T Artix-7 FPGA using the Vivado 2020.1 tool suite.

Utilization. Table 2 lists the results for resource utilization as well as the maximum frequency f_{max} obtained after synthesis and implementation. As expected, the LUT, FF, and BRAM utilization increases with the parameter sets, while the DSP utilization, governed by the NTT and MACC modules, is independent of the parameter sets.

Table 2. Resource utilization and performance on a XC7A100T FPGA

Param. Set	Core	Utilization				f_{max}	KeyGen	Sign$_{pre}$	Sign	Verify$_{pre}$	Verify
		LUT	FF	DSP	BRAM	MHz	OP/s	OP/s	OP/s	OP/s	OP/s
II	Full	27433	10681	45	15	163	8692	16905	2435	14938	18595
	Keygen	11064	7209	45	11	221	11772	–	–	–	–
	Sign	18028	9166	45	15	179	–	18557	2673	–	–
	Verify	12118	7551	45	11	200	–	–	–	18331	22819
	Cycles:						18761	9647	66966	10917	8770
III	Full	30900	11372	45	21	145	4368	7993	1375	7242	11966
	Keygen	14285	8588	45	17	205	6203	–	–	–	–
	Sign	21832	10245	45	21	174	–	9603	1659	–	–
	Verify	14911	8209	45	15	200	–	–	–	10017	16551
	Cycles:						33102	18089	105129	19966	12084
V	Full	44653	13814	45	31	140	2750	4152	1250	3868	8517
	Keygen	19319	10138	45	25	202	3954	–	–	–	–
	Sign	29331	12867	45	31	158	–	4691	1412	–	–
	Verify	17527	9984	45	23	197	–	–	–	5424	11944
	Cycles:						50982	33767	112145	36250	16462

Performance. Table 2 shows performance results for our implementations as the average over 1000 executions on random inputs. For signature verification, we report cycle counts for valid signatures only. More precisely, since the norm check of z, taking less than 100 cycles, is performed at the beginning, an invalid signature is processed subtantially faster. Besides, for signature generation, the cycle count spreads widely due to the nature of Dilithium. For the best-case scenario, in which a signature candidate is accepted after the first iteration, signing takes 19423, 26979, and 36609 cycles for Dilithium-II, III, and V, respectively.

Components. Table 3 shows the area consumption obtained after PnR for selected components. Additionally, cycle counts for the single operations are given.

4.3 Comparison to Existing Work

In out-of-context synthesis, we achieved a frequency of 311 MHz with a utilization of 524 LUTs, 759 FFs, 17 DSPs and 1 BRAM for our NTT. For NTT/iNTT, our implementation takes 533/536 cycles. In Table 4, we compare our NTT design to others. To the best of our knowledge, we are the first to report detailed performance numbers including latency for the Dilithium NTT as Ricci et al. [13] do not report cycle counts. Thus, we also include NTT implementations for different moduli and polynomial degrees. For a fair comparison, it is worth noting that the polynomial degree n mainly impacts the latency since an NTT has complexity $\mathcal{O}(n \log n)$, while the modulus size $\lceil \log_2 q \rceil$ defines the area of the arithmetic circuit which dominates the overall size.

The implementation from [13] achieves a very high frequency since it operates on the high-end Virtex-7 platform. Other implementations that target the same

Table 3. Area consumption and performance of selected components

Param. Set	Component	Operation	Utilization				Clock cycles
			LUT	FF	DSP	BRAM	
All	NTT	*Forward*	444	421	17	1	533^P
		Inverse					536^P
All	MACC	*MACC*	641	751	24	–	85^P
		Add/sub					75^P
All	Keccak	*Permute*	3708	1623	–	–	24
		Absorb					$\geq 42^M$
		Squeeze					1 per 4B
II	Matrix-vector multiplication		2129	59	–	–	2370
III			2774	49	–	–	3019
V			4591	46	–	–	4434
II	Expansion	*Expand* $\hat{\mathbf{A}}$	198	142	–	–	9647
III			1021	144	–	–	18089
V			1316	144	–	–	33767
II	Sampler	*Sample c*	312	458	–	–	946
III			411	547	–	–	1417
V			384	662	–	–	2050
II	Sampler	*Sample* $\mathbf{s_1}$, $\mathbf{s_2}$	143	44	–	–	3176
III			114	48	–	–	6750
V			163	45	–	–	5953
II	Sampler	*Sample* $\mathbf{y}$	244	43	–	–	1654
III			112	42	–	–	2147
V			469	48	–	–	3006

[P] Multiple consecutive operations are pipelineable [M] Depending on the master module

polynomial ring size $n = 256$ and target Artix-7 FPGAs are presented in [3,18]. The first one offers a similar latency like our implementation, but due to the modulus supporting only 7 layers of NTT instead of 8, the gap is larger in practice. Note that regarding LUTs and FFs, our implementation has a similar area usage despite the 10 bit larger modulus. The reason for this is our heavy usage of DSPs. Finally, we compare to three NTT implementations with a smaller gap for the modulus size, but a higher polynomial degree. As expected, these implementations have a higher latency due to the bigger n. However, we expect that our implementation would have a latency of about 3.8 μs for $n = 512$ and about 8.4 μs for $n = 1024$ at the cost of a minor increase in area usage[5]. Overall, our NTT implementation features a low LUT and FF usage and at the same time, the f_{max} is, to the best of our knowledge, significantly higher than for any other known design on Artix-7.

It is worth noting, however, that the comparison has several limitations: Our implementation results have been achieved with out-of-context synthesis and subsequent PnR, without connection to the memory that contains the polynomials. For other implementations, like [19], the authors do not report what exactly is contained in the NTT-only implementations and how the utilization and performance numbers are found, although the numbers indicate that some-

---

[5] Doubling the polynomial degree can be achieved by increasing the size of an internal counter by 1 bit.

Table 4. Comparison of hardware designs for NTT implementations

(n, q)	Platform	Utilization				f	t	Ref.
		LUT	FF	DSP	BRAM	MHz	μs	
256, 8380417	XC7A100T	524	759	17	1	311	1.7	This
256, 8380417	XCVU7P	1798	2532	48	3.5	637	–	[13]
256, 3329	XC7A35T	609	640	2	4	257	1.9	[18]
256, 7681	XC7A200T	533	514	1	3	–	17.1	[3]
256, 7681	XC7A200T	479	472	1	2	–	16.7	[3]
1024, 12289	XC7Z020	847	375	2	6	244	10.5	[19]
512, 12289	XC7Z020	741	330	2	5	245	5.3	[19]
512, 12289	V6LX75T	994	944	1	3	278	14.8	[14][E]

[E]Excluding area usage for sampler and random number generator.

how a polynomial memory is connected. The advantage of our approach, to use an out-of-context synthesis without memory connection, is that a good approximation of the real f_{max} of the *arithmetic* is given. The operational frequency for a design that features our NTT then oviously depends *additionally* on the exact memory layout of the overall design, which however is not depending on the NTT itself.

In Table 5, we compare our implementation of Dilithium-III with other relevant implementations of post-quantum signature schemes on reconfigurable hardware. In contrast to existing implementations of Dilithium for Artix-7 [16] and Virtex-7 [13] which report area utilization, frequency, and latency individually *per operation*, we would like to emphasize that in addition to our single-task cores, our full core combines and embeds all operations in a single architecture. Additionally, since our cores feature precomputation operations for signing and verification, performing these for multiple messages under the same key can be speeded up significantly. In particular, for signing, 104 μs are spent on precomputations for the single-task core at security level III. For verification, precomputations take 100 μs at security level III, so the actual verification latency is about 60 μs in that case.

Notably, our architecture outperforms existing solutions either in terms of resource utilization or throughput thus provides a compact, self-contained, and efficient solution for post-quantum secure digital signatures. In general, our design focuses on a reasonable trade-off between area consumption and performance degradation, in order to provide a modestly large and fast architecture.

Table 5. Comparison of hardware design for PQC signature schemes

Oper.	Scheme	Platform	Utilization				f	t	Ref.
			LUT	FF	DSP	BRAM	MHz	μs	
KeyGen	Dilithium-III^F	XC7A100T	30900	11372	45	21	145	229	This
	Dilithium-III	XC7A100T	14285	8588	45	17	205	161	This
	Dilithium-III^R	XCVU7P	54183	25236	182	15	350	52	[13]
	Dilithium-III^{R,H}	Artix-7	86646	17674	–	–	119	1955	[16]
	qTesla-3^H	Artix-7	111122	23398	–	–	79	45650	[16]
Sign	Dilithium-III^F	XC7A100T	30900	11372	45	21	145	852	This
	Dilithium-III	XC7A100T	21832	10245	45	21	174	709	This
	Dilithium-III^R	XCVU7P	81530	83926	965	145	333	63	[13]
	Dilithium-III^{R,H}	Artix-7	90567	21160	–	–	114	14140	[16]
	qTesla-3^H	Artix-7	126008	25984	–	–	79	7441	[16]
	GLP	Spartan-6	7465	8993	28	29.5	–	1074	[11]
	Rainbow-Ia^C	Kintex-7	27712	27679	0	59	111	18	[6]
	Rainbow-Ic^C	Kintex-7	52895	32476	0	67	90	11	[6]
	SPHINCS-256	Kintex-7	19067	38132	3	36	525	1530	[1]
Verify	Dilithium-III^F	XC7A100T	30900	11372	45	21	145	222	This
	Dilithium-III	XC7A100T	14911	8209	45	15	200	160	This
	Dilithium-III^R	XCVU7P	61738	34963	316	18	158	95	[13]
	Dilithium-III^{R,H}	Artix-7	65274	15169	–	–	114	2491	[16]
	qTesla-3^H	Artix-7	84834	17604	–	–	79	1926	[16]
	GLP	Spartan-6	6225	6663	8	15	–	1002	[11]

^{F}Full core ^{R}Round-2 parameters ^{H}High level synthesis ^{C}Core enabling signing and verification

5   Conclusion

In this work, we present the first set of FPGA implementations for all three round-3 parameter sets of Dilithium for the low-end Artix-7 platform. Our design follows a universal design goal, featuring low latency compared to implementations of other post-quantum secure signature algorithms on the one hand, but still having a low area footprint on the other hand, making the usage of Dilithium feasible for many low-cost and constrained scenarios. As a highlight, our implementations can be used as full-service processors for Dilithium, being capable of performing key generation, precomputations, signature generation, verification, arbitrary-length message digesting as well as key and signature packing and unpacking.

Acknowledgments. The work described in this paper has been supported in part by the Deutsche Forschungsgemeinschaft (DFG, German Research Foundation) under Germany's Excellence Strategy - EXC 2092 CASA - 390781972, by the H2020 project PROMETHEUS (grant agreement ID 780701), and by the Federal Ministry of Education and Research of Germany through the QuantumRISC (16KIS1038) and PQC4Med (16KIS1044) projects.

References

1. Amiet, D., Curiger, A., Zbinden, P.: FPGA-based accelerator for post-quantum signature scheme SPHINCS-256. IACR Trans. Cryptogr. Hardw. Embed. Syst. (2018)
2. Banerjee, U., Ukyab, T.S., Chandrakasan, A.P.: Sapphire: a configurable crypto-processor for post-quantum lattice-based protocols. IACR Trans. Cryptogr. Hardw. Embed. Syst. (2019)
3. Chen, Z., Ma, Y., Chen, T., Lin, J., Jing, J.: High-performance area-efficient polynomial ring processor for crystals-kyber on FPGAS. Integr. (2021)
4. Ducas, L., et al.: A lattice-based digital signature scheme. IACR Trans. Cryptogr. Hardw. Embed. Syst, CRYSTALS-Dilithium (2018)
5. Ducas, L., et al.: CRYSTALS-Dilithium - Algorithm Specifications and Supporting Documentation (Version 3.1). Technical Report (2021). https://pq-crystals.org/dilithium/data/dilithium-specification-round3-20210208.pdf
6. Ferozpuri, A., Gaj, K.: High-speed FPGA implementation of the NIST round 1 rainbow signature scheme. In: 2018 International Conference on ReConFigurable Computing and FPGAs - ReConFig 2018 (2018)
7. Fouque, P.-A., et al.: Falcon: Fast-Fourier Lattice-based Compact Signatures over NTRU - (Specification v1.2 - 01/10/2020). Technical Report (2020). https://falcon-sign.info/falcon.pdf
8. Greconici, D.O.C., Kannwischer, M.J. , Sprenkels, D.: Compact dilithium implementations on Cortex-M3 and Cortex-M4. IACR Trans. Cryptogr. Hardw. Embed. Syst. (2021)
9. Güneysu, T., Lyubashevsky, V., Pöppelmann, T.: Practical lattice-based cryptography: a signature scheme for embedded systems. In: Prouff, E., Schaumont, P. (eds.) CHES 2012. LNCS, vol. 7428, pp. 530–547. Springer, Heidelberg (2012). https://doi.org/10.1007/978-3-642-33027-8_31
10. NIST. Call for Proposals - Post-Quantum Cryptography — CSRC. Technical Report, NIST (2017). https://csrc.nist.gov/Projects/Post-Quantum-Cryptography/Post-Quantum-Cryptography-Standardization/Call-for-Proposals
11. Pöppelmann, T., Ducas, L., Güneysu, T.: Enhanced lattice-based signatures on reconfigurable hardware. In: Batina, L., Robshaw, M. (eds.) CHES 2014. LNCS, vol. 8731, pp. 353–370. Springer, Heidelberg (2014). https://doi.org/10.1007/978-3-662-44709-3_20
12. Post Quantum Cryptography Team. Post-Quantum Cryptography: NIST's Plan for the Future. Technical Report, NIST (2016). https://csrc.nist.gov/csrc/media/projects/post-quantum-cryptography/documents/pqcrypto-2016-presentation.pdf
13. Ricci, S., et al.: Implementing crystals-dilithium signature scheme on FPGAS. In: Reinhardt, D., Müller, T. (eds.) ARES 2021: The 16th International Conference on Availability, Reliability and Security, Vienna, 17–20 August 2021, pp. 1:1–1:11. ACM (2021)
14. Roy, S.S., Vercauteren, F., Mentens, N., Chen, D.D., Verbauwhede, I.: Compact ring-LWE cryptoprocessor. In: Batina, L., Robshaw, M. (eds.) CHES 2014. LNCS, vol. 8731, pp. 371–391. Springer, Heidelberg (2014). https://doi.org/10.1007/978-3-662-44709-3_21
15. Shor, P.W.:. Algorithms for quantum computation: discrete logarithms and factoring. In: 35th Annual Symposium on Foundations of Computer Science (1994)

16. Soni, D., Basu, K., Nabeel, M., Karri, R.: A hardware evaluation study of NIST post-quantum cryptographic signature schemes. In: Second PQC Standardization Conference (2019)
17. Thoma, J.P., Güneysu, T.: A configurable hardware implementation of XMSS. IACR Cryptol. ePrint Arch. (2021)
18. Zhang, C., et al.: Towards efficient hardware implementation of NTT for Kyber on FPGAS. In: 2021 IEEE International Symposium: On Circuits and Systems (ISCAS) (2021)
19. Zhang, N., Yang, B., Chen, C., Yin, S., Wei, S., Liu, L.: Highly efficient architecture of NewHope-NIST on FPGA using low-complexity NTT/INTT. IACR Trans. Cryptogr. Hardw. Embed. Syst. (2020)

Secure Implementations

Under the Dome: Preventing Hardware Timing Information Leakage

Mathieu Escouteloup[1]([⊠]), Ronan Lashermes[1]([⊠]), Jacques Fournier[2]([⊠]),
and Jean-Louis Lanet[1]([⊠])

[1] Inria, Univ Rennes, CNRS, IRISA, Rennes, France
{ronan.lashermes,jean-louis.lanet}@inria.fr
[2] Univ. Grenoble Alpes, CEA Leti, DSYS/LSOSP, Grenoble, France
jacques.fournier@cea.fr

Abstract. Numerous timing side-channels attacks have been proposed in the recent years, showing that all shared states inside the microarchitecture are potential threats. Previous works have dealt with this problem by considering those "shared states" separately and not by looking at the system as a whole.

In this paper, instead of reconsidering the problematic shared resources one by one, we lay out generic guidelines to design complete cores immune to microarchitectural timing information leakage. Two implementations are described using the RISC-V ISA with a simple extension. The cores are evaluated with respect to performances, area and security, with a new open-source benchmark assessing timing leakages.

We show that with this "generic" approach, designing secure cores even with complex features such as simultaneous multithreading is possible. We discuss about the trade-offs that need to be done in that respect regarding the microarchitecture design.

1 Introduction

Since Spectre [18] and Meltdown [20] attacks were published in 2018, the microarchitecture security is under scrutiny. Numerous attacks have now been demonstrated [4,10,22,24,35] targeting the whole microarchitecture to extract information from timing variations. These weaknesses in the design allow extracting information across different security domains: a userland application can read in kernel memory, a virtual machine (VM) can gain information on another VM, *etc.* Unfortunately, on the software side, efficient countermeasures are lacking, and radical solutions have been forcefully implemented. For example, in 2018, the OpenBSD operating system (OS) decided [15] to disable Intel Hyper-Threading (Intels' simultaneous multithreading (SMT) technology) to avoid information leakage between hardware threads (also called harts), an expensive approach that cannot be reproduced for all hardware mechanisms: disabling Intel HT leads to performance losses of up to 20% [19].

V. Grosso and T. Pöppelmann (Eds.): CARDIS 2021, LNCS 13173, pp. 233–253, 2022.
https://doi.org/10.1007/978-3-030-97348-3_13

Motivation. Solutions have been proposed in the literature [7,12,16,17,25,32, 34], but they focus on some microarchitectural components in isolation. In this paper, we outline new generic design rules based on first principles to prevent timing information leakage, and build whole cores immune to them. In particular, we explore the instruction set architecture (ISA) modifications that can help build secure designs for all cores, from simple microcontrollers to complex microprocessors.

Contributions. In this paper we propose and implement a process to build cores without microarchitectural timing leakage. After analysing the attacks in the literature (Sect. 2), we extract the design rules that must be followed for leakage-free implementations (Sect. 3). We propose an ISA modification to enable circumventing timing information leakage (Sect. 4). We implement two cores with cache memories, branch prediction or SMT, free of timing leakage (Sect. 5). We propose a security benchmark suite, *timesecbench*, that evaluate the timing leakage with respect to several microarchitectural components (Sect. 6). Our security and performance evaluations highlight the trade-offs required to design leakage-free cores (Sect. 6).

2   The Need to Redefine the Microarchitecture for Security

Sharing is one of the basic principles used in modern cores for achieving high performances, *e.g.* cache memories shared between cores or branch prediction information between programs. But sharing leaks timing information between users of the same resources, leaks which can be exploited by attackers.

2.1   Threats

Threat Model. In this paper, we consider the covert channels scenario where shared resources are used to exchange information. The attacker controls both the trojan application, sending information through timing dependencies and the spy application, reading the information. The applications are supposed to be located in different security domains. A security domain is delimited by a unique security policy: different policies define corresponding domains. Resisting to this threat implies that the system can thwart a side-channel scenario, where the attacker only controls the spy and where the trojan only leaks information unwillingly. We are interested in microarchitectural timing leakage, therefore the timing information read by the spy must only be coming from the microarchitectural state of the core when the spy is executing. Thus, all trojans that functionally leak information, by writing to memory or with a time-dependent function, are out of scope in our paper.

Our threat model is the following: the attacker wins if she is able to transmit information from the trojan to the spy. But she cannot use any architectural means of communication (architectural features are the ones exposed by the

ISA). The spy cannot measure the trojan execution time (time measurements are architectural functionalities).

Shared Resources Attacks. Different kinds of sharing have been shown to be sources of timing information leakages in modern processor architectures. Timing variations due to cache memories [6] have been known for many years, with multiple variants in numerous implementations [13]. Similar results have been achieved on different resources like branch prediction tables or translation lookaside buffer (TLB).

The resource usage itself represents an interesting information that can be recovered by measuring resource contention. Different works [3–5,29] have shown the possibility to recover information from processors with SMT support. The same kind of observation is also possible with mechanisms like cache controllers shared between cores.

In 2018, timing leakage attacks have reached a new level of complexity with transient attacks, adding the use of hardware techniques like speculation or out-of-order speculation. In Spectre [18] or Meltdown [20] and their variants [9,10,28] shared resources are used to leak information. It was an important lesson for designers: even if ignored during many years, timing leakages are still present in all modern systems.

2.2 Related Work

Since the publication of the first shared resource exploitation, new countermeasures are regularly proposed.

Hardware solutions modify the microarchitecture to ensure the security. Simply removing the problematic mechanisms is not realistic from a performance point of view [8,19]. Then, another approach is to design shared resources differently. Some solutions [11,17] try to partition cache memories among the users: each of them has now only access to its own data. It can be spatial partitioning, where the cache is split between the different users, and/or temporal partitioning by flushing the data at the end of a user's execution. Another approach is to remove the deterministic behaviour by introducing some randomization [21,26]. In this case, if timing leakages still exist, they do not depend on confidential information. Both approaches have been known for many years [30], and can also be combined to enforce the isolation [12]. Finally, proposals also concern other mechanisms like speculation [16,34] or port contention [25].

Software solutions are also studied, where the application has to directly consider the microarchitecture. Retpoline [27] tries to protect against branch target injection used by Spectre [18] by influencing and redirecting speculation when it is needed. Existing primitives for microarchitecture management can also be used in some cases. `lfence` instruction exists in some x86 implementations [1] to block branch prediction. Other primitives like `clflush` also exist to manage cache structures.

If both pure hardware or software approaches have interesting properties, they also suffer from significant disadvantages. With pure hardware solutions, the software does not have to consider security issues on the hardware side. However, no flexibility on the applied constraints is possible, harming the performances. Conversely with pure software solutions, the application must perfectly know the microarchitecture to protect itself from attacks on the hardware side, harming its portability. More importantly, it also needs a way to manage all the different mechanisms with dedicated primitives. It therefore leads to study the role of the ISA.

The **ISA** is the interface between the hardware and the software. It creates an abstraction of the hardware for the software. Here again, two strategies have been explored to modify the architecture for security purposes. Regarding the previous software solutions, a first one is to break this abstraction role to allow a better microarchitecture management from the software. This functional approach [14,33] focuses on designing a complete *augmented* ISA where hardware shared features must be directly manageable with software. In our opinion, these works all suffer from the same conceptual weakness: they consider the timing problem as a microarchitectural design issue. Instead, the problem lies in the limited ISA semantics regarding security notions: the issue cannot be solved only by flushing microarchitectural elements, at the risk of forbidding multithreaded or multicore processors, which require spatial sharing. Other works have shown the efficiency of a more abstract approach, by allowing an ISA interface to guide the resource management by the hardware. MI6 [7] adds a new `purge` instruction to flush microarchitectural state independently of the implementation. The DAWG [17] proposal offers new registers to the software to parametrize security domains in cache-like structures. In ConTExT [23], a dedicated bit is added to each page entry to indicate if transient execution is possible or not.

However, these solutions are still considering only some specific shared resources and not the problem as a whole. By focusing on microarchitectural elements in isolation, they are still missing the bigger picture: we do not want to add numerous mechanisms to finely control the cache or the speculation behaviour. This path leads to stacking of countermeasures, to complex systems, to poor portability (how to use ConTExT [23] without virtual memory?) and will severely limit the possibility one day of having formal security guarantees for the software running on such processors. Instead of fine-tuning the microarchitecture, we prefer a formal contract between software and hardware. This leads to our contribution where the fully abstract approach allows a clear organization. The ISA must allow the software to communicate its security properties to the hardware.

3   Design Guidelines

Shared resources must be designed by considering security constraints. Secure design guidelines can be crafted to avoid timing leakages by considering the attack models based on known attacks.

3.1 Definitions and Goals

We call shared resources all states or elements which can be assigned to different users. A resource is temporally shared when multiple users can request it at different times. A resource is spatially shared when multiple users can request it simultaneously. Spatial and temporal sharing are not exclusive: some resources, particularly caches, can use both. For the rest of this paper, we define a user as a security domain which must be isolated from the other ones.

In any implementation, shared resources are limited in number: this is one of the reasons they are shared. A system with multiple security domains implies that at least one piece of information will inevitably be leaked between them: the availability of the resource. If a resource is used by a security domain, it becomes unavailable for another domain. By construction, this cannot be avoided. Yet it is possible to overcome this difficulty by distinguishing between static and dynamic availability. The dynamic availability is the possibility for a resource to be used at any point in time as long as it is not already requested. Static availability is the possibility for a security domain to lock a resource for a potential future usage. When the security domain locks the resource, we say that it is allocated, in which case it is no longer available but not necessarily "used". To allow correct execution of a security domain, resource allocation must be done during its creation and kept during its whole lifetime.

While dynamic availability leaks information with precise execution timings that can be exploited with port contention attacks [4], static availability does not permit this kind of leakage. In our case, we only allow static availability as information leakage, giving the following security property:

Shared Resource Security Property. *The only information that a security domain may extract from a shared resource is the domain's own data or the resource's static availability.*

Then, the different shared resources must be modified to prevent other information leakages. These modifications needed to safely support security domains can be summarized in three main strategies: lock, flush and split.

3.2 Resource Availability: Lock

Design Guideline 1: Static Allocation. *The different minimal resources needed by a security domain must be allocated during the domain creation and locked until its deletion.*

Each shared resource can only support a limited number of security domains, which can be one (only temporal sharing) or more (temporal and spatial sharing).

Static allocation allows having the exclusivity of a resource in order to use it without execution timing leakages. Obviously, it is necessary only in systems where multiple security domains can simultaneously be executed, leading to potential spatial leakages. Allocation is simplified when only one security domain can exist at any time in the whole system: it can simply use all the different resources.

3.3   Temporal Resource Sharing: Flush

The static allocation cannot last forever and the resource must be released eventually to make a place for another security domain. The resource design must ensure that there is no leakage between the security domains, which leads to the following guideline:

Design Guideline 2: Release. *When a security domain ends, all its associated resources must be released only when all persistent states have also been erased.*

We call "persistent states" all information stored in registers or memories whether data, metadata, finite-state machine (FSM) states *etc.* All of them are associated with a security domain for which the associated data must be removed before allowing allocation from another security domain. Different works [7,33] have shown that flushing resources is efficient to make a temporal isolation barrier. Then, all temporally shared resources must support it.

3.4   Spatial Resource Sharing: Split

In some cases, lock and flush strategies are enough: *e.g.* if there is only temporal sharing. But fully locking a resource in an exclusive way during each execution can be limiting. Some resources need to handle requests from different users simultaneously. In this case, the correct strategy is partitioning, also called split. Such a resource must be able to isolate all users from each other.

Design Guideline 3: Partitioning. *A resource able to handle requests from multiple security domains simultaneously must be able to partition each domain state in its own isolated compartment. States and data cannot be shared.*

In other words, any spatially shared resource must be split between the security domains. It can be seen as resources with multiple lock slot: multiple security domains can simultaneously lock a part of this resource, but without any interaction between them.

Because split is only a form of sharing, it also has both temporal and spatial variants. In a temporal split, the resource is successively available for each user and only seems simultaneously available at a global scale. It is simply a way of transforming a partial simultaneous sharing in a local temporal sharing where lock and flush strategies are applied. With spatial split, the resource is truly simultaneously available for each user at any time. It leads to our last design guideline:

Design Guideline 3: Availability Split. *A spatially shared resource must ensure that, at any given time, its availability for any security domain is independent from the domains being served.*

Partitioning can take several forms depending on the targeted resources [11, 12,17,25,30]. To efficiently apply all these strategies, the hardware must finally be informed about the security domain switching.

3.5   Exclusive Allocation and Heterogeneity

As mentioned previously, static allocation only prevents the detection of a resource usage, not its availability. In the case of heterogeneous systems, this information can be exploited to build a covert channel. We call a system heterogeneous when all the users do not have exactly the same resources. It is a common organization in modern microarchitectures: all the threads or cores are not necessarily equivalent, *e.g.* to satisfy different performances or power constraints. Then, if the trojan allocates some resources and not others, a message can be sent to the spy: the latter can deduce the trojan allocation from measuring its own available resources. In a completely secure system without even covert channels, we can deduce the following guideline:

Design Guideline 5: Homogeneity. *During their execution, all users must be treated equally, by allocating the same resources in types and numbers.*

Obviously, strictly applying this rule can be very restrictive: no flexibility is allowed in the resource allocation. If the natural solution would be to have strictly duplicated cores with their own resources, we will present in the next section a manner to prevent this covert channel while preserving some flexibility.

4   Domes

The security domains can only be defined at the software level through the applications themselves. To enforce the shared resource security property we defined above, the hardware has to be aware of the security domains. Therefore to communicate their boundaries to the hardware, the ISA must be modified. In this section, we present our proposal to modify the RISC-V ISA.

4.1   Fine-Grained Security Domains

In current systems, we can find several implementations of security domains. They are the result of a historical evolution of the security needs due to the evolution of the threats. The mostly used and classic security domains are the privilege levels, notably separating the kernel from the userland.

However, in the case of sharing, these domains are too coarse-grained. An application may want to isolate tasks (e.g. a web server isolating several clients, a web browser sandboxing its tabs) while having only one address space. It justifies the works such as ConTExT [23] where security domains are proposed at page granularity, Time-Secure Cache [26] at process granularity or a completely new security domain notion managed by the software in DAWG [17]. This domain notion must now be used by the hardware to manage all the shared resources.

4.2   Fence or Context

Boundaries of the security domains have to be communicated from the software to the hardware. In classical systems, privilege levels are changed with a dedicated mechanism, often with specialized instructions. Similarly, we must define the mechanism that allows switching between fine-grained security domains. Before the precise ISA modifications, we must choose between two possible semantics.

The first possibility is to use stateless switches between domains called **fences**, similarly to the timing fences from Wistoff *et al.* [33]. In this case the boundary between domains is specified by a dedicated `fence.t` instruction that separates the security domains before and after the instruction. Typically, the execution of this fence must ensure that all states associated with the current security domain are flushed out of the microarchitecture. Finally, fences are particularly efficient for creating temporal security domains: each one is delimited by the previous and the next fences. But this approach does not consider spatial sharing: for example the hardware has no information to decide whether two harts are in the same security domain.

The second possibility is the use of **contexts**, a stateful switch. Each microarchitectural resource, state or data is at any time explicitly or implicitly associated with a security domain which constitutes the context. With this information, the resource can be adapted to the execution and may share states (same domains) or isolate them (different domains), both temporally and spatially. The context semantics gives more power to the microarchitecture than fences, but increases the system complexity.

Since we want a global solution able to consider all the different shared resources in the microarchitecture, we choose the context semantics. We call our specific implementation a **dome**. A dome is an execution context that corresponds to one security domain. At any given time, each hart is assigned to a unique dome but several harts can share the same dome. At the microarchitecture level, it defines which resources can be used by each hart: all instructions and microarchitectural states are implicitly or explicitly assigned to the corresponding dome.

4.3   ISA Changes for Dome Support

Adding dome support in a core requires to augment the ISA with new instructions, new registers and the corresponding hardware modifications. This proposal can be seen as an extension over the base RV32I [31]. Our goal here is to analyse the ISA with context support: their role, what is needed and the consequences. The contextualization can be implemented in different ways and only one is described in the rest of this paper. Because our proposal does not use specific features of the RISC-V ISA, the same principles can be exported to other ones like x86, ARM *etc.*

Dome Identifier. Each dome is represented by a unique number, the dome identifier, stored in a dedicated register `domeid`, one per hart. This register is read-only, since a dome cannot dynamically change its own configuration. `domenextid` is the register that indicates the identifier of the next dome when a context switch occurs. The current dome can write into this register. These registers are considered as new Machine-level control and status registers (CSRs): they are manageable by the same instructions described in the RISC-V ISA [31].

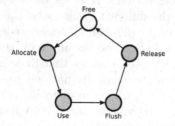

Fig. 1. Resource lifecycle with static allocation.

When our next dome configuration is ready, we need to switch to the new domain with the dedicated instruction `dome.switch`. Each resource has a lifecycle described in Fig. 1. Allocated resources have to be flushed and then released, before those needed by the new dome are allocated. At the same time, `domeid` must be updated: it receives the information present in `domenextid`. If we want to free all resources from a security domain, for example before turning the machine off with write-back caches, it is enough to switch to a new domain.

Dome Capability. Sometimes, there are not enough resources in number to satisfy the needs of each hart. For example, we may think of a system with only one cryptographic accelerator, one floating-point unit, or as in our case one multiply and divide execution unit (MULDIV) execution unit. To deal with this case, we add new registers to store the dome capabilities, specifying if the dome needs access to these few resources: `domecap` and `domenextcap`. Bits are set in these registers if the dome has or need access to some predetermined features (such as RISCV M extension) that map to hardware resources.

Upon a switch, the system will try to lock the resources corresponding to the capabilities of the next dome. Therefore `dome.switch rd` can now fail if the resources asked are not available; in case of success `rd` is set to 0.

4.4   Software Implications

In addition to having an impact on the hardware, the ISA also changes the way software must be designed.

Compiler. The RISC-V ISA naturally suggests linking a capability bit for each supported extension: because each instruction is already associated to an extension, the compiler knows when a piece of code requires a capability. As a consequence, the compiler can automatically insert the proper instructions for a dome switch (capability and all), apart from the next dome identifier. Indeed, identifying the security domains is part of the application logic.

Dome Management. In our implementation, domes are managed by the higher level of privilege, the Machine-level. It is responsible for selecting the correct IDs and capabilities for the different domes where are executed the applications. It must also perform the different switches needed. Domes are only tools to allow isolation of the software and, as any tool, they can be used improperly. Software developers have to be aware that these guarantees are offered at dome granularity. Monolithic systems are not going to take full advantages of the dome switching guarantees, while too many dome switches can make static resource allocations similar to dynamic ones. Also, since capabilities are in contradiction with the Design guideline 5, it is the responsibility of this higher privilege-level to ensure that multiple domes are not trying to communicate with resource allocation, *e.g.* abusing `dome.switch`. This can be detected with a failing `dome.switch`.

Spatial Sharing in the Single Hart Case. The cost of dome switching can be high in some scenarios. For example, in the case of an exception, all the shared resources must be flushed twice. It can be interesting to allow some spatial sharing, even in a single hart case, between an active dome currently being executed and a background dome that will eventually be returned to.

5   Implementation

To demonstrate and validate our design rules, we build several cores with a modular architecture that are evaluated in Sect. 6. We choose the Chisel language to allow a better modularity and configuration management. It becomes particularly easy to compare designs by only modifying some parameters: dome support can be enabled by switching a boolean variable to `true`. Code for our cores and the evaluations are available online: https://gitlab.inria.fr/mescoute/hsc-eval.

5.1   Target Description

Global View. To evaluate dome support in the case of a simple core but also with spatial sharing, two cores have been implemented. The first core, named Aubrac is based on a 5-stage in-order pipeline. The second core, named Salers, is a more complex dual-hart 6-stage in-order pipeline as illustrated in Fig. 2. In Salers, the two harts are running simultaneously and can be switched off using custom CSRs: one hart working alone takes all the resources and a classic superscalar execution is achieved.

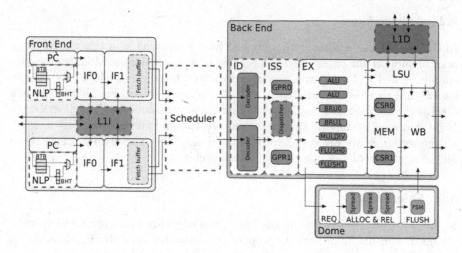

Fig. 2. Global view of the Salers core microarchitecture.

These two cores are implementations of the open-source RISC-V RV32IM ISA [31], with CSR and `fence.i` support. Both cores have separate first-level write-through cache memories for instructions (L1I) and data (L1D) with branch prediction and basic speculation mechanisms through a branch history table (BHT) and a branch target buffer (BTB). The different modifications, described later in this section, are represented with a dedicated dome unit and with existing modified components bordered with red dotted lines.

Shared Resources. These cores are designed to model multiple resource sharing, allowing reproducing a representative sample of attacks from the literature. Several temporally shared resources have to be considered in both cores. The most obvious ones are cache lines in L1I and L1D or the prediction tables. But this also applies to the pipeline, cache controllers or replacement policy registers.

Spatially shared resources are only present in the Salers core, including cache memories and execution units. Since the latter are shared between harts, port contention might occur. Particularly, our MULDIV represents a worst case: operations take many cycles (8 to 32 cycles), timing variations are possible depending on the operation (division or multiplication) and more importantly, there is only one unit for two potential users. When one hart is using this unit, if the other one needs it too, it must wait until the unit is released. This kind of problem is not exclusive to execution units, and is valid for each resource not spatially shared and present in fewer instances than the potential users. For example, port contention could be possible, in our design, with cache memories. They are spatially shared and can securely handle transactions with the pipeline, but contention is possible with the next memory level without the special care described below.

5.2 Aubrac Core

In the case of the Aubrac core, only one hart is running at a time: there is no need to support the simultaneous execution of multiple domes. Modifications are simply needed to have dome support (dedicated instruction and CSRs) and to ensure that there is no persistent traces after a dome switch. For that purpose, a dedicated execution unit implements a simplified version of the FSM described in Fig. 1. Since only temporal sharing exists here, free and allocate steps are merged: all the resources are always allocated by a dome. The release only occurs when all the resources are empty after the flush cycles.

5.3 Salers Core

In the case of the Salers core in the Fig. 2, two harts are running simultaneously. We need to ensure dome security properties even with spatial sharing. In addition to the flush strategy, resource allocation with split and lock strategies must also be implemented. We find the different modified components which now also support partitioning and a more complex dome unit, responsible for the resource allocation and release in addition to flush.

Allocation and Release. During a dome switch, allocation and release must be performed in the case of spatial sharing. To manage each kind of spatially shared resource, a mechanism called spread resource unit has been implemented. It is responsible for associating each resource with a dome depending on the received allocation and release requests. For example, we have one unit dedicated to the arithmetic and logic units (ALUs), another for the MULDIVs, *etc.*. They are all implemented in the dome unit in the Fig. 2 and are accessed before performing a `dome.switch`.

After the allocation, each resource is tagged with its corresponding dome and has a port number inside this context. Only free resources can be allocated and, to respect as much as possible the Design guideline 5, this allocation is always fixed. Then, independently of the resources available, the same number will always be allocated: only the types can change depending on the capabilities. Finally, when the execution of a dome is ended, it sends a release request to flush and free resources.

The number of implemented spread units depends on the number of spatially shared resources. During a switch, requests to release and allocate resources are sent to the spread units to respect the resource lifecycle. The final result of a `dome.switch` depends on the results of the requests to all spread units.

Spatial Sharing. Spatial partitioning has been applied for cache memories. It is a well-known mechanism to allow execution of multiple security domains in the memory hierarchy, with multiple variants. In our case, we decided to use soft-partitioning at the way-level. Then, each way is viewed by the corresponding spread unit as a different allocable resource. When a memory request is received by the cache, the dome tag of the request and the one of each way are compared to know if the data can be accessed. It is interesting to note that this is a locking strategy applied locally on each way, leading to a splitting strategy at the scale of the whole cache.

Cache controllers and memory bus to the main memory are other interesting cases in our design, because they cannot be fully duplicated nor fully locked since they are required for all executed domes. A hybrid approach between spatial and temporal sharing is used in the form of fine-grained multithreading. The controllers can be requested only during a fixed cyclic period by each dome, which has an impact on the cache miss operations. The memory bus has also been modified to support dome id transmission: the master controller is responsible for making bus contention transparent.

Based on the previously defined strategies, multiple implementations are possible for the same design: only some possible choices are described in this paper. This is the designer's role to decide where and when which mechanisms are more interesting depending on her constraints: execution units can also be time partitioned, prediction mechanisms partially shared if not fully duplicated *etc.*

6   Evaluation

6.1   Security Evaluation

Timesecbench. In order to validate the security properties of our approach, we propose Timesecbench: a security benchmark suite that measures timing leakages in various scenarios. It is inspired by the Embench [2] performance benchmark and is fully available online: https://gitlab.inria.fr/rlasherm/timesecbench. Obviously, even if the benchmarks can be customized independently of the processor, the microarchitectural mechanisms under test must be implemented. This benchmark suite can be expanded to test other mechanisms or different cores.

Six different attacks are currently available in our security benchmark targeting cache memories, branch prediction mechanisms and execution units. They have been designed with the same following covert channels scenario: a trojan tries to send information to a spy by exploiting timing information leakage due to shared resources. Inspired by the work of Ge *et al.* [14], for each attack we measure a timing associated with the trojan sending a value i (column index) and the spy reading a value j (row index).

We then apply a discrimination criterion (here minimal timing for the spy reading a given value) giving a probability for the spy to read a value j when the value sent by the trojan is i. The benchmarks are executed without any OS, cancelling most noises between tests, allowing a better control of the system and thus reinforcing the power of the attacker. From this joint probability matrix, we can compute the mutual information MI, that gives the amount of information that can be sent through the channel for a uniform distribution at input. The normalized values for our benchmarks are presented in Table 1: it gives the proportion of the trojan information that can be recovered by the spy. For example, in the L1I case, the trojan sends a 3-bit symbol through the channel (choose one set among eight), but the spy can only recover 46% of it (or 1.37 bits per symbol). The channel is closed, *i.e.* our design is secure if the mutual information is zero.

For our security analysis, the benchmarks have been executed on both unprotected and protected versions of Aubrac and Salers cores. In the case of protected designs, trojan and spy are placed in two different domes.

Benchmark Results. All the benchmark results are shown on Fig. 3. The first two benchmarks evaluate timing leakage for both cache memories L1D and L1I on Aubrac. The trojan encodes its value i by accessing the corresponding address, either by loading a value (for L1D) or by executing an instruction (for L1I). Since a `dome.switch` is performed after the trojan encoding and before the spy decoding, it is able to prevent the timing leakage as illustrated on Fig. 3. In the unprotected L1I case, the attack is not perfect as in the L1D case, due to the presence of the benchmark own instructions in the L1I cache. Two benchmarks target the branch prediction mechanisms BTB (for direct jumps) and BHT (for branches) on Aubrac. Here the trojan trains the branch predictor to ensure that only the i-th branch is accelerated by the branch predictor. Dome support is able to remove this timing leakage. The results obtained on the unprotected versions are polluted by the execution of the benchmarks themselves, that do include branches and direct jumps. One benchmark attempts to transmit information across harts on Salers through the L1D cache timing. This is similar to the previous L1D benchmark but trojan and spy are executed on two different harts. Interestingly, the timing depends on the value j read by the spy in this case. This is an overhead due to the fine-grained multithreading technique used by the memory controller. The last benchmark demonstrates that the MULDIV port contention can also be used to encode information. In this case, if we enable dome support, we cannot run this benchmark: the spy hart cannot lock the MULDIV unit, as intended. The unsecured application cannot be run.

Table 1. Normalized mutual information for the 6 benchmarks in Timesecbench with 0 for no measured leakage.

Normalized MI	L1D	L1I	BHT	BTB	Cross-L1D	Port contention
Unprotected	1.0	0.46	0.38	0.31	0.46	1.0
Protected	0.0	0.0	0.0	0.0	0.0	X

In the scenarios that have been tested, our solution has removed all leakages: timing information leakage cannot occur across security domain boundaries.

6.2   Performances/Cost Analysis

Dome support involves modifications in the whole microarchitecture. After evaluating its security efficiency, we need to analyse the impact on both performances and area. The different measurements were carried out after performing synthesis and implementation with Vivado 2019.2 (default parameters with *phys_opt_design* enabled), targeting the Xilinx ZCU104 FPGA. Sixteen configurations are compared: we vary the cache size (1 kB or 4 kB), the next-Line Predictor (NLP) support for branch prediction and the dome support, both for Salers and Aubrac. Our goal is to compare both protected and unprotected version of the same cores since performances and area overhead highly depend on the implemented shared resources. Direct comparisons with other works are not relevant: their implemented shared resources are different.

Performances Overhead. We start by evaluating the overhead in terms of clock cycles to execute the Embench [2] benchmark suite. Considering that we do not modify the critical path of our design, it is important to note that the clock frequency is not impacted in our designs. The geometric means for the different configurations are shown in Table 2. When comparing Aubrac and Salers, all the Embench benchmarks but two are taken into account: aha-mont64 gives an erroneous output and nbody is too slow and hits the simulation timeout (it involves floating point arithmetic). The single versus dual hart comparison is performed on Salers by taking into account three benchmarks (nettle-sha256, nsichneu and slre) adapted to a multithreaded core.

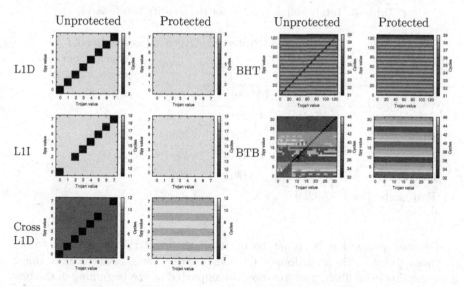

Fig. 3. Timesecbench timing matrices: horizontal variability denotes a timing leakage.

Table 2. Embench normalized timing geometric means, lower is better. Normalized with respect to the Aubrac-1kB implementation.

Cache size	1 kB	4 kB	1 kB	4 kB
	Aubrac		Salers (1 hart)	
	1.00	0.86	0.95	0.90
Dome	1.00	0.86	1.16	0.92
NLP	0.92	0.78	0.95	0.81
NLP Dome	0.92	0.78	1.07	0.82

Cache size	1 kB	4 kB	1 kB	4 kB
Salers	Single hart		Dual hart	
	1.05	0.91	0.56	0.51
Dome	1.07	0.88	0.76	0.62
NLP	1.03	0.88	0.55	0.51
NLP Dome	1.05	0.86	0.75	0.61

From Table 2, we can see that dome support has no timing overhead for Aubrac, as expected since the benchmarks run in the same security context. Yet in the Salers case, dome support can really slow down the computation due to cache partitioning as the cache size is in effect divided by two. In the worst case, we can observe a loss of 20% on the runtime when L1 caches are split without speculation. The cache influence is confirmed as multiplying the cache size by four reduces the overhead by a factor of 2 (10%).

Table 3. Total timings (cycles) for the security benchmarks

	Unprotected	Protected	Overhead%	overhead (cycles) per `dome.switch`
L1D	27256	35880	+32%	67.4
L1I	57416	64264	+12%	53.5
BHT	1756202	1796774	+2%	19.8
BTB	445544	463443	+4%	35.0
Cross-L1D	188026	134395	−29%	X
Port contention	59250	X	X	X

But our protection is meant to be used, we must therefore evaluate the overhead due to switching domes. Obviously, since `dome. switch` performs a microarchitectural flush, performances are impacted at the beginning of the new dome execution: no data is stored in cache memories and we have cache and prediction misses all the time. This can be seen on Fig. 3, where for example in the L1D case we measure in the protected case a timing of 8 cycles, corresponding to a miss, in all cases. Therefore, the cost of `dome.switch` is composed of both the time for the flush and misses due to this operation. As shown in Table 3, in these heavily domain switching scenarios, the average timing overhead is 68 clock cycles per switch for L1D and 54 for L1I.

We see that the total execution of the benchmark is significantly reduced (−29%) with dome support with respect to the unprotected case for the Cross-L1D benchmark. Upon investigation, this performance improvement is due to the better isolation between caches: one hart having a cache operation does not slow down the other hart. The performance cost of having an effective cache size divided by two is low in this case due to the extremely small program executed for this evaluation. In our designs, flushing can be done in few cycles. The cost of dome switching is mostly due to the penalty of increased misses in the microarchitectural buffers. But this is not a universal rule: for example if write-through caches allow efficient flushes, the story is different for write-back caches. For these latter caches, upon a flush the data must be written back to the upper memory level, which cannot be done rapidly.

Hence, the only parameter to modify the switch duration is the microarchitectural flush methodology. This criterion is highly dependent on the other implementation choices.

Area Overhead. Area results for each core are presented in Table 4. Lookup tables (LUTs) are necessary for the combinatorial logic whereas flip-flops (FFs) are memory elements for storing states in the microarchitecture.

Table 4. FPGA resource utilization.

Cache size	1 kB	4 kB	1 kB	4 kB
	Aubrac		Salers	
	9, 370 LUTs	×2.62	21, 000 LUTs	×2.24
	4, 408 FFs	×1.90	8, 270 FFs	×1.65
Dome	×1.03	×2.62	×1.09	×2.14
	×1.07	×1.97	×1.32	×1.99
NLP	×1.30	×2.93	×1.27	×2.58
	×1.19	×2.10	×1.21	×1.88
NLP Dome	×1.30	×2.88	×1.34	×2.67
	×1.26	×2.17	×1.52	×2.20

Finally, the area cost to mitigate security issues due to temporal sharing is only a few percents (between +3% and +0% of LUTs, in the same ballpark as fence.t's +1%[33]). The FFs increase in Aubrac core is more important (up to 7%) but must be qualified: it is mainly due to the addition of several CSRs in a small core. Moreover, considering that a switch with only temporal sharing simply performs a flush, these additional registers are not essential in this case. On the other hand, the impact is much more important when spatial sharing has to be considered because of its complexity. For the Salers core, we have a significant impact of up to 32% in the number of flip-flops. It is mainly due to new CSRs for both harts, a more complex dome unit with associated states for each resource and cache controllers with temporal split. In this case, our results are difficult to compare with other works on secure SMT [25]: we modify all the shared resources and not only the multithreaded execution units. Moreover, this overhead must be put into perspective, as SMT is mainly used in much more complex cores with expensive features like out-of-order execution.

7   Discussion and Conclusion

For many years now, timing leakages due to resource sharing have been identified as a major threat to the security of processors. Nevertheless vulnerabilities related to such timing leakages are still being found at an alarming rate. This is mainly because, so far, the proposed mitigation look at specific mechanisms of a processor architecture in isolation and not at the processor as a whole. This paper is a step in this direction.

In our approach, we first describe how the ISA has a crucial role to play in making the software communicate to the hardware the applications' security constraints. Two possible semantics, fences and contexts, are discussed. Fences are simple but limited since they cannot handle spatial sharing. Contexts, on the other hand, allow designing secure systems with a lot of liberty on the core features, at the price of more complexity.

We then introduce generic principles for designing shared resources securely whether it is temporal or spatial sharing and with different granularities: we discuss such things like shared memories (like caches), but also more subtle components such as finite state machines (e.g. cache controllers) and buses (shared between several subsystems).

We demonstrate the application of our new approach by implementing two different processors, including one with simultaneous multithreading. We analyse the impact of this new security dogma on the design of such exemplar processors. We also foresee that taking into account security will profoundly modify the canon of processor design: as an example, write-through caches are much faster to flush than write-back and should supersede the latter one in secure designs.

To evaluate the efficiency of our security approach, we propose a new benchmark that shows that the implemented features circumvent timing leakages. This benchmark tests and detects known vulnerabilities. It will be regularly updated so that it can be used to help designers validate the security of their processors at design time. But it cannot be used to guarantee that no timing leakage is present at all. In our opinion, the formalization of the hardware seems the only approach for future works to allow real exhaustiveness, a feat that can only be achieved with a clear ISA semantics to delimit security domains.

Our research shows that, if our principles can be implemented with the adequate ISA, securely implementing resource sharing within processors is possible. A future work will consist in studying the trade-offs between this security dogma, performances and design complexity (size and power). Processors with simultaneous multithreading will be a relevant use case for this, with deep resources sharing that can lead to important leakages. Particularly, an analysis of the trade-offs must be done to compare with multicore processors while maintaining a high level of security. An exploration of domes impact on out-of-order cores and many core systems must also be considered.

References

1. Managing-Speculation-on-AMD-Processors. Technical report, Advanced Micro Devices (2018)
2. Embench: a modern embedded benchmark suite (2020). https://embench.org/
3. Aciicmez, O., Seifert, J.P.: Cheap hardware parallelism implies cheap security. In: Workshop on Fault Diagnosis and Tolerance in Cryptography (FDTC 2007), Vienna, Austria, pp. 80–91. IEEE, September 2007
4. Aldaya, A.C., Brumley, B.B., ul Hassan, S., Pereida Garcia, C., Tuveri, N.: Port contention for fun and profit. In: 2019 IEEE Symposium on Security and Privacy (SP), San Francisco, CA, USA, pp. 870–887. IEEE, May 2019
5. Andrysco, M., Kohlbrenner, D., Mowery, K., Jhala, R., Lerner, S., Shacham, H.: On subnormal floating point and abnormal timing. In: IEEE Symposium on Security and Privacy (SP), San Jose, CA, USA, pp. 623–639. IEEE, May 2015
6. Bernstein, D.J.: Cache-timing attacks on AES, p. 37 (2005)
7. Bourgeat, T., Lebedev, I., Wright, A., Zhang, S., Devadas, S.: MI6: secure enclaves in a speculative out-of-order processor. In: Proceedings of the 52nd Annual IEEE/ACM International Symposium on Microarchitecture, pp. 42–56 (2019)
8. Bulpin, J.R., Pratt, I.A.: Multiprogramming performance of the Pentium 4 with Hyper-Threading. In: Second Annual Workshop on Duplicating, Deconstruction and Debunking (WDDD), p. 10 (2004)
9. Canella, C., et al.: Fallout: leaking data on meltdown-resistant CPUs. In: Proceedings of the 2019 ACM SIGSAC Conference on Computer and Communications Security, CCS'19, pp. 769–784. Association for Computing Machinery, New York (2019)
10. Canella, C., et al.: A systematic evaluation of transient execution attacks and defenses. In: 28th USENIX Security Symposium (USENIX Security 19), November 2019
11. Costan, V., Lebedev, I., Devadas, S.: Sanctum: minimal hardware extensions for strong software isolation. In: 25th USENIX Security Symposium (USENIX Security 16), Austin, TX, USA, pp. 857–874. USENIX Association August 2016
12. Dessouky, G., Frassetto, T., Sadeghi, A.R.: HybCache: hybrid side-channel-resilient caches for trusted execution environments. In: 29th USENIX Security Symposium (USENIX Security 20). USENIX Association, September 2020
13. Ge, Q., Yarom, Y., Cock, D., Heiser, G.: A survey of microarchitectural timing attacks and countermeasures on contemporary hardware. J. Cryptogr. Eng. 8(1), 1–27 (2018)
14. Ge, Q., Yarom, Y., Heiser, G.: No security without time protection: we need a new hardware-software contract. In: Proceedings of the 9th Asia-Pacific Workshop on Systems - APSys'18, Jeju Island, Republic of Korea, pp. 1–9. ACM Press (2018)
15. Larabel, M.: Intel Hyper Threading Performance With A Core I7 On Ubuntu 18.04 LTS. Phoronix (2018). https://www.phoronix.com/scan.php?page=article&item=intel-ht-2018&num=4
16. Khasawneh, K.N., Koruyeh, E.M., Song, C., Evtyushkin, D., Ponomarev, D., Abu-Ghazaleh, N.: SafeSpec: banishing the spectre of a meltdown with leakage-free speculation. In: Proceedings of the 56th Annual Design Automation Conference 2019 (DAC16), Las Vegas, NV, USA, pp. 1–6. ACM Press, June 2019
17. Kiriansky, V., Lebedev, I., Amarasinghe, S., Devadas, S., Emer, J.: DAWG: a defense against cache timing attacks in speculative execution processors. In: 2018 51st Annual IEEE/ACM International Symposium on Microarchitecture (MICRO), Fukuoka, pp. 974–987. IEEE, October 2018

18. Kocher, P., et al.: Spectre attacks: exploiting speculative execution. In: 40th IEEE Symposium on Security and Privacy (S&P'19), Los Alamitos, CA, USA. IEEE Computer Society, May 2019

19. Larabel, M.: Intel Hyper Threading Performance With A Core i7 On Ubuntu 18.04 LTS - Phoronix, June 2018. https://www.phoronix.com/scan.php?page=article&item=intel-ht-2018&num=4

20. Lipp, M., et al.: Meltdown: reading kernel memory from user space. In: 27th USENIX Security Symposium (USENIX Security 18), Baltimore, MD, USA, pp. 973–990. USENIX Association, August 2018

21. Qureshi, M.K.: CEASER: mitigating conflict-based cache attacks via encrypted-address and remapping. In: 51st Annual IEEE/ACM International Symposium on Microarchitecture (MICRO), Fukuoka, pp. 775–787 (2018)

22. van Schaik, S., et al.: RIDL: Rogue In-Flight Data Load. In: 40th IEEE Symposium on Security and Privacy (S&P'19), San Francisco, CA, USA, p. 18, May 2019

23. Schwarz, M., Lipp, M., Canella, C., Schilling, R., Kargl, F., Gruss, D.: ConTExT: a generic approach for mitigating spectre. In: Proceedings of the 27th Annual Network and Distributed System Security Symposium (NDSS20). Internet Society, Reston (2020)

24. Schwarz, M., et al.: ZombieLoad: cross-privilege-boundary data sampling. In: Proceedings of the 2019 ACM SIGSAC Conference on Computer and Communications Security, p. 15, May 2019

25. Townley, D., Ponomarev, D.: SMT-COP: defeating side-channel attacks on execution units in SMT processors. In: 2019 28th International Conference on Parallel Architectures and Compilation Techniques (PACT), pp. 43–54 (2019)

26. Trilla, D., Hernandez, C., Abella, J., Cazorla, F.J.: Cache side-channel attacks and time-predictability in high-performance critical real-time systems. In: Proceedings of the 55th Annual Design Automation Conference, San Francisco, CA, USA, pp. 1–6. ACM, June 2018

27. Turner, P.: Retpoline: a software construct for preventing branch-target-injection, January 2018. https://support.google.com/faqs/answer/7625886

28. Van Bulck, J., et al.: Foreshadow: extracting the keys to the intel SGX kingdom with transient out-of-order execution. In: Proceedings of the 27th USENIX Security Symposium (USENIX Security 18), Baltimore, MD, USA, pp. 991–1008. USENIX Association, August 2018

29. Wang, Z., Lee, R.: Covert and side channels due to processor architecture. In: 2006 22nd Annual Computer Security Applications Conference (ACSAC'06), Miami Beach, FL, USA, pp. 473–482. IEEE, December 2006

30. Wang, Z., Lee, R.B.: New cache designs for thwarting software cache-based side channel attacks. In: Proceedings of the 34th Annual International Symposium on Computer Architecture - ISCA'07, San Diego, CA, USA, p. 494. ACM Press (2007)

31. Waterman, A., Asanovic, K.: The RISC-V Instruction Set Manual, Volume I: User-Level ISA, December 2019

32. Werner, M., Unterluggauer, T., Giner, L., Schwarz, M., Gruss, D., Mangard, S.: SCATTERCACHE: thwarting cache attacks via cache set randomization. In: 28th USENIX Security Symposium (USENIX Security 19), Santa Clara, CA, pp. 675–692. USENIX Association (2019)

33. Wistoff, N., Schneider, M., Gürkaynak, F.K., Benini, L., Heiser, G.: Prevention of microarchitectural covert channels on an open-source 64-bit RISC-V core. CoRR arXiv:2005.02193 (2020)

34. Yan, M., Choi, J., Skarlatos, D., Morrison, A., Fletcher, C., Torrellas, J.: InvisiSpec: making speculative execution invisible in the cache hierarchy. In: 2018 51st Annual IEEE/ACM International Symposium on Microarchitecture (MICRO), Fukuoka, pp. 428–441. IEEE, October 2018

35. Yarom, Y., Falkner, K.: FLUSH+RELOAD: a high resolution, low noise, L3 cache side-channel attack. In: 23rd USENIX Security Symposium (USENIX Security 14), San Diego, CA, USA, pp. 719–732. USENIX Association (2014)

Enhanced Encodings for White-Box Designs

Alberto Battistello[1], Laurent Castelnovi[2(✉)], and Thomas Chabrier[2]

[1] Security Pattern, Brescia, Italy
a.battistello@securitypattern.com
[2] IDEMIA, Cryptography and Security Group, Pessac, France
{laurent.castelnovi,thomas.chabrier}@idemia.com

Abstract. Designing a robust white-box implementation against state-of-the-art algebraic and differential computational analysis attacks is a challenging problem. The study of white-box security was revamped by recent advances involving grey box attacks. Since then, many authors have struggled to protect implementations against such new attacks. New designs as well as new security notions appeared, and white-box research in general seems to have greatly benefited from such advances. The current research aims at finding the best encodings and masking schemes to resist tracing attacks. In this perspective we suggest a new encoding scheme that can be applied to white-box designs. By using a modified version of the Benaloh cryptosystem, our design introduces semi-homomorphic properties to the encoding. To the best of our knowledge, this is the first time such properties are applied to an encoding design. This allows reducing the memory requirements and providing a better resistance against tracing attacks. Our encoding is versatile and can be adapted to different ciphers, and in most cases it provides performance improvements with respect to the state-of-the-art.

Keywords: White-Box · AES · Homomorphic cryptosystem · Benaloh cryptosystem

1 Introduction

The mass adoption of connected devices, like smartphones, tablets or smart-watches, implied a deep change in the industry. From basic cellular phones, mobile devices evolved into indispensable microcomputers of everyday life. Our smartphone collects our information, verifies our identity, secures our credit card transactions, replaces our car keys, enables us to watch movies and series, and can perform many other "useful" operations.

It is thus mandatory that such smart objects provide users with enough security for the collected data. This turns out to be the role of trusted execution

A. Battistello—Part of this work was done while the first author was working at IDEMIA.

V. Grosso and T. Pöppelmann (Eds.): CARDIS 2021, LNCS 13173, pp. 254–274, 2022.
https://doi.org/10.1007/978-3-030-97348-3_14

environments (TEE) that solved the security problem by delegating the sensitive tasks to an embedded secure element (eSE). However, smartphones are far from being standardized in all their aspects. For example the same OS version can run on multiple platforms. These platforms may have different flavors of eSEs or none at all. Thus, applications must adapt the security to the device at hand. Far from being an easy task, providers must even protect the device from the legitimate user itself, which in some cases may behave wickedly.

The white-box model takes on its full meaning in such an environment, where the cryptographic implementation is exposed. The white-box model can be seen as the opposite of the black box model, where the attacker has only access to the inputs and the outputs. Indeed, the white-box model assumes that the cryptographic primitive runs in an untrusted environment. In such a scenario the attacker has full access to the device: he can access the binary code of the application and observe or interact with the device's execution, in order for example to extract the encryption key from the implementation. It is thus very difficult to provide efficient security solutions against such threats. Nonetheless, due to the mass adoption of smart-devices, solutions are required by the industry to mitigate the problem.

Besides, the market needs white-box solutions for DRMs, Pay-TV, secure storage, etc., motivating researchers all over the world to keep working on it. The competitive spirit of researchers, together with the market pressure, also motivated the creation of international challenges, like the WhiBox contest [1,2], where users are invited to submit white-box AES implementations, and each participant can try to break others' submissions. In these challenges, a white-box is considered unbroken until its key is found or its functionality reversed. Points are assigned to the participants who implement the longer lasting unbroken white-box and to those breaking the strongest ones. For example, an interesting result of the 2019 edition of the WhiBox competition [2] is that the best white-boxes withstood attacks for more than one month. Thus, despite theoretically flawed, the security offered by actual implementations can be sufficient for content which value is limited to a short-term period (like for example a live football world cup).

One of the many techniques used in the contest of white-box is the use of encodings [20], affine or non-linear functions applied to the input/output of tables, and unknown by the attacker. These random encodings provide a map from the clear world and the encoded world, and allow randomization of key-dependent data. Such countermeasures are however expensive to deploy. The designer often needs to find a tradeoff between security and complexity (as a combination of memory requirements and running time).

The purpose of our work is thus to suggest an encoding principle that can help to reduce such complexity rise, while maintaining the security at the state-of-the-art. In particular, we suggest a novel way to create encodings that are both cheap and safe. We show how to use a degraded semi-homomorphic encryption scheme, based on the work of Benaloh [6] to build non-linear encodings that provide better security against algebraic attacks as well as security against differential computation analysis (DCA). Our encodings allow dropping the use of tables for the most used operations in crytographic algorithms. Also, our proposition provides better performances for most operations by exchanging lookup table accesses with CPU operations. We provide both a security evaluation of our proposition together with an application to an AES-128 white-box. Based on our suggested AES-128 white-box, we provide memory and performances comparisons against state-of-the-art implementations.

This paper is organized as follows. Section 2 is dedicated to the state-of-the-art in white-box designs and attacks. Afterwards, Sect. 3 introduces our new encoding scheme. In Sect. 4 we provide a security analysis of our suggested white-box encoding. The complexity in terms of memory and time of our new design is evaluated in Sect. 5. Finally some suggestions for further developments of our idea are provided in Sect. 6. Section 7 concludes this work.

2   State-of-the-Art

In 2002, two seminal papers from Chow *et al.* [19,20] introduced a new way to implement cryptographic algorithms that provided some risk mitigation. Such solutions to resist white-box attacks are known as "white-box cryptography" (WBC). They paved the way for a new and very active research field for both theoreticians and practitioners.

2.1   White-Box Designs

The work of Chow *et al.* [19,20] exposed the first white-box descriptions for both DES and AES ciphers. Their design has been the white-box implementation reference since then. Chow *et al.* introduced the use of tables to perform computations. Also, similar to the randomization technique of Kilian [31], by *encoding* each table with input/output functions unknown to the attacker, Chow *et al.* provided an initial solution to the problem of obfuscating a program.

After the first white-box propositions were published, Link *et al.* suggested an improved version of the DES white-box in [36], to better resist attacks. However, several attacks that allowed to recover the key hidden in the DES white-box were proposed by Wyseur *et al.* [47] and by Goubin *et al.* [27]. In parallel, the AES white-box was broken using an algebraic attack by Billet *et al.* [7], which was further refined and generalized by Michiels *et al.* [39]. In order to thwart such attacks, other authors proposed further white-box designs of the AES-128, for example Bringer *et al.* in [16] suggested an approach based on polynomials, but their suggestion was broken by De Mulder *et al.* in [23]. In 2009, Xiao and Lai proposed an improvement of Chow *et al.* AES white-box in [48], but again, their proposal was broken by De Mulder *et al.* [22]. In 2010, Karroumi suggested in [30] to use dual ciphers to protect the AES white-box. Unfortunately such a design was also broken by Lepoint *et al.* [35].

Generally speaking, all propositions of AES and DES white-box designs have been shown to be theoretically broken in the sense that the embedded key can be extracted. For each proposition a theoretical attack was found, see for example [7, 35, 39].

In a parallel thread of work, researchers tried to clarify the security notions related to the white-box context, thus works like those of Delerablée et al. [24], Saxena et al. [44] and Bock et al. [12] appeared.

A further step in the understanding of the security of white box implementations was brought forward by the introduction, in 2015 and 2016, of two attacks borrowed from the field of physical security. These attacks were used to break AES white-box suggestions appeared meanwhile, like the work of Luo et al. [37] and Lee et al. [32]. Such attacks were fault injection attacks, presented by Sanfelix et al. [42] and side-channel analysis (a.k.a. differential computation analysis, DCA for short), by Bos et al. [14]. Eventually such attacks provided easier methods to break all previous contributions, and researchers started to shift their interest from the algebraic security, to such a physical security dimension.

Indeed, several practical attacks have further reduced the security margin provided by a white-box implementation [14, 42]. However, all is not lost, as such advanced attacks motivated the study of advanced countermeasures. During the WhiBox contest editions, for example, a few implementations stood more than one month, while the hacking community tried to break them. From such implementations stemmed new understanding and improved countermeasures (see for example [9, 13, 28, 41, 43]), that allowed to thwart, or mitigate, the attacks explained so far.

2.2 White-Box Encoding

In order to counteract such new attacks, designers suggested to adapt known embedded security countermeasures, like the masking countermeasure [29, 40]. For example the work of Lee et al. [34] suggested a masked AES white-box implementation. Although providing an undeniable improvement on the security of white-box instances, such countermeasures deteriorate white-box implementations in terms of memory and performances.

Encodings are one of the key concepts introduced by Chow et al. Despite their use in [20] to counteract algebraic attacks authors worked in the recent publications to improve the effectiveness of encodings and to provide a masking stage to the algorithm. The two notions of encodings and masking are sometimes overlapping, and an encoding scheme may act as a masking scheme, and vice-versa. Loosely speaking, masking is a technique that removes the correlation between a value and its representation by, for example, using Shamir's secret sharing [46], while encoding is the application of (secret) input and output bijections to a transformation. Thus a secret sharing scheme can be seen as the application of the XOR bijection with a mask to the identity transformation, while an encoding can be interpreted as the application of some (non) linear masking scheme like for example [17] to a secret value.

It has been shown by various authors [9, 13, 28, 41, 43] how an accurate choice of encoding is paramount to the security of the white-box. In particular it seems that the best approach, as suggested by recent works [9, 28, 33, 45] is to use a linear masking on top of a non linear one. Such countermeasures are however expensive to deploy. The designer often needs to find a tradeoff between security and complexity (as a combination of memory requirements and running time). As an example, the winner of the 2019 edition of the WhiBox competition [2] used such an encoding (as revealed by the reverse engineering attack by Goubin *et al.* [28]) and the smallest implementation was about 20 MB for an AES-128 encryption.

In the following section we suggest a new encoding scheme that provides an improved security, fast operations, and a reduced memory footprint.

3   New Encoding Design for White-Box Constructions

Our proposal is directly inspired by the Benaloh cryptosystem, suggested in [6]. The original scheme is partially homomorphic, meaning that it allows to perform only one type of operation on plaintexts in the cipher domain. We modified the original Benaloh cryptosystem while preserving the semi-homomorphic properties in order to provide a new encoding scheme. Below, we recall the mathematical background that is used in the rest of the paper. Afterwards, we provide a brief explanation of the Benaloh cryptosystem together with our suggested modifications to use it as a white-box encoding.

3.1   Preliminaries

In the rest of this paper we will use notions such as *quadratic residue*, or *higher residue*. Such notions are detailed below.

Definition 1 (Quadratic Residue). *Let $m \in \mathbb{Z}_n^*$ for an odd integer n. Then m is a* quadratic residue *modulo n if there exists $x \in \mathbb{Z}_n^*$ such that:*

$$x^2 \equiv m \bmod n.$$

If no such x exists, then m is a quadratic non-residue *modulo n.*

Definition 2 (Legendre symbol). *Given a prime p and $m \in \mathbb{Z}_p^*$, the Legendre symbol of m modulo p is denoted $\left(\frac{m}{p}\right)$ and defined as follows:*

$$\left(\frac{m}{p}\right) = \begin{cases} 0 & if\, m \equiv 0 \mod p, \\ 1 & if\ m\ is\ a\ \text{quadratic residue}\ modulo\ p, \\ -1 & otherwise. \end{cases}$$

Definition 3 (Quadratic Residuosity Problem). *The* quadratic residuosity problem *(QRP) is the following: given an odd composite integer n and $m \in \mathbb{Z}_n^*$, decide whether m is a* quadratic residue *or a* quadratic non-residue *modulo n.*

Remark 1. If n is prime, then the QRP can easily be solved by Euler's criterion: for any $m \in \mathbb{Z}_n^*$, $\left(\frac{m}{n}\right) \equiv m^{(n-1)/2} \mod n$ (see for instance [38]).

Definition 4 (Higher Residue). *Let* $m \in \mathbb{Z}_n^*$ *for an odd integer* n, m *is said to be a* d-*residue modulo* n *if there exists* $x \in \mathbb{Z}_n^*$ *such that*

$$x^d \equiv m \bmod n.$$

If no such x *exists, then* m *is said to be a* d-*non-residue modulo* n.

Definition 5 (Higher Residuosity Problem). *The* higher residuosity problem *(HRP) is the following: given an odd composite integer* n *and* $m \in \mathbb{Z}_n^*$, *decide whether* m *is a* d-*residue or a* d-*non-residue modulo* n.

Remark 2. If the factorization of n is known, then the HRP can easily be solved (see [38]).

3.2   Original Description of Benaloh Cryptosystem

The Benaloh cryptosystem, introduced by Benaloh in 1994 [6] and improved by Fousse *et al.* [25], is an extension of the Goldwasser-Micali cryptosystem (GM) [26]. The latter's security relies on the QRP, while the former's on the HRP. Where the GM cryptosystem encrypts bits individually, Benaloh's improvement allows blocks of bits to be encrypted at once. Both schemes are probabilistic cryptosystems in the sense that several encryptions of the same message under the same key yield different ciphertexts. In this section, we describe the original Benaloh's cryptosystem.

Key Generation. The public and private key are generated as follows.

- Choose a block size r and two large prime numbers p and q such that:
  - $r | (p-1)$,
  - $\gcd(r, (p-1)/r) = 1$,
  - $\gcd(r, q-1) = 1$.
- Set $n = p \times q$ and compute $\phi(n) = (p-1)(q-1)$.
- Select $y \in \mathbb{Z}_n^*$ such that, for any prime factor r_i of r:
  - $y^{\phi(n)/r_i} \not\equiv 1 \bmod n$.

The public key is (n, r, y), and the private key is (p, q).

Encryption. Given the public parameters (n, r, y) and a an element of $\mathbb{Z}_r$, the encryption E_r is defined as:

$$E_r(a) = y^a u^r \bmod n,$$

where u is a random number in $\mathbb{Z}_n^*$.

Decryption. Given decryption key (p, q), and ciphertext c, the decryption D_r is defined as:

$$D_r(c) = \log_x(c^{\phi(n)/r}) \bmod n,$$

where $x = y^{\phi(n)/r} \bmod n$.

The homomorphic property is easily verified:

$$\begin{aligned}
E_r(a) \times E_r(b) &\equiv y^a u_0^r \times y^b u_1^r \quad \bmod n \\
&\equiv y^{a+b}(u_0 u_1)^r \quad \bmod n \\
&\equiv E_r(a+b) \quad \bmod n.
\end{aligned}$$

Our work aims at using this cryptosystem as an encoding. This allows to homomorphically perform some operations on the encoded values and thus reduce the overall memory cost of the white-box. In the following, we propose some modifications to achieve our goal.

3.3 Modified Benaloh Cryptosystem

We describe and motivate in this section our adaptations of the Benaloh cryptosystem to make it suitable for using as a white-box encoding. We deal with the encoding itself in Sect. 3.4.

Key Generation. The public and private key are generated as follows.

- Choose a prime number p.
- Choose a block size $r = 2^k$ such that $k \geq 2$ and r is the highest power of 2 which divides $p - 1$.
- Select randomly y a generator of $\mathbb{Z}_p^*$.
- Select randomly $t \in \mathbb{Z}_p^*$.

The public key is (p, r) and the private key is (t, y).

Compared to the original key generation, the private key t is introduced, u is fixed to 1 and the modulus is a prime number instead of a composite of two prime numbers. For the sake of simplicity, we keep the expression "private key" despite the fact that we use our private key both for encryption and decryption.

Encryption. Given the private key (t, y) and the public parameter p, the encryption E_t is defined as:

$$E_t(m) = t\, y^m \bmod p, \tag{1}$$

where m is an element of $\mathbb{Z}_p$.

It is easily verified that:

$$E_t(m_0) \times E_t(m_1) \equiv E_{t^2}(m_0 + m_1) \quad \bmod p.$$

Compared to the original encryption, the definition set of m is extended to the entire group $\mathbb{Z}_p$.

Decryption. Given the decryption key (y, t, p, r) and the ciphertext c, the decryption function D_t is defined as:

$$D_t(c) = \log_x((t^{-1}c)^{(p-1)/r}) \bmod p, \tag{2}$$

where $x = y^{(p-1)/r} \bmod p$.

The decryption differs from the original one only by the multiplication by $t^{-1} \bmod p$.

Motivations

About the Modulus. The modulus has been chosen to be a prime number. Since our proposal will rely on the QRP and will use a small modulus, there is no security benefit in choosing a composite modulus as the QRP is easy to solve even for small composite moduli.

About the Block Size. The block size r has been chosen to be a power of 2 in order to ensure that the least significant bit (LSB) of $D_t(E_t(a + b))$ equals the exclusive-or between the LSB of a and the LSB of b. Our proposal is based on this property, with the condition $r = 2^k$ and $k \geq 2$.

About the Base. The base y has been chosen to be a generator of $\mathbb{Z}_p^*$ as it guarantees that $y^{(p-1)/r} \not\equiv 1 \bmod p$. It is a requirement from the original key generation algorithm. The secrecy of y is a consequence of Sect. 4.1.

About the Key. In our proposal, the senstive data bits will be carried by the LSB of the exponent of y. The private key t has been introduced to hide this bit. If t was not present, with only the three previous modifications to the original Benaloh scheme, the sensitive bit m could be guessed by using the Legendre symbol of $E_1(m)$, which equals 1–2 m. The multiplication of $E_1(m)$ by a uniformly random number t makes its Legendre symbol equal to $\left(\frac{t}{p}\right)(1 - 2m)$, which is equal to 1 or −1 with the same probability $1/2$.

3.4   Modified Benaloh Cryptosystem as White-Box Encoding

In this section we show how our modified Benaloh cryptosystem can be used as a white-box encoding. Our proposal relies on three well-known facts:

1. Any Boolean function can be expressed as a logical circuit composed of XOR, AND and NOT gates.
2. The sum in $\mathbb{Z}$ of two bits a and b is $a+b = (a \wedge b) \| (a \oplus b)$, where $\|$ denotes the concatenation operator.
3. The sum in $\mathbb{Z}$ of one bit a with 1 is $a+1 = a \| (a \oplus 1) = a \| \bar{a}$.

We thus propose to consider the cryptographic algorithm as a logical circuit which gates are modified-Benaloh encoded. We describe hereafter how to encode (resp. decode) the circuit's input (resp. output) and how to evaluate its gates.

Encoding and Decoding Functions

Encoding Step. To encode a bit a, the modified key generation method (see Sect. 3.3) is run and the modified encrypting function (cf. Eq. (1)) is applied to $2s + a$, where $0 \leq s < (p-1)/2$ is uniformly drawn at random. We will denote the encoding function by Enc:

$$\mathsf{Enc}(a) = E_t(2s + a).$$

Here, s is introduced to make our encoding probabilistic, as does the random u in the original Benaloh scheme. Introducing this s instead of keeping the original u, we save one entropy bit: indeed, if the bit x was encoded as $E_t(x) = t y^x u^r \bmod p$, then $E_t(x) = t y^{vr+x} \bmod p$ with $v = \log_y u$, and since $r \geq 4$ and $r \mid (p-1)$, $(vr + x \bmod p - 1) \equiv x \bmod 4$. In other words, the second LSB of the exponent of y would always be 0. On the other hand, having both u and s does not provide more entropy to $\mathsf{Enc}(x)$. Therefore, we discard u but introduce s to keep the probabilistic property of the Benaloh scheme.

Decoding Step. To decode a value $\mathsf{Enc}(a)$, the modified decryption function (cf. Eq. (2)) is applied and the result is reduced modulo 2 to get a single bit. We will denote the decoding function by Dec:

$$\mathsf{Dec}(\mathsf{Enc}(a)) = D_t(\mathsf{Enc}(a)) \bmod 2.$$

Evaluating Logical Gates

As recalled before, a circuit can be constructed using only XOR, AND and NOT gates. We describe hereafter how each gate can be evaluated under the modified Benaloh-encoding.

From now, we consider that the encodings of the bits a and b are:

$$\mathsf{Enc}(a) = E_{t_0}(2s + a) = t_0\, y^{2s+a} \bmod p$$
$$\mathsf{Enc}(b) = E_{t_1}(2s' + b) = t_1\, y^{2s'+b} \bmod p.$$

XOR *Implementation.* To compute an encoding of $a \oplus b$, it is sufficient to multiply the encoding of the two bits:

$$\mathsf{Enc}(a)\mathsf{Enc}(b) \equiv t_0 t_1\, y^{2(s+s')+a+b} \bmod p$$
$$\equiv t_0 t_1\, y^{2(s+s'+ab)+(a\,\oplus\,b)} \bmod p. \qquad (3)$$

Let us verify that indeed $\mathsf{Dec}(\mathsf{Enc}(a)\mathsf{Enc}(b)) = a \oplus b$. Let be $\alpha \equiv 2(s + s' + ab) + (a \oplus b) \bmod p - 1$. Since $p - 1$ is even, $\alpha \bmod 2 = a \oplus b$. Setting $t = t_0 t_1$, the decryption function D_t returns α reduced modulo $r = 2^k$, thus this step preserves the k least significant bits of α. Therefore, the result of the decoding function is $a \oplus b$.

It follows that an arbitrary number of XOR gates can be evaluated in a row without caring for carries, that is to say, if $\{a_1, \ldots, a_n\}$ is a set of bits:

$$\mathsf{Dec}\left(\prod_{i=1}^{n} \mathsf{Enc}(a_i)\right) = a_1 \oplus \cdots \oplus a_n.$$

It is worth noticing that only modular multiplications, hence only CPU operations, are needed to evaluate XOR gates. Thus, the evaluation of any linear function comes at no memory cost by using our modified-Benaloh encodings.

AND *Implementation.* Contrary to the XOR operation, we use tables to implement the AND operation. A naive solution is to use one table with two operands as inputs. This table is used to decode each operand, evaluate the AND gate and re-encode the result. Each table admits p^2 entries and returns a $\log_2 p$-bit value, which implies a memory consumption of $p^2 \lceil \log_2 p \rceil$ bits per table.

We present instead another solution based on right-shift tables admitting only p entries, thus reducing the memory consumption per table down to $p \lceil \log_2 p \rceil$ bits. This solution is based on the fact that when $\mathsf{Enc}(a)$ and $\mathsf{Enc}(b)$ are multiplied together, y is raised to the power $2(s + s' + ab) + (a \oplus b)$ (see Eq. (3)). Then, right-shifting it results in $s + s' + ab$. Similarly, right-shifting the exponent of y in $\mathsf{Enc}(a)$ (resp. $\mathsf{Enc}(b)$) gives s (resp. s'). By adding these three numbers, we have $2(s + s') + ab$. Thus, we obtain with our solution the encoding of the desired bit ab as $\mathsf{Enc}(ab) = E_t(2s'' + ab)$ for some t and $s'' = s + s'$.

The first step is thus to right-shift the power of y in the expression of $\mathsf{Enc}(a)\mathsf{Enc}(b)$, $\mathsf{Enc}(a)$ and $\mathsf{Enc}(b)$. The fact that $r = 2^k$ impedes these three right shifts to be performed in a homomorphic way by successive left shifts. Thus, they have to be tabulated. Each table *decrypts* its entry (instead of decoding it, otherwise the random s's would be lost), then right-shifts the result and finally *encrypts* the shifted value to which is added a random even number (see Fig. 1).

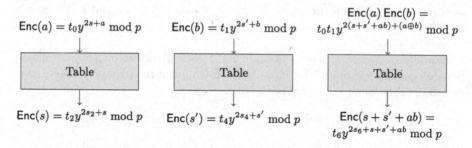

Fig. 1. Input and output of the three right-shift tables.

The output of the three tables are multiplied together to get, according to the notations in Fig. 1, $\mathsf{Enc}(ab) = ty^{2(S+s+s')+ab} \bmod p$ with $t = t_2 t_4 t_6$ and $S = s_2 + s_4 + s_6$.

NOT *Implementation.* To get an encoding of $\bar{a} = a \oplus 1$, one must multiply $\mathsf{Enc}(a)$ by any non-quadratic residue modulo p: let v be one of them, then there exists an integer α such that $v \equiv y^{2\alpha+1} \bmod p$. Thus $v\mathsf{Enc}(a) \equiv t_0 y^{2(s+\alpha)+a+1} \equiv t_0 y^{2(s+\alpha+a)+\bar{a}} \bmod p$.

Another solution for the NOT implementation can be used: it is sufficient to integrate the NOT operation to the next table. For instance, the next table can be an AND table. The evaluation of the NOT gate can thus be delegated to the next table due to the linear property of the XOR gate.

From now, sequences of binary operations composed with ANDs, XORs and NOTs can be computed under our modified-Benaloh encoding.

3.5 Using the Modified-Benaloh Encoding in a White-Box Design

Hereafter, we give a way to design a white-boxed cipher by using the modified-Benaloh encoding. As an example, we give in Sect. 5 an AES implementation using our proposal.

Overall Parameters. The modified-Benaloh key generation algorithm (see Sect. 3.3) is run to get the parameters p, r and y. They have to be common to all encoded bits within the white-box, in order for the logical gates to be correctly evaluated as described in Sect. 3.4. These parameters might be refreshed at any moment, at the cost of an extra decoding-then-encoding step on each encoded bit to switch from the former set of parameters to the new one.

Encoding Data Bits
Encoding the Key. The ℓ-bit cipher key is embedded within the white-box in a modified-Benaloh encoded form. The white-box embeds a table with ℓ entries, each one being of the form $t_j y^{2s_j + k_j} \bmod p$, where $1 \leq j \leq \ell$ and k_j is the jth key bit.

Encoding the Plaintext. The white-box turns each plaintext bit to a modified-Benaloh encoding using a 1-bit input table. Each bit of the plaintext has its own encoding table. Such tables are of the form:

$$T_i = \{\mathsf{Enc}(0), \mathsf{Enc}(1)\} = \{t_i\, y^{2s_i} \bmod p,\ t_i\, y^{2s_i' + 1} \bmod p\}.$$

Note that t_i here is fully independent from the t_j's that protect the cipher key.

Let us detail here the use of the private key t_i. We can remark that it must be the same for the two possible encodings of the same bit: suppose that we could have $\mathsf{Enc}(0) = E_t(2s)$ and $\mathsf{Enc}(1) = E_{t'}(2s' + 1)$ with $t \neq t'$ and (t, t') being different for each bit to encode. Let us consider a table that, within the circuit, decrypts its entry. As an example, it could be a table evaluating an AND gate. For this decryption step, the private key of the table entry, or a product of several of them, if the entry is a product of several encodings, has to be known. Then, when the entry of such a table would be a combination of n encoded input bits, 2^n tables (one per possible n-tuple of encoded bits) would be necessary to perform the operation delegated to the table. Therefore, the private key t_i has to be fixed per encoded bit and not per encoding.

Cipher Evaluation. Once each bit of the plaintext is encoded, the cipher, designed as a logical circuit, can be evaluated. One has just to perform binary operations on the encoded bits as explained in Sect. 3.4.

Decoding Data Bits. The ciphertext's bits are decoded from their modified-Benaloh encoded form by a table that applies the decoding function on its entries. Note that one table per ciphertext bit is necessary, as each decoding table uses a different private key from the other decoding tables.

4   Security Considerations

With our modified-Benaloh scheme, we proposed to encode each bit b as:

$$\mathsf{Enc}(b) = t\, y^{2s+b} \quad \bmod p$$

for some random numbers t and s. All logical operations between encoded bits are done in the encoding domain with modular multiplications and table accesses.

In this section we provide a security analysis of our proposal, by addressing some potential flaws.

4.1   About the Shift Tables

In this section, we study two attack paths opened by the shift tables used to evaluate the AND gates.

The input-output-squared attack. Let $n_{i,b} = t_i\, y^{2s_b+b} \bmod p$ be the Benaloh-encoded input of a shift table and $n_{o,b} = t_o\, y^{2s+s_b} \bmod p$ the corresponding output. For the sake of clarity, we set here $s = 0$ as it will not be useful in this section. Then $n_{i,b}\, n_{o,b}^2 \equiv t_i\, t_o^2\, y^{4s_b+b} \bmod p$.

The attacker can collect $n_{i,0}, n_{o,0}, n_{i,1}$ and $n_{o,1}$ and compute:

$$z = n_{i,0}\, n_{i,1}\, n_{o,0}^2\, n_{o,1}^2 \bmod p$$
$$= t_i^2\, t_o^4\, y^{4(s_0+s_1)+1} \bmod p.$$

Since y is a generator of $\mathbb{Z}_p^*$, there exists $\tau_i, \tau_o \in \{0, \ldots, p-1\}$ such that $t_i = y^{\tau_i} \bmod p$ and $t_o = y^{\tau_o} \bmod p$. This implies that $z = y^{4(\tau_o+s_0+s_1)+2\tau_i+1} \bmod p$.

If the attacker can guess the least significant bit (LSB) of τ_i from z, then he can compute $\left(\frac{t_i}{p}\right) = \tau_i \bmod 2$ and therefore b. However, whereas the LSB of $\log_y z$ is actually independent from the chosen generator y, it is not the case of its second LSB: let y' be another generator of $\mathbb{Z}_p^*$ and a be the integer such that $y = y'^{2a+1} \bmod p$; then $\log_{y'}(z) = \log_{y'}(y)\log_y(z) \equiv 2(a+\tau_i)+1 \bmod 4$. Since a can be odd or even[1], the knowledge of z does not give any information on $\tau_i \bmod 2$.

---

[1] For instance, in $\mathbb{Z}_{59}^*$, all odd powers of 2 but $2^{57} \equiv -1 \bmod 59$ are generators.

The Frequency Attack. Suppose that we want to AND two bits a_0 and a_1. Let $s_0^{(0)}, s_0^{(1)}, s_1^{(0)}$ and $s_1^{(1)}$ be four integers modulo $(p-1)/2$ and let $\mathsf{Enc}(a_0) = t_0\, y^{2s_0^{(a_0)}+a_0} \bmod p$ and $\mathsf{Enc}(a_1) = t_1\, y^{2s_1^{(a_1)}+a_1} \bmod p$. The table fed by $\mathsf{Enc}(a_0) \times \mathsf{Enc}(a_1)$ during the evaluation of the AND gate (see Fig. 1) returns some $\alpha = t\, y^{2\delta+\beta} \bmod p$ where β is a bit that equals $a_0 a_1 \oplus ((s_0^{(a_0)} + s_1^{(a_1)}) \bmod 2)$. Since $\left(\frac{\alpha}{p}\right) = \left(\frac{t}{p}\right)(1 - 2\beta)$, $\left(\frac{\alpha}{p}\right) = \left(\frac{t}{p}\right)$ with probability $3/4$ if $s_0^{(0)} \equiv s_0^{(1)} \bmod 2$ and $s_1^{(0)} \equiv s_1^{(1)} \bmod 2$, which leaks the value of $a_0 a_1$. Therefore, the LSB of the random $s_0^{(0)}, s_0^{(1)}, s_1^{(0)}$ and $s_1^{(1)}$ should be adjusted to avoid this, for instance by imposing $s_i^{(0)} \bmod 2 = s_i^{(1)} + 1 \bmod 2$ for $i = 0, 1$. In the case where such a solution would not be tractable, we suggest to implement a Boolean-masked AND to decorrelate the content of the shift tables from the bits to AND together.

4.2   About the Key

We recall that in our proposal in Sect. 3.3, the cipher key is embedded in a Benaloh-encoded form within the white-box. Encoded this way, no information can be extracted on the key just looking at its encoded form: since each key bit b has its own random private subkey t, $E_t(b)$ is indistinguishable from a random number in $\mathbb{Z}_p$ and so t acts like a one-time pad.

On the other hand, some information about the key may be revealed by the following DCA-like attack. Seeing the cipher as a logical circuit, any gate output is Benaloh-encoded with a random t unknown from the attacker but fixed over all executions of the white-box. Then any variation of the Legendre symbol of the gate output is only due to a variation of the encoded bit.

Therefore, the attacker can focus on an AND gate which inputs depend on a few key bits. By making an assumption on these key bits, the attacker can compute an expected sequence of outputs of his targeted AND gate when the input plaintexts vary. Then, by comparing this sequence to the Legendre symbols actually output by the white-box, the attacker can accept or reject his hypothesis on the subkey. Repeating this procedure with different gates depending on other key bits, he can reduce the subset of possible cipher keys.

In order to thwart such an attack, a possible countermeasure consists in implementing a Boolean-masked circuit (in addition to applying the Benaloh-encoding). The impact of the masking on the XOR gates comes at no memory cost. However, concerning the AND masking, we suggest to use the secure AND proposed by Biryukov *et al.* [8]. The impact on the number of tables is thus limited to only a factor 4.

4.3   Summary

In order to prevent the identified security issues, we decline our Benaloh-encoded white-box into two flavours:

1. *Proposition 1:* a lightweight white-boxed cipher without countermeasure,
2. *Proposition 2:* a white-boxed cipher implemented as a Boolean-masked circuit to protect vulnerable AND gates (Sect. 4.2).

We close this section with a brief estimation of the computational effort needed to defeat our propositions:

1. *Proposition 1* can be defeated by the Legendre symbol attack of Sect. 4.2. It is equivalent to a differential computational analysis (DCA) with a Legendre symbol leakage model. The results summarized in [9, Table 1] imply that the cost of the DCA Legendre symbol attack is $O(nk \log_2 p)$, where n is the length of the trace, k is the number of key hypotheses and $\log_2 p$ the cost of performing Euler's criterion.
2. *Proposition 2* can be defeated by a 2nd-order DCA if the sensitive data are shared into 2 bits. [9, Table 1] implies in this case that the cost of the Legendre symbol attack is $O(n^2 k \log_2 p)$.

5   Performances: Example with AES-128 Encryption

In this section we provide performances estimations for an AES white-box implementation designed with our two propositions with the security improvements described in Sect. 4.3. Furthermore, we compare our AES-128 white-box design performances against other state-of-the-art designs, with respect to execution time and space requirements.

The AES can be written with only elementary gates. In particular, an AES can be only composed of XOR, NOT XOR (NXOR), and AND operations. The AES requires only XOR gates to implement, except the SubBytes function that requires also AND gates. For SubBytes, we use the bitsliced software implementation proposed by Calik [18, Sect. 7] which is an improvement of the Boyar and Peralta [15] circuit. He proposed an AES SBox with 113 gates, composed of 77 XORs, 4 NXORs and 32 ANDs. Following our proposal in Sect. 3.4), only AND gates require tables. Hence, the memory consumption of an AES-128 with our proposition is $15\,360 \times p \times \lceil \log_2(p) \rceil$ bits, where $15\,360 = 32 \times 10 \times 16 \times 3$:

- 32 ANDs are required for each SBox.
- There are 10 rounds in the AES-128.
- There are 16 input bytes.
- There are 3 tables for each AND with our solution (see Sect. 3.4).

Besides, the secret key is considered to be embedded within the white-box in a Benaloh-encoded form: it corresponds to 128 tables of $\lceil \log_2(p) \rceil$ bits. Finally, the white-box requires one table to encode each plaintext bit, and one table per ciphertext bit to remove all the random masks t_i accumulated through the circuit: it corresponds to $128 \times 2 = 256$ tables of $p\lceil\log_2(p)\rceil$ bits. It leads to a total of $15\,744 = 15\,360 + 128 + 256$ tables. We can note that whatever the size of the chosen parameter p, the number of tables is always the same, i.e. $15\,744$.

In a same way, the execution time is constant and is not dependent on the size of the parameters (as long as they fit in the architecture registers). Indeed, whatever the chosen parameters of the implementation, we have $15\,744$ tables to access and $30\,520 = (92 + 128 + ((77 + 4 + 3 \times 32) \times 16)) \times 10$ XOR gates to evaluate, where:

- 92 represents the number of XORs in the MixColumns.
- 128 represents the number of XORs for the AddRoundKey.
- $77 + 4$ represents the number of XORs in the SBox computations.
- 3×32 represents the number of ANDs in the SBox computations, and the number of XORs required during the AND calculations.
- 16 represents the number of SBox in the AES-128.
- 10 represents the number of rounds in the AES-128.

It leads to an execution time of $15\,744$ table accesses and $30\,520$ short modular multiplications. The NOT gates are not taken into consideration. Indeed, we consider that these gates can be delegated to the next table of the circuit.

Table 1 gives the min and max bounds for memory consumption of an AES white-box using our proposition, where the bounds depend on the used prime number p.

Table 1. Memory consumption according to the bit size of p.

$\lceil\log_2(p)\rceil$	Memory consumption (megabytes, MB)
4	[0.07, 0.11]
6	[0.39, 0.74]
8	[2.03, 4.01]
10	[10.10, 20.14]
12	[48.42, 96.77]
14	[225.86, 451.64]
16	[1 032.35, 2 064.61]

In Fig. 2 we provide a comparison of sizes and estimated execution time of published AES-128 white-boxes and our suggestions *Proposition 1* and *Proposition 2*. The entries are sorted by publication date from the left to the right. The comparison aims at providing an overview of the evolution of white-box design sizes according to the execution time of the implementation. Figure 2 thus compares the size of a reference AES implementation [21] with the size of the white-box implementations of Chow *et al.* [20], Bringer *et al.* [16][2], Xiao *et al.* [48], Karroumi [30], Lee *et al. 1* [32], Lee *et al. 2* [34], Lee *et al. 3* [33], Luo *et al.* [37], Bai *et al.* [3], Biryukov *et al.* [9], Seker *et al.* [45][3] and this work.

The execution time estimations are obtained by using the number of LUT accesses multiplied by 0.8 ns (typical RAM access times for DDR3 memory). For the works that did not use any table, we accounted for 0.5 ns per computation (typical operation time for a 2 GHz processor).

For our implementation, we choose a 6-bit prime number. Given the remarks of Sect. 4.3, a 6-bit prime number does not significantly weaken our white-box compared to longer primes, while allowing a competitive memory footprint. Concerning memory size, the overall memory cost of the complete implementation is dominated by the AND tables. For example, by choosing $p = 53$, with the implementation described in Sect. 3, *Proposition 1* leads to an implementation of 5,014,144 bits (626.76 kilobytes), coherently with Table 1. The execution time is constant and is not dependent of the size of the prime number: $15\,744 \times 0.8 + 30\,520 \times 0.5 = 27\,855$ ns.

We remark that our new encoding allows a more efficient white-box design than the Chow *et al.* [20] one, and we also argue that our design may be adapted to a masked implementation with reduced size impact compared to the one of Biryukov *et al.* [9].

6   Further Work

In this section we provide a few ideas to further develop our encodings. We organized such ideas in two main sections. The first section suggests improvements to the side-channel security of white-boxes. Afterwards we present ideas to thwart fault attacks.

6.1   Against Side-Channel Attacks

White-box implementations are vulnerable to attacks exploiting software execution traces containing information about the memory addresses being accessed or about manipulated data. In order to complexify such attacks, one may add countermeasures. For example, one can:

- Shuffle and randomize the computations by introducing dummy operations as suggested in [10]. This can be achieved for example by computing Enc(0) × Enc(b) for some b, at random time.

---

[2] Bringer *et al.* did not provide speed figures. We used the count of monomials in Table 1 of their work and accounted one operation per monomial.

[3] Seker *et al.* did not provide memory figures. In order to obtain the memory consumption of their design we used their $(2, 1)$-masking, assumed that each gate is encoded separately (in order to avoid loops) and that each gate is encoded in 1 byte. This allows a fair comparison against for example the circuit of Biryukov *et al.* [9], where the ratio between the number of gates and the resulting size is about 6.4.

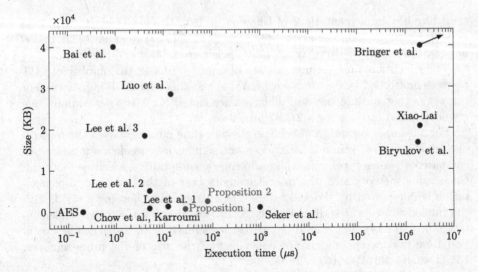

Fig. 2. Memory performances and estimated execution time of published AES-128 white-boxes.

- It is possible to mask the AES circuit prior to encoding it into tables. The impact on the size and speed would be balanced by the augmented security. We also remark that such countermeasure can easily thwart the Legendre symbol attack presented in Sect. 4.2.

6.2   Against Fault Attacks

White-box implementations are particularly vulnerable to fault attacks. An attacker can easily change the execution flow of the implementation or substitute the value of a variable [11, Sect. 7.2]. Hence, the design of a white-box must integrate countermeasures against such attacks. Typically redundancy (use of redundant representations such as a residue number system – RNS [4], or use of redundant information), error detecting or correcting techniques, or infective countermeasures [5] are used to thwart such attacks. For example, in order to introduce redundancy, one can observe that the exponents used in the encodings are values modulo r. Thus by using a composite r, it is possible to perform smaller computations modulo each prime dividing r. The result can then be recomputed by using the Chinese remainder theorem. Each of the two submodules can be used to:

- Encode the same sensitive value, which provides redundancy.
- Encode different bits of the plaintext, which provides efficiency.
- Encode the correct value on one submodule, a random value on the second one, which provides randomization.

7   Conclusion

This work addresses the problem of encoding data when building a white-box implementation. We suggest a new encoding scheme based on the Benaloh cryptosystem that allows both compactness and speed. In particular, the semi-homomorphic property of our encoding allows to drop half of the tables (in our example those used for the XOR operations) and to speed up computations by exchanging part of the tables (used for example in [20]) with homomorphic operations. We modify the Benaloh scheme in order to obtain an encoding that inherits the semi-homomorphic properties of the original design, while fitting the size constraints of the white-box context. Our new proposition allows the white-box designer to tune the performances and adapt the security of the implementation to meet its requirements.

As future work, we remark that it seems possible to enhance speed and memory consumption of our proposal. In this regard, a promising line of research is to parallelize multiplications and table accesses. Another direction for further work is the study of other homomorphic encryption schemes (e.g. lattice based). In particular, the study of fully homomorphic schemes may turn out advantageous. Indeed, we have shown in this paper that one can modify a semi-homomorphic scheme and use it as encoding. Thus it would be interesting to investigate the modification of a fully homomorphic scheme in a similar way. It could enable to enhance the security and the memory consumption by only keeping the input and output tables.

References

1. CHES 2017 capture the flag challenge - the WhibOx Contest - an ECRYPT white-box cryptography competition (2017). https://whibox-contest.github.io/2017/
2. CHES 2019 capture the flag challenge - the WhibOx contest edition 2 (2019). https://whibox-contest.github.io/2019/
3. Bai, K., Wu, C., Zhang, Z.: Protect white-box AES to resist table composition attacks. IET Inf. Secur. **12**(4), 305–313 (2018)
4. Bajard, J., Eynard, J., Merkiche, N.: Multi-fault attack detection for RNS cryptographic architecture. In: 23nd IEEE Symposium on Computer Arithmetic, ARITH, pp. 16–23 (2016)
5. Barbu, G., et al.: A high-order infective countermeasure framework. In: Workshop on Fault Diagnosis and Tolerance in Cryptography (FDTC) (2021)
6. Benaloh, J.: Dense probabilistic encryption. In: Selected Areas of Cryptography (1994)
7. Billet, O., Gilbert, H., Ech-Chatbi, C.: Cryptanalysis of a white-box AES implementation. In: International Workshop on Selected Areas in Cryptography, pp. 227–240 (2004)
8. Biryukov, A., Dinu, D., Le Corre, Y., Udovenko, A.: Optimal first-order boolean masking for embedded IoT devices. In: Eisenbarth, T., Teglia, Y. (eds.) CARDIS 2017. LNCS, vol. 10728, pp. 22–41. Springer, Cham (2018). https://doi.org/10.1007/978-3-319-75208-2_2

9. Biryukov, A., Udovenko, A.: Attacks and countermeasures for white-box designs. In: International Conference on the Theory and Application of Cryptology and Information Security, pp. 373–402 (2018)

10. Biryukov, A., Udovenko, A.: Dummy shuffling against algebraic attacks in white-box implementations. In: Canteaut, A., Standaert, F.-X. (eds.) EUROCRYPT 2021. LNCS, vol. 12697, pp. 219–248. Springer, Cham (2021). https://doi.org/10.1007/978-3-030-77886-6_8

11. Bock, E., et al.: White-box cryptography: don't forget about grey-box attacks. J. Cryptol. **32**, 1095–1143 (2019)

12. Bock, E.A., Amadori, A., Brzuska, C., Michiels, W.: On the security goals of white-box cryptography. IACR Trans. CHES 327–357 (2020)

13. Alpirez Bock, E., Brzuska, C., Michiels, W., Treff, A.: On the ineffectiveness of internal encodings - revisiting the DCA attack on white-box cryptography. In: Preneel, B., Vercauteren, F. (eds.) ACNS 2018. LNCS, vol. 10892, pp. 103–120. Springer, Cham (2018). https://doi.org/10.1007/978-3-319-93387-0_6

14. Bos, J.W., Hubain, C., Michiels, W., Teuwen, P.: Differential computation analysis: hiding your white-box designs is not enough. In: Gierlichs, B., Poschmann, A.Y. (eds.) CHES 2016. LNCS, vol. 9813, pp. 215–236. Springer, Heidelberg (2016). https://doi.org/10.1007/978-3-662-53140-2_11

15. Boyar, J., Peralta, R.: A small depth-16 circuit for the AES S-Box. In: Gritzalis, D., Furnell, S., Theoharidou, M. (eds.) SEC 2012. IAICT, vol. 376, pp. 287–298. Springer, Heidelberg (2012). https://doi.org/10.1007/978-3-642-30436-1_24

16. Bringer, J., Chabanne, H., Dottax, E.: White box cryptography: another attempt. IACR Cryptology ePrint Archive (2006)

17. Bringer, J., Chabanne, H., Le, T.H.: Protecting AES against side-channel analysis using wire-tap codes. J. Cryptogr. Eng. **2**, 129–141 (2012)

18. Calik, C.: CMT: circuit minimization team (2020). https://www.cs.yale.edu/homes/peralta/CircuitStuff/CMT.html

19. Chow, S., Eisen, P., Johnson, H., Van Oorschot, P.C.: A white-box DES implementation for DRM applications. In: ACM Workshop on Digital Rights Management, pp. 1–15 (2002)

20. Chow, S., Eisen, P., Johnson, H., Van Oorschot, P.C.: White-box cryptography and an AES implementation. In: Nyberg, K., Heys, H. (eds.) SAC 2002. LNCS, vol. 2595, pp. 250–270. Springer, Heidelberg (2003). https://doi.org/10.1007/3-540-36492-7_17

21. Cox, M., Engelschall, R., Henson, S., Laurie, B., et al.: The OpenSSL Project (2002)

22. De Mulder, Y., Roelse, P., Preneel, B.: Cryptanalysis of the Xiao-Lai white-box AES implementation. In: Knudsen, L.R., Wu, H. (eds.) SAC 2012. LNCS, vol. 7707, pp. 34–49. Springer, Heidelberg (2013). https://doi.org/10.1007/978-3-642-35999-6_3

23. De Mulder, Y., Wyseur, B., Preneel, B.: Cryptanalysis of a perturbated white-box AES implementation. In: Gong, G., Gupta, K.C. (eds.) INDOCRYPT 2010. LNCS, vol. 6498, pp. 292–310. Springer, Heidelberg (2010). https://doi.org/10.1007/978-3-642-17401-8_21

24. Delerablée, C., Lepoint, T., Paillier, P., Rivain, M.: White-box security notions for symmetric encryption schemes. In: Lange, T., Lauter, K., Lisoněk, P. (eds.) SAC 2013. LNCS, vol. 8282, pp. 247–264. Springer, Heidelberg (2014). https://doi.org/10.1007/978-3-662-43414-7_13

25. Fousse, L., Lafourcade, P., Alnuaimi, M.: Benaloh's dense probabilistic encryption revisited (2011). https://arxiv.org/pdf/1008.2991.pdf

26. Goldwasser, S., Micali, S.: Probabilistic encryption & how to play mental poker keeping secret all partial information. In: Proceedings of the Fourteenth Annual ACM Symposium on Theory of Computing, pp. 365–377 (1982)
27. Goubin, L., Masereel, J.M., Quisquater, M.: Cryptanalysis of white box DES implementations. In: International Workshop on Selected Areas in Cryptography, pp. 278–295 (2007)
28. Goubin, L., Rivain, M., Wang, J.: Defeating state-of-the-art white-box countermeasures with advanced gray-box attacks. IACR Trans. CHES **2020**(3), 454–482 (2020)
29. Ishai, Y., Sahai, A., Wagner, D.: Private circuits: securing hardware against probing attacks. In: Boneh, D. (ed.) CRYPTO 2003. LNCS, vol. 2729, pp. 463–481. Springer, Heidelberg (2003). https://doi.org/10.1007/978-3-540-45146-4_27
30. Karroumi, M.: Protecting white-box AES with dual ciphers. In: Rhee, K.-H., Nyang, D.H. (eds.) ICISC 2010. LNCS, vol. 6829, pp. 278–291. Springer, Heidelberg (2011). https://doi.org/10.1007/978-3-642-24209-0_19
31. Kilian, J.: Founding cryptography on oblivious transfer. In: Proceedings of the Twentieth annual ACM Symposium on Theory of Computing, pp. 20–31 (1988)
32. Lee, S., Choi, D., Choi, Y.J.: Conditional re-encoding method for cryptanalysis-resistant white-box AES. ETRI J. **37**(5), 1012–1022 (2015)
33. Lee, S., Kim, M.: Improvement on a masked white-box cryptographic implementation. Cryptology ePrint Archive, Report 2020/199 (2020)
34. Lee, S., Kim, T., Kang, Y.: A masked white-box cryptographic implementation for protecting against differential computation analysis. IEEE Trans. Inf. Forensics Secur. **13**(10), 2602–2615 (2018)
35. Lepoint, T., Rivain, M., De Mulder, Y., Roelse, P., Preneel, B.: Two attacks on a white-box AES implementation. In: Lange, T., Lauter, K., Lisoněk, P. (eds.) SAC 2013. LNCS, vol. 8282, pp. 265–285. Springer, Heidelberg (2014). https://doi.org/10.1007/978-3-662-43414-7_14
36. Link, H.E., Neumann, W.D.: Clarifying obfuscation: improving the security of white-box DES. In: International Conference on Information Technology: Coding and Computing (ITCC 2005)-Volume II, vol. 1, pp. 679–684. IEEE (2005)
37. Luo, R., Lai, X., You, R.: A new attempt of white-box AES implementation. In: Proceedings of 2014 IEEE International Conference on Security, Pattern Analysis, and Cybernetics (SPAC), pp. 423–429. IEEE (2014)
38. Menezes, A.J., Katz, J., Van Oorschot, P.C., Vanstone, S.A.: Handbook of Applied Cryptography (1996)
39. Michiels, W., Gorissen, P., Hollmann, H.D.L.: Cryptanalysis of a generic class of white-box implementations. In: Avanzi, R.M., Keliher, L., Sica, F. (eds.) SAC 2008. LNCS, vol. 5381, pp. 414–428. Springer, Heidelberg (2009). https://doi.org/10.1007/978-3-642-04159-4_27
40. Rivain, M., Prouff, E.: Provably secure higher-order masking of AES. In: International Workshop on CHES, pp. 413–427 (2010)
41. Rivain, M., Wang, J.: Analysis and improvement of differential computation attacks against internally-encoded white-box implementations. IACR Trans. CHES **2019**(2), 225–255 (2019)
42. Sanfelix, E., Mune, C., de Haas, J.: Unboxing the white-box. In: Black Hat EU 2015 (2015)
43. Sasdrich, P., Moradi, A., Güneysu, T.: White-box cryptography in the gray box. In: Peyrin, T. (ed.) FSE 2016. LNCS, vol. 9783, pp. 185–203. Springer, Heidelberg (2016). https://doi.org/10.1007/978-3-662-52993-5_10

44. Saxena, A., Wyseur, B., Preneel, B.: Towards security notions for white-box cryptography. In: Samarati, P., Yung, M., Martinelli, F., Ardagna, C.A. (eds.) ISC 2009. LNCS, vol. 5735, pp. 49–58. Springer, Heidelberg (2009). https://doi.org/10.1007/978-3-642-04474-8_4

45. Seker, O., Eisenbarth, T., Liskiewicz, M.: A white-box masking scheme resisting computational and algebraic attacks. Cryptology ePrint Archive, Report 2020/443 (2020)

46. Shamir, A.: How to share a secret. Commun. ACM **22**(11), 612–613 (1979)

47. Wyseur, B., Michiels, W., Gorissen, P., Preneel, B.: Cryptanalysis of white-box DES implementations with arbitrary external encodings. In: Adams, C., Miri, A., Wiener, M. (eds.) SAC 2007. LNCS, vol. 4876, pp. 264–277. Springer, Heidelberg (2007). https://doi.org/10.1007/978-3-540-77360-3_17

48. Xiao, Y., Lai, X.: A secure implementation of white-box AES. In: 2nd International Conference on Computer Science and its Applications, pp. 1–6. IEEE (2009)

PhiAttack
Rewriting the Java Card Class Hierarchy

Jean Dubreuil[1] and Guillaume Bouffard[2,3]($\boxtimes$) (iD)

[1] Serma Safety & Security, Pessac, France
j.dubreuil@serma.com
[2] National Cybersecurity Agency of France (ANSSI), Paris, France
guillaume.bouffard@ssi.gouv.fr
[3] Information Security Group, DIENS École Normale Supérieure,
CNRS, PSL University, Paris, France

Abstract. Compiling Java Card applets is based on the assumption that
`export` files used to translate Java class item to Java Card CAP tokens
are legitimate. Bouffard *et al.* [2] reversed the translation mechanism.
Based on malicious Application Programming Interface (API) embedded
in a target, they succeeded in making a man-in-the-middle attack where
cryptographic keys can leak.

In this article, we disclose that, on a pool of legitimate `export` files,
Java Card Virtual Machine (JCVM) implementations can be confused
by a CAP file verified by the Java Card Bytecode Verifier (BCV). The
disclosed vulnerability leads to Java Card class hierarchy rewriting. The
introduced vulnerability is exploitable up to Java Card 3.0.5. Recently,
Java Card 3.1.0 provides a new `export` file format which prevents this
vulnerability.

Keywords: Java Card · BCV · Inheritance tree

1 Introduction

Java Card platform [14] is the most used technology embedded in secure components [13]. Java Card is a lightweight version of Java for resource-constrained devices as secure components. Therefore, such secure component embeds a virtual machine, which interprets application bytecodes already romized with the operating system or downloaded after issuance. Due to security reasons, the ability to download code into the card is controlled by a protocol defined by GlobalPlatform [7].

To build a Java Card application, an image of the targeted Java Card Virtual Machine (JCVM) implementation is required. This image gives information about the available Application Programming Interface (API) and the class hierarchy. In this article, we focus on how class inheritance is translated during the compilation process and loaded in a JCVM platform. We show this process can be corrupted to redefine the class-tree hierarchy which leads to execute malicious code.

© Springer Nature Switzerland AG 2022
V. Grosso and T. Pöppelmann (Eds.): CARDIS 2021, LNCS 13173, pp. 275–288, 2022.
https://doi.org/10.1007/978-3-030-97348-3_15

1.1   Java Card Security Model

To install an applet on the Java Card platform, one must implement it in Java language and then build it within Java compiler (`javac`) to obtain Java `class` files. Those `class` files are not designed to be embedded in a resource-limited device. Indeed, the Java `class` files are executed as is by the Java Virtual Machine (JVM) where references are resolved by name; it is very costly in both execution time and memory space. The translated Java `class` files are named the CAP (for Converted APplet) file.

To run a Java applet on resource-constraint devices, the adopted solution is to translate reference name to token during a step made by the Java Card converter[1]. If the `class` file to convert implements features that can be used by other applications, a Java Card `export` file is also generated. The `export` file contains, for each Java reference name element, the associated token embedded on the device. Therefore, `export` files are also used by the bytecode converter during the translation process. After this translation, Java Card files are checked by the Bytecode Verifier (BCV) which statically verifies the compliance to the Java Card security rules. There is a unique CAP file by converted package, and it is signed to ensure its integrity and authenticity. On the device, the GlobalPlatform [7] layer verifies the CAP file signature. This part is described on the left part of Fig. 1.

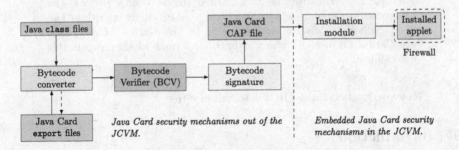

Fig. 1. Java Card security model.

After obtaining and signing the applet CAP file, the applet developer needs GlobalPlatform loading keys to load his applet or library. During the installation process, on the right part of Fig. 1, an embedded security module checks some security elements. The installed applet runs in its context segregated by the Java Card Firewall. It ensures that applet accesses only its data or specific shared features.

---

[1] The Java Card converter is included in the Java Card SDK available on the Oracle's website: https://www.oracle.com/fr/java/technologies/java-card-tech.html.

1.2 State-of-the-Art Java Card Platform Security

The Java Card platform implementation security has been thoroughly studied against software [1,3–5,8–10,12,17] attacks. Those attacks are implementation dependent and they are prevented by a BCV. The Java Card protection profile [15] requires the usage of a BCV to check the applet compliance from Java security rules.

How the BCV checks CAP files has been analysed in [6,11]. Lancia *et al.* [11] shows that the BCV does not verify the correctness of information stored twice in the CAP file. Based on this missing check, they succeed in breaking the JCVM sandbox by executing ill-formed bytecodes from BCV verified applet. This vulnerability was corrected in the BCV provided in the Java Card 3.0.5u3 toolchain.

To check the correctness of CAP files, the BCV analysis relies on export files used during the CAP file conversion. If an export file contains wrong information – information which does not correspond to the targeted JCVM – a vulnerability may occur. Disclosed by Mostowski *et al.* [12], using wrong export files, they succeed in making a type confusion upon a BCV-verified applet. Moreover, Bouffard *et al.* [2] succeed a Man-in-the-Middle attack based on malicious export files to extract cryptographic secrets. In their attack, they must install a backdoored API on a targeted JCVM and provide export files to link applet to this malicious API. Those export files replace the Java Card cryptographic API. On the targeted JCVM platform, the backdoored API makes interface with the legitimate Java Card cryptographic API and saves each key generated. However, this attack is interesting but hard to realize in practice: the attacker must force its victim to use corrupted export files whereas it is expected that any application developer use export files from Oracle's development kit.

1.3 Contribution

In this article, we generalise Bouffard *et al.*'s work [2] where we corrupt the Java Card class hierarchy. We succeed in confusing the CAP file import mechanism to force the targeted JCVM platform to use our Java class hierarchy instead of the legitimate one. As token resolution relies on runtime verification, our attack is not detected by a BCV. Therefore, we exploit the token resolution mechanism to execute malicious code on JCVM platform where each installed CAP file are checked by an up-to-date BCV.

Our contribution has been initially performed on Java Card specification 3.0.5 [14] as there is no publicly known product implementing a higher specification version. Therefore, in the paper, we use the BCV provided by the Java Card SDK 3.0.5.

We notice that the latest available Java Card SDK is the 3.1.0u5 version [16]. However, when writing this article, there is not product that implements this version.

This article is organized as follows: Sect. 2 describes the Java Card import mechanism in order to introduce the PhiAttack explained in Sect. 3. A discussion on how to counteract this attack is in Sect. 4. Section 5 concludes this article.

2   Java Card Import Mechanism

This section explains how imported packages are referenced in CAP and export files in order to introduce the exploited vulnerability.

When an application needs to call some methods from an external API, for instance the Java Card standard API, runtime must first import the package or the class containing this method. Importing classes and packages in Java Card is performed similarly to Java standard syntax as shown in Listing 1.1.

Listing 1.1. SimpleImportExample class description.

```
 1 package simple;
 2
 3 import javacard.framework.*; // Importing the whole package
 4 import javacard.framework.JCSystem; // Importing only one class
 5
 6 public class SimpleImportExample {
 7     public    byte publicField;
 8     private   byte privateField;
 9     protected byte protectedField;
10               byte packageField;
11
12     public static short getVersionExample() {
13         // Use one of the imported features
14         return JCSystem.getVersion();
15 } }
```

As explained in Sect. 1.1, outputted by the Java Card toolchain, the CAP file contains application information to be executed as is by the JCVM. The export file has everything required to use public features provided to other applications. Therefore, the export file shares public application names and associated tokens.

2.1   Import Mechanism from the CAP File Point of View

The CAP file contains information to call the external methods. We now focus on JCSystem.getVersion() method (Listing 1.1, line 14) to understand CAP file import mechanism.

The Import and the ConstantPool components are used by the Method component when calling the JCSystem.getVersion() method as shown in Listing 1.2.

Listing 1.2. A simple.cap file partial view.

```
 1 Import Component
 2   A0000000620001 // java/lang
 3   A0000000620101 // javacard/framework
 4
 5 ConstantPool Component
 6   // 0
 7   staticMethodRef 0.0.0()V; // java/lang/Object.<init>()V
 8   // 1
 9   staticMethodRef 1.8.9()S; // javacard/framework/JCSystem.getVersion()S
10
11 // ...
12
13 Method Component
14
15   .method public static getVersionExample()S 1 {
```

```
16    .stack 1;
17    .locals 0;
18
19    L0: invokestatic 1 // javacard/framework/JCSystem.getVersion()S
20    sreturn;
21    }
```

In the `Import` component (Listing 1.2, lines 1 to 3), two packages are listed: `java.lang`, indexed at 0 and `javacard.framework`, indexed at 1. Even if not explicitly imported in the Java source file, the `java.lang` package is automatically imported by the compiler.

All the imported packages are referenced by their corresponding Application Identifier (AID) value. In the `ConstantPool` component, the `JCSystem.getVersion()` method is referenced in the second entry, Listing 1.2, line 9. Value `1.8.9` is interpreted as followed:

- 1 represents the second imported package (there, `javacard.framework`),
- 8 represents the class token (`JCSystem`)
- and 9 the method token (`getVersion()`).

Class and method tokens are defined in the `export` file of `javacard.framework` package. Finally, the `invokestatic` bytecode references the second entry of the `ConstantPool` component, indicating to the JCVM where it can find the method to call.

2.2 Import Mechanism from the export File Point of View

Considering Listing 1.1, the obtained `export` file contains the declaration of:

- the `SimpleImportExample` class and reference to its super classes (in this case, only `Object` class),
- the `publicField` and `protectedField` fields. The `export` file contains: `public`, `protected`, `static` and `final` field declarations
- and the `getVersionExample()` method. As well as the fields, the `export` file contains `public`, `protected`, `static` and `final` method declarations.

In this example, we have seen that `export` file does not list the imported `javacard.framework` package. However, a package can publicly expose features that it had previously imported. This happens, for instance, when inheriting and in this case, the `export` file will trace the imported packages.

Listing 1.3. The `InheritingImportExample` class.

```
1  package inheriting;
2
3  import javacard.framework.ISOException;
4
5  public class InheritingImportExample extends ISOException {
6     public InheritingImportExample(short reason) {
7        super(reason);
8  } }
```

In Listing 1.3, a class inheriting from ISOException is defined at line 5. After converting this class, the CAP file will import the javacard.framework package as explained for Listing 1.2, based on the AID value. The export file will contain supplementary information because the InheritingImportExample class exposes all the public tokens from the ISOException class. Therefore, the following items are found in the export file:

– all the super classes of InheritingImportExample: in order, we have:

1. ISOException,
2. CardRuntimeException,
3. RuntimeException,

4. Exception,
5. Throwable
6. and Object.

– all the inherited public methods from these classes: setReason(), getReason() and equals().

Unlike in the CAP file, imported tokens in export file are referenced using their fully qualified names. For instance, the ISOException class is defined by the ConstantPool entry shown in Listing 1.4.

Listing 1.4. Partial view of inheriting package export file.

```
1  tag    :  01 (cp_utf8_info)
2  length:  00 1f
3  utf8_bytes[]: javacard/framework/ISOException
```

In this Section we have seen how imported packages are referenced in CAP and export files. In some cases, the imported package is simultaneously defined in both files. However, an asymmetry exists as the CAP file references imported packages from their AID values while the export file references them using their fully qualified names.

The BCV may not be able to ensure that the AID used in the CAP file corresponds to the package name used in the export file and this may lead to inconsistencies as explained in the next Section.

3   PhiAttack

On Java Card platforms, every package is identified by a unique AID value. Actually, nothing prevents an application developer to create its own package with the same name as an already existing package, as long as the assigned AID value to this package is not already used by another one. At compilation and runtime, this is accepted: the BCV is able to identify and discriminate the two packages ensuring that the packages are properly used and the JCVM interprets bytecode from the content of CAP files that import packages with their AID.

3.1   Setting-up the Attack

Let's consider an application developer that creates two packages, both named library but each one has a different AID, as shown in Listing 1.5 and Listing 1.6. Each package contains a class, named Phi, with a method named doSomething(). However, this method signature is different from one package to another. The difference is highlighted in <u>red and underline</u>.

Listing 1.5. library package with DEADBEEF01 AID.

```
package library;

public class Phi {
  public void doSomething() {
    // ...
} }
```

Listing 1.6. library package with DEADBEEF02 AID.

```
package library;

public class Phi {
  public short doSomething() {
    // ...
} }
```

In the Java source code, one cannot import both versions of the library package at the same time. As each package has the same name, the compilation process cannot distinguish one from the other. However, this can be achieved by forging a CAP file that imports these packages, from their AIDs. Even if such a construction cannot be obtained in a common way, it will be, however, accepted by the BCV. In this case, the BCV properly handles the two packages and it is able to differentiate the two Phi classes. Such a construction is quite weird but is actually allowed.

A third package named proxy is described in Listing 1.7. It imports library package. At compilation time, only the library package defined in Listing 1.5 is given to the Java Card toolchain. Therefore, the CAP file of proxy package imports library with DEADBEEF01 AID. The PhiProxy class only inherits from the Phi class. Therefore, the export file of proxy package references the library.Phi class and the doSomething() method with the correct signature (return type is void).

Listing 1.7. proxy package

```
package proxy;

import library.*;

public class PhiProxy extends Phi {}
```

A last package, named exploit, is created and described in Listing 1.8. This package imports two packages: library and proxy. At compilation time, the library package defined in Listing 1.6 is provided at the Java Card toolchain. Therefore, the CAP file of exploit imports library with DEADBEEF02 AID. In doExploit() method, Listing 1.8 line 7, an instance of PhiProxy is created and its reference is saved in a variable of type Phi. Finally, the doSomething() is called.

Listing 1.8. `exploit` package

```
1  package exploit;
2
3  import library.*;
4  import proxy.*;
5
6  public class Exploit {
7    public void doExploit() {
8      PhiProxy proxyInstance = new PhiProxy();
9      Phi phiInstance = proxyInstance;
10     short result = phiInstance.doSomething();
11 } }
```

Figure 2 shows the UML diagram of these packages in order to synthesise a global view of the dependencies between them.

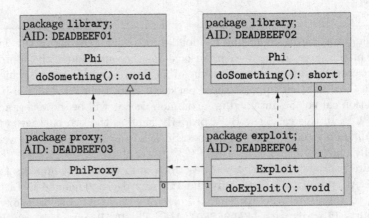

Fig. 2. UML diagram of PhiAttack.

The four packages described in this section are checked by the BCV. The obtained result is: 0 `error` and 0 `warning`.

3.2   Understanding PhiAttack

Two processes must be studied here, 1) the analysis performed by the BCV on CAP and `export` files of `exploit` package and 2) the execution flow of `doExploit()` method at runtime.

On the one hand, to verify the `exploit.cap` file, BCV makes checks as introduced in Fig. 3. In the `doExploit` method in Listing 1.8, three parts are critical:

1. At line 8, an instance of `PhiProxy` is created. The obtained reference is stored in a variable of the same type. On Fig. 3, the BCV checks this instruction `new` 0 by resolving token 0 (①) and reads the `ConstantPool` entry 0 to obtain `proxy.PhiProxy` type (②) in `proxy` `export` file.
2. At line 9 the previously stored reference is copied in a variable of type `Phi`. The compiler translates this operation by `aload` and `astore` instructions and

it does not insert `checkcast` instruction as `PhiProxy` type is a sub-class of `Phi`. From the BCV, type is ensured; `aload` instruction pushes a `PhiProxy` instance on operand stack and `astore` instruction pops a `Phi` instance from operand stack. There, the BCV validates the operation because it finds the mother class `Phi` from `library` package with DEADBEEF02 AID. At this state of the verification, the BCV cannot know that the actual mother class is in package with DEADBEEF01 AID. At runtime, as there is no `checkcast` instruction, no cast verification is performed.

3. At line 10, the `doSomething()` method is called on an instance of type `Phi`. On Fig. 3, to call this method, the `invokevirtual 1` instruction is checked by the BCV. To verify this method call, the BCV resolves token 1 (③). to obtain `library.Phi.doSomething()` method signature (④) in `library` export file.

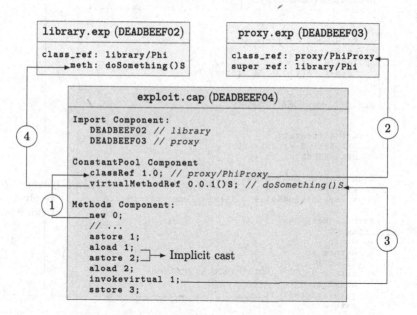

Fig. 3. BCV view when verifying `exploit.cap` file.

During the verification, the BCV performs its checks based on `export` files content:

– `proxy export` file states that `PhiProxy` inherits from a class called `library.Phi`. The missing information here is that this class must come from `library` package with DEADBEEF01 AID.
– `library export` file with DEADBEEF02 AID states that it contains a class named `library.Phi`. When verifying `exploit` package, the BCV only considers this `library` package based on the Import component of `exploit`.

On the other hand, at runtime, the JCVM tries to resolve the doSomething virtual method upon the invokevirtual 1 instruction. To do this, the class hierarchy is browsed until finding the method token. Due to the similar construction, the doSomething() methods of both library packages have the same method token value.

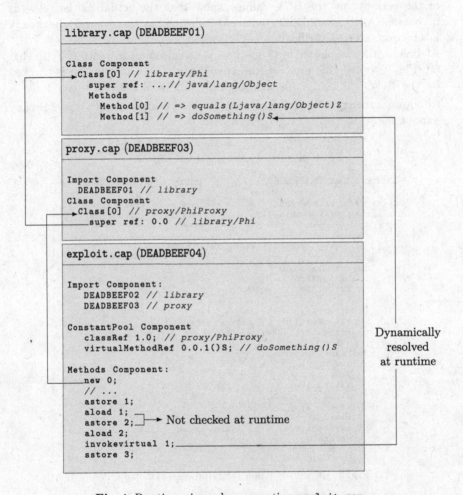

Fig. 4. Runtime view when executing exploit.cap.

From the JCVM point of view, Fig. 4, the actual class hierarchy of the currently accessed Object class:

PhiProxy → Phi (from library package with DEADBEEF01 AID) → Object.

Therefore, when interpreting the invokevirtual instruction, the found method is the one from library package with DEADBEEF01 AID: this method returns nothing (void type).

In line 10 in Listing 1.8, when returning from doSomething() method, a value is expected from the stack to store it in variable called result. During runtime, as the called method returns nothing the value is popped from an empty stack: a stack underflow is obtained.

This whole construction is allowed by the BCV because of the asymmetry in the import mechanism described in Sect. 2. In this Section, a stack underflow is demonstrated as example but various kinds of exploitation are described in Sect. 3.3.

3.3   Variations and Exploitation of Such an Attack

We have seen in Sect. 3.2 that a stack underflow attack can be performed using a specific construction that induces errors in the BCV import resolution. Using the same principle, a stack overflow attack can also be performed, by switching the two library packages.

The same principle can also be applied on the Java Card standard API. For instance, the attacker can create its own javacardx.crypto package with its own Cipher class (containing for instance methods with a different signature than expected). Using a proxy package in which a class inherits from the attacker's Cipher class, the principle described in Sect. 3.2 applies.

A type confusion attack can also be performed by replacing for instance Listings 1.5 and 1.6 by Listings 1.9 and 1.10. Indeed the confusion() method from package with DEADBEEF01 AID will be called instead of the other one, transforming the short argument in a reference type.

Listing 1.9. library package with DEADBEEF01 AID for type confusion.

```
package library;

public class Phi {
  public Object confusion(
      Object o){
    return o;
} }
```

Listing 1.10. library package with DEADBEEF02 AID for type confusion.

```
package library;

public class Phi {
  public Object confusion(
      short s) {
    return null;
} }
```

This can even be performed with the Object class itself, in java.lang package. This allows to redefine a complete class hierarchy (with Exception and all the Java Card standard API). However, it must be noted that defining Object class in a CAP file leads to set very specific values in some structures of the CAP. For instance, the super_class_ref field of class_info structure in Class component has value 0xFFFF. This value induces errors during CAP file loading on many public Java Card platforms. These errors suggest that the loader of such products is not designed to load a new Java Card class hierarchy root.

In Sect. 3.1, the two Phi classes have the same structure: they both inherit from Object and they both have the same number of public methods. However, if the number of public methods is different, calling a method in the exploit package may result in calling an actually non-existing method. Depending on the JCVM implementation, runtime may have several reactions, but overflow in the public_virtual_method_table is very likely to happen.

However, the Phi attack principle is not a full attack path by itself. Indeed the obtained overflow/underflow must still be exploited on a targeted device with a specific payload. Many state-of-the-art attacks [1,3–5,8–10,12,17] are detected by the BCV. Combined with Phi attack principle, these attacks become full exploitations that disclose sensitive assets without being detected by the BCV.

4   Discussion on Countermeasures

Our contribution was performed on Java Card specifications 3.0.5. However, when packages described in Sect. 3.1 are checked by the BCV provided by the Java Card 3.1.0 toolchain, the following log is obtained:

Listing 1.11. BCV log on proxy package

```
INFOS: [v3.1.0] Off-Card Verifier
INFOS: Export file library\javacard\library.exp is in an older export
    file format. Please update the export file to format 2.3.
INFOS: Export file proxy\javacard\proxy.exp is in an older export file
    format. Please update the export file to format 2.3.
INFOS: Verifying CAP file proxy\javacard\proxy.cap
INFOS: Verification completed with 0 warnings and 0 errors.
```

As stated in Sect. 3.1, the BCV raises no warning and no error, validating the CAP and export files. However, information about export files version is returned.

Indeed only export files in version 2.2, specified in [14], have been used. Version 2.3 is described in [16]. Nevertheless, export files in version 2.2 are still accepted by the BCV 3.1.0 as valid format, with only an information indicating that a new format is available.

Version 2.3 of export file format adds supplementary information in the file. Among modifications, a new structure is added containing the AID value, the minor and major version of each package referenced in the export file. The AID value is the missing information that prevented the BCV to detect the attack attempted in Sect. 3.1. Therefore, when export files are generated in version 2.3, the construction shown in Sect. 3.1 is successfully detected by the BCV as malformed.

Before loading one or several CAP files in a Java-Card based product, the latest version of the BCV must be executed in order to ensure that the loaded code is not malicious. However, more than just running the BCV, the entity performing the verification should also check that export files provided are in version 2.3. Ensuring the version is 2.3 allows to detect potential malicious applications to be loaded.

5   Conclusion

We show in this article how a missing information in the export file allows an attacker to abuse the BCV checks during packages import resolution. This could lead an attacker to execute malicious pieces of code within a verified application allowing to potentially break the Java Card security model.

This kind of issue can be countered by denying the use of `export` file format older than 2.3 even if the latest BCV version still accepts `export` files in 2.2 version.

The identification of this missing information in `export` files allowing to attack Java Card products opens perspective and potential future work on finding other kind of information that would be completely or partially missing.

Following our responsible disclosure policy, as far as we know, all the Java Card platform developers concerned by this vulnerability were informed before the publication of this paper.

Acknowledgments. A very special thanks to my wife, Marie-Philomène Dubreuil, who accompanied me during all these hours of work on this research topic. This attack is named after her.

Jean Dubreuil

References

1. Bouffard, G., Iguchi-Cartigny, J., Lanet, J.-L.: Combined software and hardware attacks on the Java card control flow. In: Prouff, E. (ed.) CARDIS 2011. LNCS, vol. 7079, pp. 283–296. Springer, Heidelberg (2011). https://doi.org/10.1007/978-3-642-27257-8_18

2. Bouffard, G., Khefif, T., Lanet, J., Kane, I., Salvia, S.C.: Accessing secure information using export file fraudulence. In: Crispo, B., Sandhu, R.S., Cuppens-Boulahia, N., Conti, M., Lanet, J. (eds.) 2013 International Conference on Risks and Security of Internet and Systems (CRiSIS), La Rochelle, France, 23–25 October 2013, pp. 1–5. IEEE (2013). https://doi.org/10.1109/CRiSIS.2013.6766346

3. Bouffard, G., Lanet, J.-L.: Reversing the operating system of a Java based smart card. J. Comput. Virol. Hacking Tech. **10**(4), 239–253 (2014). https://doi.org/10.1007/s11416-014-0218-7

4. Bouffard, G., Lanet, J.: The ultimate control flow transfer in a Java based smart card. Comput. Secur. **50**, 33–46 (2015). https://doi.org/10.1016/j.cose.2015.01.004

5. Faugeron, E.: Manipulating the frame information with an underflow attack. In: Francillon, A., Rohatgi, P. (eds.) CARDIS 2013. LNCS, vol. 8419, pp. 140–151. Springer, Cham (2014). https://doi.org/10.1007/978-3-319-08302-5_10

6. Faugeron, E., Valette, S.: How to hoax an off-card verifier. e-smart (2010)

7. GlobalPlatform: Card Specification. GlobalPlatform Inc., 2.2.1 edn. (January 2011)

8. Hamadouche, S., et al.: Subverting byte code linker service to characterize Java card API. In: 7th Conference on Network and Information Systems Security (SAR-SSI), 22–25 May 2012, pp. 75–81 (2012)

9. Hamadouche, S., Lanet, J.: Virus in a smart card: myth or reality? J. Inf. Secur. Appl. **18**(2–3), 130–137 (2013). https://doi.org/10.1016/j.jisa.2013.08.005

10. Lancia, J.: Java card combined attacks with localization-agnostic fault injection. In: Mangard, S. (ed.) CARDIS 2012. LNCS, vol. 7771, pp. 31–45. Springer, Heidelberg (2013). https://doi.org/10.1007/978-3-642-37288-9_3

11. Lancia, J., Bouffard, G.: Java card virtual machine compromising from a bytecode verified applet. In: Homma, N., Medwed, M. (eds.) CARDIS 2015. LNCS, vol. 9514, pp. 75–88. Springer, Cham (2016). https://doi.org/10.1007/978-3-319-31271-2_5

12. Mostowski, W., Poll, E.: Malicious code on Java card smartcards: attacks and countermeasures. In: Grimaud, G., Standaert, F.-X. (eds.) CARDIS 2008. LNCS, vol. 5189, pp. 1–16. Springer, Heidelberg (2008). https://doi.org/10.1007/978-3-540-85893-5_1

13. Oracle: Java Card Technology - Providing a secure and ubiquitous platform for smart cards. Technical report, Oracle, Security Evaluations, Oracle Corporation, 500 Oracle Parkway, Redwood Shores, CA 94065 (2012). www.oracle.com/technetwork/java/embedded/javacard/documentation/datasheet-149940.pdf

14. Oracle: Java Card 3 Platform, Virtual Machine Specification, Classic Edition. No. Version 3.0.5, Oracle, Oracle America Inc., 500 Oracle Parkway, Redwood City, CA 94065 (2015)

15. Oracle: Java card system - open configuration protection profile. Protection Profile versoin 3.0.5, Oracle, Security Evaluations, Oracle Corporation, 500 Oracle Parkway, Redwood Shores, CA 94065 (December 2017)

16. Oracle: Java Card 3 Platform, Virtual Machine Specification, Classic Edition. No. Version 3.1, Oracle, Oracle America Inc., 500 Oracle Parkway, Redwood City, CA 94065 (February 2021)

17. Razafindralambo, T., Bouffard, G., Lanet, J.-L.: A friendly framework for hidding *fault enabled virus* for Java based smartcard. In: Cuppens-Boulahia, N., Cuppens, F., Garcia-Alfaro, J. (eds.) DBSec 2012. LNCS, vol. 7371, pp. 122–128. Springer, Heidelberg (2012). https://doi.org/10.1007/978-3-642-31540-4_10

FuzzyKey: Comparing Fuzzy Cryptographic Primitives on Resource-Constrained Devices

Mo Zhang[1,4]([✉]), Eduard Marin[2], David Oswald[1], and Dave Singelée[3]

[1] University of Birmingham, Birmingham, UK
mxz819@cs.bham.ac.uk, d.f.oswald@bham.ac.uk
[2] Telefonica Research, Madrid, Spain
eduard.marinfabregas@telefonica.com
[3] imec-COSIC, KU Leuven, Leuven, Belgium
dave.singelee@esat.kuleuven.be
[4] University of Melbourne, Parkville, Australia

Abstract. Implantable medical devices, sensors and wearables are widely deployed today. However, establishing a secure wireless communication channel to these devices is a major challenge, amongst others due to the constraints on energy consumption and the need to obtain immediate access in emergencies. To address this issue, researchers have proposed various key agreement protocols based on the measurement of physiological signals such as a person's heart signal. At the core of such protocols are fuzzy cryptographic primitives that allow to agree on a shared secret based on several simultaneous, noisy measurements of the same signal. So far, although many fuzzy primitives have been proposed, there is no comprehensive evaluation and comparison yet of the overhead that such methods incur on resource-constrained embedded devices. In this paper, we study the feasibility of six types of fuzzy cryptographic primitives on embedded devices for 128-bit key agreement. We configure several variants for each fuzzy primitive under different parameter selections and mismatch rates of the physiological signal measurements on an MSP430 microcontroller, and then measure and compare their energy consumption and communication overhead. The most efficient constructions consume between 0.021 mJ and 0.198 mJ for the transmitter and between 0.029 mJ and 0.380 mJ for the receiver under different mismatch rates. Subsequently, we modify the best performing methods so that they run in constant time to protect against timing side-channel attacks, and observe that these changes only minimally affect resource consumption. Finally, we provide open-source implementations and energy consumption data of each fuzzy primitive as a reference for real-world designs.

Keywords: Fuzzy commitment · Fuzzy vault · Fuzzy extractor · Physiological signal · Key agreement · Energy consumption

© Springer Nature Switzerland AG 2022
V. Grosso and T. Pöppelmann (Eds.): CARDIS 2021, LNCS 13173, pp. 289–309, 2022.
https://doi.org/10.1007/978-3-030-97348-3_16

1   Introduction

Healthcare technology is evolving at a rapid pace. Medical sensors are getting more miniaturised, while being able to measure a broader set of people's Physiological Signals (PSs) more reliably. New generations of widely-deployed Implantable Medical Devices (IMDs) are considerably lighter and smaller compared to previous generations. Wearables are extensively used nowadays, also often within the context of health monitoring. Multiple wearable and medical computing devices can be connected to form a body area network. Besides their application opportunities within the health domain, all these devices have in common that they rely on a wireless interface to communicate with each other or with external devices such as a smartphone. This increased wireless connectivity enhances without any doubt the quality of the (remote) healthcare that can be offered to users. However, in turn, security and privacy are at stake for such medical systems. The medical data that is being monitored on the user is clearly privacy-sensitive. Moreover, the integrity and authenticity of the data, as well as remote updates or commands sent to the devices, have to be protected as well. Unfortunately, researchers have demonstrated that several medical and wearable devices available on the market currently lack security mechanisms [11, 22–24, 29].

It is therefore evident that cryptographic solutions are needed to secure the wireless interface between these devices. This includes the initial security bootstrap process to establish a secret session key to protect the wireless communication link. However, this turns out to be a challenging research problem for various reasons. First, most of these devices have strict resource constraints, e.g., limited memory and computational power. Furthermore, most IMDs are operated by a single non-rechargeable and non-replaceable battery which typically lasts between five and seven years (depending on the type of device and treatment). Once the battery is drained, the IMD is replaced through a surgical intervention that can pose risks to patients. Likewise, wearables typically contain small batteries, e.g., powered by a button cell with approximate a thousand joules. Thus, in such resource-constrained devices every single joule matters. Second, these devices often do not have any input or output interfaces, such as a keypad or a screen. Third, a subset of these medical devices, more particularly IMDs, are not even physically accessible at all, because they are implanted in the patient. Fourth, most of the wireless connections that have to be made with these devices cannot rely on any prior trust relation. This is because these network connections are not static, *i.e.*, the set of external devices one needs to connect to can change quite often. For example, during an emergency situation, the first doctor that is present (who may have never seen the patient before) might have to establish a communication link to the patient's IMD. Due to all these constraints, conventional key distribution and bootstrap techniques are not viable options: key exchanges based on public key cryptography are difficult to manage because they require establishment of a robust Public Key Infrastructure (PKI).

The use of physiological signals (e.g., a signal extracted from the user's heartbeat) has been proposed as an alternative to securely establish a key between two devices that do not have any prior trust relationship. In contrast to biometrics, where the extracted information is to some extent invariant, PSs are required to be random signals that vary over time. The security of PS-based cryptographic solutions relies on the fact that the user's PS can *only* be obtained by making physical contact with them (e.g., by touching the skin long enough). A common approach to agree on a key is for each of the devices to independently and synchronously take a measurement of a given user's PS [20, 21]. However, the measurements taken by the devices are often not identical but at best rather similar due to inherent noise introduced by the measuring process. To address this limitation, Juels et al. [15, 16] and Dodis et al. [10] introduced so-called *fuzzy cryptographic primitives*, including the fuzzy commitment [16], fuzzy vault [15] and fuzzy extractor [10], which allow two devices to agree a cryptographic key from noisy data.[1]

1.1 Related Work

Fuzzy cryptographic primitives have become the basis of several PS-based cryptographic protocols. For example, K Venkatasubramanian et al. [38], Hu et al. [14] and Reshan et al. [4] utilised the fuzzy vault for key agreement based on measurements of InterPulse Intervals (IPIs), *i.e.*, time intervals between R-peaks of Electrocardiogram (ECG) signal. Similarly, Cherukuri et al. proposed a PS-based key distribution protocol based on the fuzzy commitment that is used to securely transport a session key between two sensors [7]. Another example is the key agreement protocol by Marin et al. which uses a fuzzy extractor in combination with IPIs [21]. It is worth noting that the security of PS-based key exchange protocols has been exhaustively investigated over the past years. In particular, Calleja et al. [6] and Seepers et al. [32] demonstrated that some PS, such as those extracted from the patient's heart, might be measured remotely without the need for direct physical touch. Besides, the entropy of the PS itself has been questioned, e.g., although IPI was frequently chosen as the PS used in prior security protocols, Ortiz-Martin et al. [26] challenged that IPIs may not have as much entropy as expected. Furthermore, some PS-based key exchange protocols, such as [7, 30], have been proved to be vulnerable to certain attacks [20].

While PS-based solutions have been frequently designed and analysed, little effort has been devoted into studying the feasibility of fuzzy primitives (as the core of such schemes) in resource-constrained systems as well as how to configure them to optimise performance. This is in contrast to "traditional" cryptographic algorithms, whose efficient implementation on resource-constrained devices has been widely studied, see e.g., [12, 25, 33].

---

[1] Apart from being used in PS-based key exchange protocols, fuzzy schemes are also used in other areas such as biometrics and Physical Unclonable Functions (PUFs) [3, 5, 9, 10], where traditional cryptographic algorithms are not directly applicable.

1.2   Contributions

In this paper, we present implementations and evaluations of PS-based 128-bit key agreement based on fuzzy cryptographic primitives on an MSP430, which is a representative low-power microcontroller similar to the one used in commercial IMDs or wearables. Our main contributions are:

1. We implement and optimise six fuzzy cryptographic primitives for PS-based key exchange. Our implementation can be easily ported to different platforms.
2. We evaluate and compare the resource consumption (energy consumption and communication overhead) of each construction under various parameter settings both at the transmitter and receiver using an MSP430. We demonstrate that fuzzy primitives are feasible on a resource-constrained embedded device. We show how parameter selection affects the performance and report on the overall best-performing fuzzy primitives under different metric spaces. To the best of our knowledge, we are the first to provide a systematic evaluations of various fuzzy primitives on resource-constrained devices.
3. We implement countermeasures against timing attacks for the most efficient constructions, and show that our protected implementations reduce timing leakage below the statistical significance threshold, while only minimally affecting resource consumption.

Our source code is available under the following link: https://github.com/MrZMN/FuzzyKey .

Paper organisation. The remainder of this paper is organised as follows: in Sect. 2, we introduce the mathematical background of fuzzy primitives, commonly used components, and concrete constructions used in this paper. In Sect. 3, we explain our security assumptions and how to instantiate the constructions of fuzzy primitives. We give implementation details in Sect. 4, before evaluating the performance of all fuzzy primitives in Sect. 5. We conclude in Sect. 6.

2   Background

In this section, we describe the mathematical background required for this paper, and discuss several fuzzy cryptographic algorithms. Elementary computations are in $GF(2^m)$. In this paper, we consider $m \leq 8$ so that computations are fast on constrained embedded devices and most variables fit in one byte. A metric space M is a finite set. For each M, there is a definite integer distance $dist\,(m_1,\, m_2)$ between any two elements m_1 and m_2. The fuzzy primitives discussed in this paper rely on two different kinds of metric spaces: (i) *Hamming metric space* and (ii) *set metric space*. In a Hamming metric space, $M = F^\ell$ for an alphabet F. $dist(m_1, m_2)$ in M is the Hamming distance, which is the number of positions that m_1 differs from m_2. For example, for $M = \{0,\, 1\}^3$, $dist(\{0,\, 0,\, 0\}, \{1,\, 1,\, 1\})$ $= 3$. Besides, the number of non-zero elements in m_1 is called m_1's Hamming weight. In a set metric space, M contains all s-element subsets of a universe U. $dist()$ in M is the set difference, which is the size of symmetric difference (defined by $symdiff(m_1, m_2) = \{x \in m_1 \cup m_2 \mid x \notin m_1 \cap m_2\}$). For example, $U = GF(2^3)$ and $s = 3$, $dist(\{0, 1, 2\}, \{0, 1, 3\}) = 2$. $dist(m_1, m_2)$ is an even number when the size of m_1 and m_2 is the same.

The inputs of the fuzzy primitives working on these two metrics are different. For this paper, the input is the physiological value converted from a PS. For Hamming metric methods, the input is a bit string that can be generated by concatenating the bit representations of PSs, such as heart rates, which makes these methods flexible for different types of PS. However, because a bit string is consecutive, these methods are sensitive to dislocation and erasure errors on the measurements (e.g., due to peak misdetection when using the heart beat [31]). One bit erasure at the start of a bit string might lead to a significant increase in the Hamming distance. Set metric methods alleviate these problems to a certain extent. The input in this case is a set, and even if there are order-difference or erasure problems on set elements, the set difference will not vary substantially. However, converting one specific PS into a set whose elements are randomly distributed in U can be complicated, especially when the size of U is large.

Error Correction Codes. Error Correction Codes (ECCs) are frequently used to achieve error-tolerance in this paper. An ECC comprises *encoding* and *decoding* phases. In the encoding phase, the original data is encoded as a codeword, where some form of redundancy is added. When errors appear in the codeword, the decoding phase recovers the original data if the total number of errors is below the error tolerance limit. ECCs are represented by the triple $\{n, k, t\}$, where n is the number of symbols of the codeword, k is the number of symbols of the data ($k < n$), and t is the maximum number of errors that can be corrected in a codeword. The error tolerance is then t/n. We focus on two linear ECCs, namely binary Bose-Chaudhuri-Hocquenghem (BCH) and Reed-Solomon (RS) codes, as already recommended in the first papers on fuzzy primitives [10, 15, 16]. They provide flexible parameter selection as well as efficient encoding and decoding methods. As we will show in the next sections, an efficient ECC can greatly improve the performance of the fuzzy cryptographic algorithms.

2.1 Fuzzy Cryptographic Primitives for PS-Based Key Exchange

We briefly describe all fuzzy cryptographic primitives evaluated in this paper and show their use for PS-based 128-bit key exchange. We distinguish two types: (i) based on Hamming distance (fuzzy commitment, code-offset and syndrome) and (ii) based on set difference (fuzzy vault, improved Juels-Sudan and Pinsketch).

We denote the transmitter and receiver that agree on a cryptographic key as TX and RX, and refer to the physiological values generated by TX and RX as ps and ps'. $\xleftarrow{Ext}$ denotes extraction of ps or ps' from raw PS measurements, and $\xleftarrow{R}$ denotes random number generation. $\xleftarrow{Shuffle}$ refers to randomly mixing elements in a set, while calculating the roots of a polynomial is denoted as $\xleftarrow{roots}$. We write $(0, 1)^\ell$ for an ℓ-bit length string and $\{x, y\}^s$ for a set comprising s distinct elements. In all fuzzy cryptographic constructions described below, the first step is to extract ps and ps', which we will omit in the rest of this section.

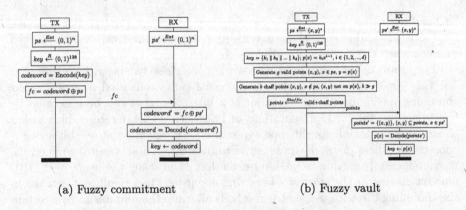

(a) Fuzzy commitment   (b) Fuzzy vault

Fig. 1. Fuzzy cryptographic primitives.

In a *fuzzy commitment* [16], TX generates a random *key* and encodes it to form a *codeword* (Fig. 1a). Subsequently, TX masks the *codeword* by XORing it with ps and then sends the resulting value (denoted by fc) to RX. Upon receiving fc, RX generates *codeword'* by XORing fc with ps'. Only if the mismatch rate between *codeword* and *codeword'* is less than the ECC's error tolerance limit, RX can successfully recover the key previously generated by TX.

The *fuzzy vault* (Fig. 1b) [15] is designed to "lock" a key using a set of features A. It can be unlocked only by using a set of features B that is sufficiently similar to A. Concretely, TX generates a key and embeds it in a univariate polynomial $p()$. Then, TX mixes and sends valid points (x, y), where x is in ps and $y = p(x)$, and invalid points (also known as 'chaff points') that do not lie on $p()$. For each received point, RX verifies whether x is in ps', and then performs polynomial reconstruction based on all the matched points. Only if the overlap between ps and ps' is sufficiently large, RX can successfully recover the key.

Both fuzzy commitment and fuzzy vault transport a key using two similar PS measurements. In contrast, *fuzzy extractors* [10] extract the key from the PS itself. Generally, the mismatches of PS measurements at TX and RX are corrected by sharing "helper data". Afterwards, both sides use the agreed PS to extract the cryptographic key with a strong random extractor (e.g., a secure hash function). We consider four fuzzy extractors in Hamming and set metrics. We omit the key extraction step below as it is the last step shared by all constructions.

The *code-offset construction* (Fig. 2a) is similar to the fuzzy commitment scheme, but here ps is the secret, while in fuzzy commitment, ps conceals the key. In particular, TX generates a random *nonce* and encodes it as *codeword* using the ECC. Then, TX sends $ss = codeword \oplus ps$. RX obtains the *codeword'* $= ss \oplus ps' = codeword \oplus ps \oplus ps'$ and can decode it to *codeword* if the mismatch rate is within bounds. Finally, RX recovers $ps = codeword \oplus ss$.

The *syndrome construction* (Fig. 2b) is based on syndrome decoding of an ECC. Concretely, TX and RX regard ps and ps' as a codeword and calculate syndromes syn and syn', respectively. TX sends syn to RX, who calculates $syn \oplus syn'$. For mismatch vector $mis = ps \oplus ps'$, $syn \oplus syn'$ is the syndrome of mis, which decodes to mis if the mismatch rate is within bounds. Then, one recovers $ps = mis \oplus ps'$. Compared to code-offset construction, the syndrome is always shorter than the codeword, reducing the communication overhead.

In the *improved Juels-Sudan construction* (Fig. 2c), TX uses the monic polynomial $p(x) = \prod_{w \in ps}(x-w)$ with roots as elements in ps and writes it as the sum $p_{high}() + p_{low}()$. TX calculates the coefficients of $p_{high}()$ and sends them to RX. Then, RX generates points (x,y) where x is in ps' and $y = p_{high}(x)$. If $ps' \approx ps$, most points will also be on $p_{low}()$, so RX can reconstruct it and obtain ps by finding roots of $p()$. Compared with fuzzy vault, the communication overhead is much lower as only some coefficients have to be sent.

The *Pinsketch construction* (Fig. 2d) is based on an ECC. For universe size $u = 2^m - 1$, a set set can be viewed as a vector $\{0,1\}^u$, with 1 at position where $x \in set$ and 0 otherwise. In this way, ps and ps' are written as two such u-element vectors v, v' whose Hamming weight is the set size s. TX and RX calculate the syndromes $sstx$ and $ssrx$ of v and v'. Afterwords, TX sends $sstx$ to RX, while RX computes $syn = sstx \oplus ssrx$. If the mismatch rate is under the error tolerance of the ECC, the syndrome decoding result of syn is the symmetric difference between sets ps and ps', which helps correct the mismatches. Because v and v' are binary vectors, BCH codes are particularly suitable [10].

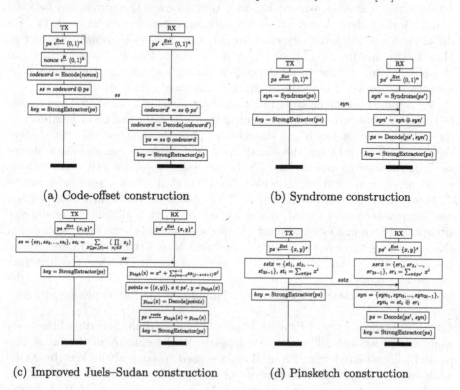

(a) Code-offset construction   (b) Syndrome construction

(c) Improved Juels–Sudan construction   (d) Pinsketch construction

Fig. 2. Fuzzy extractor constructions.

3 Design Security and Parameter Selection

To provide a systematic comparison and evaluation of fuzzy primitives for PS-based key exchange on resource-constrained embedded systems, we make several design decisions: Taking into account the limits on energy consumption and computational resources in a body-area network scenario and the fact that keys are often short-lived, we limit ourselves to 128-bit keys. Furthermore, we only consider key exchange between two devices. We note that subsequent protocol steps, such as key confirmation step to ensure that TX and RX derive the same 128-bit key, are independent of the underlying fuzzy primitive and hence do not consider those steps. We also note that fuzzy primitives are only responsible for correcting the mismatches of the PS, *i.e.*, we do not consider errors on the wireless channel, and assume that the underlying wireless protocol includes appropriate error detection and correction measures.

Adversary Model. We consider a strong adversary who knows all details about the used fuzzy primitives and has full access to the communication channel between TX and RX. The adversary can (i) perform *passive attacks* by eavesdropping on the communication and exploiting information leakage from it. For example, if ps and ps' in a fuzzy commitment are low-entropy, the adversary can statistically analyse their distribution and thus compromise the security [27]. Alternatively, correlation-based methods that leverage the correlation between communication data over *multiple* key exchange sessions can be used [17]. On the other hand, the adversary can also (ii) carry out *active attacks*, *i.e.*, act as Man-In-The-Middle (MITM) or replay old sessions. Finally, the adversary can also observe and exploit secret-dependent timing leakage e.g., the precise time between two protocol messages, both in passive and active attacks.

We assume that the measured PS cannot be modelled or predicted and cannot be remotely obtained. The latter implies that adversary can be in proximity to the user but cannot touch him directly or indirectly (because this would allow the adversary to measure the signal), nor being able to compromise a device worn by the user to measure the PS. In the research community, this *touch-to-access* access control model is widely accepted as it offers a reasonable trade-off between security and availability [24,30]. Although the security may rely on user awareness to some extent, this model ensures high availability in emergency situations where fast establishment of a secure channel to the IMD is vital. For this reason, we leave physical side-channel and other attacks with direct access (such as fault injection) out of the adversary model, as in this case, the adversary can equally measure the PS directly for key recovery. We also do not consider Denial-of-Service (DoS) attacks such as jamming or battery depletion attacks.

Countermeasures Against Passive Attacks. The underlying security of the fuzzy commitment against offline attacks depends on the entropy of the bit strings ps and ps' extracted from PS as these are used to conceal the key (by XOR) while being transported. The security of fuzzy vault relies on the fact that the adversary cannot distinguish between valid and chaff points, and hence is unable to reconstruct $p()$. For a fuzzy vault scheme with parameters g, b and d (cf. Fig. 1b), the adversary would need an average of $\binom{g+b}{(g+d)/2}/\binom{g}{(g+d)/2}$ attempts to reveal $p()$ (assuming that Berlekamp-Welch decoding is used). Therefore, the number of chaff points needs to be sufficiently large.

For fuzzy extractors, the security depends on the entropy of the PS itself as the key is directly extracted from the PS. Due to the leakage of helper data, there will be an amount of entropy loss on PS in each construction. For code-offset and syndrome constructions, the entropy loss is $(n - k) \cdot f$, where n, k come from the underlying (n, k, t) ECC, and f is the number of bits constituting each symbol. The entropy loss is $t \cdot \log_2 u$ for the improved Juels-Sudan construction, and is $t \cdot \log_2(u + 1)$ for the Pinsketch construction, where u is the universe size and t is the maximum set difference between ps and ps'. Note that the above represent worst case entropy loss values [10]. Some of them were also proven to be overly pessimistic [9]. To ensure security, we regard the worst-case values as the actual entropy loss in this paper. Because we only focus on 128-bit key agreement, if the remaining entropy of PS (the agreed PS before input to the strong extractor) is ≥ 128 bit, the fuzzy extractor is considered secure.

For correlation-based attacks, note that in the case of PS-based key exchange, the PS has to vary over time and the exchanged key (generated randomly by the device or extracted from the PS) is short-lived and different in each session [20], unlike scenarios based on non-variable materials, e.g., biometrics or PUFs. This means that correlation attacks are prevented by the nature of the application.

Countermeasures Against Active and Timing Attacks. Due to the varying key, replay attacks are by design prevented. Other active attacks (such as guessing-based ones) require the adversary to break the fuzzy primitive "online" within a single protocol session [4,18], otherwise, they at most result in failure of the key exchange and are detected by subsequent key confirmation. They can thus be prevented by generating a secret with substantially high entropy. Active attacks based on accurate measurement or modelling of the underlying PS [6] are outside our adversary model. Timing attacks can be generically prevented using constant-time implementations techniques, which we further discuss in Sect. 4.

Assumptions on Physiological Signal. The selection of the PS (e.g., IPI) and its quality as an entropy source, although an important issue, are out of the scope of this paper. However, we would like to stress that the quality of PS only affects the total measurement time, e.g., a lower quality of the entropy source means longer measurements. In order to generate the input for the fuzzy primitives, a set of pre-processing methods (e.g., quantisation and coding [26]) is applied to the raw PS measurements. However, this is out of the scope of this paper.

Assumptions on Fuzzy Primitive Input. The inputs of fuzzy primitives (*i.e.*, ps and ps' in Sect. 2.1) are extracted from some PS which is measured by two devices simultaneously. There are several factors that affect the similarity of ps and ps', e.g., the type of PS, the measurement accuracy of the sensor, and the signal processing method. To evaluate and compare different fuzzy primitives, it is necessary to consider pre-defined mismatch rates (*i.e.*, percentage of different bits/set elements) between ps and ps', which reflect the characteristics of different kinds of scenarios. In this paper, we consider three mismatch thresholds of 2%, 5% and 10%. While the authors of [39,40] reported that the mismatch rate for heart rate measurements is typically below 5%, we note that other PSs might have slightly higher mismatch thresholds. We also note that unlike BCH codes, RS codes are multi-bit-symbol based. Thus, for RS code variants, the above thresholds indicate the percentage of different symbols rather than bits. Additionally, one should note that the average bit error rate (*i.e.*, the possibility that each bit differs for two bitstrings) may be more broadly used on the Hamming metric in other application scenarios, thus, we also provide this information for each variant in Table 2 (with a maximum tolerable failure rate of 10^{-6}). This maximum average bit rate that can be tolerated needs to be considered when selecting the most appropriate error correcting code.

Here, we assume that ps and ps' are ℓ-bit strings that are random and uniformly distributed for Hamming metric methods, or sets containing s distinct elements that are uniformly distributed in a universe U for set metric methods. This assumption is only made for fairly comparing different fuzzy primitives; both fuzzy commitment and fuzzy vault naturally require the input to be uniformly randomly distributed to ensure security.[2] Additionally, if the fuzzy primitive inputs are not uniformly distributed, it is hard to quantify the entropy level of the PS and establish a unified mismatch rate threshold. Under this assumption, the initial entropy of the PS is ℓ for Hamming metric fuzzy extractors, while for set metric fuzzy extractors, it is $log_2\binom{u}{s}$ with u the size of U.

Parameter Selection. The mismatch rate between ps and ps' directly determines the error tolerance requirement of the fuzzy primitives. For Hamming metric methods, the error tolerance is the same as that of the underlying ECC (*i.e.*, t/n for an (n, k, t) code). For example, $(50, 44, 1)$ and $(20, 15, 1)$ BCH codes are suitable when the maximum mismatch rate is 2% and 5%, respectively. However, RS codes cannot provide exact 2%, 5% and 10% error tolerance because of their inherent structure. Therefore, we selected several RS constructions with error tolerance within 2% + the pre-defined mismatch rate thresholds. For example, the error tolerance of a $(31, 29, 1)$ RS code is 3.23%. As mentioned in Sect. 2, all codes stay within the field $GF(2^8)$. For set metric methods with (u, s, t) structure, where u is the universe size, s the set size and t the maximum tolerable set difference between ps and ps', the error tolerance is $t/2s$.

For each fuzzy primitive, there can be multiple feasible parameter choices under the same mismatch rate, e.g., using different configurations of ECCs may achieve the same error tolerance. The difference between them is that the repetition count might be different: Assume the total repetition count is r and the number of secret bits distributed in each iteration is i, we need to ensure that $r \cdot i \geq 128$ to achieve 128-bit security. This way, RX concatenates the secret

---

[2] However, this requirement can be alleviated with the combination of a Password Authenticated Key Exchange (PAKE), as shown in [18]. Note that fuzzy extractors can still be securely used even if the inputs are not uniformly distributed.

bits it receives in each iteration to form the 128-bit key. The security of subsequent/parallel execution based on linear codes has been proven in [9]. Note that i is the length of the key distributed per iteration for fuzzy commitment and fuzzy vault, but the remaining entropy of PS for fuzzy extractors. Consider a fuzzy commitment that is based on (50, 44, 1) and (200, 168, 4) BCH codes (both handle mismatch ≤2%) as an example. In order to distribute a 128-bit key, the former variant needs to be executed three times $(3 \cdot 44 > 128)$, while the latter only needs to be executed once. Although more iterations may be required, small parameter choices (e.g., an ECC with a small block size) almost always mean less computation and hence less energy consumption. Therefore, we test different variants under the same mismatch threshold. A variant with larger parameter choice is considered only if it reduces the number of required iterations. Besides, under each mismatch rate, the variants used by different fuzzy primitives in each metric are the same, thus help with the performance comparison.

Note that for Hamming metric methods, the number of feasible variants depends on the number of underlying ECCs that achieve the pre-defined mismatch thresholds. We give all feasible variants for Hamming metric in Table 2. For set metric methods, there are more possible (u, s, t) variants because (i) the universe size u can vary depending on how a PS is converted to a set and (ii) multiple s and t combinations can achieve the same error tolerance. In this paper, we use $u = 255$, which is the maximum universe size for the Pinsketch construction on $GF(2^8)$. We define three variants (255, 50, 2), (255, 20, 2) and (255, 10, 2) for 2%, 5%, and 10% mismatch rate thresholds. These variants are provided for reference only, and one could devise more appropriate variants for set metrics with specific mappings from PS to set. Finally, the fuzzy vault construction over $GF(2^8)$ is insecure, because the number of chaff points is ≤2^8. However, for our performance evaluation in Sect. 5, we limit ourselves to $GF(2^8)$, and note that the system can be easily extended to larger fields (e.g., $GF(2^{16})$).

4   Implementation

We implemented, ran, and measured all algorithms on a TI MSP430FR5969 LaunchPad development board [35]. This board comprises a 16-bit microprocessor with 2 kB volatile SRAM and 64 kB permanent FRAM, which is representative for low-power body area network devices (including e.g., IMDs). We also alternatively used an MSP430FR5994 development board [36] with 8 kB SRAM for certain variants that require more resources, and indicate this in Table 2. For development, we used TI's Code Composer Studio as it provides integrated functionality for on-device energy consumption measurement.

Implementation of the Strong Extractor. Considering many embedded microcontrollers, including the MSP430 used in this paper, feature a hardware AES accelerator, we opted to use a block cipher-based hash function, with AES as the underlying cipher. We selected the Hirose construction [13] for the strong extractor in our implementation. Hirose is a double-block-length hash with Merkle-Damgård structure. We measured the average energy consumption of each invocation of the Hirose compression function on MSP430FR5969 to be 1.42 µJ.

Depending on the availability of a fast hardware/software implementation, other hash functions such as SHA256 can be used instead of Hirose.

Software Development and Energy Measurement. We implemented all algorithms in plain C and mainly relied on standard C libraries so that our implementation can be easily ported to other platforms. For random number generation and hardware-accelerated AES, we used TI's driver APIs. The tested average energy consumption of generating 16 bytes when using TI's random number generator API is $2.5\,\mu$J. Certain components can be implemented in different ways. For example, there are a variety of algorithms for ECCs. We chose commonly used, efficient algorithms: for BCH and RS encoding, we used standard cyclic code encoding, and for decoding we used the Berlekamp decoding method [2,19]. For polynomial reconstruction, we used the Berlekamp-Welch algorithm.

We carried out the energy consumption measurement using TI `energyTrace` tool. This functionality allows to take accurate on-device energy measurement from the Code Composer Studio IDE. For each measurement, we averaged the energy consumption value over 100 executions of the respective algorithm. To test the error correction ability of the fuzzy primitives, we artificially added the maximum tolerable number of mismatches on the PS in the code, and then measured the corresponding energy consumption. We used TI `Ultra Low Power Advisor` tool to refactor our code and minimise energy consumption. Overall, we found that these optimisations reduced the energy consumption $\leq 10\%$.

Estimation of Communication Energy Cost. The energy consumption of a protocol between multiple devices comprises two components: (i) the energy consumption of computations; and (ii) the energy consumption of wireless communication. In this paper, we only measure the energy consumption of computation, and model the cost of wireless communication based on the number of bits to be transmitted and received. In particular, in Sect. 5, we use the experimental results of [25] for a TelosB [8], a wireless sensor node based on a 16-bit MSP430 microcontroller and a CC2420 transceiver to illustrate the impact of communication overhead on overall energy consumption. Their results show that for 75 kbps data rate and $-5\,$dBm transmit power, the average energy required to transmit one bit of effective data is $0.72\,\mu$J, and the energy required to receive this bit is $0.81\,\mu$J.

We acknowledge that a simplistic "energy-per-bit" model may be inadequate e.g., when using packet-based protocols such as Bluetooth Low Energy (BLE)[3], where the constant overheads due to the frame structure and other steps (e.g., wakeup and preparation) can be substantial. Therefore, we also provide the number of payload bits for each variant in Table 2, which can be fed into a more appropriate energy consumption model for a specific wireless protocol (e.g., informed by measurements as reported in [34]). We note that many widely used protocols support payloads large enough to accommodate all our variants in one packet (e.g., 246 bytes for BLE). This minimizes the impact of the frame

---

[3] BLE is already being used in commercial IMDs e.g., Medtronic Azure pacemakers [1].

structure, thus, when considering such protocols, the different implementations can be compared purely based on their computational energy cost.

Defenses Against Timing Side Channels. We implemented countermeasures against timing-based side-channel attacks on the best-performing variants (*i.e.*, fuzzy primitives with lowest total energy consumption under different mismatch thresholds, cf. Table 4). We found that non-constant execution time mainly arises in the ECC encoding/decoding processes through various conditional branches depending on a value being negative. To address this, we replaced all such conditional branches with Boolean operators, and used other constant-time implementation techniques, such as constant-time modulo reduction (based on Barrett reduction) and constant-time sorting.

Table 1. Effects of timing side-channel defenses on timing leakage (measured by Welch's t-test) and energy consumption.

Fuzzy primitive	Variant	TX				RX			
		Protected		Unprotected		Protected		Unprotected	
		t-value	Energy (mJ)	t-value	Energy (mJ)	t-value	Energy (mJ)	t-value	Energy (mJ)
Syndrome extractor	(31,29,1)RS	0.06	0.016	92.69	0.021	0.73	0.023	2039.85	0.029
Syndrome extractor	(31,27,2)RS	1.64	0.029	2220.64	0.037	1.67	0.043	352.48	0.053
Syndrome extractor	(63,49,7)RS	0.99	0.136	4927.79	0.198	0.80	0.237	438.42	0.308
Pinsketch extractor	(255,50,2)	1.01	0.089	242.24	0.046	0.72	0.168	733.98	0.127
Pinsketch extractor	(255,20,2)	0.77	0.052	468.67	0.044	0.91	0.208	428.64	0.201
Pinsketch extractor	(255,10,2)	0.20	0.066	298.66	0.067	6.63	0.377	236.67	0.380

We empirically verified the effects of implementing the above countermeasures, including the effect on timing leakage and energy consumption (communication overhead included). We used `dudect` [28] to evaluate the timing leakage of the TX and RX implementations running on the MSP430FR5969. The results are given in Table 1. The timing leakage of a program is evaluated by Welch's t-test in `dudect`. For each TX and RX implementation, the t-value in Table 1 was computed using 10,000 timing measurements. For a t-value ≤ 10, `dudect` regards the timing leakage as insignificant given the number of timing measurements.

It is evident that the baseline implementations exhibit strong timing leakage, while the protected variants significantly reduce the leakage below the constant-time threshold of the t-test in `dudect`. Besides, the energy consumption is not significantly increased for the protected variants. In fact, in some cases the energy consumption even decreases because of the use of Barrett reduction, which replaces the costly modulo operation otherwise implemented through division.

5 Performance Evaluation

We implemented 22 variants of fuzzy primitives in total for the Hamming metric and three for the set metric. For each variant, we measured its computational energy consumption and estimated the communication cost at both TX and RX sides, and give the input size (extracted from the PS) required to achieve 128-bit security. Table 3 shows the main building blocks used by each fuzzy primitive.

Table 2. Evaluation of Hamming and set metric methods

Error tolerance	Max. average bit error rate	Variant	# iterations	PS data (bit)	Fuzzy commitment TX (mJ)	RX (mJ)	Comm (bit)	Code-offset construction TX (mJ)	RX (mJ)	Comm (bit)	Syndrome construction TX (mJ)	RX (mJ)	PS data (bit)	Comm (bit)
2%	0.0016%	(50, 44, 1) BCH	3	150	0.022	0.079	150	0.030	0.091	150	0.052	0.084	150	36
2%	0.0146%	(100, 86, 2) BCH	2	200	0.037	0.201	200	0.045	0.215	200	0.127	0.207	200	56
2%	0.0854%	(200, 168, 4) BCH	1	200	0.082	0.389	200	0.087	0.404	200	0.241	0.394	200	64
3.23%	0.0037%	(31, 29, 1) RS	1	155	0.011	0.017	155	0.016	0.021	155	0.014	0.021	155	10
5%	0.0024%	(20, 15, 1) RS	9	180	0.029	0.107	180	0.047	0.127	180	0.070	0.120	180	90
5%	0.0273%	(40, 28, 2) BCH	5	200	0.034	0.225	200	0.046	0.239	200	0.128	0.235	200	120
5%	0.0854%	(60, 42, 3) BCH	4	240	0.047	0.344	240	0.059	0.357	240	0.221	0.354	240	144
5%	0.1728%	(80, 52, 4) BCH	3	240	0.076	0.526	240	0.085	0.545	240	0.294	0.533	240	168
5%	0.2842%	(100, 65, 5) BCH	2	200	0.080	0.505	200	0.091	0.519	200	0.306	0.505	200	140
5%	0.9005%	(220, 136, 11) BCH	1	220	0.176	0.925*	220	0.179	0.976*	220	0.725	1.096*	220	176
6.67%	0.0038%	(15, 13, 1) RS	3	180	0.020	0.027	180	0.029	0.041	180	0.026	0.039	180	24
6.45%	0.0662%	(31, 27, 2) RS	1	155	0.019	0.034	155	0.023	0.040	155	0.023	0.037	155	20
10%	0.0031%	(10, 6, 1) RS	22	220	0.060	0.141	220	0.099	0.180	220	0.103	0.180	220	176
10%	0.0407%	(20, 10, 2) BCH	13	260	0.046	0.307	260	0.073	0.331	260	0.175	0.331	260	260
10%	0.1429%	(30, 15, 3) BCH	9	270	0.044	0.399	270	0.065	0.420	270	0.259	0.428	270	270
10%	0.2904%	(40, 16, 4) BCH	8	320	0.067	0.732	320	0.085	0.745	320	0.394	0.735	320	384
10%	0.4822%	(50, 23, 5) BCH	6	300	0.074	0.786	300	0.091	0.797	300	0.452	0.785	300	360
10%	0.6855%	(60, 27, 6) BCH	5	300	0.077	0.878	300	0.092	0.896	300	0.548	0.885	300	360
10%	1.2713%	(90, 34, 9) BCH	4	360	0.131	1.713	360	0.145	1.730	360	0.965	1.724	360	504
10%	1.8153%	(120, 43, 12) BCH	3	360	0.156	2.102	360	0.168	2.110	360	1.276	2.085	360	504
10%	3.0090%	(210, 70, 21) BCH	2	420	0.288	3.340*	420	0.306	3.480*	420	2.637	4.025*	420	672
11.11%	2.4626%	(63, 49, 7) RS	1	378	0.103	0.247	378	0.107	0.252	378	0.138	0.240	378	84

Fuzzy vault						
Error tolerance	Variant	# iterations	TX (mJ)	RX (mJ)	PS data (bit)	Comm (bit)
2%	(255, 50, 2)	1	2.534	7.036*	400	4080
5%	(255, 20, 2)	1	1.354	0.640	160	4080
10%	(255, 10, 2)	2	1.906	0.238	160	8160

Improved Juels-Sudan construction				
# iterations	TX (mJ)	RX (mJ)	PS data (bit)	Comm (bit)
1	0.391	18.957*	400	16
2	0.132	2.980	320	32
4	0.073	2.320	320	64

Pinsketch construction				
# iterations	TX (mJ)	RX (mJ)	PS data (bit)	Comm (bit)
1	0.034	0.114	400	16
2	0.021	0.175	320	32
4	0.021	0.328	320	64

Table 2 shows the detailed measurement results for all considered fuzzy primitive instantiations in both the Hamming and set metric. We include the following characteristics of each variant: error tolerance, maximum average bit error rate, required number of iterations to achieve 128-bit security, computational energy cost at TX/RX (excluding communication cost), communication overhead (in bits transmitted/received), and required number of bits extracted from the PS. $*$ indicates implementation on MSP430FR5994 due to memory requirements.

In the following, we focus on the evaluation and comparison of selected variants. We include full, detailed results for all variants in Table 2. As mentioned, we base our estimation of communication costs on the values of $0.72\,\mu J$ per bit for TX and $0.81\,\mu J$ for RX [25], but also provide the number of exchanged payload bits for use with other models to estimate communication energy.

5.1   Hamming Metric Constructions

The minimum number of input bits derived from the PS is given as $n \cdot f \cdot r$, where n is the codeword length of the chosen ECC, f is the number of bits constituting a symbol, and r is the number of repetitions (*i.e.*, how many iterations of the primitive are required for 128-bit security). Depending on the specific variant, between 150 and 420 PS-derived bits are required (cf. Table 2). However, as we focus on the fuzzy primitive itself, rather than the conversion from PS to the algorithm input, we provide these values for reference only and to guide developer decisions in specific situations.

Table 3. Main building blocks of fuzzy primitives for TX and RX.

TX side	RNG	ECC encoding	XOR	Hash	Syndrome gen.	Find poly. coeffs	Gen. points on $p()$	Gen. chaff points	Shuffle points
Fuzzy commitment	•	•	•						
Fuzzy vault	•						•	•	•
Code-offset extractor	•	•	•	•					
Syndrome extractor				•	•				
Improved JS extractor				•		•			
Pinsketch extractor				•	•				

RX side	ECC decoding	XOR	Reconstruct $p()$	Syndrome gen.	Hash	Gen. points on $p()$	Filter points	Find root on $p()$
Fuzzy commitment	•	•						
Fuzzy vault			•				•	
Code-offset extractor	•	•			•			
Syndrome extractor	•	•		•	•			
Improved JS extractor			•		•	•		•
Pinsketch extractor	•	•		•	•			

Computation Costs. Fig. 3 shows the energy cost of the Hamming metric fuzzy primitives. For each mismatch threshold, we show four variants of each fuzzy primitive and note that they are adequate to indicate the overall trend. At TX side, we observe that the fuzzy commitment consumes the least energy. The cost of the code-offset extractor is generally slightly higher than the fuzzy commitment under different mismatch rates. This result is in line with our expectations, because the code-offset extractor can be seen as a fuzzy commitment with additional invocation of a strong extractor. The syndrome fuzzy extractor involves the most energy-intensive computations. This is because syndrome generation for BCH and RS codes is an expensive operation that involves repeatedly evaluating $p(x)$ given x, which requires a number of iterative operations.

At RX side, we note that the energy consumption of the fuzzy commitment is also the smallest. The difference in computational energy consumption between the code-offset and syndrome extractors is often small because both extractors share several building blocks. Note that, even if the syndrome extractor has an extra "syndrome generation" block compared to the code-offset extractor (cf. Table 3), the actual execution of these constructions is equivalent.

Regarding ECC choice, the RS code performs substantially better than BCH for mismatch rates below 5%. However, for 10% mismatch, the chosen RS code is worse than the best BCH variant. However, note that e.g., the (63, 49, 7) RS instance can accommodate up to 343-bit distribution per iteration for the fuzzy commitment, while we only require 128 bits, which is not optimal if only considering computational energy consumption.

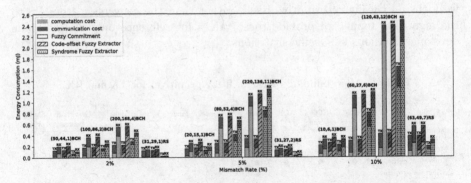

Fig. 3. Energy consumption of Hamming metric primitives.

Combined Computation and Communication Cost. When we also take the estimated communication costs into account, the syndrome fuzzy extractor outperforms the other two variants most of the time. For both fuzzy commitment and code-offset construction, the communication overhead is determined by the codeword length n of the chosen ECC and the number of required repetitions. For example, consider the (50, 44, 1) BCH variant in Table 2. In this case, the communication overhead is $50 \cdot 3$ bits, because the variant needs to be executed three times to establish a 128-bit key. In contrast, the communication overhead for the syndrome extractor depends on the syndrome length and the number of repetitions. The length of the syndrome is $2 \cdot t \cdot m$ for BCH and RS codes, where m comes from $GF(2^m)$ underlying the ECC [19]. An obvious advantage is that the syndrome is always shorter than the codeword. Considering the previous example, TX would only need to transmit $12 \cdot 3$ bits for the syndrome extractor. Overall, the variants with lowest combined computation and communication cost under each mismatch rate are shown in Table 4. The syndrome extractor has variants with the lowest total energy consumption in all conditions.

Table 4. Fuzzy primitives with lowest total energy cost on the Hamming metric (Syndrome extractor) and set metric (Pinsketch extractor).

Mismatch rate	Fuzzy primitive	Variant	Total energy at TX (mJ)	Total energy at RX (mJ)
2%	Syndrome extractor	(31,29,1) RS	0.021	0.029
5%	Syndrome extractor	(31,27,2) RS	0.037	0.053
10%	Syndrome extractor	(63,49,7) RS	0.198	0.308
2%	Pinsketch extractor	(255,50,2)	0.046	0.127
5%	Pinsketch extractor	(255,20,2)	0.044	0.201
10%	Pinsketch extractor	(255,10,2)	0.067	0.380

5.2 Set Metric Constructions

The required number of derived bits for set metric methods is $s \cdot f \cdot r$, where s is the set size, f is the number of bits constituting a set element, and r is the number of repetitions. Set metric constructions require input sizes from 160 to 400 bits (cf. Table 2), which is similar to the Hamming metric variants.

Computation Costs. Figure 4 shows the energy consumption of all considered set metric methods (cf. Table 2 for the underlying data). At TX, we observe that the fuzzy vault consumes substantially more energy than the other two methods. This is likely because TX of the fuzzy vault has to generate and shuffle a large amount of points (mostly chaff points). The TX energy cost of the Pinsketch fuzzy extractor is slightly below improved Juels-Sudan. According to Table 3, the difference in energy consumption is due to the difference between syndrome generation (note that this is not the same as the standard syndrome calculation of BCH and RS code) and the polynomial coefficient finding.

On the RX side, we find that the Pinsketch construction has the lowest energy consumption for mismatch rates below 5%, and has slightly higher consumption than fuzzy vault for 10% mismatch. The improved Juels-Sudan fuzzy extractor is always the most expensive construction under all mismatch rates, likely due to the required polynomial root finding process. We further observe that the energy consumption of this method and the fuzzy vault decrease significantly when the mismatch rate threshold increases. This is expected because both methods rely on the same complex polynomial reconstruction for mismatch correction. This involves operations on $s \times s$ matrices (s is the set size). Hence, polynomial reconstruction is efficient for small sets (*i.e.*, under higher mismatch threshold), but as the set size increases, the computational complexity increases quadratically.

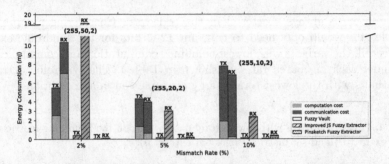

Fig. 4. Energy consumption of set metric primitives.

Combined Computation and Communication Cost. The number of transmitted bits for the fuzzy vault is $np \cdot lp \cdot r$, where np is the total number of points (valid and chaff points), lp is the length of each point, and r is the repetition count. For our universe size of 255, $np = 255$ and $lp = 16$ bits (each coordinate is one byte). In contrast, the transmission size for improved Juels-Sudan and Pinsketch fuzzy extractors is $t \cdot f \cdot r$, where t is the maximum tolerable set difference between sets and f is the number of bits constituting a set element (in our constructions $f = 8$). Hence, the communication cost of the fuzzy vault is much higher compared to improved Juels-Sudan and Pinsketch. The overall best set metric variants for each mismatch threshold are shown in Table 4. The Pinsketch fuzzy extractor performs best in terms of combined computation and communication cost in all cases. The improved Juels-Sudan has extremely high computation cost in RX, while the fuzzy vault incurs substantial communication overhead. Considering that secure implementation of fuzzy vault requires operations over $GF(2^{16})$ and transmits more points, it is likely that costs would further grow in practice.

5.3 Common Observations and Comparison with Curve25519

We observed certain common tendencies for all fuzzy primitives: for each variant, the computation energy consumption for RX is generally higher than for TX. Conversely, the communication cost is roughly the same for TX and RX. This observation is relevant when assigning TX/RX roles in more complex protocols; e.g., a low-power IMD can act as TX if the goal is to minimise energy consumption. In addition, the energy consumption of variants with larger parameter (e.g., larger BCH code) shows an increase both for TX and RX, even though the number of required repetitions decreases.

We compared the energy cost of our best-performing variants with Curve25519, one of the most efficient elliptic curve-based key exchange schemes for embedded systems. As reported in [12], one full execution of Curve25519 on MSP430FR5969 costs about 0.012 mJ (0.404 mJ if communication energy is estimated as in this paper). Thus, our methods are comparable in terms of total energy consumption. Moreover, fuzzy primitives provide security guarantees beyond a public-key scheme such as Curve25519: they can defend against MITM attacks (without certificate infrastructure) and guarantee that RX and TX are in physical proximity.

6 Conclusion

In this paper, we systematically and fairly evaluate the performance of fuzzy cryptographic primitives for PS-based key exchange under controlled conditions on a resource-constrained MSP430 microcontroller. We show how different fuzzy primitives can be securely applied to derive a 128-bit key from joint measurements of a PS, and provide implementations of each of these primitives in multiple variants. To our knowledge, we are the first to compare the computation and communication energy consumption of different fuzzy primitives for a variety of parameter choices. Among all considered fuzzy primitives, we find that Syndrome and Pinsketch fuzzy extractors overall offer the lowest energy consumption in Hamming and set metric spaces.

This indicates that fuzzy commitment and fuzzy vault used in previous PS-based key exchange solutions [4,7,14,37,38] are not optimal on constrained devices. Instead, Syndrome/Pinsketch fuzzy extractors may be preferable, with the added advantage that they neither require random number generation, which can be costly on embedded systems, nor uniformly randomly distributed inputs derived from a PS. These constructions consume between 0.021 mJ and 0.198 mJ for TX and between 0.029 mJ and 0.380 mJ for RX, including computational and communication energy. This demonstrates that PS-based key exchange methods using fuzzy primitives are feasible for a resource-constrained device, even if keys are relatively frequently exchanged. We also observe that ECCs with smaller parameter choices in fuzzy primitives have generally better performance, even if more repetitions are required. However, this might come at the cost of having more strict constraints on the maximum average bit error rate of a PS. Our work serves as a reference when applying fuzzy primitives for body-area networks and medical devices, and for other use cases such as biometrics or PUFs.

Acknowledgements. This work is funded in part by the European Union's Horizon 2020 Research and innovation program under grant agreement No. 826284 (ProTego), the FWO-SBO project SPITE, and by the Engineering and Physical Sciences Research Council (EPSRC) under grant EP/R012598/1. Mo Zhang is funded by the Priestley PhD Scholarship programme. The ECC decoding methods were based in part on the source code of Simon Rockliff [2].

References

1. Medtronic Azure pacing system. https://europe.medtronic.com/xd-en/healthcare-professionals/products/cardiac-rhythm/pacemakers/azure.html
2. Simon Rockliff's Reed-Solomon encoder/decoder. http://www.eccpage.com/rs.c
3. Abidin, A., Argones Rúa, E., Peeters, R.: Uncoupling biometrics from templates for secure and privacy-preserving authentication. In: ACM SACMAT (2017)

4. Al Reshan, M., Liu, H., Hu, C., Yu, J.: MBPSKA: multi-biometric and physiological signal-based key agreement for body area networks. IEEE Access **7**, 78484–78502 (2019)
5. Billeb, S., Rathgeb, C., Reininger, H., Kasper, K., Busch, C.: Biometric template protection for speaker recognition based on universal background models. IET Biometrics **4**(2), 116–126 (2015)
6. Calleja, A., Peris-Lopez, P., Tapiador, J.E.: Electrical heart signals can be monitored from the moon: security implications for IPI-based protocols. In: WISTP, pp. 36–51 (2015)
7. Cherukuri, S., Venkatasubramanian, K.K., Gupta, S.K.S.: BioSec: a biometric based approach for securing communication in wireless networks of biosensors implanted in the human body. In: ICPP, pp. 432–439 (2003)
8. Crossbow Technology Inc.: TelosB Mote Platform datasheet, Rev. B, https://www.willow.co.uk/TelosB_Datasheet.pdf
9. Delvaux, J., Gu, D., Schellekens, D., Verbauwhede, I.: Helper data algorithms for PUF-based key generation: overview and analysis. IEEE TCAD **34**(6), 889–902 (2015)
10. Dodis, Y., Ostrovsky, R., Reyzin, L., Smith, A.: Fuzzy extractors: how to generate strong keys from biometrics and other noisy data. SIAM J. Comput. **38**(1), 97–139 (2008)
11. Halperin, D., Heydt-Benjamin, T.S., Fu, K., Kohno, T., Maisel, W.H.: Security and privacy for implantable medical devices. IEEE Pervasive Comput. Spec. Issue Implantable Electron. **7**, 30–39 (2008)
12. Hinterwälder, G., Moradi, A., Hutter, M., Schwabe, P., Paar, C.: Full-size high-security ECC implementation on MSP430 microcontrollers. In: Aranha, D.F., Menezes, A. (eds.) LATINCRYPT 2014. LNCS, vol. 8895, pp. 31–47. Springer, Cham (2015). https://doi.org/10.1007/978-3-319-16295-9_2
13. Hirose, S.: Some plausible constructions of double-block-length hash functions. In: FSE, pp. 210–225 (2006)
14. Hu, C., Cheng, X., Zhang, F., Wu, D., Liao, X., Chen, D.: OPFKA: secure and efficient ordered-physiological-feature-based key agreement for wireless body area networks. In: INFOCOM (2013)
15. Juels, A., Sudan, M.: A fuzzy vault scheme. Des. Codes Crypt. **38**(2), 237–257 (2006)
16. Juels, A., Wattenberg, M.: A fuzzy commitment scheme. In: ACM CCS (1999)
17. Kholmatov, A., Yanikoglu, B.: Realization of correlation attack against the fuzzy vault scheme. In: Security, Forensics, Steganography, and Watermarking of Multimedia Contents X, vol. 6819, p. 68190O. SPIE (2008)
18. Li, X., Zeng, Q., Luo, L., Luo, T.: T2Pair: secure and usable pairing for heterogeneous IoT devices. In: ACM CCS, pp. 309–323 (2020)
19. Lin, S., Costello, D.J.: Error Control Coding, vol. 2. Prentice Hall (2001)
20. Marin, E., Argones Rúa, E., Singelée, D., Preneel, B.: On the difficulty of using patient's physiological signals in cryptographic protocols. In: ACM SACMAT, pp. 113–122 (2019)
21. Marin, E., Mustafa, M.A., Singelée, D., Preneel, B.: A privacy-preserving remote healthcare system offering end-to-end security. In: Mitton, N., Loscri, V., Mouradian, A. (eds.) ADHOC-NOW 2016. LNCS, vol. 9724, pp. 237–250. Springer, Cham (2016). https://doi.org/10.1007/978-3-319-40509-4_17
22. Marin, E., Singelée, D., Garcia, F.D., Chothia, T., Willems, R., Preneel, B.: On the (in)security of the latest generation implantable cardiac defibrillators and how to secure them. In: ACSAC, pp. 226–236 (2016)

23. Marin, E., Singelée, D., Yang, B., Verbauwhede, I., Preneel, B.: On the feasibility of cryptography for a wireless insulin pump system. In: CODASPY (2016)
24. Marin, E., et al.: Securing wireless neurostimulators. In: CODASPY, pp. 287–298 (2018)
25. de Meulenaer, G., Gosset, F., Standaert, F., Pereira, O.: On the energy cost of communication and cryptography in wireless sensors networks. In: IEEE WiMob, pp. 580–585 (2008)
26. Ortiz Martin, L., Picazo-Sanchez, P., Peris-Lopez, P., Tapiador, J.: Heartbeats do not make good pseudo-random number generators: an analysis of the randomness of inter-pulse intervals. Entropy **20**, 94 (2018)
27. Rathgeb, C., Uhl, A.: Statistical attack against fuzzy commitment scheme. IET Biometrics **1**(2), 94–104 (2012)
28. Reparaz, O., Balasch, J., Verbauwhede, I.: Dude, is my code constant time? In: DATE, pp. 1697–1702. IEEE (2017)
29. Reverberi, L., Oswald, D.: Breaking (and fixing) a widely used continuous glucose monitoring system. In: USENIX WOOT (2017)
30. Rostami, M., Juels, A., Koushanfar, F.: Heart-to-Heart (H2H): authentication for implanted medical devices. In: ACM CCS, pp. 1099–1112 (2013)
31. Seepers, R.M., Strydis, C., Peris-Lopez, P., Sourdis, I., Zeeuw, C.I.D.: Peak misdetection in heart-beat-based security: characterization and tolerance. In: EMBC, pp. 5401–5405 (2014)
32. Seepers, R.M., Wang, W., de Haan, G., Sourdis, I., Strydis, C.: Attacks on heartbeat-based security using remote photoplethysmography. IEEE J-BHI **22**(3), 714–721 (2018)
33. Singelée, D., Seys, S., Batina, L., Verbauwhede, I.: The energy budget for wireless security: extended version. IACR Cryptol. ePrint Arch. **2015**, 1029 (2015)
34. TI: AN092: Measuring Bluetooth Low Energy Power Consumption (2012)
35. TI: MSP430FR596x, MSP430FR594x Mixed-Signal Microcontrollers datasheet (2012). rev. G. https://www.ti.com/lit/gpn/msp430fr5969
36. TI: MSP430FR599x, MSP430FR596x Mixed-Signal Microcontrollers datasheet (2016). rev. C. https://www.ti.com/lit/gpn/msp430fr5994
37. Venkatasubramanian, K.K., Banerjee, A., Gupta, S.: Plethysmogram-based secure inter-sensor communication in body area networks. In: IEEE MILCOM (2008)
38. Venkatasubramanian, K.K., Banerjee, A., Gupta, S.K.S.: PSKA: usable and secure key agreement scheme for body area networks. IEEE T-ITB **14**(1), 60–68 (2010)
39. Venkatasubramanian, K.K., Gupta, S.K.S.: Physiological value-based efficient usable security solutions for body sensor networks. ACM TOSN **6**(4), 1–36 (2010)
40. Xu, F., Qin, Z., Tan, C.C., Wang, B., Li, Q.: IMDGuard: securing implantable medical devices with the external wearable guardian. In: IEEE INFOCOM (2011)

Author Index

Printed in the United States
by Baker & Taylor Publisher Services